A view to a kill

Sidestone Press

© 2009 G.L. Dusseldorp

Published by Sidestone Press, Leiden
www.sidestone.com
Sidestone registration number: SSP39370001

ISBN 978-90-8890-020-4

Cover Illustration: Painting by Cornelis van Dalem: 'Landschap met het begin van de Beschaving' (c. 1565). Museum Boijmans Van Beuningen, Rotterdam.
Cover design: K. Wentink, Sidestone Press
Lay-out: P.C. van Woerdekom, Sidestone Press

A view to a kill

Investigating Middle Palaeolithic subsistence
using an optimal foraging perspective

Proefschrift

Ter verkrijging van de graad van Doctor
aan de Universiteit van Leiden
op gezag van Rector Magnificus prof. mr. P.F. van der Heijden
volgens het besluit van het College voor Promoties
te verdedigen op donderdag 2 april 2009
klokke 13:45 uur

door

Gerrit Leendert Dusseldorp

Geboren op 5 augustus 1979
te Eindhoven

Promotiecommissie

Promotor:		Prof. dr. W. Roebroeks

Co-promotor:		Prof. dr. R.Corbey

Referenten:		Prof. dr. S. Gaudzinski
			Prof. dr. D. Guthrie

Overige leden:	Prof. dr. T. van Kolfschoten
			Prof. dr. A. Tuffreau
			Dr. A. Verpoorte

Contents

1 Introduction — 9
   1.1 Research design — 10

2 Neanderthal Biology — 13
   2.1 Introduction — 13
   2.2 Neanderthal evolution — 13
   2.3 Neanderthal distribution patterns — 16
   2.4 Neanderthal anatomy and adaptation — 19
   2.5 Neanderthal brains — 21
   2.6 Neanderthal dietary niche and its implications — 23
   2.7 Neanderthal lives — 24
   2.8 Concluding remarks — 27

3 Neanderthal Archaeology — 29
   3.1 Introduction — 29
   3.2 Neanderthal mobility and the study of foraging behaviour — 29
   3.3 Neanderthal archaeozoology — 32
      3.3.1 Introduction — 32
      3.3.2 The hunting vs. scavenging debate — 32
      3.3.3 Specialised hunting of ungulates — 33
      3.3.4 Neanderthals and megafauna — 35
      3.3.5 Central places: Sites exhibiting the full suite of Neanderthal foraging strategies? — 37
      3.3.6 Broad spectrum revolution, division of labour — 42
      3.3.7 Summary and conclusion — 45
   3.4 Material culture — 46
   3.5 Other aspects of Neanderthal archaeology — 51
   3.6 Summary and Conclusion — 52

4 Optimal foraging models and Neanderthal archaeology — 55
   4.1 Introduction — 55
   4.2 General assumptions and criticism — 55
   4.3 An example of an OFT model: The diet breadth model — 58
   4.4 Applications of diet breadth in the study of the Middle Palaeolithic — 60
   4.5 On reconstructing the model's parameters — 61
   4.6 Possible confounding factors in the archaeological record — 67
   4.7 Modelling Neanderthal diet breadth — 69
   4.8 Modelling hyena diet breadth — 71
   4.9 Summary and conclusion — 72

5 Biache-Saint-Vaast — 75
   5.1 Introduction — 75
   5.2 The site — 75
   5.3 Dating — 76
   5.4 Stratigraphy and archaeological horizons — 77
   5.5 The stone artefacts — 79
   5.6 The bone assemblage — 81
   5.7 The environment — 90

	5.8 Applying OFT to Biache-Saint-Vaast	92
	5.9 Discussion	99
	5.10 Conclusion	100

6 Taubach — 103

    6.1 Introduction — 103
    6.2 The site — 104
    6.3 Dating — 104
    6.4 The archaeological finds — 108
    6.5 The bone collection — 109
    6.6 The environment — 113
    6.7 Applying OFT to Taubach — 118
    6.8 Discussion — 124
    6.9 Conclusion — 126

7 Hyena foraging — 127

    7.1 Introduction — 127
    7.2 Hyena ecology — 128
    7.3 Hyena sites — 130
    7.4 Expectations for the study of Pleistocene hyenas — 132
    7.5 Case-studies — 132
        7.5.1 Lunel-Viel — 132
        7.5.2 Camiac — 137
    7.6 Discussion — 139
    7.7 Conclusion — 141

8 Discussion — 145

    8.1 Application of the diet breadth model to archaeological data — 145
    8.2 Reconstructing the model's variables — 146
    8.3 Modelling Neanderthals — 149
    8.4 This study — 150
    8.5 Application of OFT to Biache-Saint-Vaast and Taubach — 151
    8.6 The analysis in context — 156

9 Conclusion — 159

10 References — 161

Dutch Summary — 189

Acknowledgements — 197

Curriculum vitae — 199

1   Introduction

During human evolution our primate ancestors gradually switched from a diet based mainly on plant foods to one based to a significant degree on animal foods. This shift is thought to have been important in the process of human evolution, some even regard it as critical (*e.g.* Milton 2003). Many important developments in human evolution, like increasing brain-size and changes in life histories, are assumed to have co-evolved with the increasing contribution of animal products to the diet (*e.g.* Aiello and Wheeler 1995, Isaac 1978, Kaplan *et al.* 2000, Kaplan and Robson 2002, Kuhn and Stiner 2006). Theories that make evolutionary links between factors in human evolution, like brain size with other factors like foraging niche, longevity or group size, have focused mainly on comparative studies of primates and ethnographically known hunter/gatherers (*e.g.* Dunbar 1992, Hawkes *et al.* 1998, Kaplan *et al.* 2000, Reader and Laland 2002). The general validity of these theories can be evaluated by testing them on other species in the hominin family. Neanderthals are especially interesting in this respect; we shared a common ancestor relatively recently and their general body plan was similar to that of modern humans. More importantly, they had large brains, in terms of both absolute and relative size (Wood and Collard 1999, 69). If we accept the increasing anatomical and genetic evidence that modern humans and Neanderthals are separate species (*e.g.* Green *et al.* 2008, Hofreiter *et al.* 2001, McDougall, Brown, and Fleagle 2005, Ovchinikov *et al.* 2000, Stringer 2003, White *et al.* 2003), Neanderthals present us with a case of parallel evolution of large brains, the factor that is deemed to be most important in human evolution. This makes the study of the factors responsible for the similar Neanderthal evolutionary trajectory germane to our understanding of human evolutionary patterns in general.

In order to assess the role of the foraging niche in the evolution of large brains and prolonged life-history trajectories, this thesis aims to assess the efficacy of Neanderthal foraging strategies, specifically Neanderthal meat procurement. It has been argued that hunting is a very knowledge-intensive activity practised by modern humans (*e.g.* Kaplan *et al.* 2000). It is also seen as the most "complex" activity that chimpanzees (*Pan troglodytes*) engage in (*e.g.* Boesch 2003). Therefore, studying the knowledge-intensity of the Neanderthal foraging niche and its evolutionary implications for the evolution of larger brains has bearing on the theories as proposed by Kaplan *et al.*, among others since it may yield insight in the validity of their underlying assumptions.

The importance of meat in the lives of our ancestors has been the subject of heated debate within Palaeolithic archaeology. First, the crucial contribution that gathering provides to the diets of many extant hunter/gatherers has been stressed (*e.g.* Dahlberg 1981). Second, the question of how meat was obtained has been debated heatedly (for a review see Domínguez-Rodrigo 2002). Hunting is seen as complicated behaviour and this, combined with meagre archaeological evidence has led some researchers to suggest that only anatomically modern humans (AMH) were able to subsist by regularly hunting large mammals (*e.g.* Binford 1984). Scientists studying Pleistocene ecology on the other hand, have stated that subsisting primarily by scavenging was not a viable option for hominins and hence predicted hunting as the basis of subsistence (Geist 1978, Tooby and DeVore 1987).

Neanderthals occupy a peculiar position in this debate. They are very similar to AMH in general build. Furthermore, they have large brains, on average even larger than those of AMH. Moreover, the research that originally called into question the role of hunting by hominins was carried out at Sterkfontein and Bed I of the Olduvai Gorge, dealing with species at a much earlier stage in human evolution (Binford 1981, Brain 1981). Still, Neanderthals are also alleged to have procured meat mainly by scavenging (*e.g.* Binford 1988, Stiner 1994).

Gathering cannot have been as important to Neanderthals as it may have been to hominins in more tropical environments, since Neanderthals lived at temperate latitudes, where plant foods are not as abundant as in tropical and subtropical environments. Crucially, they are not available year-round (*e.g.* Roebroeks, Conard, and Van Kolfschoten 1992, 551). Moreover during much of the Pleistocene temperatures were lower than today, further limiting the availability of plant foods. Coping with winter conditions and the cessation of primary biological production in this period is an unusual problem for a primate. In addition to a greater reliance on meat to deal with this there are other imaginable solutions. For example, a species could adapt to spending the winter in hibernation, or create stores of food in order to survive this season. Modern-day primates living at temperate latitudes do not hibernate; therefore it seems unlikely Neanderthals did. Food-storage is an option that merits attention however.

Studies of the isotopic composition of the bones of some Neanderthals have shown that their diet consisted mainly of meat (*e.g.* Bocherens and Drucker 2003, Bocherens *et al.* 2005, Richards *et al.* 2000, Richards and Schmitz 2008, Richards *et al.* 2008b). This suggests that Neanderthals solved the problem of surviving the winter by a reliance on meat. However, as important as they are, the isotope-studies do not tell us how they obtained it.

In this respect it is important to note that some of the analyses that advocated the importance of scavenging in Neanderthal subsistence have since been refuted. Binford's (1988) analysis of the Grotte Vaufrey for example, was found to be flawed (Grayson and Delpech 1994). Other analyses, such as one by Stiner (1994) in Italy, did not take the collecting strategies of the excavators into consideration. At some fo the old excavations she analysed only diagnostic bones had been collected, which yielded an assemblage dominated by head parts, considered to be characteristic of a scavenged assemblage (Mussi 1999).

Compelling evidence for hunting has been found through detailed studies of bone assemblages, often done along the lines developed by Lewis Binford. Many Middle Palaeolithic bone assemblages for instance are dominated by prime aged adults, the animals least likely to die from predation, disease etc. This is a characteristic pattern of modern human hunting; it is not seen in other carnivores (*e.g.* Gaudzinski 1995, Gaudzinski and Roebroeks 2000, Steele 2004). Furthermore at many of these sites cut-marks and conchoidal fractures testify to a very intensive hominin exploitation of the fauna present at the sites (Auguste 1995a, Gaudzinski and Roebroeks 2003). There are the spectacular finds of projectile weapons; a number of wooden spears associated with the remains of about 20 butchered horses at Schöningen (Thieme 1997, Voormolen 2008), and a wooden lance found associated with an elephant carcass at Lehringen (Thieme and Veil 1985). In Syria a Mousterian point was found embedded in the vertebra of a wild ass. The direction of the impact suggests a parabolic trajectory, which means that the point probably functioned as the tip of a thrown spear, rather than a thrusted one (Boëda *et al.* 1999).

In recent years, the realisation that Neanderthals were able hunters of big game has led to the development of new hypotheses regarding differences in adaptation between Neanderthals and modern humans. The most influential of these is the hypothesis of a "broad-spectrum revolution" (*e.g.* Richards *et al.* 2001, Stiner 2001, Stiner, Munro, and Surovell 2000, Stiner *et al.* 1999). This hypothesis states that, in contrast to modern humans, Neanderthals did not efficiently exploit fast-moving small game like rodents, birds and fish. Consequently, they would have been unable to maintain the population sizes modern humans could reach in similar areas.

This development in the debate surrounding Neanderthal foraging decisions is remarkable, since during the heyday of the scavenging hypothesis, it was thought that prior to the last glacial, small animals were the only category of animals European hominins were deemed capable of hunting, as Binford (1985, 319) put it:

> *The European sites from the Rissian age (100,000 – 300,000 years ago) exhibit a very different pattern than that noted above. It is my impression that hunting seems most likely indicated for small animals and rodents, particularly rabbits, which are common in such early European sites as Lazaret (Jullien & Pillard 1969) and the earlier Rissian levels of Combe Grenal.*

In order to assess the validity of the hypotheses on co-evolution of intelligence, life-histories and foraging strategies and to evaluate current ideas on the sophistication of Neanderthal hunting strategies, the following research design has been developed.

1.1 Research design

The complete reversal of ideas on Neanderthal foraging strategies during such a short period of time illustrates the need for the development of a reliable methodology with which to interpret archaeological indications for hominin foraging behaviour in an evolutionary framework. This methodology should enable meaningful comparisons of sites from different geographical areas and of different ages. The focus should be on the bone assemblages and not necessarily on the associated tools since the tool spectrum need not necessarily be indicative of the sophistication of the hunting strategies.

A promising perspective is provided by optimal foraging theory. This theory investigates how the need of animals to maximise their fitness influences their foraging strategies. Since foraging is crucial for the survival of the individual, it is assumed that foraging efficiency will be maximised. In addition, efficient foraging can enhance fitness in more ways, for instance because more efficient foraging allows an organism more time for activities related to reproduction (*e.g.* Winterhalder 1987). Since hunter/gatherers have been subject to long periods of selective pressures it is assumed that they are as proficient and skilled as they could possibly be (Winterhalder 2001, 13-14). The application of this method to hunter/gatherers has been criticised by some cultural anthropologists (*e.g.* Ingold 2000). They feel that the application of evolutionary theory to situation with an important role for cultural transmission is problematic, since evolutionary theory is geared to dealing with genetic inheritance. The same goes for the mechanisms of selection. However, optimal foraging models have been successfully applied in a wide array of studies, ranging from the foraging behaviour of insects, to that of hunter/gatherers, to industrial fishing and to surfing the Internet (*e.g.* DiClemente and D. A. Hantula 2003, Dorn 1997, Waldbauer and Friedman 1991, Winterhalder 1987, Winterhalder 2001). These models have been designed not to represent the truth, but are simplifications that can be used to determine what factors are important in foraging choices made by hunter/gatherers (*e.g.* Shennan 2002, Winterhalder and Smith 1992).

Because in archaeology, the data at our disposal is different than in ecological and anthropological studies, this study aims to test whether we can adapt Optimal Foraging Theory in such a way that it becomes applicable to the study of Pleistocene subsistence strategies. An important consideration is that much of the information needed relates to the ecological structure of the environment, which in archaeology often has to be reconstructed. In order to minimise the uncertainties associated with reconstructing important variables, it appears most productive to use a simple model. In this study, I will focus on the Diet Breadth Model. This model predicts which species will be exploited by a given predator in a certain environment and which species will be avoided (MacArthur and Pianka 1966). Whether a species is exploited depends on many factors, such as the caloric value of a resource, the cost of tracking it, anti-predator behaviour of the prey and so on (*e.g.* Ugan 2005, Winterhalder 1987, Winterhalder 2001). If we can highlight which of these factors influenced Neanderthal foraging behaviour, we can gain insight in the way their hunting strategies were organised.

In this study I will adopt a diachronic perspective and focuson the archaeological record of northwestern Europe. For the application of this analysis areas further south, the models would have to be adapted to suit the fact that southern Neanderthals did not possess the same cold-adapted physiology as northern ones (*e.g.* Aiello and Wheeler 2003, 147). Furthermore, the energetic needs of cold-adapted modern humans, and presumably also Neanderthals, are significantly higher than those of individuals from more temperate climes (Aiello and Wheeler 2003, Steegman, Cerny, and Holliday 2002). This may have influenced the foraging tactics practised in these areas. Finally, the role of plant foods was probably more substantial in southern Europe than in northern Europe. Since taphonomic factors preclude analysis of the floral component of the Neanderthal diet, it appears most productive to study sites where the importance of plant foods was in all likelihood small.

I will first introduce the current thinking on the co-evolution of hominin intelligence, life histories and foraging behaviour. This will be followed by an introduction into Neanderthal biology and archaeology, in order to assess this predator's needs and abilities, which are important with regard to the application of the model (chapters 2 and 3). Next, some optimal foraging models will be discussed and hypotheses regarding the Neanderthal foraging niche will be developed (chapter 4). These will be tested by applying them to well-documented sites from the Middle Palaeolithic of Northwest Europe (chapters 5 and 6), and to sites produced by a competing predator, namely the cave hyena (*Crocuta spelaea*) (chapter 7). This will be done to highlight whether the modelled foraging niches of the two predators diverge and in what way. It should then become clear whether the resolution provided by the model is sufficient to provide evolutionary meaningful interpretations of foraging niches.

The archaeological focus will be on two sites, whose rich faunal assemblages span different chronological and climatic periods. This should provide insight in how Neanderthals dealt with the climatic oscillations that characterised the Pleistocene. The focus will be on palimpsest assemblages that were formed over several years, resulting in a time-averaged picture, thus filtering out variations in foraging behaviour due to exceptional circumstances. By so doing I aim to increase the reliability of the analysis in characterising the Neanderthal foraging niche. The environment will be reconstructed based on information from pollen cores, small fauna and geology. Analysis of the behaviour of the species that were present may give us insight in what kind of prey Neanderthals favoured. The species of prey that were targeted and age-structure of the hunted assemblage for example provide important clues as to hunting strategies.

The earliest site that will be analysed is Biache-Saint-Vaast in northern France. This site has been excavated, researched and published reasonably recently (*e.g.* Auguste 1992, Auguste 1995a, Tuffreau and Sommé 1988b). The site was formed during the transition of a temperate phase within the Saalian, Marine Isotope Stage (MIS) 7, to the most recent glaciation of the Saalian, MIS 6 (Sommé *et al.* 1988). The site consists of multiple layers formed during periods characterised by different climatic conditions, from cold boreal to temperate. This site may thus provide insight in the long-term dynamics of Neanderthal foraging adaptations at the transition of MIS 7 to MIS 6.

The second site that will be examined is Taubach in Germany. This site is dated to the last interglacial, the Eemian. Analysis of this site is pertinent in the context of the debate about whether or not Neanderthals were able to cope with the climax conditions of its climatic optimum (*e.g.*, Roebroeks, Conard, and Van Kolfschoten 1992, Roebroeks and Speleers 2002 *contra* Gamble 1986, Gamble 1992, Gamble 1999). Sites of a similar age are known in this region, but these represent only single hunting episodes (Gaudzinski 2004) and will not yield a reliable picture of foraging adaptations if treated in isolation. Taubach was chosen because it has yielded a large assemblage of cut-marked bones, and an abundant natural fauna that can be used to evaluate Neanderthal foraging decisions. Analysis of this site is not unproblematic however, since the bones were collected in the course of travertine quarrying activities in the 19th century. The collection is therefore biased towards diagnostic bones of the larger mammals (Bratlund 1999). The site can be compared to neighbouring archaeological and natural bone assemblages in order to determine how representative the bone assemblage is.

The insights this study gives us into Neanderthal foraging niches will be compared with a similar case-study of two Pleistocene hyena dens containing large bone assemblages from France, namely Lunel-Viel and Camiac. Camiac is dated to MIS 3, while Lunel-Viel is considerably older, dated to around 350 ka (Fosse 1996, Guadelli *et al.* 1988). The environmental data available for Lunel-Viel is unfortunately somewhat poor but the faunal assemblage shows that it was situated in a temperate environment. At Camiac, pollen analysis from hyena coprolites can be combined with the faunal assemblage to reconstruct a mammoth steppe environmental setting. These two sites therefore inform us on hyena behaviour in both temperate and colder periods and provide good comparisons for the archaeological assemblages.

Finally I will evaluate how the application of OFT to the study of Pleistocene foraging strategies can increase our understanding of Neanderthal behaviour. Moreover I will discuss how these results apply to the theories on the evolution of hominin intelligence and life histories.

2 Neanderthal Biology

2.1 Introduction

This chapter deals with the distinctive biological features of Neanderthals. Knowledge of these features will be used as a basis for the adaptation of Optimal Foraging Theory (OFT) to study Neanderthal subsistence strategies. Unfortunately, establishing such a basis is not straightforward, since specific way in which Neanderthal adaptations took shape is not always clear. First, I will introduce the evolutionary history of Neanderthals as it is perceived at present. This will be followed by an examination of their distribution patterns and how these relate to the conditions to which they were adapted. This will be combined with an overview of the skeletal clues regarding Neanderthal adaptations. Much has been written about the consequences of having a large brain for a variety of phenomena, from the organisation of the adaptive tract, to the evolution of language, to its influence on an organism's life-history. The Neanderthal brain and its effects will therefore be considered in a separate section. The combined effects of Neanderthal brain size, build, and distribution are thought to have had drastic consequences for their dietary niche, which will be discussed next. This will be followed by a discussion of the implications of the dietary niche and data on life-histories for the social organisation of Neanderthals. This will result in an overview of the specific adaptations of the "Neanderthal animal" which will be used as input for OFT models in chapter 4.

2.2 Neanderthal evolution

Neanderthals are usually seen as a distinct species of hominin, *Homo neanderthalensis*, although some scientists prefer to classify them as a subspecies of *Homo sapiens*: *Homo sapiens neanderthalensis* (see for example discussion in Ahern, Hawks, and Lee 2005, Harvati, Frost, and McNulty 2004). Because of genetic, anatomical and behavioural differences between anatomically modern humans (AMH) and Neanderthals I prefer to group Neanderthals as a separate species: *H. neanderthalensis*. Fossils of Neanderthals have been found over a wide area, from Northwest Europe to the Levant and further eastward to southern Siberia (Krause *et al.* 2007). First I will sketch the current views of the evolution of the hominin lineage in Europe.

The exact evolutionary origins of Neanderthals are uncertain. Europe has been occupied by hominins from at least 1 million years ago, but "Classic" Neanderthals are usually placed between 120 thousand years ago (ka) and the time of their extinction about 30 ka (*e.g.* Klein 2003). Several species have been proposed as being ancestral to the "classic Neanderthals". The oldest species of hominin present in Europe is *Homo antecessor*, found at Atapuerca TD 6 and Sima del Elefante.[1] This name was chosen because the discoverers thought that this species was the ancestor of both Neanderthals and AMH. The species shows a combination of primitive and derived features. The midface topography is considered to be derived and this midface form is a feature that is shared by Neanderthals and AMH (Bermúdez de Castro *et al.* 1997). At present, the species is only known from Spain, where it is present from 1.2-1.1 mya. (Carbonell *et al.* 2008).

The re-dating of the *Homo heidelbergensis* sample from Sima de los Huesos led the team to retract the hypothesis that H. antecessor could be ancestral to *H. heidelbergensis*. The Sima de los Huesos fossils show a combination of primitive traits and apomorphies (derived traits) only present in other European fossils, most notably in Neanderthals but not in AMH. This population can therefore be considered ancestral to Neanderthals, but not to ourselves (Arsuaga *et al.* 1997). The fossils were originally dated to about 300 ka, but redating has shown them to be considerably older, probably about 600 ka (Bischoff *et al.* 2007). Since there are significant dental differences between Homo antecessor, most fossils of which are dated to about 800 ka and the *Homo heidelbergensis* fossils, the research team considers it unlikely that *Homo antecessor* was the ancestor of *Homo heidelbergensis* (Bermúdez de Castro *et al.* 2004b).

---

[1] It has been suggested that these fossils belong to the same species as fossils found in North Africa that were described as *Atlanthropus mauretanicus* and should therefore be called *Homo mauretanicus* (Stringer 2003).

It is now thought that in the early Middle Pleistocene, a new species arrived in Europe, *Homo heidelbergensis* (Bermúdez de Castro *et al.* 2004b). This hypothesized new migration into Europe is supported by important changes in the character of the European Archaeological record, most notably the sudden appearance of the Acheulean at around 500 ka (Bermúdez de Castro *et al.* 2004b, Langbroek 2003, Roebroeks and Van Kolfschoten 1995). Furthermore, genetic evidence suggests a migration out of Africa between 700 and 500 ka (Templeton 2002). Most researchers think that it was this population of newly arrived *H. heidelbergensis* that would give rise to the "classic Neanderthals".

The Sima de los Huesos fossils show many Neanderthal characteristics. Moreover, the dentition of the type specimen of *H. heidelbergensis* is also very Neanderthal-like (Bermúdez de Castro *et al.* 2004b, 1423). Similarly, Neanderthal characteristics have been observed in some other fossil specimens that are assigned to *H. heidelbergensis*, such as the Swanscombe skull (Stringer 2002, Stringer and Hublin 1999). This shows that the Neanderthalisation process started at least around 500 ka. Therefore, the lineage evolving in Europe could be called *H. neanderthalensis*, evolving anagenetically in Europe from an ancestral population that could be characterised as the chronospecies *H. heidelbergensis* (Bermúdez de Castro *et al.* 2004a, 39). Hence, all archaic hominin specimens from northwestern Europe dating between 400 and about 30 ka will be considered as belonging to the species *Homo neanderthalensis*.

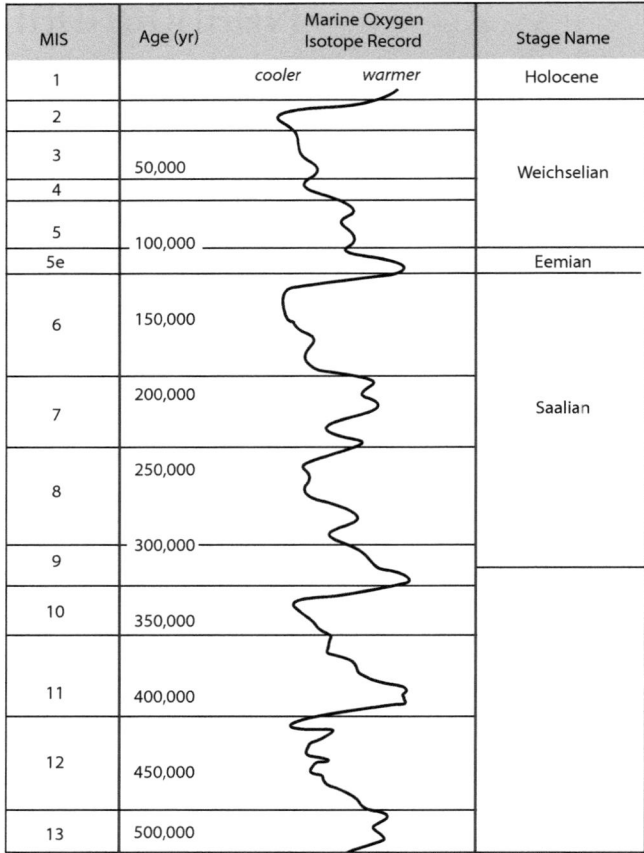

Figure 2.1: Scheme showing a climatic curve illustrating warm and cold periods during the last 500 ka. And the corresponding Marine Isotope Stages and dates. Adapted from the time chart of the AHOB project (http://www.nhm.ac.uk/hosted_sites/ahob/Chart.pdf).

There is one competing hypothesis, which states that the archaeological record changes drastically at the beginning of the Middle Palaeolithic, around 300-250 ka. Technological change is evident in the adoption of the Levallois technique for stone reduction. Furthermore, the earliest unequivocal indications for the use of fire appear in Europe. This has led some authors to presume the migration of a new species of hominin into Europe, namely *Homo helmei* from Africa (*e.g.* Lahr and Foley 1998). However, the fossils of *H. helmei* are younger than the oldest characteristic Neanderthal fossils, so they cannot be the ancestors of Neanderthals (Stringer 2002). Moreover, developments foreshadowing the Levallois technique are already seen in the European Lower Palaeolithic (White and Ashton 2003). The "*H. helmei*" scenario is therefore most likely incorrect, although contact between the African and European populations may have occurred from time to time, for example in the Levant.

In addition to their emergence, the process of extinction of the Neanderthals is also the subject of debate. An important question is whether Neanderthals were ancestral to AMH. It is now thought that the distinct Neanderthal and AMH forms arose independently in different areas. The oldest anatomically modern fossils that are known date to about 200 ka, in Ethiopia (McDougall, Brown, and Fleagle 2005). According to most authors, classic Neanderthals postdate 200 ka, showing that they are not ancestral to AMH. Moreover, typical Neanderthals persist in Europe until about 30 ka and these show no developments toward anatomical modernity (*e.g.* Klein 2003, 1526). Therefore, even though AMH and Neanderthals co-existed in some areas, there is no obvious evidence of crossbreeding.

The earliest contact between the species took place in the Levant. The earliest Middle Palaeolithic fossil known from this area is a partial skull from Zuttiyeh cave, dated between 250 and 300 ka.

However, it is unclear to what species this skull belongs. Some argue that it represents a population ancestral to *Homo sapiens sapiens*; others claim that it belongs to the Neanderthal lineage (Smith 1995). The oldest taxonomically distinct fossils in this region have been found at Tabun. The skeleton of a female Neanderthal has been excavated in layer C of this cave, as well as a maxilla, which after much debate has also been determined to be Neanderthal (Schwartz and Tattersall 2000). The layer probably dates to MIS 6, or maybe even late MIS 7 (Mercier *et al.* 1995).

AMH appear to arrive in the Levant in MIS 5, with fossils found in Skhul and Qafzeh, dated to 120 and 92 ka respectively (Mercier *et al.* 1993). All hominin fossils dated later than 90 ka from the area are Neanderthals. After about 50 ka they are finally replaced by AMH, or at least by assemblages we associate with AMH, since early upper Palaeolithic human remains are very rare in this area (Smith 1995). The interpretation of this fossil record is far from straightforward. AMH are only known from two sites and it is unclear whether they are replaced by Neanderthals after MIS 5e, although all more recent fossils are Neanderthals. It could be suggested that Neanderthals were present in MIS 6, as shown by the Tabun C fossils. The warmer climate of MIS 5 would have led to their replacement by anatomically (but not behaviourally) modern humans, who were in turn replaced by Neanderthals as the climate cooled again.

Later during the Weichselian, AMH migrated out of Africa again, finally replacing the European and Asian hominin populations. During the expansion of behaviourally modern populations across Europe there were opportunities for contact. In certain areas Neanderthals and modern humans co-existed at least for a short period of time, although its duration is unclear. Some authors think it may only have been for about 1000 to 2000 years. Dating the time of co-existence is problematic, given the difficulties inherent in calibrating ^{14}C dates at the lower limit of their range (*e.g.* Jöris and Street 2008, Mellars 2006, Pettitt and Pike 2001). Some initial Upper Palaeolithic cultures appear across Europe and at least the Châtelperronian now appears to be solidly associated with Neanderthal fossils, as shown by the find of a skeleton at Saint-Césaire and a temporal bone at Arcy-sur-Cure (Hublin *et al.* 1996). It has been proposed that the Châtelperronian was the result of Neanderthals copying the behaviour of AMH. A thorough analysis of the novelties associated with such transitional cultures suggests that the roots of these phenomena do not lie in cultures associated with AMH (*e.g.* d'Errico *et al.* 1998). In some caves interstratifications of Aurignacian and Châtelperronian layers have been proposed (*e.g.* Gravina, Mellars, and Ramsey 2005, Mellars, Gravina, and Ramsey 2007). Other analyses suggest that the interstratifications are the result of taphonomic processes (*e.g.* d'Errico and Goñi 2003, 770, Zilhão *et al.* 2006).

The timing of the extinction of Neanderthals is also uncertain. There is a paucity of well-dated AMH fossils in the time range spanning the transition from the Middle Palaeolithic to the Upper Palaeolithic. The AMH remains of Vogelherd were thought to be associated with an early Aurignacian industry, but redating has shown that the fossils are Neolithic (Conard, Grootes, and Smith 2004). Mladeč, in the Czech Republic, has yielded early Aurignacian stone tools and AMH fossils, but the fossils have been dated to the middle to late Aurignacian, at about 31 ka. Furthermore, there is ongoing discussion about whether they exhibit Neanderthal feautures (Wild *et al.* 2005). Theoretically, the early Aurignacian, which is usually ascribed to AMH, could thus have been produced by Neanderthals.

In addition to the dearth of well-dated early Upper Palaeolithic modern humans, there is uncertainty about the dates associated with the youngest Neanderthals. Very young dates, of up to 28 ka, for the Neanderthal occupation of Gibraltar have been proposed (Finlayson *et al.* 2006), and severely criticised (Zilhão and Pettitt 2006). After a thorough review of the available ^{14}C dates, Jöris and Street (2008) conclude that there are no reliably dated Neanderthal remains after 38 ka ^{14}C years before present, although industries associated with Neanderthals persist until slightly later. They assume that Neanderthals had disappeared after 35 ka ^{14}C years before present (Jöris and Street 2008).

An important site in the context of this debate is Peştera cu Oase in Romania. A mandible and a skull belonging to two individuals have been found there, dated to 35 ka. Unfortunately they are not associated with archaeological materials. Moreover, both specimens show some archaic features, not seen in AMH (Crevecoeur and Trinkaus 2004, Rougier *et al.* 2007, Trinkaus *et al.* 2003). This is apparent from the lingual bridging of the molars, which is unknown in late and middle Pleistocene hominins except for Neanderthals. The mandible has archaic molars, reminiscent of Neanderthals and other Pleistocene hominins (Crevecoeur and Trinkaus 2004, Trinkaus *et al.* 2003). This is striking, because Neanderthal dental morphological trait frequencies are unique within the hominin family. It is thought that Neanderthal dental morphology has evolved separately from the dental morphology of African populations of archaic *H. sapiens*. The phylogenetic position of this material is therefore unclear. The combination of derived modern features and archaic features may point to crossbreeding between early modern humans and Neanderthals. Alternatively, the remains may belong to descendants from primitive Middle Pleistocene Modern Humans and represent another group of humans than the earliest AMH that migrated out of Africa (Rougier *et al.* 2007). Crossbreeding of Neanderthals and AMH has also been proposed for the case of a juvenile skeleton from Portugal (Duarte *et al.* 1999).

Recently, DNA analyses have been used to suggest that admixture of genes from Neanderthals into the AMH genome did not happen. Several research groups have isolated strands of Neanderthal mitochondrial DNA. These seem to fall outside the range of modern human DNA (*e.g.* Beauval *et al.* 2005, Krings *et al.* 1999, Ovchinikov *et al.* 2000). The DNA shows that there is no closer relationship between modern Europeans and Neanderthals than between other humans and Neanderthals (Höss 2000). Initially, most of the recovered strands were short, containing only between 100 and 300 base-pairs. Nevertheless, the fact that strands from multiple individuals show that they are related, yet not identical suggests that they do not represent some form of contamination (Höss 2000, 454). Still, these results have been critisised. Some researchers suggest that the methods used were not ideal and that the effect of degradation has not been sufficiently accounted for. According to them, Neanderthals may be more closely related to modern humans than generally assumed (Guitierrez, Sánchez, and Marín 2002).

More recently, the complete mitochondrial genome of Neanderthals has been reconstructed (Green *et al.* 2008). The fact that the Neanderthal DNA differs on multiple points from that of modern humans but is internally consistent, points to the fact that Neanderthals formed a distinct evolutionary lineage. The age of the last common ancestor is difficult to reconstruct exactly from DNA analysis, but is estimated at 660 ± 140 ka (Green *et al.* 2008).

Since Neanderthal fossils have a number of apomorphies not shared with other hominins and their DNA is different from that of AMH, I see them as a separate species of hominin. I treat all European *Homo heidelbergensis* fossils as belonging to the Neanderthal lineage.

2.3 Neanderthal distribution patterns

Neanderthal fossils have been found across a large part of Eurasia, from eastern Russia to the Levant in the South and Britain in the Northwest (See figure 2.2). In the southern and eastern part of their range we cannot use Middle Palaeolithic stone tools as a proxy for the presence of Neanderthals, since Neanderthals and AMH apparently produced very similar assemblages (*e.g.* Shea 2003, Zilhão 2001). Middle Palaeolithic tools have been reported from the North European plain, for instance from Denmark (Johansen and Stapert 1995/1996). These can be confidently ascribed to Neanderthals. The northeastern limit of their range is still unclear. Some publications mention tools that may be Middle Palaeolithic from northern latitudes in Russia, but their provenance and dating are usually unclear (*e.g.* Pavlov, Roebroeks, and Svendsen 2004). Recently, Neanderthal-like mitochondrial DNA isolated from taxonomically indeterminate fossils in Siberia has extended the Neanderthal range eastwards by 2000 kilometres (Krause *et al.* 2007). The fossils and artefacts represent a period of time of hundreds of thousands of years, during which many range expansions and contractions probably took place. They do not reflect the distribution of Neanderthals at any one time, but show that Neanderthals survived in a wide range of environments during their existence.

Neanderthal fossils and tools have been found throughout a large area encompassing many different types of environment. Moreover, the climate during the period of their existence was very variable. The later part of the Pleistocene was characterised by a cyclical alternation of glacials and interglacials (See fig. 2.1). Marine and ice core isotope records have enabled accurate reconstructions of global climatic patterns, especially for the most recent glacial. (*e.g.* Andersen *et al.* 2004, Petit *et al.* 1999). For the palaeomagnetic Bruhnes chron, during which most of the substantial occupation of Europe took place we know of eight major glacial-interglacial phases. During these 800 ka at most 25 percent of the time sea-levels were high, indicative of present-day and warmer climates, but for over 75 percent of the time, they were lower, indicating colder climates (Gamble 1999, 104). Within these grand climatic cycles many shorter oscillations took place. During the Weichselian for example, we know of more than twenty abrupt changes in isotopic values of the ice cores, suggesting a very unstable climate (Andersen *et al.* 2004). The impact of these rapid oscillations on the continen-

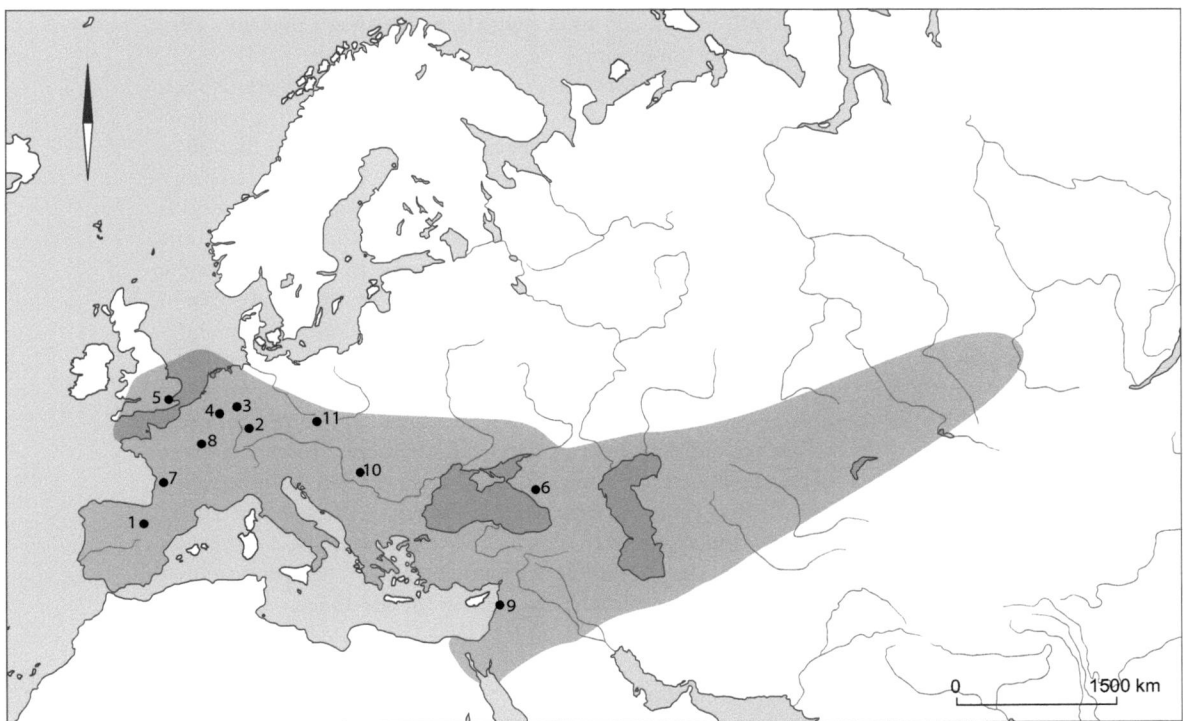

Figure 2.2: Map showing the known distribution of Neanderthal fossil specimens in grey with the location of important fossil finds mentioned in the text: 1 Atapuerca (Sima del Elefante, TD 6 and Sima de los Huesos; 2 Mauer; 3 Neanderthal, Feldhofer grotte (type specimen); 4 Sclayn; 5 Swanscombe; 6 Mezmaiskaya; 7 Saint-Césaire; 8 Arcy-sur-Cure; 9 Skhul, Tabun, Kebara; 10 Peştera cu Oase; 11 Mladeč. Neanderthal distribution adapted from (Krause et al. 2007).

tal climate and hence on human behaviour is not yet well-understood though. The resolution of pollen cores is too poor to precisely correlate all climatic events known from marine and ice cores with changes in pollen diagrams (Van Andel 2003, 13-15). In cold climatic phases climatic ameliorations did not have much impact in the northern pollen cores, but whether this is because of the resolution of the pollen cores or because climatic ameliorations had less effect at northern latitudes is unclear. What is clear though is that some ameliorations were of sufficient duration and warmth to cause the formation of palaeosols in the loess in Northern France and the Rhineland (Van Andel 2003, 15).

Reconstructing the preferred Neanderthal habitat is problematic. It is uncertain how well Neanderthals were able to deal with the cold and it is unknown what determined the limits of their distribution. Furthermore there is debate about whether Neanderthals were able to cope with the densely forested environments in interglacials in Europe. Even very early occupants of Europe were able to colonize northwestern Europe as shown by the site of Pakefield in East Anglia, dated to about 700 ka (Parfitt *et al.* 2005). The finds were accompanied by fossils that suggest the climate was warmer than it is presently. It has been suggested that these findings imply that the early hominin occupants of Europe preferred warm climates and as their habitat expanded to the North, they followed suit (Parfitt *et al.* 2005, Roebroeks 2005).

When the climatic tolerance of European hominins developed further, allowing them to survive in cold climates is not known yet. Evidence for the early occupation of northern Europe is quite scarce and many of the earliest sites like Pakefield and Boxgrove were situated in temperate environments. In the case of Boxgrove bifaces and refitting debitage have been found in mass movement gravel deposits overlying the warm sediments at the site. This implies that hominins were able to survive the cold phases of glacials at quite northern latitudes as early as MIS 12 (Roberts, Gamble, and Bridgland 1995, 171). The sites of Cagny La Garenne were also deposited in a periglacial environment in MIS 12 (Tuffreau, Lamotte, and Marcy 1997, 229-230). From MIS 8 we know a number of sites situated in a cold steppic environment, like Mesvin IV in Belgium, and Ariendorf 1 in Germany (Van Neer 1986, Roebroeks, Conard, and Van Kolfschoten 1992, 560). From this period onwards,

Neanderthals are frequently associated with remains of arctic animals, which shows that they were perfectly able to cope with cold environmental conditions.

Remarkably, Neanderthal remains are better known from relatively cold climatic periods than from interglacials. Based on the paucity of sites in the last glacial, the Eemian, Gamble has postulated that Neanderthals were unable to deal with full interglacial forests. He argues that since there are dated faunas, but no archaeological sites in Western Europe interglacial forested environments were "human deserts". This situation is illustrated best by the Eemian, since this period is represented by the strongest peak in the isotope records (Gamble 1986, 367-370). Other authors have pointed out that we do know sites from full interglacial conditions in the Eemian and that the paucity of sites is probably due more to post-depositional processes than to hominin absence in northwestern Europe. In areas where the sedimentary conditions allowed preservation of interglacial sites, archaeological sites have been found (*e.g.* Roebroeks, Conard, and Van Kolfschoten 1992, Roebroeks and Speleers 2002). Until recently, these were located almost exclusively in central and eastern Germany, which led Gamble (1986; 1992) to suggest that the climate in these areas was more continental than in Western Europe and that there were no full interglacial forests in these areas. Recently, however interglacial archaeological levels were found at Caours in the Somme valley, showing that Neanderthals were present in oceanic interglacial environments (Antoine *et al.* 2006). Some authors have even proposed that Neanderthals were actually a mediterranean species that was able to occupy the higher latitudes of Europe only in milder climatic intervals. They propose that Neanderthals were severely affected by cold climates, surviving only in Mediterranean refugia (*e.g.* Finlayson 2005, 461).

It is certainly true that Neanderthals were not able to cope with the coldest periods of glacials in northern areas. However, during the early part of the Weichselian, Neanderthals occupied the North European plain most of the time. The dates of Micoquian sites in Germany and Poland only show a hiatus during the coldest phase of MIS 4, presumably reflecting a retreat areas further south (*e.g.* Jöris 2003). In Northern France, the beginning of MIS 4 shows an occupation hiatus, but the area is re-colonised at least from 55 ka (Locht 2005). This shows that the idea that Neanderthals did not fare very well in cold-temperate areas, as proposed by Finlayson (2005) can be discarded.

It is important to realise that the most severe glacial and interglacial periods had a relatively short duration. For the longest part of the period during which Neanderthals lived in Europe climatic conditions were intermediate between warm climates resembling the modern climate and very cold conditions. During the last glacial cycle for example, only 9 percent of the time was characterised by full interglacial conditions and 17 percent by full glacial conditions. The rest of the cycle was characterised by intermediate climates, with temperate, open environmental conditions (Gamble 1986, Gamble 1992). This, according to Gamble, is the type of environment that was encountered by Neanderthals most of the time and therefore the environment they were adapted to survive in.

Guthrie (1990; 2001) has characterized the environment of Eurasia and parts of Northern America during these intermediate time-periods as a "mammoth steppe". The mammoth steppe was a unique, "non-analogue environment", in which elements of both modern day arctic environments and arid steppe environments were present. It was characterized by a low amount of annual precipitation and a cold climate, although it covered areas at temperate latitudes. Despite the cold climate, the area received a lot of sunshine, and bioproductivity was therefore high. Estimates of bioproductivity, and herbivore biomass equal those of the modern day African savannahs (over 14 tonnes/km^2 against 0.5 tonnes/km^2 for present-day forested environments) have been advanced for this kind of landscape (*e.g.* Delpech 1999). Moreover, temperatures may have been higher on average than signalled by the faunal and floral indicators that were present in the area. Guthrie (2001, 572) suggests that most of the time, the climate would have been warm enough for species adapted to warmer environments to colonise the mammoth steppe. However, the very abrupt Dansgaard/Oescher events may have periodically "set the clock back to zero" for these colonisations. Neanderthals occupied this very rich environment in large parts of their range. Although they had to withdraw to the south during the coldest glacial phases, they were very well able to cope with the environments that prevailed for most of the duration of glacial periods. An important point made recently by Stewart is that Neanderthal sites are preferentially in areas of ecological diversity (Stewart 2005, 38). This is interesting, because a comparison of mammal faunas shows that Europe's ecology in Mammoth Steppe environments was already more diverse than it is at present (Stewart 2005). This may explain why Neanderthals seemed to thrive in both temperate glacial conditions and in warm Mediterranean conditions, since both environments were diverse and productive.

The paucity of Neanderthal sites during full interglacials, as discussed above, is due at least in part to taphonomic factors (*e.g.* Roebroeks, Conard, and Van Kolfschoten 1992, Roebroeks and Speleers 2002, Speleers 2000, Tuffreau 1988c). However, since in these periods much of the biomass is locked away in tree trunks and leaves, and herbivore biomass was low, Neanderthals may have been present in smaller numbers in forested environments than on the mammoth steppe.

2.4 Neanderthal anatomy and adaptation

In order to understand Neanderthal adaptations we need to know in what respects they were different from AMH and the consequences of these differences. The basic body plan of Neanderthals was quite similar to our own, but differences did exist. The functional implications of these differences are at first sight not great; many point to a heavier musculature in Neanderthals (Wood and Collard 1999, 69). I will briefly examine the most significant differences between Neanderthals and AMH's and the possible behavioural impacts of these differences on Neanderthal ways of life.

Neanderthals evolved during a succession of glacial-interglacial cycles, the glacial part of which was much longer than the interglacial part. Neanderthals must therefore have been able to survive the periods of extreme cold, but their adaptation was presumably shaped by the long periods of intermediate climates. The extent to which Neanderthals were effectively adapted to cold environments is debated. As discussed in the previous section it has been proposed that they were unable to deal with cold climatic circumstances (*e.g.* Finlayson 2005, 461). Others maintain that their anatomy betrays drastic adaptations to the cold (Holliday 1997, 256). Two traditional indices of cold adaptation are Bergmann's rule and Allen's rule. Bergmann's rule states that within a dispersed species the populations living in colder climates will have a greater body mass. Allen's rule predicts that populations living in cold climates will develop shorter extremities. This pattern is explained by the fact that the surface area to volume ratio is minimized by these developments minimising heat loss (Holliday 1997). Neanderthal anatomy conforms to these predictions about cold-adaptation. It is thought that their barrel-shaped ribcage, and a torso that was relatively large in comparison to the limbs resulted from cold-adaptation. Their limb proportions are also different than those of AMH; especially the lower limbs are shorter than would be expected in AMH of similar size (Steudel-Numbers and Tilkens 2004). The brachial index (the relative length of the ulna compared to the humerus) of Near Eastern Neanderthals is higher than that of European ones (Aiello and Wheeler 2003, 147). Furthermore, their body mass was greater than that of AMH. This suggests that they conformed to Allen's and Bergmann's rules (Aiello and Wheeler 2003, 147). Some authors have argued that many Neanderthal features more likely resulted from biomechanical adaptations than from thermoregulatory ones (*e.g.* Churchill 1998, Porter 1999). However, some of these biomechanical adaptations, such as limb robusticity, probably had the secondary effect of being beneficial in a thermoregulatory sense as well (Churchill 1998, 58-59). This combination of anatomical features has led many to conclude that Neanderthals were cold-adapted, or even a hyperarctic species (*e.g.* Holliday 1997).

Metabolic adaptations are also significant in populations that have to cope with cold climates. In modern human populations from cold areas the Basal Metabolic Rate (BMR, the energy production of an animal in rest) may rise by some 15% compared with "normal" controls (Steegman, Cerny, and Holliday 2002, 577). Furthermore, changes in the amount of specific tissues, such as Brown Adipose Tissue, a fat that plays a part in thermoregulation, may also have been important (Steegman, Cerny, and Holliday 2002). Finally, BMR increases with increasing body weight. Neanderthals are therefore expected to have a significantly higher BMR than AMH (Sorensen and Leonard 2001).

There are some problems in viewing Neanderthals as cold-adapted, or even hyperarctic. Two are of particular interest here. First, some authors have argued that applying Allen's and Bergmann's rules to Neanderthals compared to modern humans is incorrect. These rules were originally developed to explain patterns of adaptation among individuals within a species, not to explain differences between species. Differences in limb length and robusticity between species are, according to some authors, usually better explained as reflecting differences in locomotor behaviour (Stewart 2005, 42-43). However, as stated above, conformation to these rules has also been proposed within the Neanderthal sample.

Secondly, a recent study by Aiello and Wheeler (2003) suggests that the anatomical differences between Neanderthals and AMH had little influence on their climatic tolerance. Aiello and Wheeler (2003) focus on the critical temperature, *i.e.* the environmental temperature at which an animal must start producing heat in order to keep his body temperature optimal. This can be modelled using heat conductivity and BMR. Since the maximum metabolic rate of an organism is usually three times its BMR, these estimates can also be used to model the lowest temperature at which Neanderthals can survive without additional insulation (Aiello and Wheeler 2003, 148). If average human BMR, skin conductivity equal to that of modern humans, and a standardised relationship between surface area and body mass and stature are used, the Neanderthal's critical temperature is estimated at 27.3 °C, against 28.2 °C for early modern humans. The lowest temperature at which Neanderthals could survive without additional insulation would be 8.0 °C, against 10.5 °C for modern humans (Aiello and Wheeler 2003, 148). However, if a 15% increased BMR is assumed and the additional insulation provided by increased muscularity is taken into account, the critical temperature would drop to 25.3 °C and the lowest tolerable temperature tolerable would become 1.9 °C for Neanderthals (Aiello and Wheeler 2003, 150-151). The tolerance of extremely low ambient temperatures would necessitate high metabolism and could only be maintained if Neanderthals had a high dietary intake (Aiello and Wheeler 2003, 151).

The different limb proportions may have had an effect on Neanderthal cold adaptation, but they also point to differences between the locomotion of Neanderthals and AMH. Their limbs were relatively short compared to the torso, but the limbs themselves are also different compared to those of AMH. They are much more robust and show evidence of a much heavier musculature. Moreover, their lower limbs are very short; the crural index, the relative length of the tibia compared to the femur, of Neanderthals lies outside that of the modern range (Porter 1999, 65-66). Furthermore, the Neanderthal pelvis had a different shape than in AMH. The superior pubic ramus lies further forward, meaning that in females the birth canal would also lie further forward. It is possible that this is an adaptation to giving birth to large-brained babies. However, this pattern is most pronounced in males, therefore it is usually interpreted as indicating a difference in locomotion behaviour in Neanderthals (Tattersall 1999, 15).

The cost of locomotion is largely determined by the number of steps one has to take in order to travel a given distance, which is dependent on lower limb length and on the weight being transported. The impact of decreasing lower limb length and adding weight has been modelled on modern test subjects, assuming an average travel distance of 12.2 kilometres daily for hunter/gatherers. It appears that decreasing lower limb length by one centimetre would increase the cost of locomotion by 9.89 kcal daily. Adding one kilogram of weight would increase the cost by 13.7 kcal a day (Weaver and Steudel-Numbers 2005, 220). Because Neanderthals were heavier than AMH and had shorter lower limbs, they had to expend 30 percent more energy than AMH in order to travel a given distance (Steudel-Numbers and Tilkens 2004). Modelling based on differences in limb length alone has shown that Neanderthals spent 78 kcal per day more on mobility than early Upper Palaeolithic AMH. If differences in body mass are taken into account this figure would rise to Neanderthals 215 kcal (Weaver and Steudel-Numbers 2005, 220-221). These figures indicate that Neanderthal body proportions may have had severe consequences for their capacity for travelling and their foraging radii (Weaver and Steudel-Numbers 2005, 221).

Neanderthal limb structure was thus less efficient for locomotion than that of the AMH. It was probably better suited to conferring power for example when thrusting a spear (Steudel-Numbers and Tilkens 2004, 160). Therefore, their limb structure may signal an adaptation to a way of life in which short bursts of great power were of more use than being able to cover large distances efficiently (Steudel-Numbers and Tilkens 2004, Stewart 2005). Some authors have interpreted this as indicating an adaptation to ambush hunting in wooded environments, where sprinting is more important than covering large distances (*e.g.* Finlayson 2005, Stewart 2005). It has also been proposed that it may have been an adaptation to locomotion in conditions with a thick snowcover, helping them to close in on, and kill prey. Short lower limbs favour force over speed and would therefore be advantageous in such situations (Porter 1999, 58).

We can conclude that while Neanderthal body structure complies with the predictions of Allen's rule and Bergman's rule, their different limb structure also had important implications for Neanderthal locomotion. We can confidently assume that Neanderthals had an elevated BMR in order to cope with cold conditions, since this is a universal adaptation among populations living in cold climates.

2.5 Neanderthal brains

As stated in the introduction, many theories that attempt to explain the evolution of modern human features focus on the links between brain size, life histories and diet (*e.g.* Aiello and Wheeler 1995, Hawkes *et al.* 1998, Kaplan *et al.* 2000, Kaplan and Robson 2002). This makes sense because brain size poses significant constraints on human ways of life on a variety of levels. These theories are usually based on comparative studies of modern humans and living primates. Neanderthals present an excellent opportunity to evaluate the validity of these models, since they also had large brains, but are generally regarded as a separate species from AMH. As Neanderthal evolution presents a case of parallel evolution of large brains, it can therefore be used to test current hypotheses and can yield clues as to whether other scenarios explaining the evolution of modern human life histories, brain size and foraging strategies should be developed. In this section, I will review the current theories regarding the link between brain size, foraging and hominin evolution. This will be combined with a presentation of the available evidence on these features from the Neanderthal fossil record.

Neanderthals had an average brain size of 1512 cm^3, against 1355 cm^3 in AMH (Wood and Collard 1999, 69). Since their bodyweight was larger than that of modern humans too, the relative brain size of both species is roughly equal, 3.06 in Neanderthals versus 3.08 in AMH (*e.g.* Wood and Collard 1999, 69). Not only was the Neanderthal brain absolutely larger than that of modern humans, their braincase had a different form: it was low, long and had bulging sides. These differences are significant because the form of the braincase is determined by the growth of the brain during development (Tattersall 1999, 12). There is no clear relation between brain-form and organization, so the differences in form do not inform us if and how Neanderthal brains functioned differently from AMH ones. Since this unique brain form is developed within the womb and determines the form of the braincase and adjacent features such as the inner ear, it does help us to classify fossils that at first glance do not seem diagnostic (Hublin *et al.* 1996).

Possessing a large brain is alleged to have severe consequences for childbearing and child-rearing, diet and even life-histories in AMH (*e.g.* Aiello and Wheeler 1995, Gibbons 1998, Hawkes *et al.* 1998, Kaplan *et al.* 2000, Mussi 1999). Since Neanderthals had brains of roughly similar size as AMH, they faced similar consequences. In modern humans babies with fully developed brains are too large to pass through the birth canal. This problem has been "solved" in AMH by giving birth "too early". Since fully developed babies could not pass through the female birth canal, human babies have brains that are about 25 percent of the adult size when they are born, while monkey and ape brains are about 70 percent of their adult size (Coqueugniot *et al.* 2004, Rosenberg and Trevathan 1996). Despite the early birth of babies, the fit between cranium size and birth canal size is so close that the baby's head has to rotate at several points in the birthing process in order to make use of the maximum dimensions of the birth canal (Rosenberg and Trevathan 1996, 162).

The implications of the early timing of childbirth are far-reaching. Human babies require a much longer period of intensive maternal care compared to monkeys and apes. On the other hand, their brain develops in an enriched environment, stimulating cognitive development. This is probably a requirement for the uptake of spoken language (Coqueugniot *et al.* 2004, 299-300). In biology, species that give birth to their young in a relatively helpless state are dubbed altricial species. In the case of AMH this process is called secondarily altricial, since the altricial pattern of giving birth has evolved out of more precocial patterns in our primate ancestors (Rosenberg and Trevathan 2002, 1205). This secondary altriciality appears to have evolved late in the hominin lineage. The Mojokerto child, an Early Pleistocene *H. erectus* specimen, displays an ape-like speed of brain development, with a brain of 72% of the adult size at between of 0.5 and 1.5 years of age (Coqueugniot *et al.* 2004). Analysis of a Neanderthal neonate and two infants shows that Neanderthals followed the same pattern as modern humans. Brain size at birth was similar in Neanderthals as in recent AMH babies. Neanderthal adults had larger brains than AMH, and data from Neanderthal infants suggests that this size was attained by a higher rate of brain growth instead of a longer period of development (Ponce de León *et al.* 2008).

Furthermore, the brain consists of so-called "expensive tissue", which needs large amounts of energy even when at rest. A species cannot simply increase its brain size indefinitely, because this would severely impact its energy requirements. Consequently a creature will either need to furnish,itself with a lot more calories and nutrients if it is to increase the amount of expensive tissue, or compensate for the increased size of the brain through a reduction of other expensive tissues (Aiello and Wheeler 1995). The latter strategy seems to be in evidence in human evolution. When we compare the expected amount of expensive tissues in a primate of human size to that actually present in humans, we see that the total size is the same. However, humans have a much larger brain than would be expected, whereas the gastro-intestinal tract is significantly smaller than expected for a primate of human size. Therefore, the increase in brain size during hominin evolution was compensated for by a reduction in gut-size (Aiello and Wheeler 1995, 203-204).

This seems an elegant solution, but it has far-reaching consequences. Because the smaller gut cannot digest specific types of food as thoroughly as a gut of the expected size for a primate of human size, the hominin diet must have diverged significantly from what our smaller-brained, ancestors with comparatively large guts ate. It is thought that the increase in hominin brain-size co-evolved with a greater reliance on high-quality foods, rich in energy, like tubers, fruit and meat (Aiello and Wheeler 1995, Kaplan *et al.* 2000, Milton 2003). In the temperate and cold environments in which Neanderthals lived, fruit and tubers were probably not available in large quantities. Therefore the share of meat is expected to have been very large in the Neanderthal diet.

The growth of the brain, which lasts until a child is about 4 years old, is also energetically expensive. This development is fuelled by the mother, first during gestation and afterwards during lactation (Gibbons 1998), which puts considerable strain on human mothers. After birth this strain continues as the mother lactates her child for an extended period of time. In Neanderthals, this problem is exacerbated by the higher rate of brain growth in children. A switch to high-quality foods may therefore enable children to draw more energy from their mother, without killing her (Gibbons 1998).

Another possible change in hominin dietary habits stemming from the reduction in gut size is an externalisation of part of the digestive process, for example by preparing the food using tools and more significantly by cooking it (Aiello and Wheeler 1995, Wrangham *et al.* 1999). Some authors think this change may have taken place early in the development of the human lineage. In support they cite possible evidence for the occurrence of fire at archaeological sites dated to about 1.6 mya (Bellomo 1994, Brain and Sillent 1988). Such evidence is very rare and unclear however. Only from the Middle Palaeolithic onwards do charcoal, burnt flints and hearths become common at sites, suggesting that the practice of cooking may have been the driving force behind the final phase of brain expansion in Neanderthals and archaic *H. sapiens* (Aiello and Wheeler 1995).

As has been argued, the development of large brains drastically changed the organisation of life of the species. Childbirth became more dangerous for mother and child than in our primate cousins. Especially mothers were put under severe energetic strain to fuel brain growth in their children, and the dietary needs of hominins were significantly altered. This leads us to expect that possessing large brains must have had significant adaptive advantages. Most importantly, we associate the possession of large brains with increased intelligence. The exact relationship between Encephalisation Quotient (EQ; relative brain size) and intelligence is unclear and EQ is not directly proportional to intelligence (*e.g.* Macphail 1982). It is assumed that there must have been a trade-off in which the disadvantages of having a large brain were offset by significant adaptive advantages, *i.e.* increased intelligence.

One of the inferred advantages of a larger brain, is the capacity for language. It has been proposed that in primates, brain size correlates with group size. If this correlation was also valid in fossil hominins, by about 500 ka group size had become so large that social relations could no longer be maintained only by grooming. Spoken language would enable more efficient maintaining of social bonds, since conversations can encompass a greater number of individuals (Dunbar 1992, Dunbar 2001). This hypothesis is hard to test archaeologically. Anatomically however, Neanderthals appear to have fulfilled all necessary conditions for the evolution of language. In order to use language, humans need to produce a much larger range of sounds than do chimpanzees. The human hyoid, which is descended compared to its position in the great apes, enables this (Nishimura *et al.* 2006). Hyoid bones have been preserved in *H. heidelbergensis* fossils from the Middle Pleistocene site of Sima de Los Huesos and in the Neanderthal skeleton of Kebara (Bar-Yosef *et al.* 1992, Martínez *et al.* 2008). Of course the hyoid may have been lowered in response to other evolutionary pressures and the ability to produce a larger range of sounds may have been a side-effect of this development (Martínez *et al.* 2008, Nishimura *et al.* 2006). It is striking however, that *H. heidelbergensis* at Sima de Los Huesos also had an ear with the structure needed to hear this increased range of sounds, something chimpanzees for example lack (Martínez *et al.* 2008, Martinez *et al.* 2004).

Another explanation of the value of a large brain focuses on foraging. It is thought that extractive foraging requires high intelligence, as does the mapping of complicated environments (Milton 1993, Reader and Laland 2002). According to this hypothesis, the large brain evolved simply to cope with ecological challenges. This hypothesis is supported by the fact that in primates there is a correlation between innovation frequency and brain size. Furthermore, most of these innovations take place in the foraging domain (Reader and Laland 2002). Further support for this hypothesis is the fact that in modern humans, foraging success seems to be related to experience, rather than physical strength (Gurven, Kaplan, and Guitierrez 2006, Kaplan *et al.* 2000, 160). These hypotheses need not be considered mutually exclusive; increased intelligence would certainly have been used in both domains. This is reinforced by the suggestion that similar decision-making mechanisms are used by modern humans in dealing with ecological and social problems (*e.g.* Todd 2000)

Neanderthals provide an interesting case with regard to evolutionary models for the increase in brain size. If, as I assume, Neanderthals were a separate species from AMH, their case can be used to test the validity of hypotheses about the causes of increasing brain size in human evolution.

2.6 Neanderthal dietary niche and its implications

While constraints on diet imposed on early hominins with brain sizes not too divergent from those of the common ancestor of chimpanzees and hominins may have been quite moderate, Neanderthals had roughly the same relative brain size as AMH. This means that the dietary requirements of their brain were comparable to those of AMH. A heavy reliance on high-quality food is therefore expected, especially since Neanderthals lived at temperate latitudes in climates that were at times much colder than at present. Plant growth was absent during a large part of the year, so high-quality plant foods would only have been available for a limited period each year. The only resource that was present in sufficient quantities year round was meat (*e.g.* Roebroeks, Conard, and Van Kolfschoten 1992, 551). Procuring meat is a dangerous job, however, certainly for mothers with helpless children. It is no coincidence that hunting is predominantly done by males, both in contemporary hunter/gatherer societies and among chimpanzees (*e.g.* Boesch 2003, Kaplan *et al.* 2000, Stanford 2001b). Scavenging, which has been proposed as an alternative to hunting, is also dangerous, since competition from other scavengers has to be faced (*e.g.* O'Connell *et al.* 2002, Tooby and DeVore 1987). We have seen that Neanderthals had high energetic demands because of their elevated BMR. Energetic needs of mothers with children were even more elevated, since children are not expected to take part in foraging activities and mothers therefore needed to provide them with sufficient high-quality food to fuel their growth, including the development of their expensive brains. The only type of food available to them in sufficient quantities across a large part of their range was meat. We do not know when a sexual division of labour was developed, but from the foregoing it follows that it must have been in place by the time hominins started to colonise temperate latitudes (*e.g.* Kaplan *et al.* 2000, Tooby and DeVore 1987).

The most direct method available for the reconstruction of Neanderthal diets is the analysis of stable isotopes extracted from their bones. Several types of isotope studies can be used to make inferences about diet. $^{13}C/^{12}C$ analyses can be used to discriminate between a diet based on C_4 and one based on C_3 plants. C_4 and C_3 employ different processes to fixate carbon from CO_2 in the atmosphere. Tropical grasses and most of our modern crops are C_4 plants. Most trees and forest plants, as well as temperate grasses are C_3 plants (Richards *et al.* 2001, Sponnheimer and Lee-Thorp 1999). In more northerly environments harbouring only C_3 plants, this type of analysis can be used to distinguish between the sort of environment food was obtained from, because forest plants contain slightly less ^{13}C than grassland and arctic plants (Bocherens and Drucker 2003). Furthermore, ^{13}C values can be used to distinguish between diets of terrestrial and marine origins, since marine animals show enriched ^{13}C values (Richards *et al.* 2001).

Other methods focus on the trophic level of foodstuffs. Animals prefer to use Calcium to build up their bones and discriminate against Strontium. Therefore, with each increase in trophic level, the ratio of Sr/Ca will show increased quantities of Ca. However, different plants contain different amounts of Sr, so some plant eaters may emit a carnivore-like signature. Furthermore, the amount of Sr in plants is also determined by the geological substrate, so migratory animals may blur the picture, because their signatures are averaged out (Wood and Strait 2004, 125-126). ^{15}N values can also be used to infer trophic level, since ^{15}N is preferentially selected by animals to construct proteins. Therefore, at each successive trophic level, a larger amount of ^{15}N is selected (Richards *et al.* 2001). However, this analysis can only be applied if sufficient collagen has been preserved in the bone (Bocherens and Drucker 2003, 6).

A number of Neanderthals from Belgium, France and Croatia, dating between 120 ka and 30 ka have been analysed. All isotope signatures point to a diet consisting almost entirely of animal matter (Bocherens and Drucker 2003, Richards *et al.* 2001, Richards *et al.* 2008b). ^{13}C values all suggest that prey animals came from open environments. For most individuals this was to be expected, since they lived during MIS 3 and 4. However, the oldest analysed individual lived in a warm period during MIS 5, either 5e or 5c, in Sclayn, Belgium. It was associated predominantly with remains of forest dwellers. However, its isotope signature suggests that it preyed on animals living in open environments. ^{15}N values showed that all analysed individuals were highly carnivorous, with values similar to those of hyenas, lions and wolves (Bocherens and Drucker 2003, 5-6). More recently Bocherens *et al.* (2005) have tried to apply a method that might allow the determination of the relative importance of different prey species in a predator's diet. This "multi-source mixing model" uses fractionation values of the ratio of ^{13}C and ^{15}N in the bones of different potential prey species and the predators in order to see which species probably contributed to the diet of the predators. The application of this technique to sites in southwestern France suggests that both hyenas and Neanderthals ate similar amounts of bovinae and large deer. Neanderthals seem to have focused heavily on woolly rhinoceros and mammoth, while hyenas on the other hand concentrated more heavily on reindeer than Neanderthals did (Bocherens *et al.* 2005, 80-81).

How consumed animal matter was procured cannot be determined from isotopic analyses. As pointed out in chapter 1, it was suggested in the 1980s that Neanderthals mainly scavenged for meat. More recent studies contradict this and it is now accepted the Neanderthals were successful hunters that were able to selectively hunt prime-aged prey. (*e.g.* Adler *et al.* 2006, Auguste 1995a, Costamagno *et al.* 2006, Gaudzinski and Roebroeks 2000, Steele 2004).

Remarkably, despite the fact that archaeozoology shows that Neanderthals were successful hunters, some researchers have proposed that they may have been less efficient foragers than AMH (*e.g.* Trinkaus and Hilton 1996). As pointed out, because of their heavy build and the cold climates in which Neanderthals lived, they probably had high energy demands (Sorensen and Leonard 2001). Estimations of their energy demands are about 4000-6000 kcal/day for men and between 3000 and 5000 kcal/day for women. Given the average foraging time in primates of about 5.7 hours/day (which is longer than human hunter/gatherers forage), they needed to produce between 770 and 1160 kcal per hour spent foraging. This is within the range of modern human hunter/gatherers. We can therefore assume that Neanderthals foraged at least as efficiently as contemporary hunter/gatherers (Sorensen and Leonard 2001, 491-492).

The wear on teeth that is caused by the processing of food can also tell us something about the properties of these foodstuffs. Comparisons with wear patterns in modern humans have been undertaken to deduce what kind of foodstuffs Neanderthals ate. It seems that Neanderthal teeth exhibit wear that in most cases falls neatly within the limits for carnivorous hunter/gatherers and in some cases falling within the limits for hunter/gatherers with a mixed diet. However, Neanderthal fossils show a large amount of variation that is attributed to the fact that the sample of Neanderthal fossils is derived from a large period of time and from very varied environmental conditions ranging from subtropical to arctic (Lalueza, Péréz-Perez, and D. Turbón 1996, 384). To complicate matters further, there is evidence for wear patterns caused by using teeth for non-masticatory purposes, for example tooth-picking (Lebel *et al.* 2001, Ungar *et al.* 1997).

2.7 Neanderthal lives

Large and expensive brains, high energetic needs and a diet of meat may have had important consequences on Neanderthal life-histories. Models of life-histories are based on AMH and living primates. They suggest some constraints to Neanderthal life-histories, but since they were a different species from AMH, they may have coped with the situation in different ways. Modern human life-histories differ significantly from those of other primates. The most important differences are our extended period of youth and our very long lifespans, also seen in ethnographically studied hunter/gatherers (e.g Hawkes *et al.* 1998, Kaplan *et al.* 2000, Sherman 1998). Many of the models explaining the evolution of changed patterns of life-histories in humans focus on the implications of brain size for the life-histories, which is why there may be parallels between modern human and Neanderthal life histories.

As discussed in the previous section, Neanderthal anatomy imposed heavy demands on females with children. It is believed that some kind of redistribution of food within the group must have come into place at some point during the evolution of the hominin lineage. There are two main competing hypotheses to explain how this was achieved.

First, there is the grandmothering hypothesis. This hypothesis explains the long human lifespan as an adaptation in which postmenopausal grandmothers help their daughters raise their offspring. Humans are the only known species of primate whose females have a long postmenopausal lifespan (Hawkes *et al.* 1998, 1336). This phenomenon may have evolved since, after a certain age, females would no longer be able to raise their own offspring effectively. Helping their daughters would then be a more profitable strategy, since the grandmother, mother and the mother's offspring share a large proportion of their genes (Hawkes *et al.* 1998). The role of grandmothers in foraging activities has been documented for example among the Hadza of Tanzania. Here, mothers, grandmothers and children forage as a team, with grandmothers working long hours in all seasons. Furthermore, their return rates are sometimes higher than those of their kin of reproductive age (O'Connell, Hawkes, and Blurton-Jones 1999). Moreover, male food-sharing does not play a large role within the family, since most of the best food that the males procure is shared outside the nuclear family (Hawkes 1993).

Prolonged survival after the reproductive age is rare in mammals. Therefore the grandmothering hypothesis is difficult to test. In some social mammals individuals live longer than their reproductive age but they do not appear to influence the fitness of their grandchildren. Among lions (*Panthera leo*) for example, the survival of grandchildren is only positively influenced if the grandmother is still reproductively active (Packer, Tatar, and Collins 1998). Among baboons (*Papio anubis*), presence of a grandmother does not affect the survival of grandchildren at all (Packer, Tatar, and Collins 1998). Another explanation is that natural selection on old individuals is not very strong. Therefore, the maladaptive menopause may not be selected against, since the females have already reproduced at a younger age. With the relationship of childhood, age of first reproduction, start of decline in reproduction, and age of death more or less constant across mammals, one could expect that humans with a childhood of ten years would start to show reproductive decline at forty and would live to 58 and 65 years of age. If one accepts that pre-modern mortality rates were high, this pattern might approximate hunter/gatherer life-histories (Packer, Tatar, and Collins 1998). However, in hunter/gatherers women frequently live considerably longer than this, so some selective benefits of longevity are still to be expected (Sherman 1998).

Although most species have been too poorly studied to determine the occurrence of a menopause and long post-reproductive lifespan, cetaceans represent a group of mammals that have a menopause and prolonged postmenopausal lifespan. Orca's (*Orcinus orca*) and the short finned pilot whale (*Globicephala macrorhynchus*) provide reasonably well-studied examples of this. The maximum lifespan of orcas is about 70 years, while reproduction ceases at about 45 years. In short-finned pilot whales, lifespan is about 63 years, while reproduction ceases at about 40 (Rendell and Whitehead 2001, 323). Both these species show long post-reproductive lifespans and may therefore be more relevant to testing the grandmothering hypothesis than lions and baboons with their far shorter post-reproductive lifespan (Packer, Tatar, and Collins 1998). A striking feature that orca's and pilot whales have in common is that they live in matrilineal groups, with complicated, group-specific behaviour that is probably cultural. Older females might therefore be a valuable source of knowledge that could influence the fitness of other group members, who are related to them, due to their living in matrilineal societies (Rendell and Whitehead 2001). Similar group-benefits have been proposed for long living matriarchs among African elephants (*Loxodonta africana*) (McComb *et al.* 2001).

An alternative for the grandmothering hypothesis, the "embodied capital model", has been proposed by Kaplan *et al.* (Gurven, Kaplan, and Guitierrez 2006, Kaplan *et al.* 2000, Kaplan and Robson 2002). This model focuses on the role of males and specifically of male hunting. Kaplan *et al.* have measured the caloric contribution of hunter-gatherer individuals throughout their lives. Their results show that during the long childhood children contribute far fewer calories than they consume. However, from about the age of 15 they start to produce a large surplus (Kaplan *et al.* 2000). This can be contrasted with the chimpanzee, where young individuals start producing the calories they need almost immediately after they are born. From these results, it seems likely that children need this long childhood in order to learn how to exploit their knowledge-intensive foraging niche. The surplus they produce reaches its maximum long after they have passed their physical prime. The surplus is especially high in hunting men, suggesting that this is an important factor in providing the non-producing children with their "missing" calories (Gurven, Kaplan, and Guitierrez 2006). This set-up can only work of course, if adults live long enough to provision the children, who by the age of 15 have consumed 25 percent of their lifetime energy consumption and produced only 5 percent (Kaplan *et al.* 2000, 161). High adult mortality in chimpanzees leaves too few older animals to provision the young, thus making it impossible for this species to extend the duration of childhood. Kaplan *et al.* (2000) conclude that intelligence, longevity and a high-quality diet must have co-evolved. This evolutionary process must also have had an impact on hominin social organization as well, since it is essential that the males, who produce the greatest surplus by hunting, share their food with the women raising children (Kaplan *et al.* 2000).

Both hypotheses have been based on modern humans, so it is interesting to see if either one applies to Neanderthal life-histories. I will therefore discuss the clues on life-histories that are provided by the Neanderthal fossil record. The rate of maturation of Neanderthals is an important point of discussion. On the basis of Neanderthal brain size it would seem logical that, like modern humans, Neanderthals would invest in a long lifespan, during which they can first acquire the complex behaviours needed to produce surpluses later in life, in order to finance the development of the brain in their children. It has been proposed that Neanderthals matured faster than modern humans however (Ramirez-Rozzi and Bermúdez de Castro 2004). These findings have been called into question by a different team of researchers whose results suggest that Neanderthal maturation fell within the range of variation seen in modern humans (Guatelli-Steinberg *et al.* 2005).

The maturation speed of individuals can be reconstructed using the periods of dental growth. Dental development correlates closely with life-histories. Teeth grow in layers and these layers show up as perikymata when teeth are microscopically examined. The average timespan of the formation of a layer in apes and humans is known to be about eight or nine days, but the variation in modern humans is large, although values lower than 6 days are unknown in both modern humans and apes. The maximum timespan may be up to 11 or 12 days. Within an individual, the number of days it takes to form a perikyma is constant, therefore, the more perikymata are visible in the enamel, the longer it took for the tooth to develop (Guatelli-Steinberg *et al.* 2005, Ramirez-Rozzi and Bermúdez de Castro 2004).

The two teams used different samples of modern humans for comparison. Ramirez-Rossi and Bermúdez de Castro used a sample of Upper Palaeolithic and Mesolithic modern humans and a sample of *H. heidelbergensis* and *H. antecessor* for comparison. They concluded that Neanderthals show significantly fewer perikymata than AMH, they also show lower numbers when compared to their predecessors. This leads them to conclude that Neanderthals must have matured about 15 percent faster than AMH's, reaching adulthood at about 15 years of age (Ramirez-Rozzi and Bermúdez de Castro 2004, 936-937). Guatelli-Steinberg *et al.* on the other hand compared the Neanderthals with three different samples: historical Inuit and two modern day samples, one from Newcastle and one from South Africa. It transpires that Neanderthals do show fewer perikymata than the Inuit, but there is no statistical difference with the Newcastle population. Moreover, they show significantly more perikymata than the South African population. They conclude that Neanderthal growth patterns fall within the modern human range (Guatelli-Steinberg *et al.* 2005).

Ramirez-Rossi and Bermúdez de Castro (2004, 938), propose that the high maturation rate may be an adaptation to elevated adult mortality. This is a plausible suggestion, since the many known Neanderthal fossils show signs of a highly dangerous lifestyle. For example, the pattern of bone fracture in Neanderthals is comparable only to rodeo-riders in modern humans (Berger and Trinkaus 1995). Moreover, Neanderthal palaeodemography is comparable to some populations of modern human hunter/gatherers, but a higher proportion of the population died as a young adult. This suggests that Neanderthal life expectancy was lower than in modern humans and that not many adults lived to a (relatively) old age. On the other hand taphonomic factors also influence the picture: most fossils were found in caves or rock shelters, at least in part because of preservation circumstances. If dying old adults were less frequently able to reach shelters, they may be underrepresented. Furthermore, choice for burial may have centred predominantly on young adults (Trinkaus 1995, 139). On the other hand, since life histories and brain size are strongly correlated in primates, faster maturation in a species with such large brains would be against ex[ectations (Guatelli-Steinberg *et al.* 2005).

Other studies have estimated maturation rate based on the emergence of teeth. The timing of the eruption of molars is correlated with important life-history traits (Dean 2006, 2801). The eruption of the first molar in the Scladina juvenile is thought to have taken place before the individual was six years of age, which is the time of eruption of the M1 in AMH, since the tooth was heavily worn by the time of death at 8 years of age. Moreover, the M2 had already emerged in this individual, while it emerges between 10 and 13 years of age in AMH (Smith *et al.* 2007). Therefore, the timing of tooth eruption in Neanderthals suggests that they developed faster than AMH juveniles.

Neanderthal teeth also provide insight in the levels of nutritional stress they experienced during teeth development. If there are nutritional shortages during teeth development, a defect called hypoplasia will develop. Some studies have suggested that Neanderthals exhibit more hypoplasias than modern humans, indicating more developmental stress (Guatelli-Steinberg, Larsen, and Huchinson 2004, 66). However, a comparison with historical Inuit teeth shows that Neanderthals have about the same frequency of hypoplasia. Furthermore, the number of perikymata within a hypoplasia is larger in the Inuit sample, suggesting that they are subject to more prolonged periods of stress (Guatelli-Steinberg, Larsen, and Huchinson 2004, 81). There is some evidence to suggest that Upper Palaeolithic modern humans show significantly more evidence of hypoplasia during infancy. This may point to an earlier cessation of lactation and thus earlier weaning of AMH, which might indicate a shorter inter-birth interval in Upper Palaeolithic modern humans (Skinner 1997, 690).

The combined evidence shows that Neanderthals may not have grown as old as modern humans. However, their childhood, even if it was shorter than in modern humans, is still quite long compared to that of other primates. The evidence regarding the duration of the childhood is ambiguous and contested though (compare for example Guatelli-Steinberg *et al.* 2005, Ponce de León *et al.* 2008, Ramirez-Rozzi and Bermúdez de Castro 2004, Smith *et al.* 2007). Moreover if we assume that Neanderthal children had the same rate of development as AMH children, the Neanderthal rate of growth would still be higher than in the case of AMH children because of larger body size and larger brains in Neanderthals. Therefore the need to provision Neanderthal children with large amounts of high-quality food in order to support their development is well established.

The grandmothering hypothesis does not explain how Neanderthal mothers could provision their children, since meat would in all probability be procured by men. Therefore, I prefer a model in which males provision the rest of the group. Still, an increase in longevity may have started developing in an earlier phase of human evolution, when plant foods were still an important part of the diet. This may have resulted in the modern human pattern of increased duration of childhood and increased adult lifespans of high productivity. Since old individuals were likely rarer than they are in modern human hunter/gatherer societies, we may envisage a role for them, not in the direct provisioning of children and grandchildren, but more as repositories of knowledge, like we see in elephants and whales. If groups consisted mainly of related individuals, this knowledge would still benefit an old individual's fitness, since it would be promoting her its kin's fitness. This role could be filled by both old males and females.

2.8 Concluding remarks

At the beginning of this chapter the choice to regard Neanderthals as a separate species from AMH was explained. The anatomical and genetic differences between Neanderthals are too large to merit the inclusion of the Neanderthals in *Homo sapiens*. As I will argue in the following chapter, the behavioural evidence supports this choice. Many of the characteristics of the biological niche of AMH appear to have come about because of the evolution of large brains. These characteristics include for example a high quality diet with an important role for meat and life-histories that are exceptional among mammals. These developments are also visible in Neanderthals.

Differences were present as well. Most obviously there are the increased energetic needs of Neanderthals, because of their larger bodies and, in cold climates, an increased BMR. Another difference is the higher cost of locomotion of Neanderthals as compared to modern humans. This may have had important consequences for Neanderthal foraging adaptations as we will see in later chapters. The increased rate of maturation of Neanderthal children is yet another difference that could have important consequences for foraging adaptations. Neanderthal children needed more calories than modern human children in order to be able to grow up faster and still have brains of equal size. However, there is less time available during childhood for learning, since they probably needed to contribute to the group's foraging effort from a younger age.

An important problem is the fact that Neanderthal dietary reliance on meat would lead us to assume a division of labour along sexual lines, based on primatological and ethnographical evidence. This has far-reaching consequences for the social organisation of Neanderthal society. Because of the heavy reliance on meat in the diet, it is unlikely that grandmothers played a very important role in the provisioning of their grandchildren. If this is correct, it would lead one to assume a fair amount of male parental investment (cf. Tooby and DeVore 1987). This is a problematic supposition, for ethnographical studies have shown that the meat that men procure while foraging is most often shared outside the nuclear family, contrary to what one would expect (Hawkes 1993). Furthermore, parental investment is only interesting for males if they have certainty of parenthood. Because of decreasing sexual dimorphism throughout human evolution and the need for cooperation between males while hunting, Neanderthals probably lived in multi-male groups in which a monogamous pair-bond might seem the obvious solution to this problem. In chimpanzees (*Pan troglodytes*), meat is used by males to attain access to females. Males invest a lot of time and energy in hunting, even when palm nuts are readily available and provide a higher caloric return rate and more saturated fat per weight unit than red colobus (*Piliocolobus badius*) meat (Stanford 2001b, 109). Stanford (*e.g.* 2001a; 2001b) sees meat as an important political tool for chimpanzee and it plays an important role in the formation and maintenance of coalitions in the fighting arena for the dominance hierarchy. This does not seem to be the case among most ethnographically known hunter/gatherers, where there is usually no visible dominance hierarchy. According to Stanford, when hunting success increased during hominin evolution, brain size increased and in the wake of this, group size increased as well. Therefore complex sharing conventions were needed in order to negotiate a working social life in this larger group (Stanford 2001a, 135-137). However, as shown by Kaplan *et al.* (2000) some sort of provisioning of women with children is needed in AMH and probably in Neanderthals too. Therefore, with Neanderthal carnivory in mind, we can hypothesize that whatever sharing conventions were in place in Neanderthal society, one of their functions must have been provisioning the children. The role of meat as social currency should not be underestimated and will be explored further in chapter 4. We must keep in mind that such patterns will probably remain archaeologically invisible and the biological approximations as sketched above will remain an important avenue to approach this subject.

Neanderthals were thus hunter/gatherers with life-histories resembling our own. However, their life was more dangerous than that of AMH, probably resulting in shorter average lifespans. Higher energetic needs in order to cope with the cold climate and differences in the mechanics of locomotion are other important differences between Neanderthal and AMH hunter/gatherers. The implications of these differences for Neanderthal foraging strategies will be examined in chapter 4.

3 Neanderthal Archaeology

3.1 Introduction

In this chapter I will discuss the behavioural information on Neanderthals provided by the archaeological record, with a focus on their subsistence behaviour. Before going into the interpretation of food remains found at archaeological sites, I will introduce ideas on the influence of mobility strategies on the formation of the archaeological record. This will be followed by a discussion of the hunter versus scavenging debate that was already touched upon in chapter 1. I will then present an overview of the different categories of food remains that have been recovered from Neanderthal archaeological sites and how they are currently interpreted. Archaeological theories and supporting evidence on the existence of a division of labour and differences between Neanderthal and AMH foraging strategies will also be touched upon. In addition to the information provided by food remains, we will look at how the study of Middle Palaeolithic artefacts can illuminate foraging behaviour. The insight gained in Neanderthal foraging behaviour will be combined with the information on Neanderthal biology presented in chapter 2. This information will be used together with Optimal Foraging Theory to produce testable hypotheses on how to interpret Neanderthal foraging behaviours.

3.2 Neanderthal mobility and the study of foraging behaviour

Hunter/gatherer societies are characterized by the fact that they are (almost) all mobile (Kelly 1992). This mobile way of life is caused by the fact that exploitation of an area depletes the available resources. Hunter/gatherers usually operate out of a home-base, exploiting the vicinity of this location. They generally forage no further than 10 kilometres from their camp (*e.g.* Binford 2001, 238, Vita-Finzi and Higgs 1970, 7). When foraging returns diminish, the group moves to another area. Even in situations where it is energetically possible to live at a single location, a mobile way of life is usually more efficient for hunter/gatherers (Kelly 1992, 53). The organisation of mobility has important implications for the formation of the archaeological record, which is important to realise when studying Middle Palaeolithic sites.

Mobility can be organised in distinct ways; the practised mobility strategies are usually dictated by the distribution of resources in the environment. Humans need many different resources, which are not always easily procurable from a specific place. Therefore, systems of mobility will be adopted in order to make sure that a group is provisioned as efficiently as possible with all the resources it needs. In general, the cost of movement is minimised while ensuring high return rates. Binford (1980) has described two extreme patterns which can be seen as the opposite ends of a continuum of ways in which mobility is usually organised.

At one end of the spectrum he recognised "foragers". According to Binford (1980), foragers "map onto resources". Foragers characteristically display a high degree of residential mobility. They operate out of a central place and do not usually store food, but gather what they need on a daily basis. When resources are depleted near the central place, they move their central place to a new area. Scarcity is dealt with by adjusting group size; fissioning to live in dispersed smaller groups when resources are scarce. They produce two types of archaeological sites, base camps that form the centre of activities and "locations", which are places where resources are extracted from the environment. Locations often leave few traces that are archaeologically recognisable; tools are rarely discarded at these sites (Binford 1980, 5-10). This strategy can be summarized as bringing consumers to resources (Kelly 1992, 45).

"Collectors" are characterized by a high degree of logistical mobility: they do not move their base-camp very often, but use expeditionary groups in order to procure the resources they need. These groups travel to areas quite far from the home base, and operate from a special-purpose camp to extract resources which they then transport back to the home base. This strategy is usually adopted in less diverse environments, where resources are dispersed. In this situation it is more efficient to bring the resources to the consumers (Kelly 1992). In this system, there is regular storage of food and a greater diversity of sites. Like foragers, collectors make use of home-bases and locations, but also field camps, from which expeditionary foraging parties operate. Furthermore, there are stations where information is gathered about resources, for example movement of prey animals, and collectors also produce storage facilities or caches (Binford 1980, 10-12).

Theoretically it might be possible to discern how mobility was organised by Neanderthals by looking at diversity of sites in the archaeological record, but ethnographic work has shown that the function of a site often changes over time. For example a site that is used as a home base in one season may be used as a special purpose camp after a residential move of the group has taken place (Binford 1982, 11-14). On the other hand, camps that are only used logistically may retain functional integrity in the archaeological record (Binford 1982, 16). An important observation by Binford (1982, 16) is that there is no necessary relationship between depositional periods and occupational episodes. We can therefore expect that the different occupational episodes will all become incorporated in the same palimpsest. This presents us with problems in periods as remote in time as the Middle Palaeolithic.

Interestingly, there seems to be a correlation between the organisation of mobility and the effective temperature of the area the group lives in. Apparently the lower the effective temperature, the more important logistical strategies become (Binford 1980, 14). Neanderthals were present in a wide range of environments, so they probably shifted between more logistically and more residentially organised systems of mobility. However, because the Pleistocene climate was considerably cooler than present-day climates for long periods of time and because Neanderthals were present mostly around temperate latitudes, following Binford's predictions we would expect Neanderthals to favour logistical mobility.

The archaeological record is hard to interpret with regard to Neanderthal mobility strategies. We know that they were highly mobile. This is illustrated by the fact that they moved raw materials through the landscape over quite large distances; sometimes up to well over a 100 kilometres. Some transfers of up to 300 kilometres are known in the late Middle Palaeolithic of Central Europe and more recently distances of at least 250 kilometres were reported for the site of Champ Grand in France (Féblot-Augustins 1993, Geneste 1989, Roebroeks, Kolen, and Rensink 1988, Slimak and Giraud 2007). Generally, in western Europe, most of the raw materials in Middle Palaeolithic assemblages come from within six kilometres of the site. The zone up to 20 kilometres from the site is generally the source of 5 to 20 percent of raw materials. Materials from more distant sources generally make up no more than one to two percent of the assemblage (Féblot-Augustins 1993, 214-215). Long distance transfers usually concern finished tools that are discarded at the end of their use-life. These are probably tools that formed part of an individual's "personal gear" that was used for quite some time (Kuhn 1995, 23-24). The high percentage of raw materials from within 6 kilometres of the site may reflect raw materials collected in the foraging radius.

In most areas there is a clear difference between Middle Palaeolithic and Upper Palaeolithic resource transfers. In the latter case, transport distances are often greater and quantities transported sometimes larger. In Upper Palaeolithic times raw material is sometimes transported in the form of cores and worked at great distances from their source, contrasting with the Middle Palaeolithic pattern of transporting finished tools. Additionally, in the Upper Palaeolithic, non-utilitarian objects are often also transported over cosiderable distances, like shells for beads (Adler *et al.* 2006, Roebroeks, Kolen, and Rensink 1988). This may be the result of exchange between Upper Palaeolithic people while there are no convincing indications for trade or exchange in the Middle Palaeolithic (*e.g.* Adler *et al.* 2006, Gamble 1999)

The frequency and the organisation of Middle Palaeolithic moves are difficult to distil from the archaeological record. An interesting starting point is Stewart's (2005, 38) impression that Middle Palaeolithic archaeological sites often seem to be located at places of ecological transition. Apparently Neanderthals preferred diverse environments, which enabled them to exploit a large range of resources from the base camp. This was reinforced by the fact that the environment that was present in Europe during much of the Pleistocene, the so-called mammoth steppe, was probably more productive and diverse than the Holocene environments. In the Holocene and presumably also in earlier warm climatic phases, Europe was covered in homogeneous vegetation zones, while the mammoth steppe was characterised by more mosaic vegetation patches (*e.g.* Stewart 2005, 38). This suggests that Neanderthals preferred to minimise the number of residential moves they had to make, while trying to avoid logistical activities by locating sites at places where provisioning of was straightforward. For the Levantine Neanderthal sites, a model of residential stability has been proposed, *i.e.* sites were used for extended periods of time and provisioned in bulk from extractive sites, suggesting that in some areas Neanderthals resorted to logistical mobility (Shea 2003, 181-182). The Mediterranean, an ecologically diverse and productive environment, may have represented an area where most resources could be easily procured from a residential base. Therefore they probably resorted to higher logistical mobility in order to minimise residential moves.

It seems that the southern parts of the Neanderthal range, sites generally have a higher artefact density than in the north. This may reflect more intensive occupation of these sites (Gamble 1999, 201-205). However, in the southern area of the Neanderthal range cave sites are more common than in the north. Caves are an excellent preservational environment and often harbour the remains of multiple occupations. They often yield high concentrations of artefacts that were deposited over a considerable period of time. The differential distribution of cave sites may then bias our impression of the intensity of Neanderthal occupation in the northern and southern parts of their range respectively. On the other hand, in northern caves, larger areas have usually been excavated and caves have been completely cleared in places, suggesting lower artefact densities at these sites than in the south (Gamble 1999, 201-205). This indicates that northern sites were used less intensively and therefore may have functioned in a different system of mobility.

I will assume that Neanderthals used central places. I consider these to be places where the spoils of the range of activities carried out by different group members were exchanged. Although some authors dismiss the idea that Neanderthals used central places (see for a discussion Kolen 1999, Mussi 1999). I think the archaeological record shows beyond doubt that some archaeological sites functioned as a central place. I take the following factors as indications for the function of a site as a central place:

- Site architecture like hearths.
- Large numbers of stone artefacts, reflecting many different stages in the reduction sequence.
- Large amounts of bone material, exhibiting traces of hominin modification and preferably reflecting multiple species of animal.
- Minimal indications of carnivore activity.
- Preferably different spatial location of areas of tool use and discard. The formation of trash middens.

The last criterion is one of Schiffer's important c-transforms; it posits that with more intense use of a location secondary refuse deposits will be formed (Schiffer 1972, 162).

The function of a site also influences which kinds of materials are represented. Central places probably provide the most complete insight in the range of foraging activities that were practised. However, because transport costs are usually minimised, processing of resources at locations in the field influences the representation of different activities at central places. We expect large animals to be more thoroughly processed in the field than small animals for example. With regard to stone tools, raw materials are often worked at the place where they were collected, thus some stages of tool production are underrepresented at central places.

Mobility influences more than the function of sites and which materials end up at which sites though. For example the design of stone tools may be determined to a large degree by considerations with regard to their function in a mobile way of life. In a highly mobile society, people may opt to produce highly versatile tooltypes, thus minimizing the number of different tools that have to be transported. If transport costs are less important, or if activities to which tools are geared are highly important, more specialised tools will be produced (*e.g.* Bleed 1986, Shott 1986).

All in all, the materials we find at archaeological sites are influenced by the way in which societal mobility was organised. We might expect that central places will present us with the full suite of remains connected to subsistence activities, but some activities will be severely underrepresented because of processing activities and so on. Part of the material record connected with subsistence strategies may have been left behind at other locations. Special purpose locations can yield detailed information on specific activities that were performed there, but these sites do not inform us on the importance of the activity within the full suite of subsistence behaviours. For a full picture of Neanderthal foraging strategies we need to be aware that different types of sites can provide complementary evidence.

3.3 Neanderthal archaeozoology

3.3.1 Introduction

Bone assemblages are our principal source of information about Neanderthal subsistence behaviour. In this section I will summarise the evolution of ideas on the interpretation of the archaeological record of Neanderthals. I discuss the implications of the hunting vs. scavenging debate for our interpretations of Middle Palaeolithic bone assemblages. This will be followed by a sketch of the "post-scavenging-debate" consensus, and an overview of current questions and debates in the field of Neanderthal archaeozoology. Moreover, I will present the variety of remains that have been found at Middle Palaeolithic sites, underscoring the variability of Middle Palaeolithic subsistence behaviour. I intend to highlight the most important issues in this field and end up with a basis that can be used in the development of OFT-models.

3.3.2 The hunting vs. scavenging debate

As outlined in chapter 1, research commencing in the 1970's and 1980's has pointed out that reconstructing prehistoric subsistence behaviour on the basis of archaeological bone assemblages is not as straightforward as was once thought. Taphonomic research has shown that hominin activities were often not the only activities that contributed to the formation of bone assemblages found in association with stone tools (*e.g.* Binford 1981, Brain 1981, Isaac 1983). Moreover, even when human involvement in the formation of bone assemblages could be demonstrated, traditional hypotheses about what behaviour was exhibited by these hominins was challenged. Lewis Binford proposed that

Figure 3.1: Map showing the location of the most important sites mentioned in the text: 1 Pakefield; 2 Lynford; 3 Boxgrove; 4 La Cotte de Saint-Brelade; 5 Gröbern; 6 Schöningen; 7 Salzgitter-Lebenstedt; 8 Lehringen; 9 Wallertheim; 10 Taubach; 11 Zwoleń; 12 Il'Skaya; 13 Ortvale Klde; 14 Kebara; 15 Quneitra; Grotta dei Moscerini; 17 Biache-Saint-Vaast; 18 Mauran; 19 Grotte XVI; 20 Combe Grenal; 21 La Borde; 22 Ambrona; 23 Gorham's Cave, 24 Vanguard Cave.

hominin involvement with animal carcasses was not the result of hunting, but probably of a form of marginal scavenging (*e.g.* Binford 1981, Binford 1984).

The research that started this debate was done on very early archaeological sites in Africa. Brain (1981) convincingly demonstrated that South African Australopithecines were not savage killers as previously thought. Careful taphonomic analyses of the caves in which hominin fossils were found led him to the conclusion that they, and the other animals found at the sites, had actually been preyed upon by felines. Binford (1981) meanwhile, had made a strong case for interpreting the bone assemblages at the sites in the Olduvai Gorge as the result of scavenging. These revolutionary studies questioned interpretations about early hominin hunting strategies that been taken for granted for a long time, and led to more critical studies of archaeological bone assemblages.

There were also repercussions for Neanderthal archaeology. The view propagated by Binford was that hunting animals like ungulates, did not occur in prehistory until very recently. Even Anatomically Modern Humans (AMH) in Africa, at Klasies River Mouth, dated from 125 ka to 35 ka, practised scavenging as an important subsistence strategy (Binford 1984, Binford 1985). According to Binford, only small mammals were hunted regularly at this site and hunting only became important in the later part of the sequence (Binford 1984).

Binford also analysed some European sites, namely Torralba-Ambrona in Spain and Grotte Vaufrey and Combe Grenal in France. Torralba, now dated to MIS 12 (Villa *et al.* 2005) had originally been interpreted as a site where early hominins hunted straight-tusked elephants *(Palaeoloxodon antiquus)*. Binford (1987) concluded that the representation of bones and the distribution of stone artefacts among them were indicative of elephant exploitation by hominins, but not by way of hunting. He considered this assemblage to be the result of marginal scavenging. A more recent re-analysis of this site indicates that both previous interpretations must be rejected. Taphonomic analysis shows that the co-occurrence of artefacts and bones is the result of several processes, including natural deaths, fluvial action and some hominin activities (Villa *et al.* 2005). At the Grotte Vaufrey, a French Middle Palaeolithic site dated to MIS 6 or 7 (Grayson and Delpech 1994), Binford claimed that the assemblage was also the result of Neanderthals scavenging ungulate remains (Binford 1988). In this case, re-analysis has shown that the statistics he used were faulty and that evidence to indicate that the assemblage was the result of scavenging is absent (Grayson and Delpech 1994). For Combe Grenal, Binford concluded that hunting was practised in the second phase of the Weichselian, up to 45 ka, but only on medium-sized animals; large mammals like horse and aurochs were still scavenged (Binford 1985, 320). This study was never published in detail, and hence cannot be checked.

More recently, Stiner (1994), analysed a number of Italian Middle Palaeolithic archaeological sites and concluded that they provide evidence of a largely scavenging mode of subsistence prior to 50 ka. These assemblages are dominated by head parts, thought to be the parts that are most difficult to exploit for carnivores and therefore the remains that were left to hominin scavengers. Her findings were examined by Mussi (*e.g.* 1999), who concluded that the fact that Stiner's early assemblages were head-dominated, reflected the method of bone collection used during the excavations. Apparently, the excavators focused on determinable anatomical elements, which led to a bias towards head elements (Mussi 1999, 65-66).

These findings illustrate the outcome of the debate. Careful re-analyses of many sites have shown their interpretation in terms of human subsistence strategies to be far from straightforward. Sites often have very complicated taphonomic histories and the final assemblage is the result of various processes, like fluvial sorting, carnivore activity and hominin behaviour. At sites where hominin activities are the most important contributing factor to the accumulation of the bone assemblage, hunting has proven to be the main mode of acquisition of animal matter by Neanderthals. Scavenging on the other hand was only rarely practised, if at all.

3.3.3 Specialised hunting of ungulates
Before and during the archaeological debate on scavenging, there were ecologists claiming that specialised hunting was the only strategy that could logically be practised by hominins: especially by Neanderthals living in environments with long winters, with no vegetable alternatives to meat (*e.g.* Geist 1978, Tooby and DeVore 1987). Moreover, scavenging niches are characterised by fierce competition, not only with other mammalian carnivores, but also with birds, insects and micro-organisms. Mammalian scavengers are dangerous to compete with, since most are also predators. Micro-organisms make carcasses inedible, hence obligate scavengers have digestive defences to deal

with rotting meat. Since scavenging is a competitive niche requiring specialisations, it was considered unlikely that hominins ever relied on this strategy (Tooby and DeVore 1987, 221).

As a reaction to the proposition that hominins were obligate scavengers, research into how to recognise sites that were the product of hunting intensified. A number of criteria were proposed. An obvious criterion is that a site should contain evidence for intensive hominin exploitation in the form of cut-marks or bones exploited for their marrow. Another factor deemed important was whether the hunting effort was concentrated on one species, in order to rule out more opportunistic strategies. A further indication as to the manner in which a bone assemblage was formed can be obtained by studying the age-profile of the prey animals. Different age-profiles are indicative of different strategies of acquiring meat (*e.g.* Auguste 1995a, Speth and Tchernov 1998). The composition of bone assemblages can show whether the accumulator had early access to the carcass or not. It is thought that the sequence of disarticulation of a carcass is similar in most cases. Entrails are generally consumed first, followed by the hindlegs and the frontlegs (*e.g.* Potts 1983). Head and foot parts are generally deemed least profitable for carnivores and will therefore be available to scavengers in the largest quantities. Unfortunately, this patterning is not constant, since transport and processing decisions have a large influence (*e.g.* Domínguez-Rodrigo 2002, 9-13).

A natural death assemblage is usually dominated by animals at the weakest stages of life, mostly the very young and old; this is an "attritional" age-profile. Assemblages produced by cursorial hunters tend to mimic this kind of assemblage, since they tend to focus on the weakest individuals (Steele 2002, Stiner 1994). On the other hand, a living population is usually dominated by animals in the "fittest" stages of life, since weak animals are filtered out. A death assemblage resembling the structure of a living population will only occur if a great catastrophe like a volcano or a flood kills every animal in its path (Steele 2002, Stiner 1994). Nevertheless, some predators use strategies that enable them to also target these "fit" age-classes. This is the most rewarding prey since it is in the prime of its life, but it is also the hardest to acquire and the most dangerous, for the same reasons. Ambush hunters usually prefer these prime-aged individuals (*e.g.* Husseman 2003). Only one extant species consistently targets the prime-aged adults of a population when hunting and that is anatomically modern man (Steele 2004, 307, Stiner 2002, 20). Sites that yield evidence for this kind of specialised hunting are generally thought to appear late in prehistory, after 250 ka (Stiner 2002, 34, 37). This pattern may be partly due to the fact that Lower and Middle Palaeolithic sites are usually characterised by a long and complicated taphonomic history. At older sites, taphonomic processes have had more time to blur the archaeological signature originally present. The archaeological record is therefore biased toward the younger sites. On the other hand, some sites where specialised hunting of ungulates was practised, (*e.g.* Mauran, Ortvalde Klde) were formed over a period of several years. The fact that these palimpsests show a narrow focus, and palimpsests from the Lower Palaeolithic often do not, suggests that the character of hominin hunting strategies may have changed between the Lower and Middle Palaeolithic. Specialised hunting of ungulates may therefore be more characteristic of the Middle Palaeolithic.

An early and very famous example of a site dominated by a single taxon is Schöningen, a German site dated to between 400 and 300 ka. The site was located at the edge of a small lake and has been exceptionally well preserved (Thieme 1997). Eight wooden spears were found in association with a bone assemblage containing about 20 horses as well as stone tools. It appears a family group was ambushed here, driven into the marshy edge of a lake and killed. Cut-marks on the bones are ubiquitous and processing of the carcasses was aimed at recovery of meat and marrow. Furthermore, exploitation marks pointing to the exploitation of the hides are also in evidence (Voormolen 2008). The exploitation of meat may not have been very intensive, though. Some elements show low frequencies of cut-marks. This may be caused by the fact that a complete herd of animals was available (Voormolen 2008). This site proves that from the Lower Palaeolithic onwards, hominins were able to ambush herds of large ungulates and despatch them.

Most European sites with a bone assemblage dominated by a single species and showing reliable indications of human hunting date to the last glacial-interglacial cycle (MIS 5-3). The majority of these also exhibit a clearly prime-age dominated age-profile (Gaudzinski and Roebroeks 2000). Prime-aged dominated assemblages have already been demonstrated at least from MIS 6 (Steele 2004, 314). A selection of sites thought to indicate specialized hunting of a single species can be found in table 3.1. The targeted species were dependent on local environment and climate, and range from Caucasian tur (*Capra caucasica*) in the east to Bison (*Bison priscus*) in the western part of their range. As pointed out, for some of these it can be demonstrated that the location was used

Site	Main species	MNI	NISP	Date	Refs	Remarks
Schöningen (De)	*Equus mosbachensis*	20		350 ka	(Thieme 1997, Voormolen 2008)	Lake edge, not prime dominated? (Voormolen pers. comm.)
Wallertheim (De)	*Bison priscus*	52 (59)	861 (1557)	114-108 ka	(Gaudzinski 1995)	Numbers in brackets are numbers with bones not assignable to findlayer included.
Zwoleń (Pl)	*Equus caballus*	38	239	70 ka	(Schild et al. 2000)	At confluence of small and large valley, finds spread over at least 7500 sq. m., only 523 sq. m. excavated.
Salzgitter-Lebenstedt (De)	*Rangifer tarandus*	86	2130	Oerel 58-54 ka	(Gaudzinski and Roebroeks 2000)	At confluence of small and large valley, also mammoth bone tools.
Les Pradelles (Fr)	*Rangifer tarandus*	55	1277	MIS 4-3	(Costamagno et al. 2006)	Cave site, not the hunting location.
Ortvale Klde (Ge)	*Capra caucasica*	33	3021	43-36 ka	(Adler et al. 2006)	Along migration valley.
La Borde (Fr)	*Bos primigenius*	27	410	Last/penultimate interglacial	(Jaubert et al. 1990)	Sinkhole used as trap? Higher MNI using wear stages of teeth.
Mauran (Fr)	*Bison priscus*	83	4150	Early Weichsel	(Farizy et al. 1994)	Few animals taken each year for long period of time. Only 25 sq. m. excavated of estimated area of 1000 sq. m
Il'Skaya (Ru)	*Bison priscus*	51	1334	Early Weichsel	(Gaudzinski 1996)	
Grotte Saint-Marcel (Fr)	*Cervus elaphus*	77	1031	MIS 3	(Moncel et al. 2004)	Cave site, not the hunting location.

Table 3.1: Sites dominated by a single species in the European Middle Palaeolithic.

in a similar way for a long time, with several individuals being taken each year (Adler *et al.* 2006, Farizy *et al.* 1994). The location of some sites points to strategic hunting behaviour by Neanderthals. Salzgitter and Zwoleń for example are located at "natural ambush" locations, at the confluence of small steep valleys with larger ones. Presumably the large valley was used by the prey as migration route and hominin hunters could easily select their preferred prey at such locations (Gaudzinski and Roebroeks 2000, 509-510). These characteristics point to a function as special-purpose locations in Neanderthal mobility systems. They may have been visited repeatedly, but only one specific activity is represented.

3.3.4 Neanderthals and megafauna

The considerable number of sites showing specialised ungulate hunting published in the last decades has shown that Neanderthals were perfectly capable of hunting medium to large sized ungulates. This was certainly the case during the last glacial – interglacial cycle and earlier, as proved by Schöningen. However, more dangerous animals were also an option: for example megafaunal species like mammoth and rhinoceros. There is evidence that Neanderthals were involved in processing carcasses of megafauna. As suggested by an isotopic study (see section 2.6) these species may even have been important constituents of the (late) Neanderthal diet (Bocherens *et al.* 2005). The interpretation of Neanderthal dealings with megafaunal species are not as unambiguous as is the case for ungulates. In exploiting these species, alternative strategies like scavenging may have been more profitable than in the case of smaller species. Actualistic research in Africa has shown that carcasses of megafaunal species provide the best scavenging opportunities for hominins (Blumenschine 1987). Even nowadays in Europe scavengeable resources are available for much longer than in Africa (Fosse *et al.* 2004). In colder glacial climates availability could last even longer, so scavenging carcasses of megafauna may have been a profitable strategy.

The site of Ambrona was already mentioned in the discussion on the hunting vs. scavenging debate. While it does not furnish unequivocal evidence for either hunting or scavenging of straight-tusked elephants, the co-occurrence of elephant bones, some cut-marked and stone tools does show that hominins were sometimes involved in processing carcasses of megafauna. Even though the evidence to link the elephant bones to the stone tools and thus hominin activities is scanty, there are some indications of hominin interference with the bones: one cut-marked cranium and three femora that show anthropic breakage (Villa *et al.* 2005). However, there are sites in Europe where hominin involvement with megafaunal remains was less ephemeral than at Ambrona. Table 3.2 shows a selection of sites yielding evidence of hominin involvement with megafauna.

Site	Species	Date	Remarks	Refs
Boxgrove (GB)	*Stephanorhinus hundsheimensis*	MIS 13	Prime aged, according to anecdote in (Pitts and Roberts 1997)	(Pitts and Roberts 1997, 266-267, Stringer et al. 1998)
Ambrona (Es)	*Paleoxodon antiquus*	MIS 12	Natural elephant deaths, fluvial transport of bones and stones. Some of the artefacts are abraded. Not much evidence to link artefacts and bones; (very few) cut-marks (Villa et al. 2005, 235).	(Villa et al. 2005)
Ebbsfield (Southfleet road) (GB)	*Palaeoloxodon antiquus*	MIS 11	Preliminary report, no NISP, no age. Authors are not certain about hunting.	(Wenban-Smith et al. 2006)
Aridos 1 (Es)	*Palaeoloxodon antiquus*	MIS 9 or 11	1 Individual; hominins had primary access; small stone artefact assemblage	(Santonja et al. 2001, Villa 1990)
Biache-Saint-Vaast (Fr)	*Dicerorhinus hemitoechus*	MIS 7-6	Many individuals; lots of stone tools	(Auguste 1988a, Auguste 1988b, Auguste 1992, Auguste 1995a)
La Cotte de Saint-Brelade (GB)	*Mammuthus primigenius, Coelodonta antiquitatis*	MIS 6	Two levels, both containing remains of multiple individuals; small stone tool assemblages	(Scott 1980, Scott 1986)
Lehringen (De)	*Palaeoloxodon antiquus*	MIS 5e	Much of material destroyed before recording; 1 old individual, few tools.	(Gaudzinski 2004, Thieme and Veil 1985)
Gröbern (De)	*Palaeoloxodon antiquus*	MIS 5e	1 old and diseased individual; possible scavenging; few tools	(Gaudzinski 2004)
Taubach (De)	*Stephanorhinus kirchbergensis*	MIS 5e	Old collection, at best sample of what was originally there. (Gaudzinski 2004) gives different MNI's.	(Bratlund 1999)
Mont Dol (Fr)	*Coelodonta antiquitatis*	MIS 5b	8 individuals. 6 mature. Cut marks on economically important bones	(Auguste, Moncel, and Patou-Mathis 1998, 139-140)
Buhlen (De)	*Mammuthus primigenius*	56-40 ka	Fauna dominated by young and prime-aged individuals.	(Schuurman 2004)
Asolo (It)	*Mammuthus primigenius*	MIS 4-3	1 mature female; associated flint artefacts, no cut-marks	(Mussi and Villa 2008)
Lynford (GB)	*Mammuthus primigenius*	MIS3 beginning	No cut-marks; hunting inferred from selective transport of leg bones	(Schreve 2006)

Table 3.2: Selection of sites pointing to hominin involvement with megafauna.

First, at some sites scattered throughout Europe a single carcass of an elephant is associated with a stone tool assemblage, while there is no evidence for primary carnivore involvement with the carcass. In some cases it is difficult to determine what the method of procurement of the elephant was. Neither hunting nor scavenging can be ruled out here. The interpretation of sites containing elephant remains is complicated, since at many sites no cut-marks are preserved (*e.g.* Lynford, Asolo, Lehringen). This is partly due to the structure of elephant bones which does not preserve cut-marks well (Scott 1980, 144). Therefore the character of hominin involvement with proboscideans at most sites remains unresolved.

In some cases circumstantial evidence allows us to argue for either hunting or scavenging. For example, at the German site of Lehringen, dated to the Eemian, an elephant carcass was found in association with stone tools and a wooden spear (Gaudzinski 2004, Thieme and Veil 1985). The find of a spear is quite a powerful argument in favour of an explanation in terms of hunting. The skeleton belonged to a 45-year-old male individual, so in this case an older individual was selected instead of a prime-aged individual. Another German site, Gröbern, also dated to the Eemian, yielded the skeleton of a diseased elephant. The position of its bones suggested to the excavators that the skeleton was probably scavenged. Gnaw marks indicate that wolves also had access to the carcass (Gaudzinski 2004, 204).

Other sites yielded the remains of multiple carcasses of megafaunal species, showing that in some cases megafauna was a consistent focus of hominin activities. Two of these sites, Taubach and Biache-Saint-Vaast, will be the subject of a more detailed analysis in chapter 5. At these sites the exploited megafaunal species were rhinoceroses. To illustrate, we will look into the bones identified at Taubach, a site dated to MIS 5e. The site was located in an area where travertine was formed during the Eemian. During this period, the area probably functioned as a salt lick for Merck's rhinoceros (*Stephanorhinus kirchbergensis*). The number of individuals represented in the collection, 44, suggests that this was known to hominins, who repeatedly visited the site. Hunting was focused on juvenile rhinoceroses, possibly in order to lessen the risk associated with the activity. On the other hand, other large and dangerous species were also exploited at this site. The focus of brown bear (*Ursus arctos*) exploitation at the site was on adults. Bear hunting is considered to be very dangerous. The fact that this is ethnographically known to have been the first activity to see traditional methods abandoned in favour of firearms upon their introduction serves as testimony to its risk (Bratlund 1999, 147). Moreover, even when using firearms, it is apparently advisable to use a large calibre gun and fire multiple shots when hunting bears (Charles 1997). Nevertheless, the spear found at Lehringen testifies to the possibility of direct combat.

Using devices like pitfalls and other strategies that minimise direct combat would be advantageous in the successfull hunting of megafauna. In this respect La Cotte de Saint-Brelade is an interesting site. This site is located on Jersey; the layers containing the megafaunal assemblage are dated to the later part of MIS 6 (Scott 1980, 141). Layers 3 and 6 at this site are located at the bottom of a cliff, about 35 metres high (Scott 1980, 153). Both layers contain quite large numbers of mammoth (*Mammuthus primigenius*) bones and smaller numbers of woolly rhinoceros (*Coelodonta antiquitatis*) bones. Some artefacts were found in association with these bones. The bones do not show signs of carnivore activity, while some cut-marks are present. Moreover, some of the skulls seem to have been broken to retrieve to brains (Scott 1980, 150).[2] It seems that these two layers represent two episodes of which mammoths and woolly rhinoceros being driven off the cliff to fall to their deaths, upon which they were exploited by hominins.

Sites that provide evidence of the hunting of megafauna are rare. Many sites offer only minimal indications for hominin involvement with these animals. Some sites do contain large numbers of rhinoceros bones, showing that hunting these animals was not beyond the capabilities of Neanderthals. This is supported by recent isotopic data (Bocherens *et al.* 2005).

3.3.5 Central places: Sites exhibiting the full suite of Neanderthal foraging strategies?

Specific targeting of medium-sized and large mammals has been demonstrated above. Most of the sites mentioned in the previous sections can only be interpreted as special purpose sites. They usually represent specific subsistence activities. The large number of sites showing heavy reliance on only one or a few species is sometimes used to argue that Neanderthals were inflexible foragers and had a low diet breadth (Adler *et al.* 2006, 90). Nonetheless, there are also Middle Palaeolithic sites where multiple activities are represented. The structured use of some of these sites and the indications that they were occupied for long periods of time, lead to an interpretation as central places (sensu Isaac 1978). To illustrate this type of site, I will discuss Kebara cave in Israel, a clear example of a central place that conforms to all the criteria discussed in section 3.2.

Located close to the Mediterranean coast, Kebara has been the subject of archaeological excavations for a long time. Parts of the cave were excavated from the 1930's onwards, and in the 1980s and 1990s extensive excavations with a focus on the Middle Palaeolithic occupation of the cave were carried out (Bar-Yosef *et al.* 1992), dated to between 60 and 48 ka (Bar-Yosef *et al.* 1992, 508). During this period the Levant was occupied by Neanderthals. Furthermore, a Neanderthal skeleton has been found in the cave. This find has been interpreted as a burial. The fossil is very well preserved, yielding the only known "classic Neanderthal" pelvis and the only known complete Neanderthal hyoid bone (Bar-Yosef *et al.* 1992, 528).[3]

The Middle Palaeolithic sequence at Kebara spans several metres of sediment and the bedrock has not been reached in the excavations. The sequence can be divided into two parts. First there are early, ephemeral occupations of the central part of the cave, leaving few bones and artefacts. After an erosional episode, a second phase of Mousterian occupations followed. During this phase, occupation was more substantial, with structured use of the central part of the cave and the accumulation of a bone midden near the north wall. During this phase of occupation more than 3.5 metres of sediment was deposited (Bar-Yosef *et al.* 1992, 501, 531). The industry in the Middle Palaeolithic layers is classified as Levantine Mousterian. This is a Mousterian facies characterised by a high percentage of pointed forms.

---

2   Even Binford was convinced of the absence of carnivore traces on the bones and the presence of traces of human modification pointing to dismemberment (Binford 1981, 287-288).

3   If we accept *Homo heidelbergensis* as belonging to the same chronospecies as Neanderthals, another complete pelvis and two hyoid bones are known from Sima de los Huesos (Arsuaga *et al.* 1999, Martínez *et al.* 2008). A hyoid body has also been discovered at El Sidrón (Martínez *et al.* 2008).

While the several metres of Middle Palaeolithic sediment accumulated, the space in the cave was used in a fixed and structured manner. Hearths were constructed in the central zone of the cave, probably in excavated pits (Meignen *et al.* 1998, 231). The location of these hearths remained constant for long periods of time. One concentration could be traced through a column of 60 centimetres of sediment, without the bottom being reached (Meignen *et al.* 1998, 229). Such constancy of hearths has been observed at other sites with a long stratigraphic sequence and this sort of behaviour may date back to at least MIS 9 times (*e.g.*Moncel, Moigne, and Combier 2005, 1299). However, constant use of space at a site depends on several factors. First, a change in site function may affect the use of space. Second, the form of caves may change through time, which also affects the place of hearths. Constant use of a hearth spanning multiple burning episodes in one stratigraphic level may thus already signal structured use of space suggesting the use of a site as a central place (*e.g.* Moncel, Moigne, and Combier 2005, Vaquero *et al.* 2001). In addition to the fact that the hearths in the central area of the cave at Kebara were used for long periods of time, the rest of the central area was cleared of bones, as a result they are only found in the hearths and in the midden (Meignen *et al.* 1998, 229). During the later phases of the Middle Palaeolithic occupation, most of the bones, and many of the stone artefacts were deposited in a midden along the north wall of the cave (Bar-Yosef *et al.* 1992, Speth and Tchernov 2001). This suggests that the central area of the cave was used intensively as a living space. It was regularly cleared and the waste was accumulated along the northern wall.

The recovered bone assemblage is large (see table 3.3). Most of it was deposited during the "midden-phase" of the Middle Palaeolithic occupation. The bone assemblage contains abundant traces of hominin modification like burning and cut-marks, but some carnivore damage is present too, in the form of gnaw-marks and etching of bones (*e.g.* Bar-Yosef *et al.* 1992, Speth and Tchernov 1998). Moreover, coprolites and some hyena bones point to the occasional presence of these carnivores. However, hominins were the principal accumulating agent, while carnivores exploited the bones discarded by the occupants of the site. This is shown by the fact that lithics and bones are intermingled in the bone midden. The north wall bone concentrations grade into the ash lenses of the central occupation area. The burnt bones are also found mainly in the midden, while burning took place in the hearths. This shows that the burning took place before the final deposition of the bones (Speth and Tchernov 2001, 64). Furthermore, it is hypothesised that occupation of the site was very intensive and lasted for prolonged periods of time (Shea 2003, 181). This would rule out an interpretation involving hyena denning, since hyena cubs stay close to the den for at least 15 months (Bar-Yosef *et al.* 1992, Speth and Tchernov 1998). If hyenas had transported bones, they would have transported them away from the site. The fact that soft elements are underrepresented and the bias against upper limbs points to significant attrition of the assemblage by carnivores (Speth and Tchernov 1998, 228). Finally, the early Middle Palaeolithic and Upper Palaeolithic occupations show more indications of carnivore activity than the bones of the "midden-phase". During the "midden-phase" skeletal completeness is highest, suggesting that attrition was at a minimum took place during this phase (Speth and Tchernov 2001, 65-67).

The permanent "architecture" in the cave, such as the hearths and the midden suggests that the cave was occupied in a structured, repeated and intensive way during part of its Middle Palaeolithic use-life. This notion is reinforced by the fact that exactly during this "midden-phase" there are the fewest indications for carnivore activities.

All in all, thousands of animal bones have been found in the cave, identification of which is a lengthy process (see changes in NISP given in the following publications Bar-Yosef *et al.* 1992, Speth and Tchernov 1998, Speth and Tchernov 2001, Speth and Tchernov 2003). However, the pattern of Neanderthal faunal exploitation emerging from the bone assemblages has not changed with the increase in number of identified bones; an overview of the identified assemblage is presented in table 3.3.

The main focus of Neanderthal subsistence in Kebara was on gazelle (*Gazella gazelle*) and fallow deer (*Dama dama*). This pattern is common in the Middle Palaeolithic of the Near East. The relative importance of gazelle and fallow deer at archaeological sites appears to have been influenced by climatic developments, with fallow deer more common in moist periods and gazelle better represented in arid phases. This led to the compilation of a Gazella/Dama curve to track climatic fluctuations in the region (Bate 1937), as curve still used nowadays (*e.g.* Speth and Tchernov 2003). The abundance of these species cannot be equated directly to their economic importance; since red deer (*Cervus elaphus*) and aurochs (*Bos primigenius*) are considerably larger than the aforementioned species, their

Species	Number of bones	Percentage	Percentage with "rest" excluded
Gazella gazelle	8121	38.52%	46.75%
Dama dama	4036	19.14%	23.23%
Testudo graeca	2345	11.12%	13.50%
Cervus elaphus	965	4.58%	5.56%
Bos primigenius	826	3.92%	4.76%
Sus scrofa	710	3.37%	4.09%
Capra cf. *aegagrus*	167	0.79%	0.96%
Equus spp.	137	0.65%	0.79%
Capreolus capreolus	64	0.30%	0.37%
Indet/other	3714	17.61%	
Total	21085	100.00%	100.00%

Table 3.3: The Middle Palaeolithic faunal assemblage of Kebara, based on (Speth and Tchernov 2003).

economic importance will have been larger than it seems from the NISP data alone (*e.g.* Bar-Yosef *et al.* 1992, Speth and Tchernov 2001, Speth and Tchernov 2003).

The ages of the gazelle, fallow deer, aurochs, and wild boar (*Sus scrofa*) sample present at the site have been reconstructed by analysing wear stages of their teeth. The gazelle, aurochs and boar samples are prime-age dominated. Their age-profiles fall in the range of prey ages usually associated with ambush hunting by animals. The fallow deer sample in the lower levels is dominated by juveniles, possibly because of the small sample size. In later levels it appears to be dominated by prime-aged individuals (Speth and Tchernov 1998, 231-233).

This picture of subsistence strategies is drawn from a palimpsest of bones from occupations spanning about 12 ka. In later publications, the authors have tried to track changes in the bone assemblage through time. This is difficult as the bone sample they used was collected in two different excavation campaigns that used different stratigraphic strategies. Therefore, only rough conclusions can be reached, based on analysing bone assemblages per 50 cm. spit (Speth and Tchernov 2001, 54-55). This analysis, although not very fine-grained, reveals some interesting patterns.

During the earlier part of the Middle Palaeolithic occupation of the cave, as well as during the Upper Palaeolithic occupation, the gazelle and fallow deer samples are male-dominated. This is interesting for there is an excellent body of data on the yearly behavioural cycle of fallow deer. With regard to gazelle, the data is poorer but their cycle roughly coincides with that of fallow deer cycle (Speth and Tchernov 2001, 58-60). Fallow deer males are in rut during the late summer and early autumn. They do not eat much during this period, so their condition is expected to be poor in autumn and winter. They were probably avoided as prey during these seasons. Females were in poorest condition around the period of fawning, which took place in late April or May. This suggests that the season of occupation in the early Middle Palaeolithic and Upper Palaeolithic was probably in the late spring or early summer, when females would be in poor condition. During the "midden-phase" when females dominate, occupation probably took place in the winter, or maybe the early part of spring (Speth and Tchernov 2001, 68).

Throughout the sequence aurochs and red deer exhibit a steady decline in importance, which cannot be related to climatic changes (Speth 2004, 158). Because of their size, these animals were probably highly prized by hunter/gatherers. Therefore, this pattern is possibly the result of overexploitation of these large species (Speth 2004, 158). Another indication of intensive exploitation of the environment is the fact that juvenile gazelles increase in importance throughout the sequence, while the proportion of older gazelles drops. This may reflect the fact that fewer adults managed to survive into old age and hunters may have had to make do with less profitable juvenile individuals (Speth 2004, 158-159).

The poor representation of larger species of animal is intriguing, since one would expect hunters to concentrate on the largest available species. As argued above, their weak representation may be partly caused by the fact that they had been exploited intensively. Probably not many large animals were available during the time of occupation. On the other hand, because the cave likely functioned as a central place, some of the activities carried out further afield may be underrepresented. In the case of hunting large mammals, this may relate to transport costs. At most Levantine cave sites,

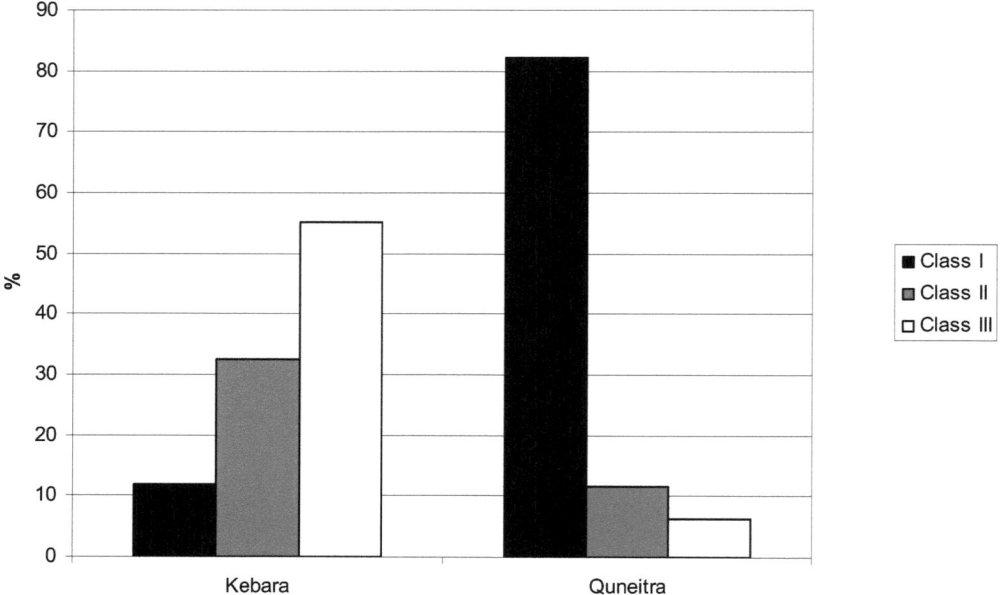

Figure 3.2: Comparison of size classes of the mammal bone assemblages of Kebara (NISP=17371) and Quneitra (NISP=320). Kebara data based on (Speth and Tchernov 2003), Quneitra data and size classes based on (Rabinovich 1990). Size class I: (Rhinoceros, Horse, Aurochs, Red deer)[4]; Size class II: (Fallow deer, Roe deer, Wild boar, Wild ass); Size class III: (Gazelle, Wild goat).

remains of large mammals are rare and fragmented (Rabinovich and Hovers 2004, 303). This can be explained by the fact that it is more rewarding to process large carcasses in the field and only transport the richer parts to the cave. For smaller animals, returning the complete animal to the site to process later may have been more rewarding, since this would give hunters more time to continue hunting (*e.g.* Winterhalder 2001, 22-23).

In the Levant this can be illustrated by comparing the faunal assemblage of a central place like Kebara with that of a hunting camp. Quneitra is an open-air site in the Golan Heights that has been interpreted as a hunting station (Bar-Yosef 1995). ESR dating of the site has yielded an average age of 53.9 ka ± 5.9 ka (Ziaei *et al.* 1990). The stone tool assemblage that was recovered at the site can be characterised as Levantine Mousterian. Finally, it has yielded a small faunal assemblage, which appears to be anthropogenic in origin (Rabinovich 1990). Large bodied animal, in particular aurochs and horse dominate the assemblage. In comparing different faunal assemblages, it is important to realise that hunted species are usually dependant on the site's environment (Rabinovich and Hovers 2004, 303). I have therefore used size categories, as detailed in (Rabinovich 1990, 209). Figure 3.2 illustrates this comparison.

This graph shows that even when a home-base serves as a place where people doing different tasks in society meet and exchange the fruits of their activities, not all activities may be represented evenly. Therefore, the analysis of sites that functioned as central places must be supplemented with information on the context in which these sites functioned, in order to assess the full suite of subsistence activities practised by a group of hunter/gatherers. Some appreciation of the importance of processing in the field can be gained by analysing the representation of skeletal parts of large animals at home bases. In the case of selective transport of remains of these animals to the site, one would expect economically valuable parts, like the hindlimbs to be overrepresented (*e.g.* Chatters 1987, 343, Rogers and Broughton. 2001). On the other hand, if a carcass is filleted, none of its bones will reach the central place (Rabinovich and Hovers 2004, 303). Therefore, we need to consider all the components of a settlement system when studying subsistence behaviour.

---

4   Equids from Kebara have been grouped with class II, since *E. hydruntinus* is the most common equid present (Bar-Yosef *et al.* 1992, 517). However, some *E. caballus* and *E. tabeti* are also present at the site. There is no published data that enables me to distinguish between these species. I chose to classify red deer as a class I mammal, however, since *E. hydruntinus* is grouped by Rabinovich (1990) as size II, this might also be valid for red deer. In that case Kebara has even fewer class I animals.

Ungulate hunting can be expected to be underrepresented among groups using special purpose hunting sites. At central places, toolkits may be produced and maintained, while at special purpose camps we may only see a short period of their use. Furthermore, different provisioning strategies may have been pursued by different members of the group. A central place is expected to reflect the activities of all group members. This makes the study of central places important, especially with regard to the activities of women, who are usually assumed to be excluded from hunting large mammals and whose activities will only very rarely be reflected at other types of site (*e.g.* Kelly 1992, Kelly 1995).

Resources that could be gathered as an alternative to the dangerous activity of hunting large mammals are plants and smaller, less dangerous, animals. Foraging for plant foods is difficult to detect archaeologically, but there are indications that these resources were important in Kebara. We know from anthropology that at temperate and tropical latitudes plant foods usually comprise quite a large part of hunter/gatherer diets (Bar-Yosef 2004, 337). Furthermore, carbonised wild pea seeds were found in the lower levels of many hearths in Kebara and a possible grinding stone was found in the Middle Palaeolithic levels of the cave. Moreover, pistachio nuts, acorns, grass seeds and legumes have been identified in samples (Albert *et al.* 2000, 934, Bar-Yosef *et al.* 1992, 530-531).

Information on prehistoric plant use can also be obtained by looking at phytoliths contained in the sediments of archaeological sites. Phytoliths are silicate bodies that are part of a plant's tissue; they are resilient to degradation and identifiable up to family level. In Kebara, the analysis of the families of plants that were present in the samples suggests that a major proportion of the plants that were brought into the site were used as fuel. Nevertheless, some of the samples located away from the hearths show that significant quantities of plants were also brought in for purposes unrelated to fire (Albert *et al.* 2000, 946).

In view of the fact that the climate was colder than nowadays for much of the Middle Palaeolithic foraging for plant foods was very marginally attested at most sites located at more northern latitudes. Kebara exemplifies that, given the opportunity, Neanderthals exploited this kind of food resource.

The collecting of small animals has recently started to receive attention in Middle Palaeolithic archaeology. It is thought that the exploitation of small animal biomass led to increased population densities (*e.g.* Kuhn and Stiner 2006, Stiner 2001, Stiner, Munro, and Surovell 2000, Stiner *et al.* 1999). Exploitation of small animals rises in importance in the Mediterranean from the late Middle Palaeolithic. At Kebara, many tortoise bones are present in the bone assemblage, accounting for more than 11 percent of the total number of identified bones. Moreover, most of the tortoise bones discovered in the early excavations by Stekelis have not yet been analysed and are therefore not represented in that number (Speth and Tchernov 2002, 472). The species represented at Kebara is the spur-thighed tortoise (*Testudo graeca*), which can be found throughout the Mediterranean. This species exhibits a lot of variation in size throughout its range. In general, eastern populations are considered larger than western populations. The weight of the species is estimated by (Stiner 2005) to be between one and two kg., but they can grow significantly larger according to her. The tortoises found at Kebara were used by humans: they are found mainly in the midden concentration and 7.3 percent of the bones shows signs of burning, which is a higher percentage than that encountered in the ungulate sample (Speth and Tchernov 2002, 473). The burnt bones suggest that they were cooked by placing them belly-up in the fire, since most signs of burning are found on the outside of their carapace, while their limbs and plastron show much less evidence of burning (Speth and Tchernov 2002, 474). The collection of turtles represents another kind of activity than the hunting represented by the large mammals found at the cave. This can be classified as gathering rather than hunting, because, aside from their carapace, tortoises do not have true anti-predator defences (Besides urinating on you if you pick them up). The economic importance of this activity must not be underestimated, since even though it concerns small animals, they were obviously collected in large numbers.

Researchers measured the diameter of the tortoise humeri, which is directly proportional to the weight of the tortoises. From this they concluded that Middle Palaeolithic tortoises were significantly larger than Upper Palaeolithic ones, a trend that has been attributed to overexploitation in the Upper Palaeolithic by Stiner (*e.g.* Stiner *et al.* 1999). Tortoises continue to grow their entire lives; therefore heavy exploitation will be reflected in declining dimensions, since the average lifespan of the animals of the population will decrease. However, part of this trend can be attributed to a deterioration of the climate in this period, which resulted in slower growth (Speth and Tchernov 2002). More interesting is the fact that tortoises also show a decline in dimensions during the midden phase of the Middle Palaeolithic, the period of most intense occupation. Again, climate may be a factor in this decline, but overexploitation is a distinct possibility too (Speth and Tchernov 2002, Speth and Tchernov 2003, 17).

Summing up, this site shows that the subsistence behaviours of Neanderthals were not only geared towards the exploitation of one or two species of large mammals. The site shows the exploitation of a broad range of species. Hunting mammals was complemented with collecting tortoises and plant foods, as shown by charred seeds, fruits and analysis of phytoliths. The combined analysis of central places like Kebara and hunting stations that yield evidence on the exploitation of larger mammals, supplementing the bone assemblages from central places, appears to be productive. We can conclude that in the Levant, Neanderthals exploited a broad range of resources. However, in terms of caloric value, hunting of mammals remains the most significant economic activity.

3.3.6 Broad spectrum revolution, division of labour

The exploitation of tortoises and plants at Kebara brings us to an important issue in the study of Palaeolithic subsistence strategies: whether a division of labour was in place in Middle Palaeolithic foraging. If we accept contemporary hunter/gatherers and hunting chimpanzees as a valid analogy we can assume that Neanderthal women did not in general take part in hunting large mammals. This can be combined with the admittedly scant evidence for different musculature in the arms of Neanderthal men and women as discussed in chapter 2. Based on ethnographic parallels we would expect their activities to be geared towards the harvesting of plants and small animals. However, as discussed in a series of papers by Stiner *et al.* these activities are not well represented in the archaeological record (*e.g.* Kuhn and Stiner 2006, Stiner 2001, Stiner, Munro, and Surovell 2000, Stiner *et al.* 1999). In this section I will discuss the available evidence for Neanderthal exploitation of resources other than large mammals. Moreover, some of the taphonomic factors influencing recognition of the exploitation of these resources are discussed.

According to Stiner *et al.* (Stiner, Munro, and Surovell 2000, Stiner *et al.* 1999) the exploitation of small animals rises in importance only in the late Middle Palaeolithic. Moreover, Neanderthals concentrated on slow-moving easy-to-catch prey like tortoises and shellfish. These species reproduce very slowly and their exploitation resulted in a drop in prey sizes. Only AMH in the Upper Palaeolithic concentrate heavily on fast moving prey like birds and small mammals. Since small animals and plants present lower return rates per unit, efficient strategies are needed to make exploiting these resources worthwhile (*e.g.* Stiner 2001, Stiner, Munro, and Surovell 2000, Stiner *et al.* 1999). Such activities may have been carried out by AMH women, since they are much less dangerous than hunting ungulates. According to Kuhn and Stiner (2006), Neanderthal women probably did not carry out complementary tasks in the realm subsistence, but assisted the men with the less dangerous activities in the hunting domain.

Although the economic role of these resources may appear negligable, their introduction in the hominin diet may have had far-reaching consequences. Since small animals are present in higher population densities than large animals they represent a large total amount of biomass. Moreover, mammals and birds have high reproductive rates. If AMH were able to exploit these species effectively, this enabled them to increase their population density further and bounce back more rapidly from population crashes than Neanderthals (*e.g.* Stiner 2001, Stiner, Munro, and Surovell 2000, Stiner *et al.* 1999). This has been proposed as a reason for the replacement of Neanderthals by AMH by Stiner *et al.* It is a problematic proposition to test, since research has traditionally focused on large mammals. Therefore the full extent of exploitation of small animals by Neanderthals remains unclear.

As argued in chapter 1, this provides an interesting illustration of the changing views of the abilities of hominins. In the 1980s it was thought that hunting large mammals would be beyond the capabilities of Neanderthals and even early AMH (Binford 1984, Binford 1985). Hunting of smaller mammals, like rabbits, was deemed to be important however (*e.g.* Binford 1985, 319). Nowadays the hunting of ungulates is well documented for Neanderthals, but evidence for the capture of small fast-moving prey is thought to be rare in their archaeological record. There are good arguments in favour of the current view, however. First there is the fact that this kind of prey is rarely described in site reports, so it may truly not have been important for Neanderthals. Second, the technology required for the efficient capture of such prey, *e.g.* snares and traps, requires a considerable amount of planning, technical knowledge and investment. Third, indications for hominin exploitation of small prey are usually rare. Often the presence of small mammals in cave deposits can be attributed to the activities of carnivores like lynxes or raptors (Hockett and Haws 2002, Lloveras, Moreno-García, and Nadal 2008).

On the other hand there are indications for Neanderthal interference with fast moving small prey. At Kebara for example, birds are represented in the bone assemblage, but have not been studied with regard to subsistence. They are only used for environmental reconstruction, and bone counts are not given (Bar-Yosef *et al.* 1992, 517). Nevertheless, bird bones have been found in the intensively used central area of the cave. This suggests that the bird remains were deposited in the hearths by hominins. Their relative importance is hard to assess however (Meignen *et al.* 1998, 229). This brings us to a fundamental problem in evaluating this kind of hypothesis. The study of small animal bones, or the lack thereof, shows that post-depositional processes and research interests bias our picture of Neanderthal subsistence activities.

Most of the instances of Neanderthal involvement with other resources than large mammals are from the southern part of the range. This is to be expected, since extant hunter/gatherers in tropical and Mediterranean ecozones rely heavily on vegetable foods (Bar-Yosef 2004, 337). Neanderthals show a preference for diverse environments in the European part of their range. The fact that distances between feeding patches in the Mediterranean are generally smaller than further north may have made it an ideal environment for Neanderthals subsisting on a broader diet (Roebroeks 2003, Stewart 2005). Even though the role of plant foods in the north was in all likelihoodsmall, it must be kept in mind that modern Arctic peoples sometimes use plants quite intensively (Arts and Deeben 1981, 98).

Remains of plant foods are hard to detect archaeologically, since they mostly do not preserve very well. In some cases charred plant remains may provide an indication of plant exploitation. As discussed above, at Kebara charred pea seeds, legumes, acorns and pistachio's are present in samples. Pine nuts have been found at Gorham's cave in Gibraltar (Barton *et al.* 1999, 16). This resource may have been available across a large part of the Neanderthal range, even at higher latitudes. Furthermore, it is known to have been a rich source of calories for historic hunter/gatherers, for example in the Great Basin in the United States (Kelly 2001, 49).

Moreover, plants sometimes produce microfossils like phytoliths and pollen, which do preserve well but linking these to Neanderthal foraging strategies is more complicated. Pollen for example are designed to be transported by the wind, so their presence at sites only tells us that specific plants were available, not that they were actually used by Neanderthals. Phytoliths are part of the fabric of the plant so they are not transported widely. Still, care must be taken, since they can be transported into a site by water action for example (Albert *et al.* 2000). Furthermore, they can only be classified in broad groups and usually not at species level (Madella *et al.* 2002). At Amud, in the Levant, study of phytoliths has enabled researchers to conclude that, as at Kebara, plants were introduced in large quantities for purposes other than to serve as fuel. They were also able to determine some specific groups of plants that were exploited by the Mousterians, namely palm trees and figs. Both of these may have been exploited for their fruits (Madella *et al.* 2002, 712).

As discussed previously, small animals have been divided by Stiner *et al.* in two categories, slow and fast moving prey (*e.g.* Stiner, Munro, and Surovell 2000, Stiner *et al.* 1999). The exploitation of slow-moving prey, like tortoises and shellfish, is generally deemed to be within the capabilities of Neanderthals. However, the categorisation of small animals in two categories, fast and slow seems a little too simplistic. For example, one of the resources listed by Stiner *et al.* with the slow moving prey is ostrich (*Struthio camelus*) egg. This resource, may not be very fast-moving itself, yet may be quite dangerous to procure, since the eggs will be defended by the parents. Reptiles are also put in the slow moving category by Stiner *et al.* While this is certainly true for tortoises, some sites also yield evidence for the exploitation of other reptiles, like snakes and legless lizards, which are nowhere near as slow-moving as tortoises. Furthermore it has been proposed that these resources only become important in the later phase of the Middle Palaeolithic. This is not an absolute pattern though. For example, at Hayonim cave in Israel, tortoise and legless lizard (*Ophisaurus apodus*) are well represented in levels dated to MIS 7 (Stiner, Munro, and Surovell 2000, Stiner and Tchernov 1998).

It is striking that a resource like shellfish was rarely exploited, even though Neanderthals were present in coastal or near coastal settings. Heavy exploitation of aquatic resources is often equated with behavioural modernity (*e.g.* Bar-Yosef 2004, 138-139), but shellfish exploitation hardly requires very complex behaviour. In the Middle Palaeolithic, shellfish exploitation is in evidence at sites in the Levant, Italy and Gibraltar (*e.g.* Barton 2000, Stiner *et al.* 1999). The scale on which shellfish were exploited is hard to assess. In Grotta dei Moscerini, shellfish exploitation was practised during ephemeral occupations of the cave (Stiner 1994, 194-196). One episode of shellfish collection at Gibraltar also represents a very short visit to the site (Barton 2000). More recent work at Gibraltar has yielded a diversified faunal assemblage, with molluscs accounting for 17% of the identified faunal assemblage (Stringer *et al.* 2008). This shows that mollusc exploitation was incorporated into the standard suite of hominin foraging practices at this site.

The exploitation of aquatic resources will be underrepresented in the archaeological record, due to the fact that sea-levels were lower than at present for about 75% of the duration of the Neanderthal occupation of Europe (Gamble 1999, 104). Many coastal sites will are therefore submerged nowadays. The relatively small importance of shellfish exploitation may also be caused by the fact that the Mediterranean is not a prolific producer of shellfish (Vita-Finzi and Higgs 1970, 2).

Small, fast moving prey species, like rabbits and birds, were supposedly not heavily exploited in the Middle Palaeolithic. Leporid bones are reported at some sites, however if they are present, the possibility has to be considered that they were brought into the site by other animals, like raptors, or lynxes (*e.g.* Hockett and Haws 2002).

Since Stiner first put the issue of small mammal exploitation on the agenda, some evidence that Neanderthals did not leave this category of prey alone has surfaced. Cut-marked rabbit bones are now in evidence from as early as 1.2 mya at the site of Sima del Elefante in Spain (Blasco 2008, 2839). Comparison of the Terra Amata rabbit sample with assemblages formed by various predators shows that predators did not deposit the Terra Amata assemblage. Furthermore, at least one of the rabbit bones exhibits a cut-mark, pointing to a hominin origin for the assemblage (Valensi and Guennouni 2004). Leporids are present in small quantities in Middle Palaeolithic sites in Italy as well (Stiner, Munro, and Surovell 2000). In Spain, exploitation of leporids is also evidenced at several Middle Palaeolithic sites. Likewise ther rodents were exploited from time to time. Their use may not always be related to subsistence though. For example cut-marks on marmot bones found in Riparo Tagliente seem to point to skinning as the main activity performed by the hominins exploiting them. Therefore exploitation may have been geared primarily towards provisioning themselves with fur instead of food (Thun Hohenstein 2006).

Birds also fall in this prey category. According to Stiner *et al.* they only become important in the Upper Palaeolithic. On the other hand, as illustrated by Kebara above, birds are present at Middle Palaeolithic sites. They are frequently used as environmental indicators and often said to be "present" in site reports. NISP data are usually not given. There are some Middle Palaeolithic sites at which birds have been exploited though. Most of these are located in the Mediterranean. However, cut-marked duck bones have also been found at Salzgitter-Lebenstedt in the north (Gaudzinski, pers. comm). Moreover, swan was exploited at Bolomor cave in Spain (Blasco 2008).

Aside from shellfish, aquatic resources are very rare at Middle Palaeolithic sites. This impression is bolstered by isotopic studies (*e.g.* Richards *et al.* 2001) Most of the known examples of exploitation of aquatic resources date to the late Middle Palaeolithic, but there are hints that aquatic resources were exploited earlier on as well. Terra Amata and the Grotte du Lazaret have yielded fish remains for example. At Terra Amata shellfish have also been recovered (Boone 1976, Desse and Desse 1976). Indications for the exploitation of other marine resources are rare too. At Gibraltar marine mammals like the monk seal (*Monachus monachus*) and dolphins were exploited occasionally (Finlayson and Pacheco 2000, Stringer *et al.* 2008).

Freshwater resources are conspicuously absent from Neanderthal sites. This is doubly surprising, as many open-air sites that have been excavated were located in lacustrine or riverine environments. Some animals associated with these environments were exploited though; at Taubach for example cut-marked beaver bones were found (Bratlund 1999). At a few sites, such as the Grotte Vaufrey and the site of Orgnac, large quantities of freshwater fish have been found: (Desse and Desse 1976, Le Gall 1988). At the site of Koudaro I in the Caucasus tens of thousands of salmon bones (*Salmo strutta labrax*) were found. According to the researchers, bears are unlikely to have been the accumulating agent, since they usually eat their prey at the spot where they catch it, and do not transport it (Liobine 2002, 48).

In general, it seems that exploitation of small fast moving prey was indeed rare in the Middle Palaeolithic. However, there are factors that influence our view of this category of subsistence behaviour. First, as pointed out earlier, our research focus seems to centre on the more spectacular, larger prey categories. Second, proving the exploitation of these small species may be more difficult than that of large mammals. Most importantly, their bones are much smaller, which may influence the chances of recovery, especially in older excavations where sieving was not practised regularly. Third, ethnography shows that small animals tend to be subjected to much less processing than larger animals. Usually they are simply eaten whole (*e.g.* Fernandez-Jalvo, Andrews, and Denys 1999). This is supported by the presence of human gnawing marks on rabbit and bird bones at Gorham's cave in Gibraltar (Stringer *et al.* 2008). Finally, non-mammals have a different bone structure that may influence traces of exploitation. Bird bone for example only rarely preserves cut-marks, which is attributed by some to its brittle nature, causing it to break often, rather than exhibit surface modifications (Livingston 2001, 286).

The case of aquatic resources is even more problematic. As pointed out, for 90% of the time, sea levels were lower than they are today and many coastal sites will be submerged. Furthermore, there is a preservation bias against fish bones. They are less dense and therefore more prone to destruction by geological processes. Apparently, fish bones are not present or underrepresented even when the preservation of bone from other taxa is good (*e.g.* Whitbridge 2001, 19). Moreover, some species of fish store fat in their vertebrae, causing the bone to be dissolved by the release of the fatty acids after the fish has died. This problem is particularly serious in fish like salmon and eel, which will therefore be strongly underrepresented in the archaeological record (*e.g.* Beerenhout 2001, 252).

3.3.7 Summary and conclusion

The archaeological picture of Neanderthal subsistence strategies is still far from clear. However, research conducted in the last decades has provided much new and interesting evidence on Neanderthal interactions with animal species. The suggestion that Neanderthals were obligate scavengers has been refuted for the sites where evidence for this strategy was once perceived. An even more powerful refutation of this hypothesis is provided by the ever increasing number of sites where Neanderthal foraging efforts were concentrated on prime aged individuals of a single species. Opportunism cannot explain this behaviour. Neanderthals apparently planned their foraging efforts well, which resulted in their obtaining the most rewarding prey available and in many cases many individuals of this prey. Evidence for planned behaviour is also provided by the fact that Neanderthals often chose strategic locations for this kind of hunting, as exemplified by Salzgitter and Zwoleń and La Cotte de Saint-Brelade. The evidence for this pattern of activity is spread over a large area and at least indubitable for the later part of the Middle Pleistocene. The site of Schöningen suggests that if more early sites with excellent preservation conditions are excavated, the evidence for specialised hunting may be extended further back in time.

Exploitation of megafauna is also in evidence. However, the focus on prime-aged individuals is less clear in this category of prey and a site like Gröbern may represent a scavenging episode. At Lehringen, an old individual was exploited, while in Taubach of hunting focussed on young rhinoceros. On the other hand, sites like Biache-Saint-Vaast do provide evidence for hunting of prime-aged individuals. An obvious explanation for the fact that focus is not merely on prime-aged prey in this category is the fact that these very large animals are also very dangerous. Furthermore, since even young and old individuals still represent a lot of food, return rates will be high regardless of the exploited age-category. Moreover, Lehringen and Gröbern are dated to the Eemian. In this climatic optimum with dispersed resources an encounter strategy could be practised. Since locationsof these animals could be much less accurately predicted than those of herd animals on the mammoth steppe, that probably followed reasonably fixed migration routes, chance encounters may have determined prey choice. If valuable prey was encountered, it was exploited, since continuing tracking might not result in an encounter with better prey.

Site function also plays a role in our perception of Neanderthal subsistence strategies. This was illustrated by comparing kill sites to sites that may have functioned as a central place. Here we see that in places Neanderthal subsistence strategies were more varied than we would have anticipated only on the basis of sites providing evidence for specialised hunting. In many cases the range of exploited species is best represented at the central places. On the other hand, transport decisions influenced the representation of different prey categories. At this kind of site, there is evidence for activities that we would not see at large mammal exploitation sites, such as the exploitation of plants and small animals for example.

The exploitation of small animals may not have been very significant, as exploiting larger prey would be economically more rewarding. As discussed, the extension of subsistence strategies to also encompass this prey category has been the subject of a series of recent papers, mostly by Stiner *et al.* (Stiner 2001, Stiner, Munro, and Surovell 2000, Stiner *et al.* 1999). It is thought that the ability to effectively exploit small prey may have been a fallback strategy that was employed when other prey was overexploited. It enabled populations to live at higher population densities and may also have enabled them to recover more speedily from population crashes. Ultimately this practice may have played a role in the replacement of Neanderthals by AMH.

The archaeological record shows that while Neanderthals exploited small prey, this was not a very common activity. Mostly they focused on slow-moving species, which are easy to exploit. However, there are indications for the exploitation of fast moving mammals, birds and maybe even fish. Moreover, the archaeological recovery methods are arguably very biased toward larger animals. Additionally, bias against some non-mammal groups like fish and birds may be even stronger because their bone does not preserve as well. Finally, the scarcity of evidence for exploitation of these species does not enable us to draw many conclusions as to the importance of this kind of behaviour in Neanderthal foraging strategies. However, it does show that these activities were not necessarily beyond the capabilities of Neanderthals.

3.4 Material culture

In addition to bone assemblages, material culture may also be helpful in the study of subsistence strategies. The earliest known stone artefacts from Gona in Ethiopia, dated to 2.6 mya are associated with cut-marked bones, suggesting a close association between the use of stone tools and the consumption of animal tissue from the inception of stone tool use (*e.g.* Domínguez-Rodrigo *et al.* 2005). In this section, emphasis will be on stone artefacts, because they are the most abundant category of finds in the archaeological record. We must keep in mind however, that stone tools represent only a part of the tool spectrum in known ethnographic cases and that these tools function as part of a larger technological repertoire, which in the case of the Middle Palaeolithic, has unfortunately not been preserved as well as the stone component.

Material culture is used in two important domains of subsistence behaviour. First, weapons are used in the acquisition of food items. Second, material culture may play a crucial part in processing food items. Using material culture in processing resources can substantially lower their handling costs and even make available resources whose exploitation would otherwise not be feasible. An obvious example of this is the use of stone tools to get at bone marrow, a practice which may have conferred significant advantages on hominins from the Plio-Pleistocene onwards (Blumenschine 1987). Large amounts of artefacts in Middle Palaeolithic assemblages, like many flakes, scrapers, bifaces and so on, appear to have been used in processing activities. Most of the tooltypes that we encounter appear to have been geared primarily towards processing resources animals and not capturing them (Kuhn 1998, 217).

Tools used in the procurement of animals may be hard to distinguish in the Middle Palaeolithic. Yet, an important contrast between hominins and carnivores is the fact that hominins have no natural weapons to aid them in the capture of animals. Hominins lack the big claws and teeth, and also the ability to attain the high speeds that predators reach when capturing animals (*e.g.* Webb 1989). Therefore, material culture must compensate for the lack of natural "weapons". In this chapter, I will first delve into the evidence we have for the use of hunting weapons during the Middle Palaeolithic. This will be followed by a discussion on the functions tools had in processing food.

The Middle Palaeolithic is traditionally defined by the use of the Levallois technique in stone tool production. This denotes a specific technique of core reduction, which enabled the knapper to accurately control the form of the product he was knapping. Levallois flakes, blades or points could then be further shaped into specific tool types. This does not mean that the Levallois technique was universally used during the Middle Palaeolithic. It is present at many, but by no means all, Middle Palaeolithic sites, and the relative importance of Levallois products within assemblages varies tremendously. Assemblages of a Lower Palaeolithic (Mode I) character were still produced during this period as well (*e.g.* Stringer and Gamble 1993, 150).

The range of tooltypes that is known from Middle Palaeolithic sites is small compared to later periods (Stringer and Gamble 1993). Moreover, guide fossils clustering in a limited area or time period are largely absent. Many tooltypes are used over large parts of Eurasia for hundreds of thousands of years with no visible development towards newer, more "advanced" types (Gamble *et al.* 2004, 210). Variability between assemblages is based on the percentages of different techniques that are being used in their production and different ratios of the tooltypes. Many explanations for the general character of Middle Palaeolithic stone tool assemblages have been proposed. The variability is attributed to the many considerations that may have played a role in Neanderthal tool production, like economic considerations about raw material use and tool curation.

The fact that Neanderthals made a small range of tooltypes suggests that their technical capabilities were not very great. This is not necessarily true though. Comparison of standardization of Levantine Mousterian (dated to 200 ka, so presumably not produced by AMH) and Upper Palaeolithic burins shows that Upper Palaeolithic toolforms are no more standardised. Therefore, one can conclude that Neanderthals were as good at imposing a form on their raw materials as AMH's (Marks, Hietala, and Williams 2001, 26).

Moreover during the latest stage of Neanderthal existence some interesting patterns occur when one regards the assemblages they produced. In some parts of their range Neanderthals continued to produce Mousterian assemblages, on the Iberian Peninsula for example. In other parts of their range, "transitional industries" have been excavated. These industries were initially labelled Upper Palaeolithic and it was assumed that they were produced by AMH groups. More recently, researchers have proposed the possibility that they were produced by Neanderthals. Most of these industries are not associated with taxonomically identifiable fossils. The Châtelperronian, a blade-based industry from France, has however yielded Neanderthal fossils (Hublin *et al.* 1996, Mercier *et al.* 1991). Similarly, a Neanderthal molar has been found in Greece, associated with an "Initial Upper Palaeolithic" industry (Harvati, Panagopoulou, and Karkanas 2003). There are other similar industries, like the Ulluzzian in Italy and the Szeletian and Bohunician in Central Europe that are sometimes tentatively associated with Neanderthals, even though no diagnostic fossils have yet been found in association. These findings suggest that Neanderthals were capable of behaviour that we would more readily associate with AMH.

Here I will go into Middle Palaeolithic artefacts as constituting a relatively uniform group, even though there is a lot of variation in the composition of assemblages. It is important to keep in mind that some of the variation may be caused by the different functions for which the assemblages were used. The dominant toolforms of most Middle Palaeolithic assemblages are different forms of sidescrapers. Furthermore, denticulates are ubiquitous, other forms present include bifaces, points and Levallois products that may also be modified (*e.g.* Stringer and Gamble 1993, 151).

Studying methods of subsistence through the material culture used in subsistence strategies can be problematic for several reasons. First, we do not know the function of many toolforms. Therefore we cannot measure the importance of different subsistence strategies, by looking at how ubiquitous the different tools used for these strategies were. Since the range of tooltypes was small, we can assume that most tools were used in a very versatile way for a number of different activities. This may be the result of considerations to do with the system of mobility that was practised. If residential moves were frequent we would expect the weight of the transported toolkit to be minimised. Furthermore, specialization of tool production may also be related to the economic importance of the activity for which the specialised tool will be used. If the activity is very important and will take place at a predictable time than tools may tend to be "overdesigned" in order to minimize the chance of failure of the technology. For less important or less predictable tasks it is often not worth the investment to produce overdesigned tools and more versatile tools may be used for the occasion (Bleed 1986).

Interestingly, a correlation between the degree of technological specialization exhibited by groups and the latitude at which they live has been observed ethnographically. Apparently groups are more specialised in more northern latitudes, while more generalised technologies are usually seen closer to the equator (Henrich 2004, 207). Middle Palaeolithic sites do not exhibit such a gradient. This may be due to low population densities which resulted in a small pool of people from which to learn technological skills. Simpler skills may be copied more faithfully in these situations (Henrich 2004). The development of complicated technologies may have been hindered in Middle Palaeolithic societies, which probably consisted of small groups, living in low population densities.

There are a few tool categories that were used as weapons. One very early candidate are the Oldowan manuports. These seem to cluster around certain weights, which would maximize their potential as thrown objects, suggesting a use as primitive projectile (Cannel 2002). A similar use has been proposed for spheroids and subspheroids found in the Olduvai Gorge, whose dimensions are a bit smaller than those of throwing stones known ethnographically. This is to be expected, since the body size of the Oldowan hominins was smaller than the body size of modern humans (Isaac 1987, 13) These implements are well-known from Oldowan times, but they persist up until final Mousterian times in Africa, Europe and the Near East and apparently the dimensions of later spheroids are more like those of the ethnographically known throwing stones (Isaac 1987, 13, Lorblanchet 1999, 117).

However, thrown stones are not the kind of weapon we would expect to be wielded when practising specialised hunting of prime-aged ungulates and megafauna. More advanced kinds of weapons have been found in the archaeological record though. The earliest possible example of spear use is a putative impact mark of a projectile found on a horse scapula at the 500 ka site of Boxgrove in England (Roberts 1999, 378). More famous are the eight wooden throwing spears found at Schöningen, dated between 300 and 400 ka (Thieme 1997). Another example, already mentioned, is the wooden lance found with the carcass of an elephant at Lehringen, dated to the last interglacial (Thieme and Veil 1985). Unfortunately, wood is rarely preserved, so we do not know how ubiquitous these weapons were. Nevertheless, the Schöningen spears appear to have been well-balanced throwing weapons (Rieder 2003). Therefore, their producers were probably experienced in their manufacture.

In addition to rare finds of wooden objects, stone tools may have functioned as weapons. It has been hypothesised that Levallois points were used as spear points. These suspicions were confirmed when in Syria, a part of a Levallois point was found embedded in a vertebra of a wild ass. This find is dated as older than 50 ka and is believed to represent Neanderthal behaviour (Boëda *et al.* 1999). On the basis of kinetic tests it is impossible to distinguish whether this was the result of a thrusted or a thrown weapon, but since the point entered by a parabolic trajectory it is suggested that the weapon must have been thrown. The finding of the Levallois point in an animal bone is a promising discovery, since this is a stone projectile point that we can recover archaeologically. However, Levallois points cannot be seen as projectile points *pur sang*. They were apparently used for a wide variety of purposes. Many points show traces of wear related to butchering, or even working plant foods, suggesting that these items could have a variety of functions (Meignen *et al.* 1998, 234-236, Plisson and Beyries 1998, 7).

Tools classified as points are rare in the European Middle Palaeolithic (*e.g.* Villa and Lenoir 2006). Comparison with African Middle Stone Age assemblages suggests that this may be partly due to the system of classification used in Europe. This system results in many pointed forms being classified as scrapers. Especially the category "convergent scrapers" contains many forms that could very well have functioned as points (Villa and Lenoir 2006, 91-92). Research on these tools from the Near East shows that some of them may have been used as points. At Grotta Breuil in Italy, convergent scrapers were described as showing traces of piercing activities near the point (*e.g.* Lemorini 1992). Moreover, the dimensions of some of these scrapers, together with those of some Levallois points fall within the range of dimensions of ethnographically known points of thrusting spears (Shea 2006, Villa and Lenoir 2006). Therefore, ethnographic data suggests a use as points for thrusting spears.

Furthermore, experimental work and work on paleoindian kill-sites has led to the identification of features that may help in identifying points that were used as weapons. First, bulbar thinning to prepare the point for hafting was often observed. More importantly, damage concurrent with projectile use on pointed forms has been analysed. This takes the form of step-fractures, burin-like fractures and spin-off fractures at the tip of the point (Villa and Lenoir 2006, 112-113). This kind of damage has been observed on Levallois points from sites in the Levant, and more recently in southwestern France and Italy (*e.g.* Hardy *et al.* 2001, Meignen *et al.* 1998, Villa *et al.* 2009, Villa and Lenoir 2006, Shea, 1995 #253).

We know that hafting was practised by Neanderthals, for use-wear analysis that has revealed traces of hafting on stone tools (*e.g.* Hardy *et al.* 2001). More spectacularly, at the German site of Königsaue, two pieces of birch pitch have been unearthed. One of these pieces, probably dating to MIS 5a, exhibits a hominin fingerprint as well as the impression of a flint blade on one end and impressions of wood cells on the other hand, indicating its use as hafting material (Koller, Baumer, and Mania 2001, 386-388). A very recent find are flakes still covered in the tar that was used to haft them, which were discovered scattered between the remains of an 18-19 year old elephant in Italy, dated before MIS 6 (Mazza *et al.* 2006).

The importance of the use as projectiles of convergent scrapers and Levallois points is a subject of discussion. In some cases Levallois points were simply the preferred end-products of stone working and that form does not necessarily indicate their use as spear points. Some researchers think that the use of pointed forms as spear points was so rare as to be negligible (*e.g.* Plisson and Beyries 1998). There are some factors that prompt rethinking this point of view. At Kebara, for example,

35% of the points in the assemblage showed evidence for hafting, suggesting that this function may not have been very rare after all (Bar-Yosef *et al.* 1992). Furthermore the absence of characteristic impact damage does not mean that points were not used as missiles. Experiments have shown that when aimed well, and provided no bone is hit, points will not be damaged. Furthermore, if points are damaged, repairs can be made whereby the damage is removed (Frison 1989). Furthermore, use-wear analysis only shows the last activity that was performed. Ethnographically, examples are known where spearheads are used to butcher prey (Shea 1993). This would lead to a butchering wear (which is common at some sites), while the tool was also used as projectile to procure the animal. This does not solve the problem, however, especially since it cannot explain traces of wood-working on these types. We know that points were sometimes used as weapons, but not always.

Most tools that we know from the Middle Palaeolithic were probably used for processing rather than hunting. However, we do not know the exact activities for which most tools were used. Use-wear studies have been used to gain insight in this, although they generally only differentiate between very broad categories of use. Use-wear studies are sometimes combined with residue analysis; a technique that tries to identify ancient residues on a tool's working edges. This combination may lead to more specific results. Residue analysis only works on tools deposited under very specific conditions. In most environments, residues will deteriorate quickly (Langejans 2006). Such studies were applied to some Middle Palaeolithic sites. They have revealed that the stone tools have been used for a wide range of activities and the processing of many different materials (*e.g.* Beyries 1988, Gijn 1992, Hardy 2004, Hardy *et al.* 2001, Lemorini 1992, Meignen *et al.* 1998, Plisson and Beyries 1998). There is much evidence for wood-working, not only in warm Mediterranean climes, but also at northern sites like Biache-Saint-Vaast (Beyries 1988). Siliceous plants were also worked at some sites (Hardy 2004). Furthermore, there is abundant evidence at many sites for involvement with animal matter, be it bone, meat or hide (*e.g.* Beyries 1988, Gijn 1992, Meignen *et al.* 1998).

An important problem with regard to both use-wear and residue analysis is the fact that post-depositional processes can produce results that mimic traces of use. For instance, "wood-working" polish is also created by friction with wet sediments, not only by processes that leave stratigraphic traces like cryoturbation, but also by minute movements in the matrix (*e.g.* Levi-Sala 1986). Residues on stone tools are assumed to be the precipitate of the prehistoric activities for which they were used. This is not always the case however, they may be modern contaminants. Furthermore, not all contaminants need be modern, they are also present in the sediment and these may also end up on stone implements during deposition (Langejans 2006, Langejans 2007).

The reliability of use-wear and residue studies can be improved when a number of criteria are met. For example, it is important to break down residues on stone tools by location. Residues that could be interpreted as being the result of hafting would need to be located at the base of a stone tool for example. Residues related to tool-use should be located near the edges of the tool. Furthermore, the fact that a residue was related to the use of a tool becomes more probable if there are multiple similar residues on the tool. Single residues can easily be the result of contamination. If multiple, similar traces are present, the likelihood of them being related to the use of the tool increases (*e.g.* Lombard 2005). Moreover, in cases where use-wear and residue analyses were performed independently of one another on the same tools, the results of the analyses tended to corroborate each other (*e.g.* Hardy *et al.* 2001, 10973-10974).

In most cases, plant residues preserve better than animal residues. The importance of plant working may thus be exaggerated in residue-studies (Lombard and Wadley 2007, 161-162). Seeing that plant materials are virtually absent in the rest of the archaeological record, the identification of plant residues on Middle Palaeolithic stone tools still is invaluable. For example, at Starosele in Crimea, 31 artefacts were analysed and plant residue was found on 21 of them (Hardy *et al.* 2001, 10974). This may also indicate that, although sedimentary action can mimic use-wear traces of plant and woodworking, some of these traces do reflect past activities. Use of stone tools on soft plant materials may point to processing of foodstuffs. However, these plants may also have been used as fuel, or for other purposes, such as the construction of shelter and bedding (Hardy 2004, Madella *et al.* 2002). Grinding stones have only been reported in a few rare cases, like at Kebara (Bar-Yosef *et al.* 1992, 531). Therefore, there are only a few indications for the consumption of plant foods through Middle Palaeolithic material culture.

As mentioned, woodworking is attested often by use-wear studies. This may point to the collection of firewood, but, probably also to the use of stone tools to shape wooden tools. The manufacture of a wooden spear is considered to be much more time consuming than manufacturing a stone tip for example (Villa and Lenoir 2006, 106). Tools were frequently used for woodworking are *encoches* and denticulates (*e.g.* Lemorini 1992, 21-22). One could also envisage these tools being used when polishing spear shafts.

With regard to the processing of animal materials, some results of residue analyses are very spectacular. At La Quina, blood residue was found on a stone tool. DNA analysis was performed on this blood and apparently the DNA showed that the blood belonged to wild boar (Hardy 2004, 560). More blood and mammal hair was found on other stone tools, as was one feather fragment of a falconiform bird (Hardy 2004, 555). At sites in Crimea, feather residues of falconiform and anseriform birds in addition to blood residues were found on points that also exhibited traces of hafting. (Hardy *et al.* 2001). These findings are extremely germane to the study of subsistence, especially in view of the debate surrounding the Middle Palaeolithic exploitation of small animals.

Traces of for example hide-working are very interesting for the study of subsistence, since they point to the exploitation of resources from animals other than meat. However, tools for making clothes, like awls and needles, are absent in the Neanderthal archaeological repertoire. With regard to processing animals, use-wear studies usually point to cutting meat, while other traces of wear are sometimes present but not very common (*e.g.* Kuhn and Stiner 2006, 958). On the other hand, as argued in chapter 2, Neanderthals must have been able to insulate themselves somewhat. Skinning marks found on marmots in Italy and bears at Biache-Saint-Vaast, mentioned earlier provide additional evidence for the exploitation of animals because of their fur.

The impact of these artefacts and their implementation in on foraging strategies is difficult to determine. Without stone tools certain foodstuffs would be unavailable to hominins, as in the case of bone marrow. Another resource presenting similar problems may have been tortoises; by using tools, their armour could be defeated, an innovation that probably dates to Oldowan times (*e.g.* Roche *et al.* 1999, Sept 1992). Using tools in order to fillet animal prey was likely an important activity. Technology that enabled better processing in the field, which in turn made exploiting larger prey more efficient by significantly reducing transport costs, would be crucial during the evolution of hominin hunting strategies (*e.g.* Rabinovich and Hovers 2004).

Another category of material that has often been preserved and might have been used as a raw material for artefacts is bone. Bone tools are usually considered as part of the Upper Palaeolithic repertoire, but in the Middle Palaeolithic they were used as well, albeit much less intensively. At many sites bones were used as *retouchoirs* and anvils for flaking purposes (Moncel *et al.* 2004, 279). More formal tools were sometimes also made out of bone. At Salzgitter-Lebenstedt for example, around 30 bone daggers were fashioned out of mammoth ribs and fibulae. Furthermore, a well-made bone point was found at the site (Gaudzinski 1999, Gaudzinski and Roebroeks 2000). In some cases bone was used in a similar way as stone. In Italy for example bifaces have been found, flaked on elephant bone (Gaudzinski 1999, 216). Tools were made from bone but not very commonly.

Furthermore bone was sometimes also used as a combustible. This is not necessarily due to of a shortage of wood, but because bone has different burning properties. Where wood gives a quick burst, bone can simmer for hours (Moncel *et al.* 2004, 279). In the colder periods wood may have been very scarce in Northern Europe. In this situation bone's suitability as fuel may have increased its value for human use and therefore given large animal resources added value. However, bone needs a lot of heat to ignite it in the first place, so just bone will not have been sufficient for Neanderthals when building a fire. Quite large quantities of other material would have been required in order to get the fire started (White 2006, 561-562).

In conclusion, the biggest problem in analysing Middle Palaeolithic stone tools is the fact that no clear link between specific tool types and specific functions can be demonstrated (*e.g.* Bisson 2001, 166). As mentioned earlier, points, that to us seem suited to use as projectiles sometimes show use-wear indicating use in different domains, such as wood-working. This variability of tool use and the uniformity of the stone tools throughout the Middle Palaeolithic have led researchers to posit that tools were used for generalised tasks (Bisson 2001, 166-167). Tools made from other materials are relatively rare, so we do not know exactly how organic materials complemented the Middle Palaeolithic toolkit. The abundance of wood-working residue and wear traces, combined with the well crafted wooden spears from Schöningen do suggest that organic materials were an important part of Middle Palaeolithic culture.

3.5 Other aspects of Neanderthal archaeology

We have now dealt with the two main categories of remains that are found at Neanderthal sites, namely bones and (stone) tools. In this section I will discuss some other aspects of their archaeological record that have not been breached yet. I will briefly touch upon the issues of site architecture and upon some evidence of surprising "high-tech" behaviour found in the Middle Palaeolithic.

Investment in site architecture, especially in northwestern Europe, was minimal. If one is planning to stay at a place for a short period of time, less investment will be put into it; therefore this rarity is at least partly related to the organisation of Neanderthal mobility. At present, there are a few circular stone configurations known from the late Middle Palaeolithic. These are by no means elaborate huts, just small stone circles, or maybe windbreaks (Kolen 1999). Shelter was apparently sought in abris and caves, but in the absence of natural features, it was only very rarely constructed in a way that is visible archaeologically. Shelter in caves may have been quite important for Neanderthals though, for example as a safe haven when giving birth (Mussi 1999, 64-65).

The most common elements of "architecture" at a site in the Middle Palaeolithic are hearths and ash lenses signifying fireplaces. At some sites, there is evidence for differentiation among these. One such example is Abric Romani in Spain. At this site, different kinds of fire features have been identified. For example, there are flat hearths and pit hearths that were constructed in natural depressions. These hearths are believed to have fulfilled different functions. In some cases stones were found in hearths that are believed to be the result of human activities, and may have been used for heat-banking (Vaquero *et al.* 2001). In one case, surviving wood casts in the travertine sediments of the cave enabled the reconstruction of a tripod over a hearth (Vallverdú *et al.* 2005, 168-169). This feature, in combination with cut-marks on bones suggesting the cutting of long strips of meat, has been taken by the authors as a strong indication that meat was dried there (Vaquero *et al.* 2001, 168-169). In Grotte XVI in France smoking of fish has been proposed as function of hearths, since they were in part fuelled with lichen (Wong 2000). At other sites, hearths were used to roast vegetable resources, as mentioned for Kebara and Gorham's cave. In Douara in Syria a hearth with a diameter of 5 metres has been found, containing hackleberry fruits and large quantities of charred plums (Bar-Yosef 1995, McLaren 1998). In the Near East stones do not seem to have been used for cooking and or providing warmth. However, as mentioned above at Abric Romani stones do occur in hearths, therefore this is not an absolute pattern. At many sites burnt bones occur, so cooking of meat was probably also routinely practised.

In addition to providing fire to cook or conserve foodstuffs, another function of hearths is simply to provide warmth. In this regard it is peculiar that hearths or ash lenses are uncommon at Middle Palaeolithic sites. This is even the case at open-air sites in northern France that were occupied during the early part of the last glacial (*e.g.* Locht 2005). This shows that Neanderthal cold-adaptation may really have been critical to their survival, but also suggests that Neanderthals really were capable of providing good insulation (cf. Aiello and Wheeler 2003), even though there is not very much evidence for it. Still, there is good evidence for the exploitation of animals for their fur, as discussed in sections 3.3.6 and 3.4 (Auguste 1995a, Thun Hohenstein 2006).

"High-tech" behaviour seems to be represented by the production of birch pitch for the hafting of stone artefacts. This was already practised before 250 ka (Mazza *et al.* 2006). It requires very precise control of the fire's temperature, which needs to be between 340 and 400 °C for prolonged periods of time. If the necessary heat is not generated, no pitch is produced, but should temperatures rise above 400 °C the tar will be destroyed by charring (Koller, Baumer, and Mania 2001, 393). This points to the fact that, even though most fireplaces show up archaeologically as lenses of ash, Neanderthals were very capable of managing the fire they produced.

In addition to "high-tech" behaviour there is another category of behaviour that is proposed to be characteristic of our own species. This is ritual behaviour, seen as one of the few things that sets *Homo sapiens sapiens* apart from other animals. There is not much to suggest ritual behaviour in the Neanderthal archaeological record. Figurative art is absent for example. On the other hand, there is some evidence for behaviour that we would identify as ritual in modern humans. For example, Neanderthals buried at least some of their dead. However, analysis of the mortality profiles of a large sample of Neanderthals suggests that they practised "differential age related burial" (Trinkaus 1995, 139). In other words, some classes of individuals were more likely to be buried than others. Furthermore, personal ornamentation in the form of beads has been reported at a number of Châtelperronian sites (Zilhão 2007, 24-27). Since the stratigraphic provenance of these ornaments is unclear and they were recovered in old excavations, their attribution to the Châtelperronian is not certain though (*e.g.* Roebroeks 2008, 923).

3.6 Summary and Conclusion

In conclusion, it is safe to say that our best source of information regarding Neanderthal subsistence strategies are the bone assemblages found at their sites. Spears, like those from Schöningen and Lehringen show us that they hunted, but these artefacts are very rare. Stone tools are to some degree enigmatic. They obviously played a central part in Neanderthal lifeways (*e.g.* Kuhn 1998), but many of them were not used in the procurement of the food. Points are an exception, since they do seem to have been used as tips of hunting weapons (Boëda *et al.* 1999, Hardy *et al.* 2001, Villa and Lenoir 2006). This was not their only function however, since they sometimes exhibit use-wear related to other activities, like butchery, or even woodworking (Beyries 1988, Meignen *et al.* 1998). Implementing stone tools in the processing of food will have made exploitation of animal resources much more efficient. Their exact effect on foraging strategies is hard to estimate, however.

The use-wear and residues pointing to plant-related activities of course form a welcome extension of the knowledge about these activities that we had gathered through the discovery of wooden spears and at some sites, like Kebara and caves on Gibraltar, the recovery of roasted seeds and peas. The problem with this line of evidence is that use-wear and residue studies are not infallible. Sedimentary movements can produce gloss similar to that of for example woodworking. Furthermore residues can also result from contamination and there seems to be a preservation bias towards plant residues over animal residues.

The main problem regarding the study of stone tools for subsistence purposes is the fact that there does not seem to be a clear relationship between toolform and -function. Most studies of stone tool types show that similar tools have very diverse types of wear; they are thus not specifically geared towards a single activity. This versatility in tool function may be related to the mobile way of life practised by Neanderthals. When mobility is high, minimising the weight of transported tools becomes an important consideration. This is seen ethnographically, where high degrees of residential mobility correlate with less variable toolkits (Bleed 1986, Shott 1986). On the other hand, ethnographically there is also a correlation between latitude and toolkit variability, with variability increasing with latitude (Blades 2001, 11, Henrich 2004). This correlation seems not to apply to Neanderthal toolkits, which do not appear more variable in the more northern parts of their range and seem generalised compared to modern human toolkits. This may be attributed to the fact that Neanderthals may not have been very logistically mobile, because of the high cost of locomotion they faced. In contrast, most modern human hunter/gatherers living in temperate and cold climates are logistically mobile.

Stone artefacts were part of a larger toolkit, which included tools made from organic materials. These are of course rarely recovered, but provide clues of good technical capabilities. The hafting of stone tools using birch tar is one example, as are the wooden spears found at Schöningen and Lehringen another. Since the manufacture of wooden tools like spears may have been much more time-consuming than the manufacture of stone artefacts (*e.g.* Villa and Lenoir 2006), we must keep in mind the possibility that we are seeing only part of the Neanderthal toolkit. The stone tools may have functioned as expedient, easily replaceable components of the toolkit in which relatively little energy was invested. The wooden component may have been very important with regard to Neanderthal activities and may even have been more extensive than the stone component of the toolkit.

As discussed, at most sites, the absolute majority of stone tools were made of raw materials that can be found within 6 kilometres of the site. This may reflect the inhabitants' foraging radius (sensu Binford 1982). A small proportion, usually not more than 20%, of the tools are made of raw materials from farther afield. These may reflect tools that were produced while staying at a previous central place and that were taken along when a residential move took place. The very small number of tools that are made of raw materials from further afield may be tools that were part of a person's personal gear and "survived" several residential moves (Kuhn 1995, Roebroeks, Kolen, and Rensink 1988). It has been suggested that Levallois points would be especially suited to be part of the personal gear, since they provide a maximum amount of cutting-edge and are therefore well-equipped to deal with a host of unforeseen circumstances (Wallace and Shea 2006).

The finished tools transported over large distances may thus show us the size of the total area that was used by a group. In Western Europe maximum distances only rarely exceeded 100 kilometres (Féblot-Augustins 1993, Féblot-Augustins 1997, Roebroeks, Kolen, and Rensink 1988). However, recently distances of over 250 kilometres were recorded for a site in France (Slimak and Giraud 2007). In Central Europe the maximum recorded transport distance is up to 300 kilometres (Féblot-Augustins 1993, Féblot-Augustins 1997). These distances are greater than the maximum migration distances known ethnographically, which are no more than 200 kilometres (*e.g.* Arts and Deeben 1981, Féblot-Augustins 1993). This may indicate that a Neanderthal band needed a larger territory to subsist on than AMH groups.

The very versatile stone artefact evidence in the archaeological record can be combined with the faunal (and to a much lesser degree floral) remains present at archaeological sites. The faunal remains, as we have seen, suggest sophisticated exploitation of the largest animals around. Prime-aged hunting is in evidence for ungulates throughout the Neanderthal range and to a lesser degree also for megafauna. Evidence for the exploitation of smaller prey is rare in most cases. In the south, slow-moving prey is quite heavily exploited at some sites and fast-moving prey is present at some sites. Post-depositional processes may have influenced the evidence for these activities. However, compared with the large faunal remains present at sites, the economic importance of these activities cannot have been very significant.

We can conclude that Neanderthals were top-carnivores, living in rich environments for the largest part of their existence. Their sites are usually located in the more bountiful parts of the environment (Stewart 2004, Stewart 2005). Furthermore, it has been posited that the Mediterranean environment may have been more suitable for Neanderthals than the more northern parts of the European continent, because its environment is richer and more diverse (*e.g.* Roebroeks 2003). This may be supported by the observation that sites in the southern part of the Neanderthal range, in general yield more finds than those located more to the North (Gamble 1999, 201-205). Together with the heavy reliance on local raw materials, reviewed above, these factors suggest that Neanderthal land-use focused heavily on "magnet-locations" in the landscape. This kind of land-use pattern has been proposed by Binford for Middle Stone Age AMH in Africa (Binford 1984). He saw this kind of behaviour as reflecting hominins with little foresight, whose movement would be tethered to locations where there was a stable supply of the resources they needed (Binford 1984, 262).

Such a focus on magnet-locations becomes very understandable, once we take into account the fact that Neanderthals had to deal with locomotion that was energetically expensive, as mentioned in chapter 2 (Steudel-Numbers and Tilkens 2004). Their foraging radius would have been smaller and therefore the areas around their sites would have been depleted faster than is the case for modern human hunter/gatherers. The consequences of dealing with a smaller foraging radius become more severe since Neanderthal energetic demands were likely higher than those of AMH's (Sorensen and Leonard 2001, Steegman, Cerny, and Holliday 2002). Therefore it would have been important to minimise the amount of mobility that was practised and maximise the returns they got from the landscape by inhabiting its most productive parts. This strategy seems to have been successful considering the stable use of locations for sometimes thousands of years, as suggested by sites like Mauran, La Borde, Biache-Saint-Vaast, Kebara and others (*e.g.* Roebroeks and Tuffreau 1999, 129). In the south we know many sites, often in caves and abris that may have functioned as home bases. In the north, there are more open-air sites. Some of these were revisited often; others however, show evidence for only short occupations. Most of these sites are quite low-density scatters and structures, like hearths are rare , at these kinds of sites (*e.g.* Locht 2005, 34-35). This shows that not all sites were fixed points in a yearly round that was faithfully adhered to for thousands of years. However, some sites were definitely stable points in the yearly moves.

"Pull factors" for Neanderthals may have included shelter in the case of many abris and caves and animal resources in the case of many revisited open-air sites. This picture is of course coloured by biases. Sites in caves preserve better and archaeologists often look preferentially for cave sites for example. On the other hand, the fact that many open-air sites are low-density accumulations, showing little investment in structures like hearths may support this view. Other factors may be harder to determine in archaeology. For example, in glacial environments, it is very likely that the availability of fuel might have been a limiting factor to Neanderthal presence in areas, more so than for example available biomass (*e.g.* White 2006, 561-562). Another guiding factor for Neanderthal presence might be raw material availability. In general, raw material sources are limited areas in the landscape, while food resources can be found all over the landscape. Therefore mobility systems will have been influenced by raw material sources. Embedded foraging may have included moving to areas rich in a predictable resource, raw material, and foraging in these areas for food resources which would have been as available there as in areas without suitable raw materials (Daniel 2001, 261).

All in all, Neanderthal behaviour remains enigmatic. The virtual absence of innovation, of a succession of different tool types invented, used for some time and phased out in favour of new types is strange since it does seem to characterise all modern human cultures that come after the Neanderthals. It could even be interpreted as showing the absence of the so-called "ratchet-effect", which is thought to be responsible for the cumulative nature of human culture (Boesch and Tomasello 1998). This could lead to the supposition that Neanderthal cultural transmission was less effective than, or at least different from our own. Glimpses of "high-tech" behaviour from the archaeological record challenge these ideas. The same is true for the seemingly very effective hunting methods that were practised. All in all, the species practicsed a successful way of life that was different from ours in the harsh environment of Pleistocene Europe. In the following chapter I will discuss ways in which we can try to model this behaviour in order to gain further insight into it.

4 Optimal foraging models and Neanderthal archaeology

4.1 Introduction

In the previous chapters, the biological and archaeological evidence regarding Neanderthal subsistence behaviour were reviewed. In this chapter I will outline a theoretic framework that will be used to analyse Neanderthal and hyena bone assemblages. As argued in chapter 1, Optimal Foraging Theory (OFT) provides a promising perspective for the study of Neanderthal subsistence strategies. OFT is a theoretical approach dealing with foraging strategies, stemming from behavioural ecology and economic science (*e.g.* Rapport and Turner 1977). It is designed to evaluate the way in which an individual's behaviour affects its evolutionary fitness. It shows how natural selection influences foraging strategies and as such provides a framework within which foraging strategies can be interpreted (*e.g.* Barrett, Dunbar, and Lycett 2002, Krebs and Davies 1997, Winterhalder and Smith 1992). OFT assumes that foraging is important for an animal's survival and reproductive success. Therefore, models are designed that aim to study which ecological circumstances would favour the development of observed foraging behaviours (Winterhalder and Smith 1992, 23).

Different types of model have been designed, depending on the environmental situation and the factor deemed most important for an animal's reproductive success. Archaeological data are of a much lower resolution than the ecological data for which OFT models were originally designed. Consequently, it is most productive to focus on simpler models requiring less fine-grained data. Most of these focus on how a forager can maximise his caloric intake in a given environment. This is a simplifying assumption since Neanderthals may have pursued other goals as well. However, this simplification enables us to use OFT models to produce testable hypotheses about what foraging behaviour we would expect Neanderthals to exhibit given our knowledge of their behaviour and environment.

The first goal of this chapter is to introduce the model that is best suited for archaeological application: the diet breadth model. The chapter will begin with an introduction of the general principles of OFT, the diet breadth model and criticism that has been levelled at OFT. This will be followed by a review of previous archaeological applications of OFT. The information the Pleistocene record yields with regard to the application of OFT will be discussed as well as the problems posed by the record. After this discussion the primary aim of the chapter is to develop a strategy that will allow us to apply the diet breadth model to the Pleistocene archaeological record. I will propose ways in which the variables of the model can be approximated using the archaeological and palaeontological record. This approach will be tested in the following chapters.

4.2 General assumptions and criticism

The central assumption of evolutionary ecology is the fact that relationships between animals and their environment are under evolutionary selection. Therefore an animal's foraging behaviour can be understood as shaped by natural selection in order to maximise fitness. With a proper knowledge of the environment and the specific needs of a species, models can be constructed that predict how animals will behave (*e.g.* Krebs and Davies 1997, MacArthur and Pianka 1966, Winterhalder and Smith 1992). Furthermore, it is assumed that, because of natural selection, over time foragers will have evolved to become as proficient at foraging as possible (Winterhalder 1987, 314). Foraging strategies are thus assumed to maximise the evolutionary success of the forager. It is important to keep in mind that the optimal situation is a working assumption (*e.g.* MacArthur and Pianka 1966, Winterhalder 1987), used to construct models that can test whether behaviour is optimised toward the acquisition of a certain commodity, like food. If the observed behaviour does not conform to the model's predictions, the hypothesis is rejected. In this case an alternative hypothesis explaining the observed behaviour must be formulated.

Before I go into the models themselves, it is important to realise what kind of questions OFT models can answer. Animal behaviour can be explained at several different levels; Tinbergen (1963) delineated four categories of explanation for animal behaviour, which are known as his "four whys". These four categories can be divided in two groups: proximal causes of behaviour and ultimate causes of behaviour. Proximate causes explain the function of actions for at the level of the individual. Ultimate causes explain the evolutionary causes of behaviour at species or population level. Archaeological research, especially in the Palaeolithic can often only explain patterns at Tinbergen's ultimate level. Proximate explanations require far greater resolution.

At the ultimate level, behaviour can be studied with regard to its functional cause: explaining the function of behaviour in terms of fitness for a species. The other explanation in this category is the phylogenetic explanation. This explanation focuses on how the evolutionary history of a species has influenced the behavioural solutions employed by a species (*e.g.* Barrett, Dunbar, and Lycett 2002, Krebs and Davies 1997, Tinbergen 1963). OFT models are designed to study behaviour and explain it at an evolutionary level. They are especially promising for the functional study of behaviour. The application of OFT to archaeological sites is expected to illuminate which factors were responsible for the behaviour exhibited by Neanderthals in different settings. On the other hand, by applying OFT to different periods of time we may also be able to track the development of strategies through time and thus gain insight in the phylogenetic development of behaviours.

The use of OFT models to explain human foraging behaviour has been criticised by some, because the underlying assumptions are deemed to be problematic. First, it is not clear how foraging behaviour correlates exactly with reproductive success. Therefore, in OFT models a proxy is used that is thought to correlate with reproductive fitness. This proxy is called the currency. Usually, the currency is energetic gain. It is thus assumed that maximising energetic returns from foraging activities correlates positively with the fitness of the forager. This currency tends to be a good predictor of foraging decisions (*e.g.* Waite and Ydenberg 1996, Winterhalder 1987). This assumption is certainly not universally valid, however. Optimisation of behaviour may have been selected for other elements. These can be factors like rare but essential nutrients, gaining social prestige or the reduction of risks (*e.g.* Bliege Bird and Smith 2005, Hockett and Haws 2005, Ludvico, Bennett, and Beckerman 1991). Therefore, the fact that OFT models usually focus on caloric gain can be problematic. Malnutrition is of course an important problem, with great consequences for an animal's fitness. Nevertheless, humans need 50 essential nutrients, and it has been proven that a more diverse diet lowers infant mortality and prolongs life-expectancy (*e.g.* Bliege Bird and Smith 2005, Hockett and Haws 2005, Ludvico, Bennett, and Beckerman 1991). This problem can be solved by constructing models using different currencies. This makes it possible to test whether behaviour was geared toward optimising other commodities.

A second issue is that it is often unclear how foraging behaviours are transmitted. In OFT models, inter-generational transmission of foraging behaviours is a working assumption. Natural selection on these inherited traits ensures that foraging behaviour is optimised over time. When applying OFT to human foragers, anthropologists often object that inheritance in humans is not only genetic but also cultural. Of course this is also the case in many animal species. This results in the objection that, it is unclear whether any reproductive advantages of a good forager will be transmitted to its offspring (Ingold 2000, 30). This makes the assumption that natural selection has resulted in fitness-maximising foraging behaviour over time problematic (*e.g.* Ingold 1992, Ingold 2000).

Of course, culture as a mechanism of inheritance, is also subject to selection. This selection simply operates differently from natural selection at a genetic level (Barrett, Dunbar, and Lycett 2002). This is exactly the advantage of cultural over genetic inheritance. It allows a population to deal with change much faster than would be the case if it could only adapt genetically. Especially in long-lived animals, genetically adapting to changing circumstances would take a long time and bring with it the demise of large parts of the population. Therefore, culture can be seen as an evolutionary mechanism that facilitates fast behavioural change (*e.g.* Potts 1998).

Furthermore, in hunter-gatherers, these cultural behaviours do have clear reproductive benefits. Anthropological studies show that good hunters have greater reproductive success and more extra-marital affairs (*e.g.* Kaplan and Hill 1985, Smith 2004, Smith, Bliege Bird, and Bird 2003). There are also much more subtle consequences of foraging behaviour that, due to evolution being a long-term process, will filter out the people with less potential for efficient behaviour, whether this is genetic or cultural. For example, many consequences of malnutrition of foetuses may only become apparent later in life. So a child that was nutritionally stressed in the womb can appear to be very healthy, but later in life there may still be significant health consequences that inhibit fitness and reproduction (*e.g.* Lummaa 2002).Therefore in cases with cultural transmission it is still in a forager's best interest to forage efficiently. For the offspring of unsuccessful foragers, the fitness consequences may be less severe when foraging is inherited culturally instead of genetically. In a cultural society, offspring can acquire skills from individuals other than their parents. Therefore, they may be able to become more successful foragers than their parents.

An additional argument for why OFT models work is because they are grounded in economic principles (*e.g.* Rapport and Turner 1977). Foragers may not be consciously maximising their evolutionary fitness, but they are expected to serve their own interests as well as possible and thus to forage as efficiently as possible. On the other hand, it is clear from cultural anthropology that humans do not function solely as rational, purely self interested actors. Cultural norms may not prescribe optimisation of foraging strategies but in most cases, food is a valuable social currency. Therefore it is expected that human foragers make rational choices when foraging and they will not consciously practise very unrewarding strategies. It is known from ethnography that much behaviour of hunter/gatherers is rational in nature (*e.g.* Mithen 1988, Winterhalder 2001). Hunter/gatherers are not constantly computing equations in order to arrive at decisions. In many situations, rules of thumb are used and these have been selected for because they work well in most cases (Winterhalder 2001, 32). Simple heuristic mechanisms for decision making have been observed in many animals and also in modern humans. These mechanisms are used not only by hunter/gatherers, but for example also by employees in insurance companies (Todd 2000). We can thus assume that humans generally make decisions in a system of "bounded rationality". They will not consider the infinite number of possible courses of actions, but will decide rationally based on simple heuristic mechanisms (Todd 2000, 941)

In the course of hominin evolution, the greater reliance on cultural traits brought with it natural selection on traits that are associated with functioning in a cultural society. This may be visible in the steady increase in brain size in the human lineage. As has been argued in chapters 1 and 2, since large brains enable better foraging skills, natural selection on foraging skills was an important factor in this process (*e.g.* Kaplan *et al.* 2000). Furthermore, selection probably worked on decision making processes, favouring individuals that were able to make appropriate choices in foraging situations. Selection on decision making mechanism would be relevant, since not everyone's fitness benefits from similar decisions. There are clear conflicts between fitness interests of men and women for example. This selection has therefore resulted in the fact that in genetically similar populations, behaviour can be differentiated (Hawkes 1993, 342).

In the end, these simplified models predict behaviour in a surprisingly wide variety of contexts, as pointed out in the introduction, for instance in foraging by insects, or surfing the internet (DiClemente and D. A. Hantula 2003, Waldbauer and Friedman 1991). This alone indicates that using optimal foraging as a "working model" is a valid approach. The mechanisms by which these behaviours are transmitted across generations may be unclear, but OFT can still be used to predict behaviour (Smith 1983, 627). Application of OFT-models can thus be justified by what has been called "playing the phenotypic gambit" (Barrett, Dunbar, and Lycett 2002, 9). The model is used to predict behaviour. If its predictions work out, it is assumed that the explanation that foraging behaviour is organised in order to optimise a certain currency is valid. The mechanisms of transmission of behaviour are ignored. Of course research into the mechanisms of transmission of behaviour and the interplay between genetic and cultural inheritance is important, but these problems lie within Tinbergen's proximate level of interpretation. OFT models are not designed, nor equipped to answer questions at this level.

In conclusion: The application of OFT-models is a starting point of analysis. It enables us to check how well the simplistic assumptions of OFT explain the foraging choices that are reflected at archaeological sites. If the predictions fit the attested behaviour well, the archaeological context may provide explanations on any deviations. If the fit of the model's predictions and the archaeological assemblage is poor, we are left with two explanations. First, caloric value may not have been the currency that was maximised at the site. Another currency can be proposed and a new model can be constructed if this is the case. In this way, OFT provides an avenue of research that can illuminate what factors were important in the development of Neanderthal foraging behaviours. It has to be combined with the archaeological context in order to check how valid the predictions of a certain model are. A second possibility is that the model itself is not valid. If the variables or the categorization of different categories of food used in the model differ from the variables upon which the occupants of a site based their foraging decisions, a different model must be adopted to study the foraging behaviour reflected at the site.

4.3 An example of an OFT model: The diet breadth model

After these general considerations, it is time to look at the models themselves. The most basic optimal foraging model is the diet breadth model. This model was designed to predict which species a predator exploits and which species are ignored in a given environment. It assumes that the predator lives in a homogenous environment, and that prey items are dispersed and encountered randomly. For example, a predator can choose between two species of prey, one of which is considerably larger than the other. In this case one would expect that the predator to concentrate on the larger prey, since it would provide him with more food. However, prey is encountered at random; the smaller prey will also be encountered. The diet breadth model predicts what a predator will do in this situation. If large prey is ubiquitous, the smaller species will be ignored, since exploiting it will waste time that could be spent more profitably on searching for prey of the larger species. The small species will only be exploited in situations where the large species is not encountered often enough. If the return rate of foraging for only the large species drops below the return one gets when exploiting both species, the smaller will be incorporated into the set of exploited prey (*e.g.* MacArthur and Pianka 1966, Winterhalder 1987, Winterhalder 2001).

The diet breadth model therefore predicts an optimal set of prey items that should be exploited when encountered, while other species should be ignored. Whether a species is incorporated in the optimal set depends on the profitability of its exploitation. This depends on three factors: the "value" of the species, the abundance of the species in the landscape and the cost of hunting it. Because it is assumed that a predator randomly encounters prey, the advantage of this model is that it does not require fine-grained environmental reconstructions. Most other OFT models do and are therefore not easily applicable to the archaeological record (Sheehan 2004, 170). Therefore, although this model is simplistic, it can be applied in the absence of fine-grained reconstructions of the distribution of plant and animal resources through the Pleistocene landscape. This model predicts that the prey in the optimal set will always be exploited when encountered, while prey not in the optimal set will always be ignored. The order of profitability of the available prey types is called the ranking.

In the diet breadth model, the available resources are ranked on the basis of their profitability. When using caloric value as a currency, this is the yield of the prey minus the energy that the forager had to invest in order to acquire it (Bettinger 1991, 84-85). For different currencies, different ranking can be compiled.

The energy invested in acquiring an animal is usually divided into search cost and handling cost. A forager incurs search cost while searching for food in the environment up until the moment he encounters a resource (MacArthur and Pianka 1966, 603, Winterhalder 1987, 316). The probability that an animal of a specific species is encountered is called its encounter rate; it depends on the population density of the prey species. Search time is dependent on the encounter rates of all the prey species in the optimal set. The more species are included in the optimal set, the more time spent searching for suitable prey will decrease. It is important to realise that the inclusion of a species in the optimal set does not depend on the abundance of the species itself. It depends on the abundance, or rather lack thereof, of higher ranked species. Only if searching for higher-ranked species becomes too costly will additional species be added to the diet, no matter how abundant the lower-ranked species are.

When an animal is encountered it has to be pursued, dispatched, processed and sometimes transported back to a camp or nest. The cost incurred in these activities is called handling cost. This is not a simple function like search time. The handling cost of an animal depends on both the predator's abilities with regard to pursuing and killing prey, and the prey's anti-predator strategies (MacArthur and Pianka 1966, 604). Butchering and transportation costs can also be influenced by the predator's abilities. As a general rule it can be assumed that handling cost goes up when more prey species are added to the diet. This is because species that are hard to catch will generally be lower ranked. Moreover, because hunters grow less specialised when more species are added to the diet, which will have negative repercussions for hunting and processing efficiency (MacArthur and Pianka 1966, Winterhalder 1987).

Which prey species are included in the "optimal set" and exploited upon encounter depends on the abundance of the most rewarding prey. Ideally, a forager will only exploit the most profitable

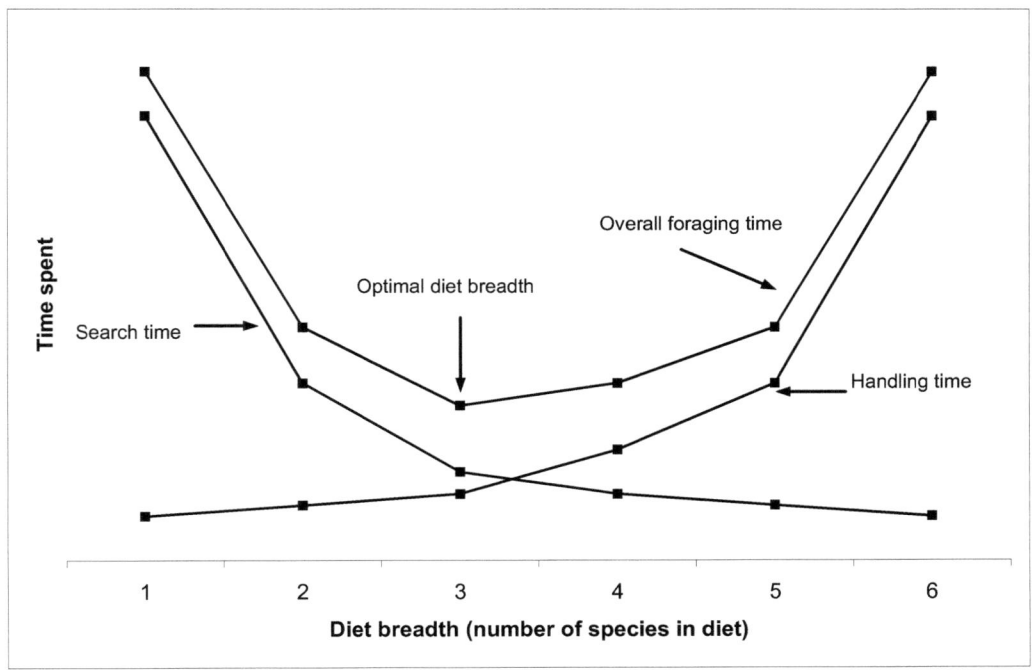

Figure 4.1: Hypothetical illustration of diet breath model. Adding species to the diet lowers search time, but raises handling time. In this situation exploiting the three most rewarding species minimizes time spent per amount of energy acquired. Graph after Bettinger (1991) and MacArthur and Pianka (1966).

species. Only if he cannot be reasonably sure that it will be encountered frequently enough will he add less lucrative species to the menu (Bettinger 1991, Winterhalder 2001). This will result in lower search time, but in a higher handling cost and consequently a lower return rate for the added species. The optimal set will be the number of species that result in the lowest overall search and handling time, as illustrated by Figure 4.1.

The simplest versions of the diet breadth model assume that if a prey species in the optimal set is encountered it is always exploited. Adaptations of the model have also been constructed. It has been proposed that the dichotomy between species that are exploited and species that are ignored may be modelled more realistically. To this end, the contingency model has been formulated (Bettinger 1991, 85-86). This model states that a prey species that is in the optimal set, but is not the highest ranked species, may or may not be exploited when encountered. It would be most logical for a forager to weigh the expected cost of continued searching for the highest ranked species against the profit he will make from the prey at hand. If the prey at hand is more rewarding than the expected cost of continued searching, subtracted from the yield of the preferred prey, the prey at hand will be exploited by the forager (Bettinger 1991, 86).

It is expected that the optimal set changes when one of the parameters of the model changes. Both search time and handling time of species may change and these changes will influence the composition of the "optimal set" of prey items. Search time will change when prey becomes more or less abundant for example. This can be a reflection of climatic change, but also of human impact. A species can become rarer if it is overexploited, in which case it is expected that lower-ranked species will be added to the diet (Jones 2004, 308). It is thus important to realise that addition of items to the diet depends not on their own abundance, but on the abundance of higher-ranked resources (Bettinger 1991, 87). If the prime prey is rare, other prey may be exploited more heavily, not because the forager prefers this species, but because of its high(er) encounter rate relative to the very low encounter rate with the highest ranked prey. This means, for example, that when new predators enter competition for a resource, diet breadth may be increased as the density of the resource gets lower, but it will not be dropped from the optimal set (MacArthur and Pianka 1966, 604).

Handling time is determined by the abilities of the prey and the predator. This variable can change for example through evolutionary developments of either prey or predator. More interesting for archaeology are the influence of technology and the development of hunting strategies on the handling costs of species. Increased knowledge of prey behaviour can for example affect its handling time and therefore its return rate in such a way that it becomes elevated to a higher rank. The same is the case with technological developments. One important example of technology affecting handling costs is seen in mass-collecting of small animals. Technology in the form of nets or traps may make the exploitation of small animals with low individual return rates very profitable, because they can be collected in great quantities (Stiner *et al.* 1999, 193, Ugan 2005).

As mentioned above, the diet breadth model is very simplistic and other models have been constructed on the basis of assumptions that are in many cases more realistic. Most animals for example do not live in a homogenous environment. In order to deal with heterogeneous environments, a refined diet breadth model has been developed, namely the patch choice model. This can be applied if fine-grained knowledge of the structure of the environment is available. In this case foragers are confronted with a range of patches that differ in energetic value and the amount of energy and time needed to exploit them. The different patches are ranked, much in the same way as prey types in the diet breadth model (Bettinger 1991, 88-89). The most important decision that hunter-gatherers face in patchy environments is when to leave a patch. They typically do not remain in a patch until it is depleted, usually choosing to leave at the moment return rates drop below the level where expected return rates in another patch minus the cost of moving result in higher returns overall. However, since moving to a patch whose status is unknown is risky, hunter-gatherers will sometimes remain at a given patch longer than expected (Bettinger 1991, Winterhalder 1987). In such decisions, transport cost is very important: if transport costs are high, hunter-gatherers will tend to become generalists, exploiting most resources as they are encountered in a patch. When transport costs are low they tend to specialise in few high ranked prey items and prefer departure to another patch earlier (Ingold 2000, 30).

If resources are distributed in patches, a very important variable is the predictability of their location in time. When the status of patches is predictable, people will leave their old patch sooner than if it is unpredictable. The assumptions that these models are based on usually state that patches are scattered through the landscape randomly and that they are encountered randomly. But hunter-gatherers typically have a good knowledge of the landscape and of the habits of their prey. They invest in this knowledge, and this pays off, because foraging becomes more predictable. Therefore patches and prey are not encountered at random. Furthermore, the fact that most foragers now face influences from the policy of the nation-state they inhabit implies that they are often forced to make less than optimal choices (Winterhalder 1987, 320).

Many other kinds of OFT models have been constructed, for example, models that predict group size, or resource transfers within a group and so on (*e.g.* Winterhalder 2001). These are very hard to test against the archaeological record. Therefore I will focus on the diet breadth model. This model is well-suited for research into the determining factors of prey selection in the Pleistocene. In the following sections, I will outline how the diet breadth model can be used on the sites that were selected for this analysis.

4.4 Applications of diet breadth in the study of the Middle Palaeolithic

The notion of diet breadth is not new in the study of Middle Palaeolithic subsistence. For example, the concept of diet breadth has regularly been invoked when comparing Middle and Upper Palaeolithic subsistence (*e.g.* Grayson and Delpech 1998, Richards *et al.* 2001, Stiner, Munro, and Surovell 2000, Stiner *et al.* 1999). It is often implied that Neanderthals had a smaller diet breadth than anatomically modern humans (AMH), who were therefore able to displace Neanderthals. This perspective on the problem is very interesting, but some aspects of the published studies are problematic. In this section, I will review these previous applications and point out some problems. In sections 4.5 and 4.6 I will discuss how these shortcomings can be corrected.

An important hypothesis with regard to changing diet breadth in the Late Pleistocene was put forward by Stiner *et al.* (Stiner 2001, Stiner, Munro, and Surovell 2000, Stiner *et al.* 1999). The central idea of her thesis is that anatomically modern humans were able to replace Neanderthals because modern humans were able to exploit small fast moving, fast reproducing prey more efficiently. This "broad-spectrum revolution" enabled modern humans to maintain higher population densities and recover faster from demographic crashes. This is an interesting hypothesis and, as pointed out in chapter 3, the evidence for exploiting this type of prey is indeed rare at Middle Palaeolithic sites. Stiner bases her hypothesis on research at a number of Mediterranean sites, in Israel, Turkey and

Italy. Her assertion that leporids and birds are generally better represented in Upper Palaeolithic levels at these sites seems to be true. However, leporids and birds are not absent at the Mediterranean sites of Middle Palaeolithic age, both in the sites she studied or at those examined by others (Tortosa *et al.* 2002). Moreover, the importance of small fauna seems to increase late in the Upper Palaeolithic in the western Mediterranean. For France it has been proposed that exploitation of small animals does not become important until the Magdalenian (Costamagno and Laroulandie 2004). Therefore, the increase in diet breadth and especially the increase in the importance of small mammals do not always coincide with the arrival of AMH.

Related to this hypothesis is a high-tech approach that has been used to highlight the differences between Middle and Upper Palaeolithic foraging behaviour: isotopic analysis. An important study by (Richards *et al.* 2001) compares middle to late Upper Palaeolithic foragers to Middle Palaeolithic ones. This study shows that in some cases, Upper Palaeolithic humans added resources to their diet that were absent from the diets of the analysed Middle Palaeolithic fossils, like fish. However, the Middle Palaeolithic fossils that were analysed were all recovered in Western Europe (Belgium and France) and the Mediterranean (Croatia). The upper Palaeolithic specimens to which they were compared were recovered in Russia, the Czech Republic and Britain. Moreover, they are all dated to the middle Upper Palaeolithic. Therefore, foragers operating in very different situations are compared. Since diet breadth will be adapted to a forager's specific environment, the outcome of this comparison does not necessarily tell us much about the foraging capabilities of Neanderthals and modern humans, it only informs us what solutions were chosen by different hominins in different circumstances.

Researchers have also looked at diet breadth for reindeer-dominated fauna in France (*e.g.* Grayson and Delpech 1998, Grayson and Delpech 2003). In this research, conflicting conclusions have been reported. Some authors say that the Upper Palaeolithic assemblages are characterised by increasing specialisation on one species (i.e. narrower diet breadth) (Mellars 1996, Mellars 2004), whereas other researchers do not detect a change in diet breadth until the Magdalenian (Grayson and Delpech 2003, Grayson and Delpech 2006).

None of these analyses, present a fine-grained environmental reconstruction, nor is a ranking of species available in the environment constructed. The absence of environmental reconstructions makes it difficult to evaluate whether increasing representation of species at archaeological sites reflects an increase in diet breadth, or a decrease in encounter rates with more highly ranked species. Conversely, an increasing representation of reindeer (*Rangifer tarandus*) at Upper Palaeolithic sites may indicate specialised hunting of this species, but could also signal increased encounter rates with this species, and decreased encounter rates with more highly ranked species, due to climatic factors (*e.g.* Grayson and Delpech 2008, 353-354). These studies therefore do not apply the diet breadth model as rigorously as is needed in order to draw with inferences on the foraging choices made by the hominins that produced the assemblages.

4.5 On reconstructing the model's parameters

As argued above, archaeological applications of the diet breadth model are different from "real-time" studies, that mostly predict which species a predator will exploit. Since data on prey densities and prey and predator capabilities are often available, search and handling cost can be reliably reconstructed. The archaeological record on the other hand confronts us with the results of foraging behaviour. Therefore we can assume that the diet breadth reflected at archaeological sites is the optimal diet breadth. The goal of this study is therefore to use OFT to reason back from the end result of foraging behaviour to gain insight into the variables determining the diet breadth. Search cost and handling cost are variables that are influenced by the sophistication of foraging tactics. The aim of using OFT is thus to gauge how Neanderthal behaviour influenced these variables and the profitability of exploiting available species. We will combine the known diet breadth with other known or reconstructable variables. This will enable us to model search cost and handling cost. The advantage of such a simplified model is that it will permit us to construct clear scenarios. These hypothetical scenarios will be tested against the archaeological record, which will allow us to refine them and use them in order to reconstruct Middle Palaeolithic foraging behaviour. In this section I will go into the factors that can influence the different variables of the diet breadth record and how this in turn can influence the foraging strategies that were practised. This will be followed by a section on the application of the theory within Neanderthal archaeology.

The most important variable that we need to understand is the currency that was optimised by Neanderthals, since this determines both how Neanderthals ranked their prey and what motivated their foraging decisions. Most OFT scenarios assume that caloric value is the most important factor guiding foraging decisions. On the other hand, there are many other options, like rare but essential nutrients, or socially motivated currencies. Therefore very complicated foraging patters can in some cases be expected. Plants represent a relatively poor source of energy, but they provide the building blocks for vitamins A, C and E. These are also present in animal livers, but not in great quantities in other tissues. Liver consumption is problematic, because it can lead to toxic levels of vitamin A (Hockett and Haws 2003, Hockett and Haws 2005). Another example is provided by birds. They are excellent suppliers of fats and may yield twice as many calories per 100g of flesh than for example mammals or fish. Marine animals produce carbohydrates and lipids generally not available from terrestrial resources (Hockett and Haws 2003, 212). Moreover, some resources may not even be targeted for dietary purposes, but for other commodities like fur or feathers (Jones 2004, 311). As many sites seem to present evidence of hunting large and dangerous animals, social prestige may also have played a role.

In some areas food can be so abundant that rather than foraging success, other activities like searching for mates, are important in determining fitness (Schoener 1971, 372-373). In such cases foraging is still done effectively, rather than maximising the amount of calories that is acquired, the amount of time spent foraging is minimised (Rapport and Turner 1977, 369). This may result in a wider diet breadth than would be expected when adopting the caloric value of a species as currency.

Furthermore, it may be the case that distinct groups in society rank foods differently. OFT hypothesizes that foraging strategies are optimised in order to optimise reproductive success. In human and also primate society, males often have different reproductive goals than females, which results in the two sexes practising different foraging strategies. (*e.g.* Bird 1999, Stanford 1999). The currency that is used to rank resources may thus not be uniform within a foraging group.

It is often thought that women's foraging is geared mainly towards provisioning the family, while the more risky to acquire big game is hunted by men and shared more widely than just among members of the nuclear family. The reasons for this difference are debated. Some researchers have argued that males share more widely in order to build a network upon which they can fall back when their hunting returns are disappointing. Big game would be the ideal food for such strategies, since it is too large for one family to eat all at once (*e.g.* Isaac 1978, Winterhalder 2001, 27). Others think that males may use their foraging spoils more to further their own political interests and may invest in order to increase their mating possibilities. It is thought that for males, mating with multiple women will almost always have a higher reproductive payoff than investing in increasing the chances of survival of their offspring. Therefore they will often choose to invest in potential partners (Bird 1999, 67). This seems to be supported by the fact that proficient hunters have greater access to extramarital affairs (Kaplan and Hill 1985, 132).

Females have other reproductive priorities. Firstly, they have certainty of parenthood of their offspring. Therefore their main foraging goal will be providing for their offspring. Furthermore, since nutrition can influence ovulation, pregnancy and lactation, foraging success or failure has more severe reproductive consequences for women than for men. Therefore it will in all probability be a higher priority for women to minimize short-term fluctuations in foraging success instead of maximizing the average returns (Jochim 1988). This means that women are expected to concentrate on abundant, low risk resources, such as plant foods.

Since the political and social role of food is very hard to test archaeologically, I will take caloric value as the starting point of my enquiry. The use of caloric value as a currency that is maximised may be simplistic but its application is reasonably straightforward. Caloric value however, is not as easily quantifiable as it appears. Body mass is generally a good indicator of caloric value. However, this is not an absolute law. As discussed, birds provide almost twice as many calories per 100g of meat than do mammals (Hockett and Haws 2003, 212, Ugan 2005, 75). In terrestrial mammals, the relationship between body size and caloric value holds up. Not only because larger animals provide more meat, but also because the meat of larger animals contains more fat (Rabinovich and Hovers 2004, 301). Since terrestrial mammals form by far the most important category of food remains found at Middle Palaeolithic sites, I will focus on body mass as a proxy for a prey's caloric value and thus its ranking.

Moreover, using this currency, deviations from the predicted patterns can be picked up, highlighting that foraging decisions were based on different factors. These will then be investigated bearing in mind the possibility of different currencies. In some cases the ranking according to caloric value and rankings based on other or multiple variables will not differ very much, however. This problem of equifinality cannot be solved by the application of the diet breadth model in isolation. By examining the archaeological context and data on for example butchery patterns we may be able to discern additional factors based upon which foragers ranked the available species.

When the caloric ranking is constructed, handling cost and search cost must be modelled in order to predict how they influence prey choice. Handling cost is an interesting variable, since Neanderthal foragers could have consciously modified it. It is a complicated factor to reconstruct, since this variable is a composite function of the predator abilities in pursuit and processing costs, and the prey species' skills at evading capture (*e.g.* MacArthur and Pianka 1966, 603). Therefore, developments in a predator's behavioural repertoire can in some cases significantly alter the return rate of a prey species and thus its ranking. Furthermore, the ranking of species may vary across individual foragers. For example, hunting skill and therefore pursuit costs of certain prey species may improve with experience, resulting in different rankings of prey species between age-groups (*e.g.* Walker, Hill, and McMillan 2002).

The most obvious way in which handling cost of prey species can be altered is by using technology for their exploitation. As shown in the previous chapter however, relating Middle Palaeolithic tools to subsistence strategies is far from straightforward. Furthermore, while technology may influence return rate it may also require a considerable amount of investment. Therefore it need not always be the most profitable solution for foragers. Increased investment in more sophisticated technology will not always yield large increases in return rates. Hence it can be more rewarding to keep technology simple (Ugan, Bright, and Rogers 2003).

An interesting example of lowering handling costs using technology and the problems connected to recognising this in Neanderthal archaeology is the case of mass collecting of small animals. When one is able to catch many of small animals simultaneously, for example by driving them into a trap, handling cost can be significantly decreased. Therefore mass collection can, in some cases, lead to return rates that match, or are even higher than those of encounter hunting of large mammals (Ugan 2005). Mass collection presents an exception to the rule that the inclusion of prey does not depend on its own abundance, but on the abundance of the higher-ranked prey types, since the return rate of mass collecting is dependent on the abundance of the prey. If population densities go up, so do return rates. Basically, it can "overtake" originally higher-ranked species (Madsen and Schmitt 1998, 447).

On the other hand, an important factor determining the handling costs are processing costs. These can account for a large percentage of the total handling cost of a species. For example, for large mammals processing can amount to between 1.3 and 40% of the total handling costs, in on-encounter hunting. In general, small animals require more processing per calorie than large animals (Ugan 2005, 82). This leads to an important point. It is often assumed that if animals are mass-collected, handling costs can be lowered sufficiently to make this more rewarding than encounter hunting of large mammals. For certain species this is the case, but generally mass collecting is not enough and efficiency gains must also be made in processing (Ugan 2005, 84). It appears that mass collecting of especially birds and mammals does not significantly improve return rates. Mass collecting does pay off in invertebrates and fish. This is because processing costs of large fish and insects are low, while they are not in mammals and birds (Ugan 2005, 78-80). Furthermore, a lot of time often has to be invested in the drives, nets etc., used in mass collecting, thus increasing the handling cost of mass-collected animals. On the other hand, trapping can be combined with other foraging activities and it is known that other resources are often exploited during animal drives. These are usually not quantified however, but this may result in an increased return rate for these activities.

As argued in section 3.3.6, the exploitation of small animals is an important topic in the study of Middle Palaeolithic subsistence. Mass collecting shows that in some cases exploiting these species is very profitable. Problematic is the fact that much of the material culture that could be used in catching animals, like snares or traps will have been made of organic materials. These will be next to invisible archaeologically. Furthermore, technology like gill-nets may take weeks or even months to produce, and for this investment to be worthwhile the tools must be used for a long time (*e.g.* Kelly 2001, 45). In mobile societies, investing in such technology may not have been worthwhile. In order to deduce what choices Neanderthals made we have to be aware of the problems surrounding lowering of handling cost. Since we know what species were exploited at sites and we can rank them on the basis of body size, we may be able to come up with educated guesses about the exploitation strategies used by Neanderthals.

Mass collection is just one example of how ranking of animal species can be altered by strategic and technological change. Ideally we would like to see a link between technology and exploited prey species. If changes in technology are accompanied by changes in the species that are represented at sites this provides an indication of changes in handling cost. It can also happen that animals that are in the exploited set change in ranking because of changes in the behavioural strategies used in their exploitation. This is a development that is more difficult to detect archaeologically. It might show up in changing representation of prey species through time. In the case of Middle Palaeolithic archaeology, the versatility of the stone tools may point to an absence of specialised technology in order to hunt specific prey. If different species of animal require different kinds of hunting or processing tools, the cost of the technological investment in the tools may influence prey choice. In some cases it can be more profitable to invest in a tool for a more common species, but one that will certainly be encountered, than in a tool for a species that may or may not be encountered (Ugan, Bright, and Rogers 2003, 1323). On the other hand, in order to exploit large mammals, generic tools will generally suffice for different species.

In the end, we will have to evaluate this variable largely on the basis of the species that are represented at the archaeological sites. In this study, handling cost will be modelled by using simple attributes of prey behaviour. If anti-predator behaviour of the available species does not influence their representation at archaeological sites, this indicated that strategies were in place to counter these behaviours. If species with well-developed anti-predator behaviours are absent from sites, we can infer that Neanderthals preferred species that were easier to catch.

A final influence on handling cost that does not receive much attention in most applications of the model is the transport cost of harvested resources. Hunter/gatherers need more than one resource, therefore they often operate out of a central place that is located in order to minimize the total transport cost of all crucial resources (Winterhalder 2001, 21). As discussed in chapter 3, the large amount of materials deposited at some sites over long periods of time seems to point to their use of these sites as a central place or home-base. This assumption is debated (*e.g.* Kolen 1999), but in this study I will assume that their foraging did have a focus at a central place from which the surrounding environment was exploited.

From the central place, the area closest to the site is usually exploited first. The more the area surrounding the site gets depleted, transport costs increase. As return rates become lower as resources in the site's vicinity become depleted, at a certain point a residential move will be in order. However, transport costs of certain resources can be lowered, for example by processing in the field, so only the most valuable elements of a resource are transported (Winterhalder 2001, 22). Transport costs can have important repercussions for hunting decisions in the field. It may become less interesting to capture large prey when one is further away from the base-camp for instance. Moreover it may lead to investment in processing equipment, in order to process the resource as fully as possible in the field, thereby minimizing transport costs. Developments in processing strategies can also influence handling cost and thus the ranking of species.

The third variable in the model is search cost. This is determined by the encounter rate with the prey. In the diet breadth model, the environment is assumed to be homogeneous, and encounter with prey is assumed to be at random (*e.g.* MacArthur and Pianka 1966). Therefore manipulation of the search time through knowledge of prey behaviour is assumed to be absent. In this case, variations in search time for the highest ranked species will have direct repercussions for the diet breadth. This is an unrealistic assumption with regard to Neanderthals; since we can assume that they knew how animals behaved and could therefore influence their encounter-rate with prey species. Hopefully, deviations from the expectations will enable us to determine how sophisticated Neanderthals were at manipulating encounter rates with high-ranked prey species, for example when certain high-ranked species are represented in higher proportions than one would expect based on reconstructed population densities.

One obvious example of influencing handling cost can be found in the exploitation of plants. The location of plants is stable, in contrast to that of animals. Especially long living plants like trees, will be at known locations for many years. This knowledge can be used to minimize search time to values close to zero. On the other hand, the harvesting of plants does have to be timed, since the moment at which they bear fruit depends on circumstances during the growing season. In order to harvest efficiently, it is best to arrive at the plants, before seeds or fruits have fallen to the ground, where they may become lost and before animals like birds arrive to harvest the plants (*e.g.* Kelly 2001, 49, 54). Similar strategies can be applied to the locations of animals. Especially migratory animals may be at easily predictable locations, enabling predators to manipulate search costs.

In conclusion, the research strategy that appears most productive is to compare the resources present in the environment, ranked according caloric value, with the exploited resources present at archaeological sites. This is the approach that is adopted in this study. I will focus predominantly on the faunal aspect of foraging strategies. This focus is dictated by taphonomic considerations but is defensible as meat appears to have been the most important component of the Neanderthal diet.

Therefore, we need to reconstruct the animal communities that were present in the vicinity of archaeological sites, so we know what species there were to choose from. As a starting point for this reconstruction we will use the analysed assemblages themselves. Because the sites that were selected were palimpsests, species that were not exploited by Neanderthals may be present in small numbers in the assemblages as a result of non-human processes. We will try to compare a species representation with a reconstructed population density. This will enable us to signal whether a species is represented in the same proportion as it would be encountered in the environment. If an animal is rare in the environment, but present in large numbers at the analysed sites we can conclude that is was exploited. If a species is underrepresented, we can conclude that it was not usually exploited at the site. Any bones of these species in the assemblage may be explained by other factors, as part of the "background fauna", or they may represent an exceptional foraging episode.

Reconstructing the species' population density will allow us to reconstruct encounter rates and therefore search cost of the species present. This is a tricky proposition however, since many of the species are extinct nowadays and it appears that Pleistocene environments do not have analogues in the present. In general, the population density of mammal species is correlated with body weight (*e.g.* Eisenberg 1990, Silva, Brimacombe, and Downing 2001, Silva, Brown, and Downing 1997). This correlation allows us to arrive at rough estimates of population densities of the available prey species.

Body weights of the species under consideration need to be obtained in order to construct a ranking of the available species. Various authors provide body weights of both fossil and extant species (*e.g.* Brook and Bowman 2004, Louguet-Lefebvre 2005, Macdonald 2006, Owen-Smith 1988 [1992], Pushkina and Raia 2008, Waguespack and Surovell 2003), values that will be combined to provide rankings for the selected archaeological and palaeontological sites. They will also be used in order to reconstruct the population densities of the species, following the equations provided by Silva, Brimacombe, and Downing (2001).

Handling cost of prey species is hard to reconstruct, but an inventory can be made of basic behavioural parameters. Based on this information, some insight into logical targets for exploitation should be gained. The ranking that is constructed can then be compared to the species present at an archaeological site. The final step is to evaluate how well the species that were exploited were predicted by the model.

First, we will look at size of the prey species. Among mammalian carnivores, body size is related to the maximum size of their prey (Radloff and Toit 2004). Therefore the size of prey is an important characteristic for the handling cost of prey species among mammalian predators in general. We can calculate the maximum prey size for a mammalian predator of 65 kg.[5], to be 300 kg.[6] Species weighing over 300 kg. will therefore be considered difficult to hunt for Neanderthals. This means that if prey larger than 300 kg. was hunted by them we can assume that they developed behaviour that allowed them to breach this important threshold. One of the ways in which this can be achieved is by coordinated group hunting (Radloff and Toit 2004).

Secondly, we will look at whether the species of prey was a carnivore. It is assumed that carnivorous species are more difficult to hunt successfully than herbivorous species, since carnivores are equipped with "weapons" like claws and teeth to kill prey (*e.g.* Webb 1989). Hunting these species will therefore be a dangerous endeavour.

Thirdly, we will look at whether the species of prey are solitary or living in groups. This is an important handling cost variable, since it appears that many species living in groups do so mainly in order to reduce the risk of predation (*e.g.* Barnard 2004, 407-416). Minimising this risk is achieved

---

5   The weight of an average male Neanderthal (Sorensen and Leonard 2001).
6   The equation used is log(prey body mass) = 1.46(log predator body mass) − 0.17 (Radloff and Du Toit 2004, 415).

by "safety in numbers", because a predator has many potential victims, the risk for any individual is lowered. Moreover, living in groups also has the effect of increasing handling costs for predators. More individuals are on hand to spot approaching predators and when grouped, can even attack and chase away predators. Therefore if Neanderthal prey species lived in groups we can deduce that Neanderthals had developed behaviour to deal with this increase in handling cost.

In order to apply the model we also need to decide which variable we use to measure the abundance of species in archaeological assemblages and thus the importance of its exploitation in the foraging strategies of the hominins that deposited the assemblage. The number of bones identified to species level is usually expressed in Number of Identified Specimens (NISP). This measure has some disadvantages when comparing different species and assemblages though. First, different species of animals have different skeletons. Some species'skeletons have more bones than others, which means that these species may be overrepresented (Lyman 1994, 98, Reitz and Wing 1999, 60-62). Second, some animals may be processed in the field more fully than others, which will result in an underrepresentation of the processed species at central places (Lyman 1994, 111). Moreover if a bone is fragmented, several pieces of the same bone may be identifiable. This may also lead to overrepresentation of species. However, if bones are processed very intensively, the degree of fragmentation may result in the fact that no fragments belonging to the bone may be identifiable by an analyst (Lyman 1994, 281).

In order to get a more realistic view of the represented animals in an assemblage, many archaeozoologists calculate the Minimum Number of Individuals (MNI). This index specifies how many individuals must at least have been present to account for the NISP of a species (Lyman 1994). This counters the differential representation of species due to the fact that there are different numbers of bones in their skeleton. Moreover, the best represented element of a species is selected in order to calculate the number of represented individuals, so this measure also counters the differential representation of species due to different processing procedures. MNI as an index is problematic too. Most importantly, this index is not always calculated or provided in reports. Moreover, some archaeozoologists use a different definition of MNI and thus a different way of calculating it (Lyman 1994, 100, 104). Some critics even argue that using MNI as a measure of species abundance is logically flawed and should not be practised (*e.g.* Plug and Plug 1990). Even if these problems can be resolved, MNI results in an overrepresentation of rare species. Of some species often one or two fragments are present in an assemblage (Auguste 1995a, 157). Therefore it is not the ideal index to compare different bone assemblages.

Another variable that is sometimes used in order to compare the relative importance of animal species in an assemblage is bone weights. This may circumvent some problems associated with other indices. For example, the degree fragmentation of bone in a collection has less effect on the weight of bones of a species than on the NISP. Moreover, differences in size of animals and thus of economic importance will not be visible in either NISP or MNI, but they will be reflected in the weight of the bones. Unfortunately, many processes profoundly influence the weight of specimens, for example heating, but also processes in the soil during deposition (Reitz and Wing 1999, 170). Moreover, not many studies of Palaeolithic bone assemblages provide the weight of the recovered bones.

Other indices are also available, but, like the weight of the bones, they are not listed for the sites that were selected for this study. Moreover, these are all derived measures and are not always calculated in the same way. Therefore in this study it was decided to use NISP as the measure of species abundance at a site. In order to correct for the problems of overrepresentation the archaeological context can be taken into account. For example looking at skeletal completeness will inform us whether certain species are overrepresented in the NISP. Moreover, the different composition of artiodactyl, perissodactyl and carnivore skeletons is known (Lyman 1994, 98, see table), so we can correct for overrepresentation of species as a result of their different skeletal composition.

With regard to the application of the diet breadth model it is important to realise that abundance in terms of NISP or MNI does not inform us as to a species' rank. Well-represented species need not be the highest ranked, they are simply most often encountered. The highest ranked species may be rare and therefore only sporadically encountered.

Based on the predictions of the model and the archaeological reality, the following research questions emerge. First, whether the ranking based on caloric value is reliable, or whether we need to explore other currencies in order to predict Neanderthal foraging decisions. This may well be the case, since the mammoth-steppe has been envisaged as an area rich in large mammal biomass, so calories may not have been scarce. A second interesting query is whether we can see the results of manipulating handling costs. The prime example of manipulating handling costs may be the inclusion of small prey in the diet, but also of large dangerous prey. If handling cost of these species can be manipulated so that they can be hunted relatively safely, this may lead to their inclusion in the diet. Looking into this problem is also interesting in a longer temporal perspective, in order to see if for example changes in technology and behaviour coincide with shifts in diet breadth (cf. Stiner, Munro, and Surovell 2000, Stiner *et al.* 1999). Third, manipulation of encounter rates is also an interesting factor. Identifying signs of manipulation of encounter-rates may be more complicated. If species turn up in higher proportions than expected this would be a likely explanation. But this interpretation also depends on the accuracy of the environmental reconstructions used. Furthermore, if the highest ranked prey also happens to be relatively common this kind of pattern may not be easily visible in the archaeological record.

4.6 Possible confounding factors in the archaeological record

The application of the diet breadth model to the archaeological record is not straightforward. Certain taphonomic factors influence the composition of bone assemblages and constrain the research questions we can answer by studying them. First, there is the problem of temporal resolution. Sites are often palimpsests, containing the remains of multiple, and possibly many separate occupations and foraging episodes. Ranking of resources need not have been uniform over all these episodes. This means that we will lose sight of short-term variations, like seasonal fluctuations in prey ranking, because these ecological phenomena operate during a shorter time than is perceptible in the archaeological assemblages (*e.g.* Lyman 2003). These differences will be almost impossible to deduce from zooarchaeological assemblages.

On the other hand, the temporal scale of the archaeological record also presents us with advantages. Since short-term fluctuations will have been averaged out in palimpsests, it will be possible to reconstruct the strategy that Neanderthals developed to deal with their environment in the long term. Furthermore, an important criticism of foraging models in biology is the fact that they try to study the role of foraging in an animal's evolutionary fitness, but usually OFT models study short-time optimisation, while fitness is a lifetime measure (cf. Smith 1983, 638). Because of the temporal resolution of the archaeological record, applying OFT in prehistory always deals with the long-term results of foraging strategies, and can therefore show how long term developments of foraging strategies may influence a population's fitness. This issue can be turned into a methodological strength by focussing on palimpsests and research questions that adress long-term developments.

Another issue when studying bone assemblages is the fact that the behaviour responsible for their accumulation may produce assemblages that do not reflect the full suite of foraging activities equally. An obvious problem concerns the vegetable contribution to the diet, as has been discussed in section 3.3.6. The fact that Neanderthals lived during cold climatic phases may alleviate the problem, since plant foods are less important in colder climes. Moreover, as shown in chapter 2, the Neanderthal remains that have been isotopically analysed in order to reconstruct their diet suggest that plant foods were insignificant components of their diet (*e.g.* Bocherens and Drucker 2003, Bocherens *et al.* 2005, Richards *et al.* 2000, Richards *et al.* 2008b). Therefore we can assume that, especially for the colder areas of the Neanderthal range and in cold periods, plant foods will not have been very important economically. Even when we focus on the faunal component of the diet only, the archaeological record is likely to be biased. As discussed in section 3.2, hunter/gatherers lead a mobile way of life, producing different types of site. Therefore we need to take into account differences in site function and differences in seasonal occupation. Bone assemblages must not be studied in isolation, but should be compared with other sites from comparable regions and time periods. Furthermore, looking into additional features, such as bone assemblages and site architecture found at sites may provide clues as to the function of sites.

Intricately connected with the problems posed by the organization of mobility are transport decisions. In transport of food, the long-standing assumption is that limbs, especially the hindlimbs of carcasses, are the most highly prized parts of an animal and that these will therefore be transported to central places (*e.g.* Bunn and Kroll 1986, Potts 1983). Especially with increasing distance and/or carcass size, selection for the most valuable parts should become obvious (Monahan 1998, 406). The problem is that in practice, this assumption does not seem to hold true in a large number of cases (*e.g.* Domínguez-Rodrigo 2002). There is no standard transport sequence and therefore no standard pattern of bone accumulation, but there are important differences between different hunter/gatherer groups. As seen in the previous chapter, these kinds of decisions can have profound implications for the representation of species and activities at specific sites.

Still, there are some general patterns in the way in which carcasses are treated; with animals of different sizes often being treated differently (*e.g.* Bunn and Kroll 1986, Rabinovich and Hovers 2004). It is thought that smaller animals, especially if they are caught near a central place, will be transported to the camp in their entirety. The reasoning behind this is that because a round trip with the carcass would be less time and energy consuming than processing in the field and transporting processed parts to the camp. Larger animals will often be processed in the field, but the extent to which they are processed and which parts will be transported depends on many factors, for example predation risk or cultural preferences (*e.g.* Domínguez-Rodrigo 2002, Monahan 1998). Problems may arise if transport distances increase. When a forager encounters a resource, in deciding whether to exploit it, he has to consider that he can only carry a set quantity. So if he then were to encounter another, more valuable resource, he might not be able to exploit it, or would have to drop whatever he already had, making its exploitation a wasted effort. Of course, containers can alleviate this problem to a degree (Winterhalder 2001, 22). Still, this factor may cause a forager not to exploit species in the optimal set in some cases. Because of the problems regarding transport costs, care has to be taken when interpreting archaeological bone assemblages, because in the most severe case, if meat from large mammals was filleted, no bones may have been transported back to the site at all (Rabinovich and Hovers 2004, 301).

Finally, there is the difference in foraging strategies between individuals or subgroups of society. Most problematic in this regard are the different reproductive interests of males and females. Applying the diet breadth model to the archaeological record will not enable us to resolve matters at that resolution; it can only shed light on the foraging strategies at the level of the groups responsible for forming an archaeological site. In the Neanderthal situation, if we accept the evidence for a division of labour between sexes and the role of males as hunters of big game as discussed in the previous chapters, this might lead to a problematic situation, especially in cold phases in the northern parts of their range. The mammoth steppe was rich in low quality plant foods and animals subsisting on plants in this environments needed guts geared to fast processing of large amounts of food (Guthrie 2006, 208). This means that including a large amount of plant foods in the Neanderthal diet is effectively ruled out. This severely limits women's foraging possibilities. Although hunting or trapping of small animals especially is an activity that they might have practised, small animals are uncommon at many Neanderthal sites. This may mean that males could almost monopolize food distribution in some environments and this may have been a very important social currency. This situation does exist in some contemporary hunter/gatherers living at high latitudes too, but in these cases women forage for alternative resources like fish and small game in order to procure resources (Kelly 1995, 264, 267). In warmer periods and more southern environments, plants may have played a larger role in the diet. This may have had consequences for the use of food as a political tool, but also at a more basic level for the organization of mobility and male hunting strategies.

In all likelihood, food, and especially meat had an important role in the social life of Neanderthals. We can assume that it was used in order to cement bonds between people and maybe also as a tool used for reproductive purposes. One thing about Neanderthal society is important in this respect, however. It is often suggested that Neanderthals were less capable of maintaining extensive social networks and alliances than anatomically modern humans, based on evidence for long-distance trade, or lack of it (*e.g.* Gamble 1999, 267, 416). This leads to the hypothesis that the role of meat within local society may have been less extensive than what we see in contemporary hunter-gatherers. Gift-giving or exchanging may not have been very important and the social role of meat may thus have been less important than what we might expect based on modern human hunter-gatherer societies. Therefore, more food may have been used for provisioning females and children.

It is clear that we must take into account the role of taphonomic and behavioural processes when interpreting archaeological bone assemblages. Selection of suitable sites for analysis may allow us to overcome some of these problems. However, other factors like transport decisions will have been a universal factor in Neanderthal foraging behaviour.

4.7 Modelling Neanderthal diet breadth

Combining the diet breadth model with our knowledge of Neanderthal behaviour as discussed in chapters 2 and 3, we can formulate a number of hypotheses on the way that Neanderthal adaptations influenced their diet breadth. Of course Neanderthals operated over a large area under different climatic regimes and therefore diet breadth will have been variable and adapted to the regional environmental circumstances. In this section I will advance hypotheses on Neanderthal diet breadth that will be examined in the following chapters.

Two factors of Neanderthal biology are likely to have had an important impact on their diet breadth. First there is the fact that locomotion in Neanderthals was energetically more expensive than it is in modern humans because of their comparatively short lower limbs. Second, Neanderthals required more energy compared to modern humans, because of the fact that they were larger and, especially in cold environments, because they likely had a higher BMR.

Since locomotion was expensive, Neanderthals are expected to have had smaller foraging ranges than modern humans. Return rates of prey-items would drop faster as distance from the site increases than they do for modern humans. Especially small animals would only be worth pursuing when encountered close to the camp. The further from a camp foraging took place the more energetic gain one would need in order to compensate the high locomotion cost. This leads us to expect that in a similar environment, Neanderthals would practise foraging with a smaller diet breadth than modern humans. Higher transport costs also increase the importance of processing resources in the field. Since processing will affect transport cost, it is expected that this will have been an important strategy pursued by Neanderthals in order to minimise this cost.

Neanderthals had a larger body weight and lived in colder environments than AMH. Therefore it is thought that their BMR will have been significantly higher than that of AMH (Sorensen and Leonard 2001, Steegman, Cerny, and Holliday 2002). This does not automatically have consequences for Neanderthal diet breadth. The diet breadth model states that species will be added to the diet as long as the animal's return rate is higher than the average return rate for all higher ranked prey items including the expected search time for the higher-ranked items (Smith 1983, 628). Consequently diet breadth is not solely dependent on the energetic needs of the predator, but also on its abilities to search and find prey. On the other hand, Neanderthals will get into trouble sooner if for some reason finding and dispatching prey becomes more difficult. Furthermore the point at which combined search and handling cost start to outweigh the energetic gain will also be reached earlier by Neanderthals than by anatomically modern humans. The most important consequence of Neanderthals' energy demands is the fact that energetic returns are more likely to be a constraining factor in Neanderthal foraging strategies. Therefore it is even more likely than in modern humans that energetic value was in fact the currency maximised by Neanderthals. This has another implication, namely that Neanderthals were probably unable to cope with the same range of environments as anatomically modern humans. Especially the more marginal, less productive areas and maybe also a patchy landscape in which much travelling may have been necessary in order to fulfil their diverse needs may have been shunned.

Both these factors, but especially the cost of locomotion will have influenced the system of mobility that was practised by Neanderthals. The most obvious consequence of the increased cost of locomotion is that the area that can be profitably exploited from a central place will be smaller for Neanderthals than for modern humans. If we take the energetic budget spent on locomotion to be constant across mammals, then the average round trip for Neanderthals, applying the formulas provided by Steudel-Numbers and Tilkens (2004), would be 12.9 km when using the highest estimates of Neanderthal energetic requirements and 10.5 using the moderate estimates (Steudel-Numbers and Tilkens 2004, Weaver and Steudel-Numbers 2005).[7] Among modern human hunter/gatherers, there is a lot of variation in the length of foraging trips. The maximum listed by Binford (2001) is 30 km, the average distance is about 12.2 kilometres. If we take the estimate of moderate activity levels in Neanderthals to be comparable to the situation in hunter/gatherers, we see that the average distance of a foraging trip is significantly smaller.

---

7 According to table 4 in (Steudel-Numbers and Tilkens 2004), based on limb length and body weight, Neanderthals probably used up 12.39 ml O_2 per meter. Since using 1 ml of O_2 translates as burning 0.004801 kCal, (Weaver and Steudel-Numbers 2005), Neanderthals used 0.05948 kCal per meter. Energetic estimates given by (Weaver and Steudel-Numbers 2005) are 4480 kCal/day for moderate and 5500 kCal/day for extreme activity levels in Neanderthals. According to them these would translate into energy budgets of 627 kCal and 770 kCal per day respectively.

What would be the implication for the mobility practised by Neanderthals? First, a smaller area is exploited around each site, which means that resources in the foraging radius will be depleted faster than among AMH. Therefore, residential mobility will have been higher. Another way to deal with this issue is by limiting group size. If less people need to be fed, resources will be depleted at a slower pace and residential mobility will be lower (Binford 2001, 239-241). Higher locomotion costs also have implications for transport; it seems logical to minimize the weight of things that need to be transported in order to save energy. Therefore, transport of food to and from sites will be affected. One would expect high degrees of processing in the field in order to minimize the weight to be transported. On the other hand, if a large number of animals, or very large animals were caught, one might also expect the base camp to move to the meat, instead of the other way around. This would lead us to expect higher residential mobility and also somewhat weakens the assumption of central-place foraging. However, since many European sites containing large mammals show activities spanning extended periods of time, there is an indubitable spatial focus in Neanderthal foraging.

As argued in the previous section, this study will focus on the faunal component of Neanderthal subsistence strategies. Hunting is a risky hunting strategy however. In many hunter-gatherer societies the high-risk/high-yield foraging strategies of males are buffered by women's foraging for low-risk plant foods. If such a division of labour was in place among Neanderthals, we would expect the women to forage for plant foods. The importance of plant foods is very hard to determine, but the evidence from the southern part their range discussed in the previous chapter shows that, in some settings it played a significant role in the diet. However, in more northern areas, especially in glacial environments, relying on plant foods is an unlikely foraging strategy. Another risk-reducing possibility is increasing diet breadth and also exploiting small animals (*e.g.* Kelly 1995). As shown in chapter 3, this latter strategy appears not to have been very important for Neanderthals. In the colder phases one might therefore expect women to engage in the less dangerous tasks associated with hunting larger mammals. Among modern day hunter/gatherers, women's assistance in tracking animals is an important factor determining a male's hunting success for example (Biesele and Barclay 2001). Aiding in the less dangerous tasks of driving animals into an ambush has also been proposed (Kuhn and Stiner 2006, 958-959).

We have one important indication that Neanderthals did manage to buffer the risk of fluctuations in hunting returns as well as modern humans. This is provided by the analysis of Neanderthal teeth, discussed in chapter 2, which shows that the incidence of hypoplasias in their teeth is comparable to that of modern-day Inuit. In addition, the number of perikymata showing hypoplasias is lower in Neanderthals than in Inuit, pointing to shorter periods of nutritional stress among Neanderthals (Guatelli-Steinberg, Larsen, and Huchinson 2004).

Since the exploitation of a broad set of small animals was not the solution adopted by Neanderthals, they must have used a different strategy to buffer the risk of fluctuations in the returns of hunting large animals. One logical strategy is to exploit areas less intensively, and leave before prey density drops significantly (*e.g.* Kelly and Todd 1988). This would enable high returns, but only in the short term, since large-bodied species are generally present in low population densities. Consequently, this would lead to a drastically elevated degree of residential mobility. This would enable Neanderthals to focus on the very largest animals only. However, since large species have a slow rate of reproduction, they are easily overexploited. Therefore such a strategy would only be viable if Neanderthals were present in low population densities too. Another way of buffering short-term fluctuations in hunting returns would be by developing ways to store meat. Drying meat is not very complicated apparently, hanging it out to dry for two days appears to be sufficient to preserve it for some time and this process furthermore reduces the weight of the meat by up to 60% (Kelly 2001, 56). Since Neanderthals are known to have focussed on large animals, storage of surplus meat is a likely strategy.

In warmer periods and richer areas diet was likely broadened. However, as argued by Stiner *et al.* (Stiner 2001, Stiner, Munro, and Surovell 2000, Stiner *et al.* 1999), it is striking that Neanderthals did not exploit small, fast-moving prey as intensively as some modern humans. This is not necessarily related to differences in capabilities though. The fact that small fast game was not exploited more heavily may be due to reliance by women on "top-end" resources. Neanderthal foraging may have been characterised by focussing on a very narrow set of species. Slow moving species like tortoises and shellfish, which were exploited by Neanderthals, may have had much lower handling costs and therefore much higher return rates than fast moving species. Therefore, in warmer conditions, the widening of the diet to include plants and slow moving species might lead to the expectation that residential mobility would have decreased. However, even when foraging for low-risk resources, Neanderthals would have focused on the items with the highest return rates. They are thus expected to maintain higher rates of residential mobility compared to AMH under these circumstances.

This is compounded by the fact that these slow-moving animal species generally are slower reproducing species than fast moving prey like small mammals or birds (*e.g.* Stiner *et al.* 1999). Still, because of their role as top-carnivores and their heavier build, Neanderthals were probably present in lower population densities than modern humans. Combined with the hypothesis that they were more residentially mobile, it may have been possible for them to exploit these populations without their return rates dropping too dramatically. Over-exploitation of some species of small prey probably did occur in the late Middle Palaeolithic; however, this becomes much more apparent in the Upper Palaeolithic. It may also be a critical difference between Neanderthal and AMH foraging strategies, which do often show a greater reliance on small game: they may therefore have been able to exploit territories more intensively than Neanderthals could.

Another expectation that ties in with this proposed higher residential mobility is a reliance on simple, versatile and transportable toolkits. Because their residential mobility was high, it may not have been very rewarding to invest in "fixed" technology such as snares and traps, even if they were able to produce these. Tools for very specific activities will only have been made if the predictable returns were high enough and the activity was executed regularly enough to warrant this specialised investment. This may be the case with nets for fishing or trapping birds, whose construction costs are thought to be very high. Therefore unless densities of birds or fish were high enough to warrant construction of nets, we should expect more simple technologies to predominate.

If residential mobility was high it would be important for Neanderthals to optimise the weight to be transported. Therefore we expect Neanderthal tools to be versatile, in the sense that one tool could be used in the exploitation of multiple resources. This could be achieved by focussing on simple technologies, geared towards the category of prey that was most profitable, which would in most cases be large mammals. Artefacts like spears are used for other activities like fishing among modern hunter/gatherers, but specialised equipment for these activities may have yielded to little to warrant the investment. If residential mobility was lowered in richer environments, investment in trapping and snaring technology is expected to become more rewarding. This lowering of residential mobility would be expected in more temperate climatic phases. On the other hand, in forested environments, biomass is very hard to exploit for animals and hunter/gatherers, since most of it is locked up in the trees (*e.g.* Binford 2001, 106). In this situation as well, concentrating on the largest animals around, would have been the most profitable course of action. Since these animals would be present at low densities residential mobility would still be high. Trapping and snaring would thus presumably to have occurred mostly in the biomass rich southern parts of the Neanderthal range.

Testing these expectations will not be straightforward. A lot of the expectations hinge on high residential mobility because of a focus on large game. However, because of the temporal resolution of the archaeological record, it will be hard to deduce whether sites are palimpsests representing multiple short periods of use, or whether sites were used for a longer time and hence residential mobility was not very high. If we succeed in reconstructing likely population densities for the exploited species we can put constraints on the interpretative scenarios. Furthermore, it will be important to try to determine whether the picture of subsistence strategies presented by a site is representative of what Neanderthals were doing in that kind of environment. This can be achieved by comparing the sites to sites in similar settings. This will show whether for example small game is under or over-represented at sites under consideration.

4.8 Modelling hyena diet breadth

As pointed out in chapter 1, this study aims to evaluate the benefits of applying OFT to Middle Palaeolithic assemblages by also using it to analyse foraging strategies of Pleistocene cave hyenas (*Crocuta spelaea*). In order to do this, we need to reconstruct the model's parameters for this species too. This species is closely related to spotted hyenas (*Crocuta crocuta*) (Rohland *et al.* 2005) and analysis of their behaviour allows us to assemble a model for cave hyenas. It appears that spotted hyenas are similar to Neanderthals in at least two important respects. They were of roughly similar size, cave hyena being slightly larger. Second, both were social carnivores. In contrast to living primates, however, spotted hyenas and presumably cave hyenas are adapted to scavenging and hunting (*e.g.* Tooby and DeVore 1987). Since Neanderthals and Cave hyenas were sympatric in large areas and they appear to have been successful in the Pleistocene, it is expected that their niches were differentiated. For OFT to prove a useful tool, it should be able to differentiate between their niches.

In order to apply the diet breadth model for cave hyenas we will use the same approach as we did in Neanderthals. We have selected sites with large bone assemblages for analysis. It is hoped that they provide us with time-averaged results of hyena foraging strategies. We will use the reconstructed weights of the prey species to construct a ranking of the available prey species. Again, we will start using caloric value of the available species as the currency that hyenas tried to maximise. Moreover we will use the same simple characteristics to try to model handling costs. Encounter rates will also be modelled using reconstructed population densities.

It is proposed that applying the same model, we should be able to see differences in selection of prey between Neanderthals and cave hyena. If this is not the case we need to either refine the model's parameters, or use a different method of analysis to study Pleistocene foraging behaviours.

4.9 Summary and conclusion

The application of OFT to the archaeological record is a promising approach. OFT provides a framework that links foraging behaviour to evolutionary fitness and as such can be used to evaluate the dramatically changing ideas surrounding the evolution of hominin foraging. The goals for this study are simple. We will use a simple version of the diet breadth model to see how well OFT predicts Neanderthal foraging decisions.

The currency that we will use is prey size as a proxy for the caloric value of the prey. This currency works well in ethnographic studies (Winterhalder 1987, 319-322), although it does not fully explain foraging decisions in all cases. After comparing archaeological bone assemblages with the constructed ranking, we can evaluate whether this currency predicts the results of foraging behaviour well. If this is not the case, other currencies will be considered. If other currencies do not explain the set of exploited species we may assume that Neanderthals ranked species differently, because they were able to influence the return rate of certain species by manipulating the search and/or handling cost of certain species. We will use simple proxies to model encounter rate and handling cost. The encounter rate will be modelled using reconstructed population densities. If species that were rare in the environment are abundant at sites we can assume that Neanderthals were able to focus on these species because of an intimate knowledge of their behaviour. Handling costs will be modelled using simple proxies to gauge whether species were dangerous or hard to approach. If they are well represented in assemblages despite these factors we can assume that the foragers were able to overcome these difficulties. The results of the application of the diet breadth theory to Neanderthal sites will then be compared to the results of similarly analysed hyena dens. It is hoped that differences in their respective niches can be recognized and, ideally that the reasons underlying these differences can be explained.

Based on the foregoing some hypotheses with regard to the foraging strategies used by Neanderthals can be formulated. In interglacial periods, if the environment was dominated by closed forests, available biomass for Neanderthals was low. Most biomass would be locked up in trees, so the combined amount of edible plant foods and herbivores was likely limited. I assume that this led to low Neanderthal population densities. Fluctuations in hunting returns could not be buffered by female foraging for plant foods in most seasons. Therefore residential mobility is expected to have been high. Herbivores providing high return rates would have been hunted in an area and residential moves would have been made before the return rates of this activity dropped considerably. In this scenario foraging activities are expected to be concentrated on the largest species. Since fluctuations in return rate needed to be minimised in contingencies smaller species would also have been exploited.

During warmer periods the environment may have more open than it is nowadays as has been proposed by Gamble (1986, 1999) for the Eemian of occupations in Germany. This may have been caused by continental conditions in Germany. However, the presence of megaherbivores may also have resulted in more open environments in Atlantic climates. The presence of horses at some sites may support this view. In these environments, more animal biomass may have been available. Furthermore, animals may have been less dispersed, but may have moved more in herds with predictable locations. This may have led to an increase in Neanderthal group size. Smaller ungulates may have been exploited more readily in such environments, thus widening diet breadth and lowering residential mobility. Whether these developments took place is dependent on how much more animal biomass was available in the environment.

In mammoth steppe environments, biomass was likely very high (*e.g.* Delpech 1999). Moreover, in open environments, animals are likely to be concentrated in larger herds (*e.g.* Guthrie 1990, 155). Therefore, the higher amount of available biomass allowed Neanderthals to be present in larger groups, but may also have necessitated larger hunting parties in order to deal with the fact that most prey was now concentrated in herds. In these richer conditions diet breadth will have been lowered, since encounter rates with high ranked prey were probably favourable. On the other hand, in conditions of affluence, other considerations may become important. The time spent foraging may have been a valuable commodity itself. In these larger groups, the fitness of individuals could have been better served if time was allocated to other activities, such as investing in bonding with mates (*e.g.* Schoener 1971). In this situation diet breadth may therefore be kept wide in order to increase encounter rates with suitable prey, resulting in shorter foraging time and leaving more time available for other activities. I propose that in this situation a focus on the most ubiquitous ungulates may be developed. On the other hand, if women's foraging was unimportant in these environments, successful foraging could also have been linked to fitness benefits. In these circumstances prestige may have played a role in foraging decisions.

In Mediterranean environments, the role of plant foods and small animals and therefore the role of women's foraging increases. These conditions may also be termed affluent and in these circumstances Neanderthals may have strived to minimize foraging time and therefore have focussed on broader diets. Prestige hunting in these circumstances is less likely, since women are more able to fend for themselves. An additional factor in widening the diet breadth is the fact that residential mobility may be lowered since fluctuations in the abundance of prey species in the optimal set can be better buffered, seeing that more species can be exploited. This in turn has implications for investing in more specialised technology. These investments become more rewarding in this situation. The widening of diet breadth may then reinforce itself, since investing in a more elaborate toolkit may allow for the profitable exploitation of more species.

Hyena foraging is expected to be more diversified than Neanderthal foraging. Scavenging animals may result in more species being exploited, since if a carcass is encountered, handling cost is drastically lowered, because no pursuit or kill has to take place. This means that even small carcasses may be profitably exploited. This may also be reflected in the age classes of exploited prey, since weak age classes will be overrepresented if this foraging tactic is used. On the other hand, spotted hyenas are capable hunters, and in rich environments, scavenging is not a very important foraging strategy (see chapter 7). It is expected that in warm periods scavenging was more important than in cold periods when the environment was more open and more herbivore biomass was available. This means that in colder periods, the average prey size may increase when compared to warmer periods. It is thought that because hyenas hunt by pursuit, weaker age categories may be overrepresented when compared to hominin hunting, since it is hypothesised that hominins were more likely to be ambush hunters.

In the next chapters we will test these hypotheses by analysing selected sites dating to the Middle and Late Pleistocene of northwestern Europe. Of course this is a small sample of sites, but it will give a good indication of whether application of the diet breadth model in this form is a fruitful approach to studying Pleistocene subsistence strategies.

5   Biache-Saint-Vaast

5.1 Introduction

The previous chapter set out to develop a way in which the diet breadth model can be applied to the archaeological record. In this chapter and the next, I will test whether applying the model to archaeological assemblages yields satisfactory insights. The focus of this chapter will be the bone assemblage of the French site of Biache-Saint-Vaast.

Biache-Saint-Vaast is an open-air site in the north of France with several occupation levels. These levels were deposited during the transition of Marine Isotope Stage (MIS) 7 to MIS 6. The site was discovered in 1976 during building activities. Excavations took place between 1976 and 1982 (Tuffreau 1988a). The sedimentological sequence of the site consists of fluviatile sediments at the base, overlain by Saalian and Weichselian loess. The archaeological levels are found in the higher reaches of the fluviatile sediments and in the lower part of the loess sequence (Sommé 1988, Tuffreau 1988c).

The bone assemblage that was excavated at the site numbers over 200.000 specimens, 20.000 of which were identifiable. The majority of the bone assemblage comes from a single occupation level, level IIA (Auguste 1992, Auguste 1993, Auguste 1995a). Many of the bones show cut-marks, demonstrating that hominins played an important part in the formation of the assemblage. Moreover, a large Mousterian assemblage was recovered from the site. Finally, two hominin skulls have been found at the site. Only one of these skulls has been studied. The taxonomic determination of this fossil is not completely clear. It was originally classified as pre-Neanderthal, but shows apomorphies that have led it to be classified as an early Neanderthal or a Neanderthal *sensu lato* in more recent studies (*e.g.* Dean *et al.* 1998, Hublin 1998, 301, Schwartz and Tattersall 2002). The bone assemblage of the site is dominated by aurochs (*Bos primigenius*) followed by brown bear (*Ursus arctos*) and narrow-nosed rhinoceros (*Dicerorhinus hemitoechus*) (Auguste 1992, Auguste 1993, Auguste 1995a). Interestingly, the representation of the species changes through the archaeological levels. This allows us to study how the analysis using Optimal Foraging Theory (OFT) reflects the changing environmental circumstances.

This site has the advantage that it was excavated relatively recently, using modern excavation methods. This means that in contrast to Taubach, which is the focus of the following chapter, aspects such as the spatial distribution of finds have been studied at Biache-Saint-Vaast (*e.g.* Tuffreau and Marcy 1988a). These circumstances permit a higher resolution of environmental reconstruction than at Taubach. Unfortunately, only one volume of the monograph has been published to date. The treatment of the bone assemblage in this publication is preliminary and limited to only three levels (Auguste 1988b). Papers have been published on the bone assemblage, but they sometimes contain conflicting data.[8] Moreover, the bone assemblage of the richest level, IIA, has not been published in great detail.

In this chapter I will first provide the stratigraphic and geological context of the archaeological site. The artefact assemblages of the most important archaeological levels will be presented, after which I will provide an overview of the published bone assemblages. Then I will place the site in its local and regional environmental context. Subsequently I will attempt to apply Optimal Foraging Theory (OFT) to this site. I will endeavour to use OFT to develop a scenario explaining the foraging strategies practised by the site's occupants.

5.2 The site

The site of Biache-Saint-Vaast is located in the *département* Pas-de-Calais in northern France, in the vicinity of the city of Arras. It was discovered in 1976 during the extension of a factory and following the discovery, a rescue excavation was initiated. By the time the excavation got underway, the sediments containing the find levels had already been removed from 1500 m² of the 2000 m² building

---

[8]   For example, in terms of NISP, (Auguste 1993) provides a percentage of about 50% of Aurochs bones, while in (Auguste 1995a) it is close to 70%.

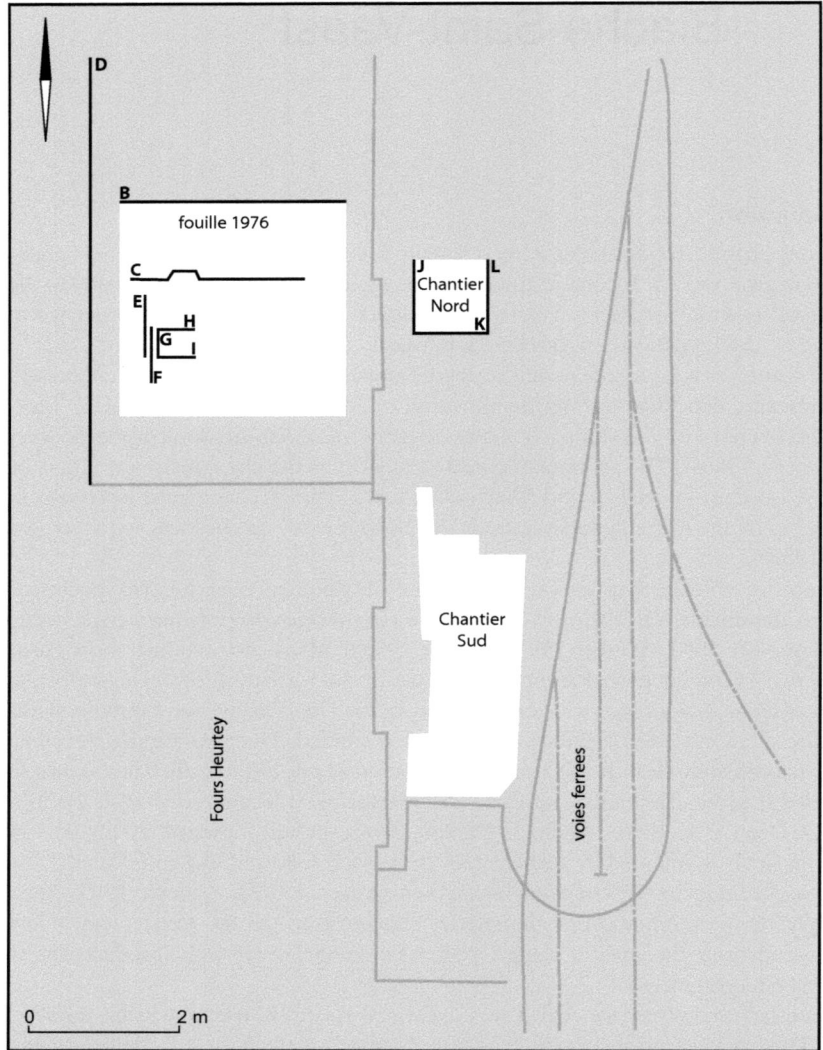

Figure 5.1 Plan of the location of the excavation trenches at Biache-Saint-Vaast. Based on (Tuffreau 1988a, 22).

site (Tuffreau 1988a, 15). From 1977 onwards, a research excavation was started on a neighbouring part of the factory terrain. Up to 1982 about 600 m² was excavated in this project (Tuffreau 1988a, 17-18). In total, three locations have been excavated at the site. One location was excavated during the rescue project in 1976, while during the research project carried out from 1977 onwards two other locations were excavated (see figure 5.1 for a plan of the excavated areas). The archaeological stratigraphy in the different excavation zones is not uniform, due to the complicated geological history of the site.

Geologically, the site is located in the zone where North European plain meets the chalk plateau of the Artois (Sommé *et al.* 1988). A calcareous plateau is located to the northwest of the site. The site itself sits on the edge of a river-terrace in the Scarpe valley It is situated between 56 and 44 metres above sea-level (Sommé *et al.* 1988, 115).

5.3 Dating

The site is thought to date to an interglacial within the Saalian, MIS 7. This is based on a combination of direct dating, and (bio)stratigraphic factors. Six burnt flint tools from level IIA were dated using thermo luminescence (TL). This yielded an average date of 175 ± 13 ka. This analysis was performed on flints that had been excavated several years previously and must therefore be regarded

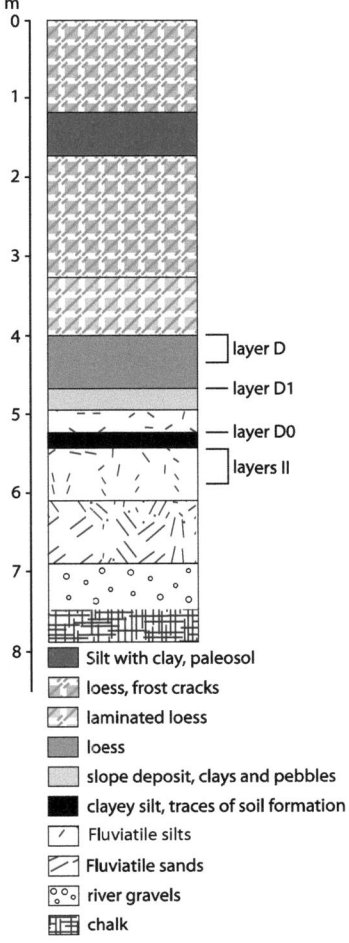

Figure 5.2: Schematic stratigraphic column of Biache-Saint-Vaast, with the position of archaeological levels. Based on (Sommé 1988, 32).

with caution (Louguet-Lefebvre 2005, 101). One of the hominin skulls, found in level IIA, was dated using gamma-ray spectrometry, yielding an age of 253 +53/-37 ka. A bone from the same level was dated using U-Th; this yielded an age of 182 +46/-31 ka (Louguet-Lefebvre 2005, 101). MIS 7 is thought to have lasted from 245 until 190 ka. The direct dates therefore roughly coincide with this period (Louguet-Lefebvre 2005, 101). Nevertheless, the combined evidence from the stratigraphic sequence, the pollen-spectra and the malacological and micromammal remains, shows that no interglacial climatic optimum is represented in the archaeological layers.

An important indication for the date of the archaeological levels is the fact that the fluviatile sands the bottom of the sequence, represent a climatic optimum (See figure 5.2 for a schematic overview of the stratigraphic column of the site). This unit contains *Corbicula fluminalis* molluscs (Tuffreau and Sommé 1988a, 311-312). This species is indicative of interglacial conditions, but is not known from the Eemian (Meijer and Preece 2000). Moreover, the *Arvicola* fossils at the site indicate that it is younger than Maastricht Belvédère in the Netherlands, which is dated to MIS 7 (Roebroeks 1986, 86). The archaeological levels document the transition to colder climes, with at least two climatic ameliorations represented in the levels (Tuffreau and Sommé 1988a, 311).

The paleosol just under 1 metre in figure 6.1 also provides vital clues with regard to the dating of the site. This unit, which is only preserved in a small part of the Chantier Sud, is a paleosol which can be correlated to the Sol de Rocourt/Sol de Warneton in the regional stratigraphy. This soil complex is dated to the Eemian interglacial and thus provides a *terminus ante quem* for the underlying layers (Sommé 1988, 34-43). The underlying layers appear to show a fairly continuous sequence of loess deposition, although some erosional events appear to have taken place in the upper part of the sequence (Sommé *et al.* 1988, 116-117). If the loess deposition really was of a continuous nature, this implies that the layers underlying the paleosol date to the second cold phase of the Saalian, MIS 6. This is supported by the fact that the underlying loess contains deep frost cracks (Sommé 1988, 34). The fluviatile units, documenting warmer conditions would then date to an interglacial or interstadial earlier than the Eemian.

The combination of the direct dates with the stratigraphic evidence discussed suggest the site must be dated during the transition of MIS 7 to MIS 6, or during the early part of MIS 6.

5.4 Stratigraphy and archaeological horizons

Multiple archaeological levels have been excavated at the site of Biache-Saint-Vaast (see figures 5.2 & 5.3). The stratigraphy of the site is complex, as a result of tectonic processes and many small faults are visible in the profiles, especially in the *Chantier Nord* (Tuffreau 1988c, 127). Moreover, the succession of archaeological levels in the *Chantier Sud* is different from that of the northern part of the site. I will summarize the information about the stratigraphic sequence here, with an emphasis on the most important archaeological levels.

The archaeological levels are situated in the lower part of the sedimentary sequence. The most important archaeological levels were designated (from oldest to youngest) IIA, IIα, II base, D0, D1 and D. The sediments in which level IIA to D0 are situated are fluviatile. They were probably deposited in shallow slow-moving to standing water. Level D1 and D on the other hand, are situated in wind-blown loessic deposits. This had consequences for the preservation of the faunal remains in these levels, which are chemically weathered (Auguste 1988b).

Fluviatile gravels have been deposited at the base of the sequence, on top of the cretaceous chalk substrate. This level is overlain by cross-bedded medium to fine-grained yellowish fluviatile sands containing, chalk granules. This level is capped by fine-grained fluviatile sediments, dubbed "tuff" in the literature and designated as Unit 2b. This unit contains the archaeological levels IIA and, slightly higher IIα in the Chantier Nord. In the Chantier Sud it harbours levels H through F (Sommé 1988, 30-31). The unit consists of very calcareous yellowish fluviatile silt, with calcareous

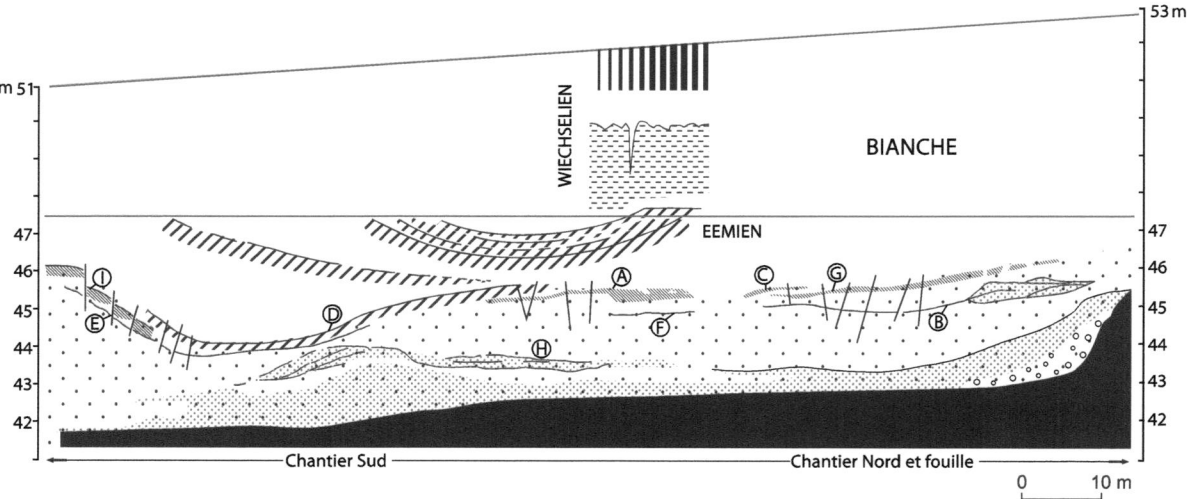

Figure 5.3: Stratigraphic profile of Biache-Saint-Vaast showing the position of the important archaeological levels. Based on (Tuffreau 1988c, 131).

concretions distributed in discontinuous bands. This level was formed by periodic low-energy calcite-rich fluviatile sedimentation (Sommé et al. 1986, 189).

Unit 2b contains the most important archaeological levels of Biache-Saint-Vaast, among which level IIA, the richest level at the site. This level is in the lowest stratigraphic position in the Chantier Nord. In the Chantier Sud, levels H, G and F were found in lower stratigraphic position, but they did not yield much behavioural information. Level IIA consists of large numbers of bones and flint artefacts, densely packed together. The level is dark in colour, at least in part because of the presence of charcoal in the sediments. This dark colouration has led to the identification of animal hoof prints and one possible hominin footprint in the upper reaches of the layer. It has been excavated over an area of about 150 m2 (Tuffreau 1988c, 123). Above level IIA, in parts of the area covered by the rescue excavation and the Chantier Nord bone fragments and flint artefacts have been found. They were separated from the finds of level IIA by sterile sediments. These have been assigned to a different level, IIα (Tuffreau 1988c, 123).

Unit 2b is topped by Unit 3 (at a depth of 5 metres in fig. 6.1), a thin unit that shows traces of soil formation. Unit 3 comprises two different facies. They were deposited in different sections of the river bed as the river moved away from the site. The lower facies of this unit, Unit 3a, consists of slightly clayey silt, with a high humic content and showing severe signs of bioturbation, pointing to soil formation (Sommé 1988, 31). Level II base was excavated in these sediments. This layer was present in the whole area of the 1976 rescue-excavation and has been excavated over an area of 340 m2 (Tuffreau 1988c, 123-127). Unit 3b has been documented in depressions, mostly in the Chantier Sud (see figures 5.2 & 5.3). This layer is made up of of silts, less clayey than those of 3a, grey-brown in colour. This deposit represents a hydromorphous paleosol, which contains the archaeological level D0 (Sommé et al. 1986, Tuffreau 1988c). In other parts of the Chantier Sud, level E was recognised. It is in a comparable stratigraphic position as level D0. Level E actually consists of multiple thin archaeological levels. In part of the trench the separate levels are not discernible, they are therefore grouped as one level E (Ameloot-Van der Heijden 1989, Tuffreau 1988c).

In the Chantier Nord, much of the fine-grained fluviatile sediments were eroded away by the river. Levels IIA and II base were only present over roughly 20 m2 in this trench (Tuffreau 1988c, 237). In the part of this trench where the sediments were still in place, Unit 3a and 3b were observed in sequence. Because both these units are paleosols, they must have been stable surfaces for quite some time. This leads the excavators to conclude that the archaeological level D0 must have been deposited some time after level II base (Sommé 1988, 31).

Above Unit 3 the mechanism of sedimentation changes. Unit 4, a slope deposit consisting of clays and pebbles, filled in the basins that were left in the area after the phase of fluviatile sedimentation ended. During this phase of sedimentation, the top of the underlying unit 3 was also partly eroded, and reworked materials from Unit 3 are found in Unit 4 (Sommé 1988, 31). This level is overlain by a level consisting of silt, but with high proportions of sand and clay, unit 5. This level is distinctly humic. The lower part of the unit consists of a coarse-grained horizon that overlies the tuff in parts of the site and covers the deposits of unit 3 that have been deposited in basins in the old riverbed (Sommé *et al.* 1986, 190). The archaeological level D1 is situated in this zone (Tuffreau 1988c, 129).

Higher up in this unit, the archaeological level D was located (Sommé 1988, 34). Level D1 coincides stratigraphically with a diffuse scatter of small limestone and flint pebbles. Archaeological materials have only been recognised in small parts of this scatter, over an area of about 115m2 (Tuffreau 1988c, 129). Level D is separated from Level D1 by sterile sediments of variable thickness. Level D has been impacted by numerous tectonic faults. Its size is about 120 m2.

Apart from the D levels, other archaeological levels have been recognised in the Chantier Sud; most of these yielded few archaeological materials and some of them have been partly destroyed by a brickyard that occupied the site before the current factory had been built. Furthermore, their faunal assemblages have not been published in detail (Auguste 1988a, Auguste 1988b, Auguste 1992, Auguste 1993, Auguste 1995a). Because of the absence of information on the faunal assemblage from levels H, G, F, E and D0, these levels will not be considered in the OFT analysis of this study.

The archaeological levels in the fluvial deposits are thought to have been the deposited in a short time and to have been buried shortly after deposition. Due to the large amount of material that was discovered in level IIA, the excavators presume that this level was accumulated over the course of multiple episodes of occupation. However, sedimentation was rapid and traces of weathering are absent from the bones. Therefore these episodes must have taken place over a relatively short period of time (Tuffreau 1988c, 131).

5.5 The stone artefacts

The archaeological levels of the site have yielded large stone artefact assemblages, especially level IIA. Since its assemblage is the largest one present at the site, the stone tool technology of Biache-Saint-Vaast has mainly been discussed on the basis of the assemblage from this level (*e.g.* Boëda 1988, Sih and Milton 1985, Tuffreau 1988b, Tuffreau and Sommé 1988a). This should not obscure the fact that the other levels contain lithics too and that these sometimes point to different activities being performed. Additionally, since levels II base, D1 and D appear to represent short periods of occupation, spatial analysis in these levels is thought to reveal the spatial organisation of the activities that were performed there.

In all levels, the great majority of artefacts were made of local flint. It may have been available in the river banks, on or very close to the site. On the other hand, the cortex of the used nodules does not show traces of weathering by fluviatile transport, suggesting the exploitation of primary flint deposits. These may have been exposed in chalky taluses in the vicinity of the site, however at the site itself the flint deposits would have been buried under 12 metres of alluvium. Therefore, the exact provenance of the raw material is unclear (Tuffreau and Marcy 1988b, 365).

Only the lithic remains with a clear stratigraphic provenance and a length of more than 30 mm. were studied from level IIA. This results in a studied assemblage of 3231 artefacts weighing 133.43 kg. (Tuffreau 1988b, 171). All but four of the studied artefacts were made out of flint. Although the Levallois method was practised at the site, the Levallois index of the assemblage is not very high (15.71). Another striking characteristic is the high blade index of the assemblage. However, the pieces classified as blades usually have a length/width ratio of less than two. Of Levallois products, 62.21% of the striking platforms was prepared, while this was only 30.78% in the non-Levallois products (Tuffreau 1988b, 171). The the percentage of flakes showing cortex on the dorsal side is high (44.9%). Moreover, most flakes were small, with about 80% of flakes being under 40 mm long and only 1% having a length in excess of 80 mm. The large flakes were preferentially selected to be transformed into tools. Moreover, in addition to the size of the blank, elongation of the product also appears to have been an important characteristic in the selection for tool production. In the blanks selected for tool production, this ratio generally exceeds 2 (Tuffreau 1988b).

Technologically, many Levallois products are present in the assemblage, but "classic" Levallois cores with one preferential plane of flake removal are absent (Boëda 1988, 186). Instead Levallois products were produced using either uni- or bipolar cores that yielded multiple overlapping flakes of predetermined form (Boëda 1988, 186-187). This shows that innovations were introduced to the traditional Levallois method during the late Middle Pleistocene (Tuffreau 1992, 63). This development had consequences for the morphometric characteristics of the blanks produced, most importantly the fact that the length-width ratio of the flakes was increased. However, during the life history of the core the laminar character of the products diminished (Boëda 1988, 213).

Tools are comparatively rare in level IIA. It is thought that the assemblage represents a lightly used industry, because high quality raw materials were present in close proximity of the site (Dibble 1995, 344). In the assemblage, Levallois products were preferentially selected as blanks for tool production. Typologically, Mousterian tools dominate the assemblage. The number of Mousterian tools further increases if the large number of "naturally backed knives" is included. Most of the Mousterian tools are tools with convergent sides (40.20%), followed by single (18.71%) and double (10.23%) scrapers (Tuffreau 1988b, 172). In addition to the Mousterian tools, denticulates are also present in quite large numbers (10.81%). Some *outils de type paléolithique supérieur* like burins and truncated flakes have also been recovered from this level (Tuffreau 1988b, 172).

Although the assemblage is dominated by tool types with convergent sides, many of these tools are not classified as formal points. Levallois points account for 1.24% of the assemblage, retouched Levallois points for 0.87% and pseudo-Levallois points for 1.75%. Mousterian points are more common, they account for 5.84% of the assemblage and 7.89% of the tools are elongated Mousterian points (Tuffreau 1988b, 182). As mentioned in chapter 3, Villa and Lenoir (Villa and Lenoir 2006, 91) have argued that other forms that in traditional typology would be designated as scrapers may well have been used as spear points. They specifically mention convergent and *déjeté* scrapers. Together with Mousterian points these are said to be abundant in the assemblage from level IIA, accounting for 23.39%. Therefore, points, which could be considered to have played a role as hunting weapons may not be as rare in the assemblage as might seem to be the case at first glance. In 64% of the cases, the blanks from which these tools were produced were Levallois products (Tuffreau 1988b, 174). Interestingly, the convergent forms present in the assemblage were very standardised. The excavators think that this may be because they were produced to be hafted (Tuffreau 1992, 65).

The assemblage from level IIA is very much like the Mousterian of Ferrassie type. It has a significantly higher percentage of tools with convergent edges and has therefore been dubbed *Mousterien de type Ferrassie de faciès Biache* by the excavator (Tuffreau 1988b, 178). The emphasis on the production of scraper types is thought to have stimulated the production of elongated products, which caused the high blade index (Dibble 1995, 344).

The assemblage from Level II base was similar to that from Level IIA (Tuffreau and Marcy 1988a, 234). A striking category of finds in this level is a large number of flint nodules, many of which are unmodified. Most of them are also concentrated in a discrete zone of the site. Furthermore, the majority is of poor quality flint. Therefore it is unclear whether this represents some kind of raw material cache, or whether the blocks may have had a different function, such as use as a pavement (*e.g.* Tuffreau and Marcy 1988a, 233). Some of the smallest nodules found may have been deposited by natural processes. However, many of the blocks are large and heavy and some of them exhibit negatives of flake removals. Therefore, most of the material probably has an anthropic origin. Some other characteristics of the stone assemblage may point to the most likely interpretation of these remains. First, in the debitage category, cortical flakes are very common (17.4%). Second, many cores are "informe" or "casson" (Tuffreau and Marcy 1988a, 234). This may point towards an interpretation of the abundance of unmodified nodules as the result of raw material collection and testing at the site. The shaping of formal cores and production of tools would then have taken place outside the excavated zone.

The spatial distribution of the finds allowed the identification of different zones or activity areas. In addition to the zone dominated by flint nodules, two areas at the site show a predominance of flintknapping remains, while the largest area of the site is dominated by faunal remains (Tuffreau and Marcy 1988a, 259). Taking into account the composition of the lithic assemblage, level II base has been interpreted as representing a level where fauna were dismembered and consumed. Within the fauna-dominated zone, two empty areas were excavated, whose significance remains unclear.

Level D1 yielded a stone assemblage of almost 3000 pieces, dominated by small debitage products. Almost 50% of the flakes has cortex. The Levallois index of the assemblage is low and as in levels D0 and E, Levallois flakes are not preferentially used as blanks for the production of tools. The non-Levallois cores in the level are of limited dimensions and exhausted, prompting the excavators to speculate that raw material provisioning may have been difficult at the time of occupation. In this respect it is strange that Levallois flakes are so rarely modified in this level. The assemblage has been described typologically as "Mousterian with denticulates" (Marcy and Tuffreau 1988b).

Level D1 contains two concentrations. The richest concentration was found in the southern part of this level. Here, a concentration of Levallois-like debitage and naturally backed knives co-occurs with the majority of the level's faunal remains. The poorer northern concentration contains a largely empty zone of about 12 m². This zone is bordered by flint nodules that weigh 700 grams on average. This contrasts with the average weight for flint nodules found in level D1 in general, which is 260 grams. This has led the excavators to propose that this empty zone may represent a shelter (Marcy and Tuffreau 1988b, Tuffreau and Marcy 1988b).

Level D yielded a small lithic assemblage. Only two Levallois cores were present in the level, as well as 18 Levallois flakes, of which 15 were broken. Moreover all of these flakes were very small. Only 5 tools were present and these were badly manufactured, with the exception of one Mousterian point. The normal debitage also has small dimensions, 75% of flakes being smaller than 40 mm. All in all, level D represents an ephemeral occupation in view of stone tool deposition. The bone assemblage that was recovered in this level was relatively large, with almost 500 pieces (Marcy and Tuffreau 1988a).

Use-wear analysis has been undertaken on some of the recovered artefacts from Level IIA (Beyries 1988). The results of this analysis are interesting, yet not unproblematic. The results of the analysis can be divided in two categories. Evidence with regard to hafting of tools and evidence with regard to the use of the working edge of artefacts.

Hafting was an important element in the repertoire of tool use represented at the site. Moreover, hafting is restricted to certain types of tools, while other types lack hafting traces. Hafting was practised exclusively on symmetric tools with convergent sides. More importantly, all the short tools with convergent sides were hafted as was 90% of the elongated tools with convergent sides (Beyries 1988, 230). This shows that hafting was important with regard to the functioning of these tools. This may support arguments put forward by Villa and Lenoir (2006) that some of the convergent scraper types may have functioned as spear points.

Strangely, most of the traces of use on the working edges of the tools point to woodworking. Only the short, non-convergent scrapers show wear related to animal butchery (Beyries 1988, 230). This contradicts the hypothesis that many of the convergent tools could have functioned as spear points. It even suggests that most tools did not have any relation to the faunal remains. However, as discussed in chapter 2, traces of woodworking can also be the result of sediment movements (Levi-Sala 1986). As shown by the numerous tectonic faults in the profiles this process was intense at the site. Therefore, this evidence cannot be accepted at face value.

According to (Tuffreau and Marcy 1988b, 306), indications for the use of fire at the site are limited to some pieces of burnt flint and bone that have been found in level II base, while level D1 also yielded a few pieces of charcoal. This statement is contradicted in (Tuffreau 1988c, 123), where it is said that level IIA was clearly recognisable as a dark layer because of the large amounts of charcoal that were present in the level. The use of fire therefore was probably a regular event during the deposition of level IIA, while in the other levels, it was rarely used or absent.

Very striking is the fact that level IIA represents a "lightly used industry" (Dibble 1995), in most other levels there are indications that raw materials were quite scarce. This is shown by the limited dimensions of cores and debitage and the fact that many cores are almost exhausted (Ameloot-Van der Heijden 1989, Marcy and Tuffreau 1988b).

5.6 The bone assemblage

The bone assemblage recovered at this site is large, containing over 200.000 pieces, about 20.000 of which could be determined to species level (Auguste 1988b, Auguste 1992, Auguste 1993, Auguste 1995a). Since the excavation was done in recent years under controlled circumstances, in contrast to sites that were excavated earlier, like Taubach (see chapter 6), recovery of faunal materials was less biased. Unfortunately, there are some problems associated with the bone assemblage from this site. Several papers have been published, providing varying amounts of detail about the bone assemblages per level. Only the bone assemblages of levels D1, D and II base have been published in detail, i.e. listing the Number of Identified Specimens (NISP) of all the identified species (*e.g.* Auguste 1988b, Auguste 1992). The most important problem connected to the study of this site is the fact that the level with the largest bone assemblage, Level IIA has not been published in detail. A number of publications of the zooarchaeology of this site treat all the bones as a single assemblage, despite the fact that they were recovered in several levels documenting differing environmental conditions (*e.g.* Auguste 1993, Auguste 1995a, Auguste 2003, Auguste and Patou-Mathis 1994). Fortunately, a separate study of the megaherbivores of the site provides additional information about the numbers of identified bones per level (Louguet-Lefebvre 2005). The number of identified bones varies between publications, presumably because as research progressed additional remains were identified.

With regard to the species represented at the site, there are also some problems. Most important is the case of large bovids. Many of the bovid bones could not be determined at species level, but may have belonged to either Bos or Bison. I have not come across the exact numbers of bones determinable to species level for bovids in the assemblage as a whole. However, Bison (*Bison priscus*) has only been mentioned in the species list in (Auguste 1992), while the species lists in (Auguste 1988a, Auguste 1988b, Auguste, Moncel, and Patou-Mathis 1998, Louguet-Lefebvre 2005) only contain aurochs. Other publications like (Auguste 1993, Auguste 1995a, Auguste 2003) do not contain an exhaustive list of the species represented in the assemblage, but they only mention aurochs for the site and not bison. Therefore, I will assume that the large bovid represented at the site is aurochs and that bison is either absent or at least very rare in the assemblage.

The degree of hominin exploitation of the different species at the site as a whole has been researched. However, it is not always quantified, therefore it has been necessary to accept qualitative statements of the archaeozoologists as in: "aurochs bones are more intensively cut-marked than those of rhinoceros." Moreover, the degree of carnivore damage to the bones is also not quantified. From the information that is presented, it is clear that hominins were the accumulating species at Biache-Saint-Vaast though.

In this section, the focus will be on the information available for the assemblage of the site as a whole and the treatment of the dominant taxa. Only for levels II base, D1 and D are more detailed data available. Therefore these levels will be discussed separately. Analysis of the assemblage as a whole is defensible, since level IIA alone yielded 89% of the identifiable bone materials at the site. Moreover, the levels with the other large assemblages IIα (about 5% of the total assemblage) and IIbase (about 2.5% of the total), were deposited in similar environmental circumstances. The large mammal assemblages in these levels are poorer in species, but generally of similar character to the assemblage from level IIA (see table 5.1).

Figure 5.4 illustrates the relative importance of the different taxa in the bone assemblage from this site. Several authors erroneously list bovids as accounting for 70% of the assemblage, following Auguste (Auguste 1995a). Other publications list different values (*e.g.* Auguste 1993, Auguste 1995b), with bovids only accounting for less than 50% of the assemblage. This percentage is also borne out by the actual NISP figures provided by Auguste (Auguste 1995a). Therefore the widely cited value of 70% bovids must be the result of an accounting error. Table 5.1 shows the composition of the faunal assemblage per archaeological level at the site in terms of species. The total number of identified bones is listed as well. It is obvious that level IIA is the most important level both in terms of the number of species identified and in terms of the NISP.

The site is thus dominated by three groups of species. In terms of NISP, bovids account for 50%, bears for 33% and rhinocerotids for 15% of the assemblage. The remaining 15 species account for only 3.5% of the NISP. If we look at the MNI values, the picture changes slightly, as shown in figure 5.5. Aurochs is most important still, followed by bear and narrow-nosed rhinoceros. However, the other species that were represented by small numbers of identified bones increase in importance now.

Changes in species representation occur during the sequence and reflect climatic changes (Sommé *et al.* 1988, 118). In general, the fauna points to a mosaic environment. Some of the species, like cervids and especially wild boar (*Sus scrofa*), which is present but rare, point to the presence of forested areas. Others, like narrow-nosed rhinoceros and equids, point to an open environment (Auguste 1992). With regard to the application of OFT, treating the faunal assemblage of Biache-Saint-Vaast as a single entity is hazardous. Climatic and environmental change may have resulted in altered rankings of the species involved or in the broadening of hominin diet because of changes in search time.

5 Biache-Saint-Vaast

	I	H	G	F	En	IIA	IIα	IIbase	D0	D1	D
Sus scrofa					■	■		■	■	■	
Cervus elaphus	■					■	■	■	■	■	■
Megaloceros giganteus		■				■	■	■			
Capreolus capreolus					■	■		■	■	■	
Bos primigenius	■	■		■	■	■	■	■	■	■	■
Dicerorhinus hemitoechus	■	■			■	■	■	■			
Dicerorhinus mercki		■	■		■	■					
Dicerorhinus sp.		■	■	■	■	■	■	■			
Coelodonta antiquitatis										■	■
Equus mosbachensis	■			■	■	■		■	■	■	■
Equus hydruntinus					■	■					
Palaeoloxodon antiquus		■				■				■	
Canis lupus						■					
Vulpes vulpes											■
Felis silvestris											
Panthera spelaea						■					
Ursus arctos		■			■	■	■	■			
Ursus deningeri					■	■					
Ursus sp.	■			■		■					
Aonyx antiqua						■					
Martes cf. martes						■					
Castor fiber		■									
	25	118	7	12	227	18321	1099	514	118	85	105

Table 5.1: Species lists of Biache-Saint-Vaast and total NISP per level. Black cells signify the presence of the species in the level, white cells signify absence. After (Louguet-Lefebvre 2005).

Rhinocerotidae	NISP	Percentage	Ursids	NISP	Percentage
Dicerorhinus hemitoechus	1066	34.3	Ursus arctos	2243	31.98
Dicerorhinus mercki	121	3.89	Ursus deningeri	226	3.22
indet	1921	61.81	indet	4544	64.79

Table 5.2: Number of ursid and rhinocerotid bones determined to species level and only determinable to genus level. Rhinocerotidae after (Louguet-Lefebvre 2005), ursids after (Auguste 2003, 139).

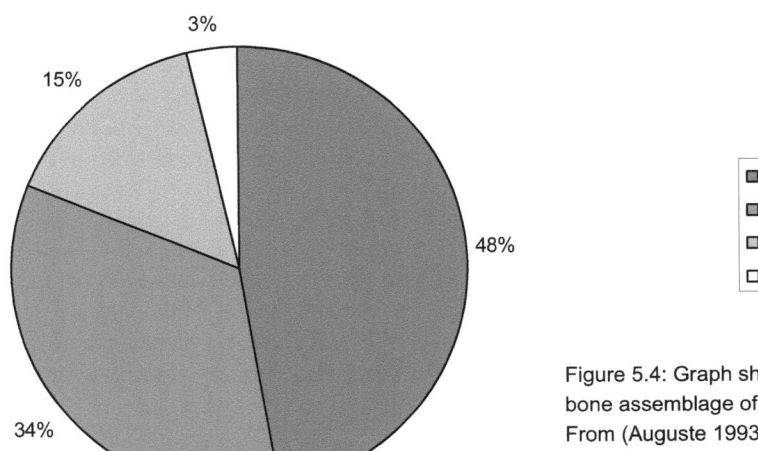

Figure 5.4: Graph showing the composition of the bone assemblage of the site as a whole by NISP. From (Auguste 1993).

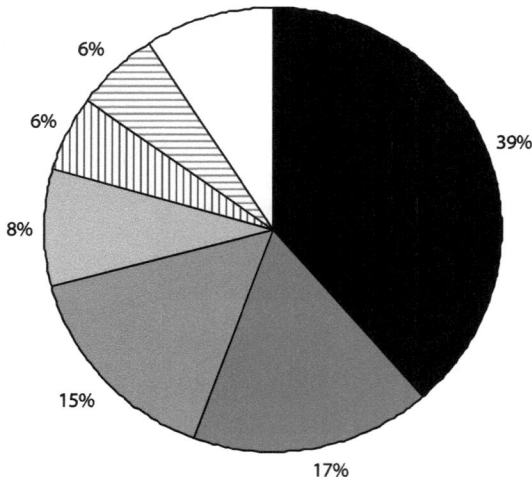

Figure 5.5: Graph showing the composition of the bone assemblage in terms of MNI. After (Auguste 1995a).

An additional problem with regard to the identification of bones to species level is the presence of several species belonging to the same family. This problem is important in ursids and rhinocerotids. Two species of bear and three rhinoceros species are present at the site. The bears that are present are the extant brown bear and Deninger's bear (*Ursus deningeri*), which is the ancestor of the cave bear (*Ursus spelaeus*). In the most important occupation levels, narrow-nosed rhinoceros and Merck's rhinoceros (*Dicerorhinus mercki/Stephanorhinus kirchbergensis*) are present. In the uppermost levels of the site, woolly rhinoceros (*Coelodonta antiquitatis*) has been found. In both taxa, over 60% of the bones could not be assigned to a specific species (Auguste 2003, Louguet-Lefebvre 2005). (See table 5.2). Similar problems may be expected in the identification of the different species of cervids. Especially large Pleistocene red deer (*Cervus elaphus*) and giant deer (*Megaloceros giganteus*) are sometimes confused (Gaudzinski pers. comm.). However, since the number of bones belonging to species other than bovids, ursids and rhinocerotids is small, problems with regard to the identification of cervids have no significant consequences for this analysis.

Level IIA contains remains of 20 species (see table 5.1), 88.8% of the identified bones comes from this level. The NISP-values of the rhinocerotids and proboscideans from this level have been published and are listed in table 5.6 (Louguet-Lefebvre 2005). The species represented attest to a temperate climate with closed and open spaces in the environment. Species like roe deer and wild boar are characteristic of temperate forests, while species that point to a more open environment like equids and narrow-nosed rhinoceros are also present. Moreover, a large number of carnivore species is present.

Level IIα has yielded the second largest bone assemblage. This assemblage represents about 5% of the identified bones of the site, it also yielded one of the hominin skulls found at the site (Rougier 2003). Table 5.1 shows that the number of species in level IIα is smaller than in level IIA. Most conspicuous is the fact that the two species of horse are absent in this level. Additionally, most of the carnivores are missing in the assemblage, except for the ursids (Louguet-Lefebvre 2005). Since carnivores are generally rare in faunal assemblages, this is probably an artefact of the fact that this assemblage is smaller than the assemblage of level IIA.

Level IIbase contains the largest bone assemblage that has been published in detail (Auguste 1988b, Auguste 1992), (see table 5.3). Compared to level IIA, the non-ursid carnivores are missing, as are wild boar and straight-tusked elephant (*Palaeoloxodon antiquus*). As in the assemblage of the site as a whole, bovids are the most important group in level II base. They are followed in importance by ursids and rhinocerotids. In Auguste (1992), a larger number of identified bones is listed, but the NISP data are only quantified at family level, not at species level. The percentages in which the different taxa are represented remain roughly the same. The species list in the 1992 paper has also changed slightly, with fallow deer (*Dama dama*) reported in (Auguste 1988b), reclassified as giant deer on account of the remains being too large (Auguste 1992, 55).

The faunal assemblage from level IIbase shows numerous traces of hominin activities (see table 5.4). Most importantly, cut-marks are present on a large number of bones. Furthermore, a small number of bones is calcinated, suggesting they were heated. Moreover, the bones are very fragmented, and the majority of osseous finds from this level are splinters (Auguste 1992, 61). No data on the frequency of carnivore modification on the bones is presented. The data on human modification however, show that hominins were a major agent in the accumulation of the faunal assemblage from this layer.

5 BIACHE-SAINT-VAAST

	Level D		Level D1		Level IIbase	
Species	NISP	MNI	NISP	MNI	NISP	MNI
Rhinocerotids	9	1	19	1	47	3
Equus caballus	24	3	9	1	18	1
Equus hydruntinus	2	3	1	1	7	1
Equid	-	-	1	1	-	-
Bos primigenius	23	2	5	1	27	3
Bos or Bison	12	1	13	3	129	5
Cervus elaphus	10	1	16	1	15	2
Capreolus capreolus	-	-	-	-	7	1
Dama dama	-	-	-	-	1	1
Cervid	4	1	3	1	4	1
Ursid	-	-	-		78	4
Canid	2g	1	-		-	-
Herbivore	13g	1	-		6	5
Others	7	1	18	1	73	0-6
	106		85[9]		412[10]	

Table 5.3: NISP and MNI counts per species for levels IIbase, D1 and D, based on the data in (Auguste 1988b).

Family	NISP	calcinated	cut-marked	% cut-marked
Rhinocerotidae	65	0	9	13.85
Equidae	31	0	1	3.23
Bovidae	207	4	53	25.6
Cervidae	40	0	3	7.5
Ursidae	92	2	38	41.3
Non-attributed	74	0	10	13.51
Splinters	3149	48	123	3.91

Table 5.4: Indications for hominin activities on the bones found in level IIbase. From (Auguste 1992, 64).

In terms of MNI, the represented classes change slightly (Auguste 1992) (see table 5.5). Bears dominate the assemblage with at least ten animals represented, while bovids and rhinocerotids follow with 8 individuals. Auguste (1992, 63), provides a breakdown of the age-structure of the populations in level II base in juveniles, adults and old individuals. Following these categories, adult individuals form the majority in all taxa. This suggests hominin hunting was the major contributing agent in the deposition of this level's faunal remains.

Level D0 has yielded a mammal assemblage indicative of temperate conditions (Louguet-Lefebvre 2005, 109), see table 5.1. Analysis of the malacological and pollen samples from this level points to deteriorating climatic conditions however (Sommé *et al.* 1988, 117). Remarkably, wild boar is present in this layer, while it was absent in II base. Wild boar is a temperate species and its presence, like that of roe deer (*Capreolus capreolus*) suggests that conditions were not too harsh. On the other hand, the precursor of Deninger's bear and *Ursus* sp. are absent in this layer.

Above level D0 the mechanism of sedimentation changes, these levels have been deposited in wind-blown loessic sediments. This has left the bones exposed to weathering processes. These bones have altered surfaces and therefore a study of anthropic traces on the bones is impossible (Auguste

---

9   Auguste (1988b) mentions 79 determined remains, whereas adding up the numbers in his table leads to 85. This is also the number that Louguet-Lefebvre (2005) lists.

10 Auguste (1988b) writes that there are 397 determined pieces. Adding up the numbers in his table gives 412. Adding up the numbers from tables 16.II to 16.VII also gives 412.

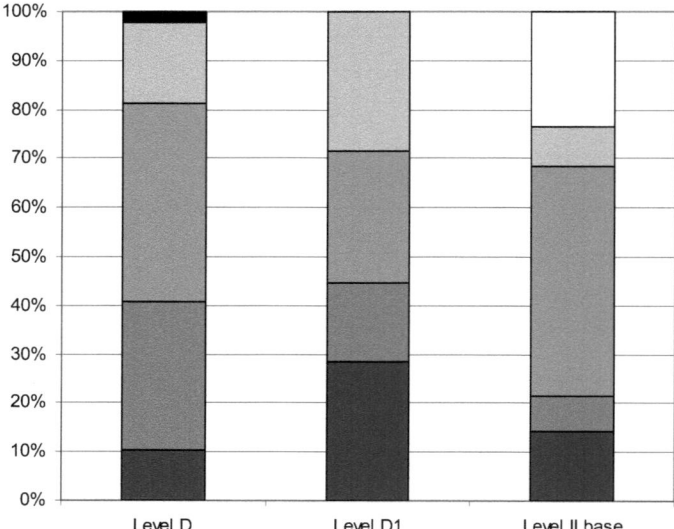

Figure 5.6: Graph showing the taxa represented in level IIbase according to (Auguste 1988b) and (Auguste 1992).

Table 5.5: Population structure in MNI of the taxa represented in level IIbase. From (Auguste 1992, 63).

Taxon	Young	Adult	Old
Rhinocerotidae	1	6	1
Equidae	1	2	1
Bovidae	1	6	1
Cervidae	1	5	0
Ursidae	1	7	2

1988b, 150). Moreover, weathering has led to a biased preservation of the bone assemblage: more durable elements, especially teeth, seem to be overrepresented in these levels (Auguste 1988b, 152-153). The association of the bones and the archaeological remains is therefore less secure for these levels than for the underlying levels.

The faunal remains from level D1 were distributed in two spatial concentrations. A rich concentration in the southern part of the excavated area and a poorer, less sharply demarcated northern concentration. The distribution of rhinocerotids and the cervids seems to be limited to the southern concentration, while bovids and equids are more widespread (Auguste 1988b, 151). In the southern concentration, the bones co-occur with a dense artefact concentration. The stone tools suggest knapping activities, but in this concentration, a large number of naturally backed knives is also present. This suggests that dismembering activities also took place here (Marcy and Tuffreau 1988b, 283). The association of lithics and faunal remains is less obvious in the northern concentration. This zone is poorer in archaeological remains and what remains there are, are more widely dispersed here (Marcy and Tuffreau 1988b, 287).

Most striking about the bone assemblage from level D1 is the absence of bears. They are among the dominant taxa at the site, accounting for a third of the total NISP. Moreover they are present in all underlying levels (see table 5.1). Another striking feature is the fact that the species of rhinoceros that is represented in this level changes with regard to the previous level. From level D1 onwards, narrow-nosed and Merck's rhinoceros are no longer present but the cold-adapted woolly rhinoceros appears.[11] In addition to these changes with regard to previous levels, roe deer is not present anymore, nor is giant deer. Wild boar, like roe deer a temperate species, has also vanished in this level. Bovids also decrease in importance in this level, while equids and rhinocerotids increase in importance. In all, the fauna thus has a more cold-adapted character than in the underlying levels.

The faunal remains of level D also show a bipolar distribution. This level has yielded a rich northern concentration and a poorer southern concentration. The latter concentration contains mostly small bones that are highly fragmented, while the former contains mostly larger, more complete specimens (Auguste 1988b, 151). The association of the fragmented remains with hominin activities is doubted by Auguste, (Auguste, 151), even though elsewhere he uses the degree of fragmentation of bones (Auguste 1992, 61) as support for hominin interference with the bone assemblage. The larger, northern concentration is spatially associated with a diffuse scatter of lithics, al-

---

11   The determination of the rhinocerotids in this level has changed in recent years Auguste (1988b) lists narrow-nosed, merck's rhinoceros and *Dicerorhinus* sp. Louguet-Lefebvre (2005) lists woolly rhinoceros for levels D1 and D.

though the densest concentration of artefacts in this level is located more to the south (Marcy and Tuffreau 1988a).

The faunal assemblage in level D is not much different from that of level D1. In terms of represented taxa we see that cervids and rhinocerotids decrease in importance, while equids and bovids increase in importance. The increase of equids in this level and in level D1 is taken to indicate an opening up of the environment. This would fit with a decreasing representation of cervids, since they are mostly associated with more closed environments. The decrease of woolly rhinoceros cannot be explained in this way, since it is thought to have been adapted to cold and open environments.

Louguet-Lefebvre (2005), has studied the megaherbivores represented at the site in detail. She lists the exact numbers of identified megaherbivore bones per level (see table 5.6). Only in level IIA were remains present in sufficient numbers for its quantitative study to have any significance. Nevertheless, the rhinoceros remains from the other levels seem to support the inferences that can be drawn from the remains from level IIA (Louguet-Lefebvre 2005, 114).

Level IIA has yielded 554 teeth belonging to narrow-nosed rhinoceros. These have been used to compile a population structure of the narrow-nosed rhinoceross represented in this level. Louguet-Lefebvre (Louguet-Lefebvre 2005, 114) illustrates her findings with a graph. However, using the data in her appendix, the graph looks different (compare the graphs in figure 5.7 with the data from her appendix in table 5.7). The important difference between the graphs is a differing total number of individuals. Louguet-Lefebvre (2005, 114) mentions an MNI of 41 in the text accompanying the graph, adding up the numbers yields 35. Moreover, using her appendices, the proportion of adult individuals is higher than in the graph she uses, while the number of juveniles and young adults is higher in her graph. The general image from the representation of the different age classes using the data from the appendices is that of an assemblage dominated by infants and young adults.

Species	I	H	G	F	En	IIA	IIα	II base	D0	D1	D	Total
Palaeoloxodon antiquus	-	6	-	1	1	13	-	-	-	1	-	22
Coelodonta antiquitatis	-	-	-	-	-	-	-	-	-	22	12	34
Dicerorhinus hemitoechus	1	8	-	3	12	942	77	21	2	-	-	1066
Dicerorhinus mercki	-	3	-	-	4	101	8	4	1	-	-	121
Dicerorhinus sp.	-	9	5	-	52	1703	98	37	17	-	-	1921
Total megaherbivore	1	26	5	4	69	2759	183	62	20	23	12	3164
Total NISP	25	118	7	12	227	18321	1099	514	118	85	106	

Table 5.6: NISP counts of megaherbivores. From (Louguet-Lefebvre 2005, annexe 3a).

Age Class	I	I/II	II	II/III	III	III/IV	IV	IV/V	V	V/VI	VI	VI/VII	VII	VII/VIII	VIII
Number	6	1	1	0	1	4	9[12]	4	8	3	1	2	0	0	0

Table 5.7: Number of narrow-nosed rhinoceros teeth per age-class, based on the data from (Louguet-Lefebvre 2005, annexe 2a)[13].

Indications for hominin activities are present on the bones as well. About 15% of the rhinoceros bones from level IIA show indications of hominin activities in the form of cut-marks and heliocoidal fractures on fresh bone (Auguste, Moncel, and Patou-Mathis 1998, Louguet-Lefebvre 2005). According to Auguste, (Auguste, 162) 623 rhinoceros bones show cut-marks, which amounts to 19.8% of all rhinocerotid remains on the site. Unfortunately, I was unable to ascertain whether there are any indications about which age-classes show traces of hominin activities. Of 108 fractures

---

12 One tooth (R10296) is from layer IIb.
13 In annexe 2c, Louguet-Lefebvre (2005) lists 9 D3 inf left as the base for her MNI. In annexe 2a, only 8 are listed however.

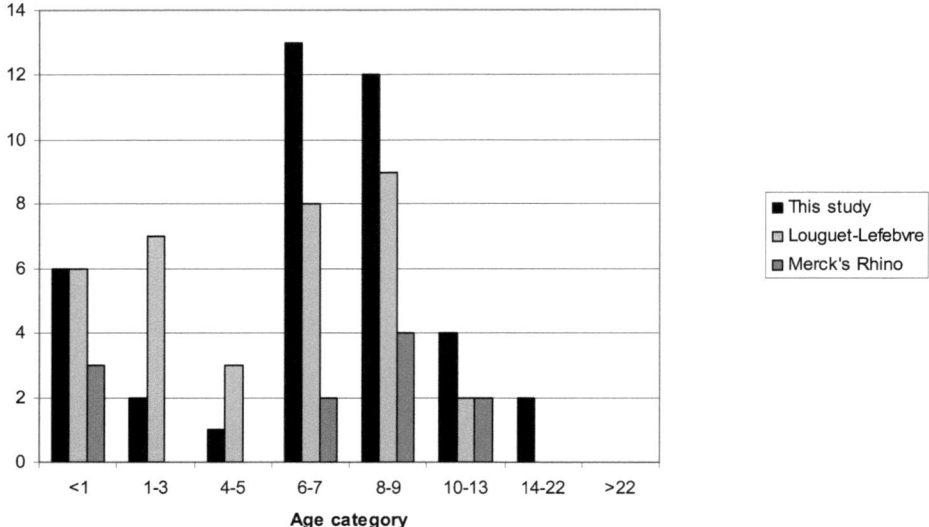

Figure 5.7: Age structure according to graph from (Louguet-Lefebvre 2005, 114) and reconstructed using her appendices. Teeth assigned to two categories were put in the oldest class.

on 98 longbones and longbone fragments from level IIA studied by (Louguet-Lefebvre 2005, 116-118) 37% are of anthropic origin. Breakage patterns differ greatly by bone type. 52% of humeri and 65% tibiae were fractured, while only 21% of radii and 16% of femora were broken open by hominins. Most broken femurs and tibia's show post-depositional breakage (Louguet-Lefebvre 2005, 116, 119). All in all, fragmentation of rhinoceros bones is much less intensive than of bear and bovid bones at Biache-Saint-Vaast (Louguet-Lefebvre 2005, 116).

Traces of carnivore activities are present on about 5% of the rhinocerotid bones. However, four out of the nine fragments with carnivore traces studied by (Louguet-Lefebvre 2005, 122), show cut-marks too and the placement of the latter suggests that hominins had primary access to the carcasses.

Bears are a second important category of prey represented at Biache-Saint-Vaast. Although hunting of bears has long been controversial, the number of remains found at this site and the frequency of traces of hominin exploitation on the bones seems to preclude other interpretations. As shown in table 5.2, 7013 ursid bones have been found, the majority of the identifiable bones belonging to brown bear, the remainder to Deninger's bear, a precursor to the cave bear (Auguste 2003). Deninger's bear was the larger of the two species represented at the site (Auguste 1988b, 147). Furthermore, it is worth noting that the brown bears recovered at the site were significantly larger than their current European homologues (Auguste 2003, 140).

In all, 107 individuals are said to be represented at the site. The population structure for level IIA is illustrated in figure 5.9. It is clear that adults are in the majority in both the brown bear and Deninger's bear categories. Moreover, in brown bears it seems that males are slightly better represented than females. The age profile of Deninger's bear suggests unnatural causes for the accumulation of the bones for this species as well, so we may assume that this species too was exploited by the occupants of the site. In addition, 2496 of the bear bones exhibit cut-marks (Auguste 1993, 55). According to Auguste (1995a, 161) the majority of cut-marks is found on brown bear bones. The placement of the cut-marks reveals some interesting patterns. In terms of absolute numbers of cut-marks, the majority of cut-marks is present on skulls, ribs and humeri. However, if we look at the percentage of a type of bone recovered that is cut-marked, we see that 73% of all ulnae are cut-marked, followed by 65 % of radii, 61% of proximal phalanges, 61% of scapulae and 57% of hip bones (coxal) and humeri. This is taken to indicate that hominins were after the body parts that yielded the greatest amount of meat (Auguste 2003, 139). Additionally, some of the cut-marks on the skulls, mandibles, phalanges and metapodials suggest they were produced while skinning the animal in order to remove the fur (Auguste 2003, 139).

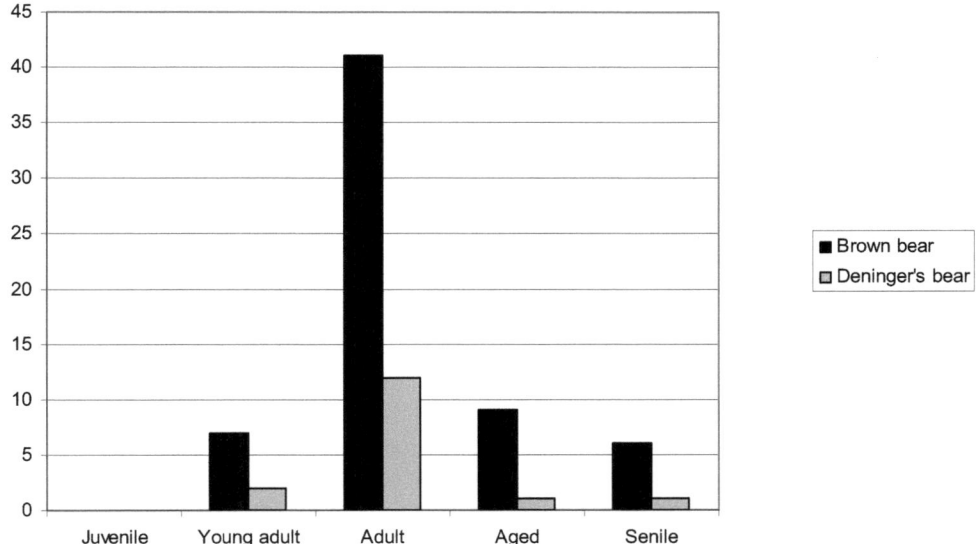

Figure 5.8: Age profile of Deninger's and brown bear from level IIA. Based on data in (Auguste 2003).

Bear bones were also fractured to exploit their marrow. However, reports on breakage patterns are slightly confusing. Louguet-Lefebvre (2005, 116, 123) reports that bear bones are more intensively fractured than rhinoceros bones. This leads her to propose that bears were hunted in spring and that marrow was an important resource because the meat on the animals was very lean in this season. Auguste (2003, 139) studied a few hundred fragments of diaphyses of longbones and found heliocoidal fractures on only 56% of them. According to him, this frequency of breakage is less intensive than that on aurochs bones at the site, which leads him to suggest bear hunting in autumn and a focus of hominins on the fat meat and the fur instead of on the marrow (Auguste 2003, 139-140).

With regard to skeletal part representation of bear bones at the site, many elements that represent little or no nutritional value, like metatarsals and metacarpals, are present in the assemblage. This can be explained by two factors. First, as discussed in section 4.6, different classes of mammals have different numbers of hand and foot bones. Carnivores have five digits, while in herbivores the number of metacarpals/tarsals is reduced, so there are more of these elements to start with. Second, the fact that fur was sought after by the Neanderthals producing this bone assemblage shows that other considerations than pure nutritional value influenced the bone deposition of this species (Auguste 1995a, 161).

Bovids are the dominant group in the assemblage of the site as a whole, representing almost 50% of the total NISP count. In the assemblage as a whole, 196 individuals are represented. The vast majority (145) falls into the "adult" age class in (Auguste 1993, 56-57, Auguste 1995a, 158, Auguste and Patou-Mathis 1994). In some cases, it is also possible to ascertain whether they belonged to male or female individuals. In terms of MNI, males are more prevalent than females with 49 males being represented at the site against 34 females (Auguste and Patou-Mathis 1994, 22). 3072 or 31% of aurochs bones found at the site show cut-marks (Auguste 1993, 55). Moreover, aurochs bones were systematically fractured, apparently more so than ursid and rhinocerotid bones from the site (Auguste 1995a, 161). Most of the cut-marks point to butchery and dismemberment of the carcasses. Nevertheless, some cut-marks on the skull and extremities show that in some cases skinning was also practised (Auguste 1995a, 162).

With regard to the skeletal part representation at the site, all elements of aurochs and of rhinoceros are represented, although the elements of high nutritional value are relatively more numerous (Auguste 1995a, 160-161). The fact that the other elements are present as well suggests that relatively complete carcasses were introduced to the site. Considering the size of these, animals, this suggests that they were killed in the close vicinity of the site (*e.g.* Valensi and Psathi 2004, 263).

Cut-marks on other species than bears, rhinoceros and aurochs are said to be rare (Auguste 1995a, 162). For level II base, as pointed out earlier, cut-marks are present on equids and cervids as well, although percentages are quite low when compared to especially bovids and ursids.

An interesting component of the bone assemblage is formed by shed antlers. About 300 shed antlers belonging to red deer (*Cervus elaphus*) and giant deer have been recovered from the site. They appear to have been the focus of collection by hominins and to have been used as retouchoirs (Auguste 1993, Auguste 1995a). Some bones were also used as retouchoirs (Auguste 1993, 59).

On the basis of the cervid remains, the seasons of occupation of the site have been determined. According to Auguste (1995) and Louguet-Lefebvre (2005), antlers of roe deer, red deer and giant deer show that the site was occupied in autumn and in early spring. I assume that they use the presence of shed antlers as indication for an occupation in early spring, since roe deer and red deer shed their antlers at the end of winter. However, since these were collected by hominins they may also have been curated and cannot be taken as an unproblematic indicator of seasonality. Occupation in autumn may be signified by the fact that bears are not exploited for their marrow, but their meat. In early spring, bears would have recently woken from their hibernation and they would be very lean. Consumption of their meat would confront hominins with the problem that the digestion of lean meat would actually take energy instead of supply it (*e.g.* Speth and Spielmann 1983). In this scenario, only exploiting the marrow would make sense. In the autumn on the other hand, bears accumulate fat reserves in anticipation of hibernation and hence exploitation of bear meat would be very rewarding in this season.

The assemblage as a whole represents a clear-cut case of human hunting of aurochs, bear and narrow-nosed rhinoceros. Cervids and equids may have been exploited less frequently, if the cutmarks from level II base reported in (Auguste 1992) can be extrapolated to the other levels. At least 196 aurochs are represented, together with 87 brown bears and 61 narrow-nosed rhinoceros (Auguste 1995a, Auguste 2003, Louguet-Lefebvre 2005). Moreover, cut-marks are abundant on the bones of these species, exploitation of bone for its marrow content is in evidence and the age profiles show an adult-dominated mortality profile in all three cases.

There is more detailed data for the most recent levels. Level II base shows an assemblage like the one recovered from IIA, except for the absence of wild boar and straight-tusked elephant. The modifications on the bones remove all doubt as to the non-natural origins of a large part of the assemblage. Sadly, the bones from levels D1 and D are more weathered and a systematic study of modifications on these bones has not been published. What is striking is that bears are absent in these assemblages, even though they were present in all other levels. The climate was changing during the time of deposition of this level, but bears, especially brown bears seem to be a catholic species that should be able to deal with the conditions suggested by the presence of other animals in the assemblages from these levels. The increase in the number of horse remains and the displacement of species of *Dicerorhinus* by woolly rhinoceros indicates a colder climate. Climatic fluctuations may also have played a role in the composition; however, species lists alone as shown in table 5.1 are not enough to gauge the kind of climate and environment that is represented by the assemblage. Especially the proportions of cervids, wild boar and equids would be interesting to know in this respect.

The site thus represents a place hominins visited for a prolonged period of time. The site therefore gives insight in the ranking of prey that formed the basis of hominin foraging strategies over some time, which is why the application of OFT on the bone assemblage appears to be a productive endeavour.

5.7 The environment

In this section I will discuss the available information regarding the environmental circumstances at the time of occupation of Biache-Saint-Vaast. The sedimentary sequence and the large mammal fauna, both of which have already been discussed in terms of the information they provide about the character of the archaeological occupation, may also provide environmental information. In addition, pollen and molluscs will be used to gain insight into   the environment around the site. Pollen data provide information about the character of the vegetation cover in the wider environment, while molluscs indicate the local environmental conditions.

The sedimentary sequence at the site documents the transition from MIS 7 to MIS 6. The different archaeological levels are thus situated in an environment that is gradually becoming colder. However, climatic ameliorations have been documented in the sequence. The sedimentary units are illustrated in figure 5.2; here I will discuss the climatic information we have for the different units in chronological order.

The lowest unit consisting of fluvial gravels did not yield any important climatological information. With Unit 2a, the character of sedimentation changes, and fluvial sands and silts are deposited. The malacological sample in the lowest reaches of Unit 2a contains mostly heavily damaged molluscs that are difficult to identify. Significantly however, in these levels *Corbicula fluminalis*, a species characteristic of warm climatic periods is present (Rousseau and Puissegur 1988, 94).

In Unit 2b, Corbicula fluminalis is no longer present. The malacological sample is dominated by species characteristic of aquatic and marshy environments. Moreover, the species that are present seem to indicate a climate that was cooler than today (Rousseau and Puissegur 1988, Sommé *et al.* 1986). This is supported by the analysis of pollen recovered from this level. The percentage of arboreal pollen in the samples is between 55 and 75%. If arboreal pollen are represented by over 10 percent in a pollen spectrum it is taken to signify that the environment was covered by a closed forest. This percentage thus suggests an open environment with stands of trees.

The arboreal pollen is dominated by the "boreal group" of pine (*Pinus*), birch (*Betula*), spruce (*Picea*) and willow (*Salix*). However more temperate species like alder (*Alnus*), hazel (*Corylus*), hornbeam (*Carpinus*), beech (*Fagus*), oak (*Quercus*), lime (*Tilia*) and elm (*Ulmus*) are also present. These species are usually not present during the early part of interglacials, which points to a date at the end of a warm cycle (Sommé *et al.* 1986, 193). In the top part of the unit, the part containing the archaeological level IIA, the molluscs show that the river is moving away from the site. Species indicative of aquatic and marshy conditions diminish markedly. Furthermore, species indicative of forested and semi-forested environments increase in importance. The species in the sample indicate a climate like that of today (Rousseau and Puissegur 1988, 95). This is confirmed by pollen analysis. The arboreal pollen is now dominated by *Quercus*, accompanied by *Fagus*, *Carpinus* and *Corylus*. *Pinus* and *Betula* remain present however (Sommé *et al.* 1986, 193). The large mammal fauna of level IIA shows the presence of forest-dwelling species, but their presence coincides with species that are adapted to more open, steppic environments, like equids and narrow-nosed rhinoceros.

On top of Unit 2, Unit 3 represents a period of soil formation in the fluvial deposits as the riverine influence at the site diminishes even more. This is shown by the fact that mollusc taxa indicative of aquatic and marshy environments drop to about 3.5% of the sample. The climatic indications provided by the samples in Unit 3a, which harbours the archaeological level II base, are similar to those for the top of unit 2b, the species present point to temperate conditions and an environment of largely open forest (Rousseau and Puissegur 1988, Sommé *et al.* 1986).

The interpretation of the environmental indications from level 3b is slightly problematic. This unit contains the archaeological level D0. The mollusc sample recovered here documents a transition to cold climatic conditions. Species indicative of open environments dominate, while species characteristic of forested environments disappear and species indicative of semi-forested areas decrease in importance (Rousseau and Puissegur 1988, Sommé *et al.* 1986). The large mammal assemblage, in which roe deer and wild boar are still represented, suggests that forested areas were still present in the wider surroundings of the site. The pollen sample is not very informative as to the character of the environment during the formation of this level. Only 118 pollen grains have been recovered and of this sample, 63.5% was arboreal. The arboreal pollen was dominated by boreal species; only 20% belonged to temperate species (Munaut 1988, 82).

Unit 4 consists of slope deposits originating from higher up the terrace. It contains reworked sediments from Units 2 and 3 (Sommé 1988, 31). The climatological information from this layer is ambiguous. Micromorphological analysis shows that frost-related features are very pronounced in this unit (Van Vliet-Lanoe 1988, 73). Moreover, remains of pollen and molluscs become rare in the sediments, suggesting that the environment was harsh (Sommé *et al.* 1986, 193). On the other hand, it may represent a relatively short erosional event, which deposited a large amount of sediment (Sommé *et al.* 1988, 99).

According to the pollen analysis, level 5 and therefore the archaeological levels D1 and D were formed during a feeble climatic optimum. Since the pollen counts are very low (Munaut 1988, 84-85), pollen are not a reliable source of information about the environment during the formation of these levels. Therefore I will give precedence to the results of the malacological analysis with regard to the reconstruction of the environment.

On the basis of malacological analysis, the lower limit of Unit 5 appears to represent a period of severely cold conditions. The malacological sample from this stratigraphic unit, containing the occupation level D1, indicates a very open environment. Higher up in Unit 5 the climate improves slightly. The environment during the deposition of the archaeological level D was characterised by a herbaceous prairie with some stands of trees in the environment (Rousseau and Puissegur 1988, 98). This climatic amelioration is also visible in the loessic deposits of Unit 6 that were deposited on top of Unit 5. By the time Unit 7 was deposited, the environment was completely devoid of trees.

For the most important occupation levels, IIA, IIα and II base, we can conclude that the climate during the time of occupation was temperate if a bit colder than today. The pollen indicate that grasses were of moderate importance in the environment. Open forest appears to have been the dominant vegetation type. The circumstances appear to have been more continental than nowadays, with larger seasonal variation in temperature. The character of the vegetation cover may have differed per level, with forest being most important in level IIA, IIα showing a humid but open environment and level II base being deposited in a largely open environment but with significant forested areas (Louguet-Lefebvre 2005, 110). It is worth noting that based on cenograms, level IIα would have the least tree cover of the three archaeological levels in Unit 2, while horses, traditionally an important indicator for steppe-like environment, are absent here. The environment probably did have an important steppic character, even in level IIA times. This is shown for example by the dominance of narrow nosed rhinoceros over Merck's rhinoceros. The latter was adapted to browsing in forested environments, while the former, with higher crowned teeth and thicker enamel was more adapted to grazing in open environments (Louguet-Lefebvre 2005, Van der Made in press).

During the deposition of level D0, the climate starts cooling significantly and the environment becomes very open. The molluscs indicate an open steppe, where trees are *quasi-inexistant* (Rousseau and Puissegur 1988, 98). The signal of the molluscs may be of mostly local importance: as discussed, the large mammal assemblage indicates the presence of forested areas in the environment.

These malacological data for Unit 5 are supported by the large mammal fauna that were recovered from these levels. The only rhinocerotid present in these levels is the woolly rhinoceros for example. Moreover the importance of equids increases in these levels (Auguste 1988b, Louguet-Lefebvre 2005).

We can thus assume that the earlier archaeological levels at the site were deposited during the latest phases of MIS 7. The occupations of D and D1 were probably formed during a stadial in MIS 6. Pollen cores from the Massif Central document a feeble optimum after the first cold phase of MIS 6 (Reille *et al.* 1998). Moreover a flowstone from Clamouse cave in France shows a period of growth that has been correlated with an amelioration in Mediterranean pollen cores. This amelioration was dated to between 162.3 ka and 169.1 ka (Plagnes *et al.* 2002). This may represent a short period in which occupation of the northwestern areas of Europe took place as documented in two occupation levels at Biache-Saint-Vaast.

5.8 Applying OFT to Biache-Saint-Vaast

I have now discussed the composition of the bone assemblage from the site as well as the environmental circumstances at the time of occupation. On the basis of these data, we will analyse the faunal assemblage using the diet breadth model. The focus of this analysis will lie on the assemblage as a whole. It will be followed by a discussion on the developments with regard to diet breadth in levels II base, D1 and D. I will first construct a ranking of the species that were available for exploitation. This will be followed by reconstructing the population densities in order to gain insight in the encounter rates with the different species. Finally, the handling cost is reconstructed. I will then analyse how well the practised diet breadth is explained by the diet breadth model.

The large mammal assemblages and climatic indicators suggest that these levels were deposited during relatively temperate conditions. The climate was more continental than it is nowadays, resulting in a more open environment, but species like wild boar and roe deer were present in the environment, suggesting an important forest component. The presence of megaherbivores like narrow-nosed and Merck's rhinoceros and straight-tusked elephant may have resulted in the forested areas being structured with tracks and open spaces (*e.g.* Haynes 2006). A rich carnivore guild was also present during these times, with lion (*Panthera leo spelaea*), wolf (*Canis lupus*) and brown bear.

An important aspect with regard to the application of OFT is the function of the site within the foraging system. Level IIA is thought to represent a spot where hominins repeatedly hunted animals in a riverine environment (Auguste 1995a, Auguste 2003). Of the three dominant species, all parts of the skeleton are represented, implying that the site functioned as a hunting location. Because of the size of the species that are present, processing of the carcass at the kill-site is expected to be essential if the spoils are to be transported to a base camp. Consequently, at a site like La Borde (Auguste

1995a, 160, Slott-Moller 1990, 51), elements with high nutritional value are very poorly represented, in contrast to elements of little nutritional value. This site probably represents a kill site from where meat-bearing elements were transported away. At Biache-Saint-Vaast on the other hand, meat-bearing elements from bison and rhinoceros seem to be slightly overrepresented. Moreover, processing of bones evidently took place on the spot, so animals were probably killed in the vicinity of the site. The site probably played a larger role than that of a hunting station, since the meat bearing parts were evidently not transported elsewhere. This, combined with the large amount of lithic materials present at the site, suggests that the site may have functioned as a central place, where animals were processed, but also where toolkits were maintained, using the abundant local flint deposits.

The levels higher up in the sequence show an overrepresentation of teeth and skull parts, especially in level D1 and D. This is partly due to less favourable conservation conditions in these levels (Auguste 1988b, 153). Hominin occupations here were probably more ephemeral, attested by a much lower density of finds compared to level IIA. Level D1 shows knapping activities, but the co-occurrence of the densest lithic concentration containing naturally backed knives with the most significant concentration of bones suggests butchery also took place in this level. In level D, both stone artefacts and bones are represented in low numbers. This level probably represents a very short visit to the site. The composition of the faunal assemblage suggests that the site did not function as a specialised hunting camp during these occupations since no taxon is dominant in the assemblages. Therefore, we can assume that the site does not represent the result of one specialised activity in the repertoire of its occupants. On the other hand, this is not certain. Because the fauna is less clearly associated with hominin activities, some of it may just be background fauna and be unrelated to the occupation of the site. We therefore need to keep in mind the fact that levels D1 and D are of a different character than the preceding levels when analysing them.

As discussed in chapter 4, OFT assumes that foraging decisions are governed by the desire to maximise the takings of hunting activities. First we therefore need to construct a ranking of the available prey species in descending order of their profitability. I assume that Neanderthals focussed their hunting activities on maximising the caloric return rates of their hunting activities instead of other variables, like prestige or rare nutrients. Since weight is a good proxy for caloric value among mammals, I constructed a ranking of the available species based on their reconstructed body weights. This ranking is shown in table 5.8. A problem that was encountered when constructing this ranking is the fact that for some species different authors list widely varying body weight estimates (Brook and Bowman 2004, Louguet-Lefebvre 2005, Pushkina and Raia 2008). In the case of extinct animals, I compared the weights with of extant relatives in order to gauge whether provided estimates are realistic. As a basis I used the weights listed in (Brook and Bowman 2004). In those cases where I rejected their estimates, the source is given in a footnote.

In many species, Pleistocene individuals had larger body sizes than their Holocene counterparts. This is the case in equids for example which show a steady reduction in size throughout the Middle and Late Pleistocene (*e.g.* Eisenmann 1991). Larger body sizes have also been reported for Pleistocene bovids and cervids (Gaudzinski pers comm.). However, body size of these animals also varied in response to more short term developments, like changes in climate (Delpech 1999). In the case of Biache-Saint-Vaast, attention is given to the values reported by (Louguet-Lefebvre 2005), who worked on the assemblage, in order to arrive at a realistic ranking.

When we compare the exploited species with the constructed ranking (table 5.8), we see that narrow-nosed rhinoceros and aurochs are ranked highly. Brown bear is somewhat lower down in the ranking as seventh heaviest species. The near absence of the heaviest species, straight-tusked elephant is striking. All in all, 22 bones belonging to this species have been found at the site. No signs of exploitation have been reported for the bones of this species. We can therefore not assume that the species was important in hominin foraging activities.

The interpretation of the remains of Merck's rhinoceros is complicated. If we assume that bones determined as belonging to Dicerorhinus sp. represent similar narrow-nosed rhinoceros and Merck's rhinoceros in the same proportions as the bones that could be determined to species level, this would result in a NISP count of about 330, or about 1.6% of the total Biache-Saint-Vaast assemblage (using the numbers and percentages from Auguste 1993, 56). The representation of Deninger's bear presents us with a similar quandary. If we assume that brown bear and Deninger's bear are represented in the same proportion in the bones that were determinable to Ursus sp. as they are in the assemblages that were identifiable at species level, this would lead to a NISP of 650, or about 3% in the total assemblage from Biache-Saint-Vaast (using the data from Auguste 2003).

Rank	Species	Weight	NISP[14]
1	Palaeoloxodon antiquus	5500	22
2	Dicerorhinus mercki	2000	2791
3	Dicerorhinus hemitoechus	1600	317
4	Bos primigenius	600[15]	9771
5	Ursus deningeri	559[16]	642
6	Megaloceros giganteus	450[17]	na
7	Ursus arctos	400	6371
8	Equus mosbachensis	272[18]	na
9	Cervus elaphus	200[19]	na
10	Panthera spelaea	195[20]	na
11	Equus hydruntinus	188	na
12	Sus scrofa	89	na
13	Canis lupus	45	na
14	Capreolus capreolus	23[21]	na
15	Aonyx antiqua	13[22]	na
16	Vulpes vulpes	5	na
17	Felis silvestris	5	na
18	Martes cf. martes	1.4	na

Table 5.8: Ranking of species present in the assemblage of Biache-Saint-Vaast. In the NISP-column, for species with na, no NISP figure was available.

Louguet-Lefebvre (2005) analysed all rhinoceros diaphysis fragments from level IIA, for cut-marks and has not distinguished between narrow-nosed rhinoceros and Merck's rhinoceros. It is therefore possible that bones belonging to this species also showed traces of hominin exploitation. Unfortunately, the age-profile (illustrated in figure 5.8) that can be constructed from the data in Louguet-Lefebvre (2005)'s appendix 2a is not conclusive, although it suggest adults are the best represented age-category. According to her, an MNI of at least 30 is needed to lend significance to such a profile. In the case of Merck's rhinoceros the MNI is 10, therefore we cannot lend too much significance to this age-profile. In the case of Deninger's bear, cut-marks are present. Moreover, they show that Deninger's bear bones were processed in the same way as brown bear bones (Auguste 2003, 138). In addition, the age profile provided in Auguste (2003) (see figure 5.8) suggests that the animal population represented at the site did not die of natural causes. Again, the number of individuals on the basis of which this profile was compiled (MNI=16) is too small to derive many conclusions from this profile.

I propose that both species were at least occasionally the focus of hominin exploitation. First, both these species are large and thus probably rare in the environment. However, if we take into ac-

---

[14] In the case of Ursids and rhinocerotids I assumed that the number of bones only determined at genus level consisted of both species in the same proportions as in the number of bones that could be assigned to a species.

[15] My estimate. According to Van Vuure (2003), aurochs weighed roughly the same as modern bison. The estimate provided by Brook and Bowman (2004) (269 kg.) and Louguet-Lefebvre (2005) (531 kg.) were considered too low. Macdonald (2006) provides the following weights: for American bison (Bison bison) females: 545 kg., males 818 kg. For European bison (Bison bonasus) males: 800 kg.

[16] Brook and Bowman (2004) do not list Ursus deningeri, so I used the estimate listed in Louguet-Lefebvre (2005).

[17] Estimate taken from Louguet-Lefebvre (2005). Estimate provided by Brook and Bowman (2004) (700 kg.) is higher than all other estimates I encountered, the estimate from Louguet-Lefebvre seems more reasonable, although Pushkina and Raia. (2008) provide a lower one (387 kg.).

[18] Brook and Bowman (2004) do not list Equus mosbachensis so I used the estimate listed in Louguet-Lefebvre (2005).

[19] Estimate taken from Pushkina and Raia. (2008) since Brook and Bowman (2004) provides a very high estimate (500 kg.).

[20] Estimate taken from Louguet-Lefebvre (2005) since the estimate listed in Brook and Bowman (2004) seemed excessive (380 kg.).

[21] Estimate taken from Pushkina and Raia. (2008), since Brook and Bowman (2004) provide a very high estimate (90 kg.).

[22] Estimate taken from Louguet-Lefebvre (2005) since the species is not listed in Brook and Bowman (2004).

count the fact that in addition to bovids, ursids and rhinocerotids 15 species are represented at the site and that these species make up 3.5% of the NISP, Merck's rhinoceros and Deninger's bear are well represented. Both species account for several hundred bones. Moreover, cut-marks are present on Deninger's bear and likely occurred on Merck's rhinoceros. On top of this, the age profiles of both species show a dominance of mature individuals.

The targeting of aurochs is to be expected, since it is a highly-ranked species in terms of weight. The dominance of this species over the other targeted species of narrow-nosed rhinoceros and brown bear can be explained in terms of encounter rate. The larger a species, the lower its population density generally is. This means that hominins probably encountered aurochs much more often than narrow-nosed rhinoceros.

Giant deer was not exploited for nutrition. Its NISP is not listed in published articles, but is probably low. Moreover, in this species, as well as in red deer, antlers are overrepresented in the assemblage. A large part of the NISP of this species is therefore taken up by elements without nutritional value (Auguste 1993, 61). This poor representation is unexpected, since larger animals like rhinoceros are represented as well as the smaller brown bear. The species is therefore in the range of species by weight that was regarded as a target by hominins.

Brown bear was slightly smaller than giant deer, but obviously an important species. It accounts for 34% of the assemblage. The exploitation of this species is unexpected at first sight, since a heavier species, giant deer, was not exploited. Still the difference in size between both species is small. Moreover, according to Auguste (2003, 140), the specimens from Biache-Saint-Vaast were larger than modern day brown bears.

As discussed, the distribution of exploitation marks on species, other than on the dominant taxa, is not quantified in published works (Auguste 1995a, 162). Nevertheless exploitation marks on other species are present, but said to be rare. As shown in table 5.4, level II base yielded some indications of exploitation on cervid and equid bones. If these results are applicable to the assemblage as a whole, these species were at least opportunistically exploited in level IIA. In this case it is striking that these species are not present in the assemblage in larger numbers. This cannot be explained by a factor like population density, since these species are expected to be present in much higher numbers than the species that were the focus of intense hominin exploitation activities.

The exploited prey classes show that the ranking of prey on the basis of animal weight is a good predictor of foraging decisions. The focus of foraging was clearly on the heavier species that were present in the environment. Still, it does not explain all foraging decisions. Most striking is the absence of signs of exploitation on by far the heaviest species available, straight-tusked elephant. In addition, we would expect giant deer to be exploited, since it is heavier than brown bear.

As discussed, the poor representation of some species may be a result of low population densities. It seems for example that Merck's rhinoceros was exploited at Biache-Saint-Vaast. This species was adapted to browsing in forested environments, and its poor representation at Biache-Saint-Vaast may therefore have been caused by its rarity in the vicinity of the site. Possibly, encounters simply did not take place very often, resulting in the small share of bones of this species in the assemblage.

In order to check whether a low encounter rate was the cause of the poor representation of other species, I have reconstructed the population densities of the species that were present in the assemblage. Reconstructing population densities of a Pleistocene community is a difficult endeavour, since some of the species are extinct nowadays and the composition of animal communities in Pleistocene assemblages

Species	Density (ind/km²)
Palaeoloxodon antiquus	0.075
Stephanorhinus kirchbergensis	0.15
Bison priscus	0.31
Ursus spelaeus	0.384
Megaloceros giganteus	0.413
Ursus arctos	0.19
Equus caballus	0.505
Cervus elaphus	0.717
Panthera spelaea	0.063
Crocuta crcocuta	0.04
Sus scrofa	1.243
Panthera pardus	0.045
Canis lupus	0.053
Capreolus capreolus	3.119
Lynx lynx	0.118
Castor fiber	3.685
Meles meles	0.331
Lutra lutra	0.616

Table 5.9: Reconstructed population densities of the species present in the Biache-Saint-Vaast assemblage, using the equations provided by (Silva, Brimacombe, and Downing 2001, 477).[23]

---

23   The equations used are: Herbivores: Log D = 1.42 − 0.68(Log M); Carnivores: Log D = 1.41 − 1.83(Log M) − 0.34(Log M²) + 0.28(Log M³). No equation is provided for omnivores. I treated Deninger's bear as a herbivore, and brown bear as a carnivore.

has no modern analogues. However, across mammals there is a significant correlation between body weight and population density (*e.g.* Eisenberg 1990, Silva, Brimacombe, and Downing 2001, Silva, Brown, and Downing 1997). This does not explain all variability in population densities, but does seem to be the major variable explaining population densities in mammals (Silva, Brimacombe, and Downing 2001, 475-477). A second important variably is the dietary specialisation of an animal species (Eisenberg 1990, Silva, Brimacombe, and Downing 2001). Based on the population densities of extant mammals, equations have been deduced, which allow the calculation of a species population density, based on its body weight and dietary niche, the two most significant factors influencing the population density. The reconstructed densities are listed in table 5.9.

It is immediately apparent that all exploited species at the site were present at low population densities compared to species that we traditionally view as game, like red deer, boar and equids. Some population densities may be overestimated though. As argued, Merck's rhinoceros may have been adapted to different environments. Therefore its population density may have been lower than estimated in the area since it had to compete with other herbivores that were better adapted to the circumstances surrounding the site, most notably narrow-nosed rhinoceros.

The poor representation of Deninger's bear may have a similar cause. Deninger's bear is the evolutionary precursor to cave bear. Isotopic studies have shown that the latter species preferred foraging in forested areas. Brown bear from the same site on the other hand yielded an isotopic signature that points to foraging in open areas (Bocherens and Drucker 2003). If Deninger's bear shared this adaptation with cave bear, than it may have been at a disadvantage in the open environment surrounding the site.

With regard to straight-tusked elephant, there is no reason to assume that the environment in level IIA times was particularly unsuited for this species. Although it is generally associated with warm climatic phases and woodland vegetation (Stuart 2005), it is thought to have had an intermediate dietary adaptation, with both browsing and grazing contributing to the diet (Palombo *et al.* 2005). Therefore I will assume that this species was not extraordinarily rare during the time of occupation of Biache-Saint-Vaast, but occurred in normal population densities. If this species had been exploited upon encounter we would therefore expect it to be better represented at the site. The population density of this species is expected to be roughly half that of narrow-nosed rhinoceros, yet only 22 bones belonging to this species have been excavated, as opposed to more than 1000 belonging to narrow-nosed rhinoceros. A low encounter rate can therefore not explain the near-absence of this species at the site. The only other possible explanation for its rarity is that, when exploited, the species was thoroughly processed in the field resulting in little transport of proboscidean bones to the site. Since signs of exploitation are rare on proboscidean bones, due to the porous bone surface (Mussi and Villa 2008, Scott 1980), the signs of exploitation could be absent on the small sample. This option cannot be discarded, yet in view of the large number of rhinoceros bones at the site, I deem it unlikely that regular exploitation of straight-tusked elephant result in only 22 bones ending up at the site.

Encounter rate also cannot explain the paucity of giant deer bones in the assemblage. Giant deer is often thought of as a mixed browsing and grazing species whose presence indicates a reasonably open environment (Bratlund 1999, 78). Therefore, the environment of the site suited this species quite well. Moreover, the species is larger than brown bear, which was heavily exploited, so it falls in the range of species that were hypothesised to be worth exploiting by the hominins responsible for the bone assemblage. Because of its herbivorous adaptation it is expected to be present in higher population densities than the smaller but omnivorous brown bear.

If we extrapolate the presence of cut-marks on equids and cervids in level IIbase to the assemblage of level IIA, we can assume that these species (and maybe giant deer too) were exploited. The small number of bones belonging to these species, as well as the reported scarcity of marks on the bones, suggest that the exploitation of these species only took place on rare occasions. The reconstructed population densities are high compared to those of the species that were heavily exploited. Therefore, whether foraging in forested environments or in open environments, hominins are expected to encounter cervids and equids more often than any of the exploited species. This shows that these animals were not exploited upon encounter, but only in exceptional circumstances.

Species	> 300 kg.	Carnivore	Living in group	
			Male	Female
Palaeoloxodon antiquus	+	-	-	+
Dicerorhinus mercki	+	-	-	-
Dicerorhinus hemitoechus	+	-	-	-
Bos primigenius	+	-	-/+	+
Ursus deningeri	+	+	-	-
Megaloceros giganteus	+	-	-/+	+
Ursus arctos	+	+	-	-
Equus mosbachensis	-	-	+	+
Panthera spelaea	-	+	-/+	+
Cervus elaphus	-	-	-/+	+
Equus hydruntinus	-	-	+	+
Sus scrofa	-	-	-?	+
Canis lupus	-	+	+	+
Capreolus capreolus	-	-	-/+	+

Table 5.10: Reconstructed handling cost attributes of the species in the Biache-Saint-Vaast assemblage.

Handling cost is the remaining component of the diet breadth model. This is an important variable in determining the actual return rate of exploiting specific animals. As discussed in chapter 4, this variable depends on both the predator's and the prey's capabilities. In order to estimate how difficult hunting of the available species would be I looked at three important characteristics: prey size, whether the prey species was carnivorous and whether or not the prey species lived alone or in groups. These factors are important determinants of handling costs of species in nature. There is a relationship between a predator's size and the maximum size of the prey it hunts. For a mammal of the same size as a Neanderthal, maximum prey size would be estimated at 300 kg. (Radloff and Toit 2004). Lower risk of predation is one of the most important reasons why animals are thought to live in groups (Barnard 2004). And hunting carnivores is considered very dangerous since these animals are equipped to hunt and kill other animals (For a discussion on why I selected these variables, see chapter 4). Table 5.10 lists the handling cost attributes for all species that were present in the bone assemblage.

These attributes explain some of the peculiarities in the spectrum of exploited species. The absence of elephant exploitation can be explained by the fact that they are very much heavier than 300 kg. Of course predators may be able to hunt larger prey than would be expected in light of their size by hunting in groups for example (Radloff and Toit 2004), but this animal is almost 10 times the expected maximum prey size for Neanderthals. Moreover, the females and young animals live in herds, which are harder for hunters to tackle than solitary animals.

This explanation is supported by the fact that in narrow-nosed rhinoceros the focus of exploitation seems to be on juveniles and young adults. The occupants of the site may thus have preferred somewhat smaller animals to full-grown adults. In addition, rhinoceros are usually solitary species.

The poor representation of giant deer cannot be easily explained by these attributes. Females probably lived in groups, which provides an argument against their exploitation. Except during rut, males did not live in groups. Although male giant deer are large animals, they are smaller than aurochs. Male aurochs were preferred over females, possibly since these are solitary creatures, but female aurochs are also well represented in the assemblage. Therefore, hunting giant deer, especially in the case of the males was certainly within the capabilities of the site's occupants.

The exploitation of horses is peculiar with regard to the handling cost attributes, since these animals are large and live in groups, which are hard to corner and despatch. Moreover, hunters will be detected more easily by social than solitary animals since there are simply more individuals that are on the look-out. Exploiting equids is therefore an activity that one would expect to be done in a planned, specialised fashion, while the low percentage of horse bones in the assemblage probably reflects opportunistic activities.

Like giant deer, male red deer probably lived solitarily most of the time; their exploitation is therefore likely to occur in an opportunistic fashion. Females live in herds, although herd size is smaller than in the case of horses. Moreover, because of the reduced visibility in forested environments, the animals may be more easily ambushed. Taking all these factors together leads to the expectation that opportunistic hunting of cervids is quite feasible, in contrast to hunting equids.

As discussed, the environmental conditions during the deposition of level II base were similar to the conditions represented in level IIA. The species represented in this level are also similar to those of level IIA, except for the fact that wild boar and most carnivores are absent. This is assumed to be a reflection of the smaller sample size. The intensity of hominin use of the animal bones is highest in ursids, followed by bovids and then rhinocerotids. In terms of absolute numbers bovids are the best represented group, followed by ursids and rhinocerotids. Cervids and equids are well represented, accounting for 9% and 7% of the total number of identified bones respectively. As shown in table 5.4, a few of the bones of these groups even show cut-marks. All in all, the situation that is reflected by the assemblage as a whole does not change significantly, although the diet breadth may have increased a little, with cervids and equids being slightly more routinely exploited.

During the accumulation of level D1, the most important development is the disappearance of ursids. The environment during this phase seems to have been much colder and more open than during the deposition of the previous levels. This may account for the absence of Deninger's bear, which was adapted to forested conditions. It is not sufficient to account for the absence of brown bear, which is a catholic species. The presence of red deer and aurochs leads me to assume that brown bear was able to survive in the environment of the site at this time. This development may therefore reflect a drastic change in hominin foraging strategies, in which a dominant species was dropped from the optimal set.

The analysis of these levels was done using the NISP figures provided by (Auguste 1988b). Due to the degree of fragmentation, is should be noted that the MNI's from the levels are low (see table 5.3). We must therefore be cautious in attaching too much importance to the findings from the levels. Both levels were truncated by the construction of the factory, so the faunal assemblages represent only a part of what was originally there (Auguste 1988b, 151). Moreover, the predominance of dental and cranial remains suggests that taphonomic processes have also deleted part of the assemblage. In this analysis I will assume that the species representation in terms of NISP is representative of the original assemblage.

The assemblage is small, so we cannot attach much importance to the increase in importance of rhinocerotids, equids and cervids. The decrease of bovids is dramatic, especially since there is one taxon less represented in the assemblage. It is hard to interpret however. Moreover, the degree to which the bones were exploited by hominins is unclear because they are more heavily weathered than those deposited in lower lying levels. With regard to rhinocerotids it must be mentioned that the represented species, woolly rhinoceros, was significantly heavier than the species present in the older levels. It is said to weigh 2900 kg. by Brook and Bowman (2004) and 2800 kg. by Louguet-Lefebvre (2005).

Level D also contained a small assemblage. It shows a decrease in rhinocerotids and cervids, while bovids and equids increase in importance compared to level D1. The cervids may have become rarer, because of the cold and open conditions, to which they are less suited. This is not sufficient to explain the decrease in importance of rhinocerotids. It is tempting to interpret the developments in terms of new hominin foraging strategies. The increased reliance on equids may signal a specialisation of foraging on animals living in herds that move through the landscape along predictable routes. Concentrating on dispersed solitary animals like rhinoceros may have proved to be a less effective strategy in the now fully open environment. The location of the site at a "t-junction" of river valleys may have placed it at an important spot near migration routes of bovids and equids.

It appears then that the diet breadth of the occupants of the site was narrow. Three species were exploited upon encounter: narrow-nosed rhinoceros, male aurochs and brown bear. The status of Merck's rhinoceros and Deninger's bear is less certain. I assume that they were also exploited when they were encountered, but that they were simply present in smaller numbers and therefore were encountered only sporadically. The exploitation of cervids and equids is problematic. They were certainly not in the "optimal set" of species; otherwise they would be more abundant in the assemblage. However, they were exploited at least occasionally.

This analysis has shown that using OFT to analyse a Pleistocene bone assemblage leads to insight in the factors that played a role in hominin foraging decisions. As pointed out in chapter 4 a ranking based on animal weights is a simplification, yet the species in the "optimal set" in level IIA are large species. Using simple proxies to gain insight in search time and especially handling cost does point to additional factors that could influence hominin strategies. The developments in levels II base, D1 and D are harder to explain. The bone assemblages are smaller and the occupations were a lot more ephemeral than the occupations represented in level IIA. In level II base we see an increase in the role of cervids and equids with regard to the dominant taxa. It may be that the encounter rate with more highly ranked species decreased, which led to these taxa playing a more important role in the hominin diet.

5.9 Discussion

The bone assemblages of this site document the transition from a warm period to a glacial. The environmental conditions at the site change from a landscape covered by open forest. Climatic conditions were not yet very cold at least during the formation of the lower levels of the site, so issues of insulation and sheltered places for camps were not yet too important. The later levels of occupation represent colder conditions, but the presence of species that are traditionally associated with forested environments, like aurochs, shows that conditions were not extreme. The site is located at a "t-junction" of river valleys, on the northern edge of the valley. The location afforded access to a large area of the low-lying river valleys, which probably served as the major migration routes for both hominins and animals. The sheltered river valleys are also the locations that are likely to have been covered by forest. The exposed plateaux probably had a less lush plant cover, since conditions here were more severe.

Because of the enormous amount of material recovered in level IIA, the excavators do not think that this level can be the result of one occupation. Rather, they interpret the site as the result of repeated occupations of similar character. Other levels, like II base, D1 and D are thought to be the result of discrete occupations. The excellent condition of the bone surfaces in level IIA does suggest that the material was not left exposed for a long time. The bones do not show any signs of weathering at all. Based on actualistic research in East Africa, it is thought that this corresponds to bones having been buried within 5 years. In more northern environments, weathering takes place more slowly (Fosse *et al.* 2004), but influences like carnivore ravaging, trampling and sorting of elements by durability do not seem to have played an important role in the final composition of the bone assemblage. I expect the bone assemblage of level IIA to reflect only a few occupations and not a palimpsest that is the result of activities spanning more than a decade.

The assemblage that is present at the site reflects a stable foraging system relied on three groups of animals: large bovids, ursids and rhinocerotids. Diet breadth was thus small and the focus of hunting was, as expected, on the heavier species available. On the other hand, it is clear that weight was not the only consideration determining foraging decisions. This is shown most clearly by the absence of straight-tusked elephant in the assemblage. Since this species is by far the largest species available to the occupants of the site, one would expect it to have been heavily exploited. I propose that, had it been exploited, even if it was more thoroughly processed in the field than rhinoceros, it would be expected to be better represented at a site with such a huge bone assemblage as Biache-Saint-Vaast.

The simple assumptions that I used to model increased handling cost are very coarse grained. The threshold of 300 kg. that I used to classify a species as dangerous is based on the expected maximum prey size for a mammal of the same size as a male Neanderthal. All species in the regularly exploited set are larger than 300 kg. This shows that the occupants of the site had developed ways of dealing with large prey. In mammals, predators are known to be able to increase the maximum size of prey that is successfully hunted by operating in groups (Radloff and Toit 2004). However, the extreme size of the prey that Neanderthals hunted at this site is unlike anything seen in mammalian carnivores. This suggests that Neanderthals were able to hunt in groups in a co-ordinated manner.

Whether animals live in groups or not does seem to be an important consideration but it is clear from both later levels and other Pleistocene sites, like Schöningen that hominins were able to dispatch animals living in herds in the Middle Pleistocene. Therefore, the decision to concentrate on solitary animals is part of a strategy, representing a conscious choice by the foragers. Apparently, the added difficulties of surprising a herd and dealing with the anti-predator behaviours of a herd were not the most optimal choice in the situations represented by the level IIA assemblage.

Modelling search time is a complicated matter. OFT assumes that encounters with animals occur at random. This can be modelled by reconstructing the population densities of the available species. This has proven difficult however. Within mammals, population density and body size are correlated, but at species level, actual densities may differ up to an order of magnitude from the predicted values (Silva, Brimacombe, and Downing 2001, Silva, Brown, and Downing 1997). Therefore, the reconstructed densities can only be taken as a very rough indication of the Pleistocene values. They can indicate in which proportions different species of animals may have been present in the environment. If the site was located at the edge of a range of a species' distribution, the environment may not have been the ideal environment for a species and the population density may have been lower than estimated here.

At Biache-Saint-Vaast this may have been the case for Merck's rhinoceros. Their poor representation in the bone assemblage is hard to explain using OFT, except when assuming that they may have been at a disadvantage in this environment with regard to narrow-nosed rhinoceros. This leads us to a major problem in the reconstructing of the optimal set of prey animals for Pleistocene foragers. Merck's rhinoceros may have been more highly ranked by foragers than narrow-nosed rhinoceros and other well represented species. It may simply not have been encountered very often. This is also the explanation I propose for the rather poor representation of Deninger's bear in the assemblage.

Therefore, high handling costs as proposed reason for the absence of straight-tusked elephant in the assemblage can only be accepted with reservations. This is a very large species that will only have been present in very low population densities, even in environments to which it was well adapted. If the environment of Biache-Saint-Vaast was not optimal for this species, then its populations may have been very thinly spread on the ground. It may thus have belonged in the set of animals that would be exploited on encounter, but during the period of time represented in level IIA it may simply not have been encountered during the times at which the site was occupied.

On the other hand, the assumption that encounters with prey animals happened at random is not tenable for Neanderthals. This was an intelligent species of hominin that was able to observe and learn the types of behaviour exhibited by prey species, it is therefore reasonable to assume that they were able to manipulate their encounter rates with prey species. This is in evidence in the Biache-Saint-Vaast assemblage, which demonstrates a reliance on a small number of prey species, all of which were large and therefore not present in very high numbers. Moreover, they focussed on specific categories of individuals of the preferred species. In aurochs they focussed on adult males, in bears they simply preferred adults, while at least with regard to narrow-nosed rhinoceros they apparently preferred juveniles to young adults. Since this focus of hunting was maintained in a consistent manner over time, resulting in an assemblage in level IIA representing hundreds of individuals, it appears that the occupants of the site were very capable of encountering the preferred prey categories in a consistent manner. I take this as an important argument to support the propositions I have made with regard to the influence of handling cost as the reason for the absence of such species as elephant and lion.

A striking species that is absent is giant deer. I find its absence difficult to explain in terms of search cost, since this species appears to have been well attuned to the environment that is indicated for level IIA. In terms of handling cost, the absence of females is understandable, since they presumably lived in herds. The absence of males is peculiar, however, since these were presumably solitary for most of the year and are heavier than brown bear, a species that was exploited. Two explanations can be proposed. First, the season of occupation may have coincided with the rut. During this time the males presumably lived in harem-groups. Second, the season of occupation may have taken place just after the rut. Males were solitary at this time of year. However, since they apparently do not feed during rut they will have been very lean and their ranking may therefore have dropped. The second hypothesis would agree with occupation in autumn as proposed by Auguste (1995a) and Louguet-Lefebvre (2005). Moreover, in this season, ranking of bear would be elevated since bears would be building fat reserves to survive their hibernation.

5.10 Conclusion

The main level of Biache-Saint-Vaast, level IIA, reflects the result of part of a foraging system that was stable over a number of years. The site has been dated to the period of transition between MIS 7 and MIS 6, reflecting circumstances intermediate between interglacial and pleniglacial. These are exactly the circumstances to which Neanderthals were adapted according to Gamble (1986, 1987).

The hunting activities clearly represent a preference for solitary prey of large size. Narrow-nosed rhinoceros probably reached their maximum size at the age of 9 (Louguet-Lefebvre 2005,

122). Moreover, it seems that young individuals leave their mothers side at about six years of age (Louguet-Lefebvre 2005, 123). This means that we are dealing with hunting of young solitary individuals. These were probably the most vulnerable, since they were not yet very experienced, but no longer accompanied by an adult. Another hypothesis that has been advanced, namely hunting of females and their young, probably in early spring (Auguste, Moncel, and Patou-Mathis 1998, 183) cannot be rejected, since a large number of infants is present and even one pregnant female (Louguet-Lefebvre 2005, 123). On the other hand, high infant mortality is common in nature anyway, so it is possible that (a large) segment of the infants were part of the natural background fauna and not connected to hominin hunting activities. In aurochs and bears, adults formed the focus of the hunting activities that are represented at the site.[24] In aurochs, the focus was on males only, presumably since they are solitary and live in small groups, while the females and calves live in larger herds. Moreover, the males represent much more meat, so in terms of caloric value this focus also concurs with the predictions made by OFT.

Of the unexploited species, the absence of giant deer is hardest to explain convincingly. A possible reason may have to do with the season of occupation of the site. There may be one additional factor that can be invoked in explaining their absence while the smaller brown bear was present. Their absence need not be explained by a decreased ranking of giant deer because of seasonal circumstances. Brown bear may have had an increased ranking based on factors other than its weight. First, Auguste has remarked that the position of cut-marks on brown bear bones suggest exploitation of these animals for their fur. This may have given the yield of this species more value than giant deer. Second, the killing of such dangerous animals may have provided prestige for the hunters. This may mean that giant deer was not in the optimal set, because it did not possess such added value. Third, if hunting bears took place in autumn, their ranking would be elevated because of their high fat content.

Level II base shows that equids and cervids were occasionally exploited. Moreover, exploitation marks are said to be present on bones of other species in level IIA. If foraging was practised using an optimal set that was exploited on encounter, one would expect these smaller species to be better represented in the assemblage. They may have been the lowest ranked species, but were probably encountered most often. This may be explained by assuming that foraging activities specifically targeted the highest-ranked species. As discussed in chapter 4, when encountering a low-ranked animal, a forager can evaluate whether the cost of continued foraging for more highly-ranked species would be more productive. Therefore, we can assume that the occupants of the site often decided to leave cervids and equids alone in favour of continued attempts at encountering more highly-ranked species.

The interpretation of developments in levels II base, D1 and D is quite complex. First, these levels do not present a time-averaged insight in activities. They represent short occupations and therefore short-term fluctuations in the environment may influence the represented species. The fact that the assemblages, especially of levels D1 and D are very small makes this problem even more serious.

On the other hand, the disappearance of bears from the diet in level D1 is a dramatic development. However, since the genus is the second best represented at the site as a whole, it is probable that their absence in these small assemblages at least reflects a decreasing importance of bears in the hominin foraging strategies. Deninger's bear is already absent in level D0 and its disappearance may be correlated to the changing climate and the disappearance of forest in the vicinity of the site. In my opinion, certainly in view of the other species that are still present, like aurochs and red deer, the environment was not unsuitable for brown bears at this time. The disappearance of ursids led to a relative increase in importance of all other taxa, except for bovids. This is also a peculiar development, since it was the dominant species at the site as a whole and accounts for a very large part of the bone assemblages of the previous and subsequent occupation. Their drop in importance may simply reflect a temporary decrease in encounter rates. In general, medium-sized ungulates living in herds become more important during the later occupations.

The developments in foraging tactics represent a changing situation, where demands of hominins were probably fulfilled more easily by a different focus of hunting activities. The presence of animals in large herds may have been easier to predict in the open environment. Moreover, herd

---

24 On the other hand, the method of compiling age-profiles used by Auguste may not be very secure. According to him adults were also the best represented category in rhino, while subsequent research by Louguet-Lefebvre (2005) revealed a focus on the younger adults and juveniles.

size of many animals increases as the environment grows more open (cf. Guthrie 1990). Therefore, herds may have represented increasingly large amounts of meat.

Exploiting species living in herds requires a large group, strategic behaviour and communication in order to co-ordinate the hunt (*e.g.* Farizy *et al.* 1994). However, this is also necessary for a small predator to kill prey as large as they did during level IIA times. In more open environments, hunting solitary and dangerous animals may have been less productive than increasing group size and concentrating on herds of ungulates. The fact that the animals in the herd are smaller than one rhinoceros is compensated by the fact that one can exploit many of them in one go. Moreover, in contrast to bears, ungulates are much less dangerous to hunt.

6 Taubach

6.1 Introduction

Taubach is a travertine site in Germany, located near the city of Weimar. The site became renowned for its archaeological materials in the 19th century. It gained international fame because large amounts of Pleistocene bones belonging to extinct species were found here. The bones at this site are very well preserved and show extensive traces of human modification, in the form of traces of burning and cut-marks (reported in: Bratlund 1999). In addition to the large collection of bones, the site also yielded a distinctive stone tool assemblage. Similar assemblages have also been found at other interglacial sites in Central Europe and the "Taubachian culture" has therefore been defined on the basis of these assemblages (Valoch 1984).

This site allows us to address several important issues. First, the main find horizon of the site is traditionally dated to Marine Isotope Stage (MIS) 5e, the Eemian interglacial. As discussed in chapter 2, the character of human occupation of northwestern Europe during this period is the subject of debate. Some authors have proposed that Neanderthals could not deal with an interglacial climax environment, because available herbivore biomass was low and dispersed, compared to the more open environments of colder periods (*e.g.* Gamble 1986, Gamble 1992). Others attacked this hypothesis, arguing that the paucity of sites dating to this period is better explained by taphonomic factors (*e.g.* Roebroeks, Conard, and Van Kolfschoten 1992, Roebroeks and Speleers 2002). Taubach is one of the few sites that can be studied to address this question. In this chapter we will test whether analysing diet breadth at this site yields insight into the way in which Neanderthals coped with interglacial circumstances. Moreover, we may be able to confirm or reject the predictions regarding Neanderthal foraging behaviour in temperate environments put forward in the previous chapter.

Another issue is the importance of megafaunal species in the assemblage. Like at Biache-Saint-Vaast, rhinoceros is one of the most important animal groups represented in the assemblage. At this site, the dominant species is Merck's rhinoceros (*Stephanorhinus kirchbergensis*). It was slightly larger than the largest extant rhinocerotid, the white rhinoceros. The bones of this species exhibit abundant cut-marks. This site therefore presents us with the possibility to test the idea that specialised hunting of big game is unknown ethnographically (Haynes 2002, 208). From this it has been concluded that foraging for megafauna is never an optimal choice when considering only its caloric value (*e.g.* Wroe *et al.* 2004, 308).

There are some disadvantages connected with a case study of this site however. First, the site was discovered in the 19th century. The presently known collections were also formed in this period, especially in the 1880's and 1890's (Bratlund 1999). Since collectors were focused on identifiable bones and apparently also focused on certain more exotic species, this leaves us with a biased collection of bones (Bratlund 1999, 82-83). On the other hand, some small species are present in the collection, especially the presence of small beaver bones seems to point to the fact that the ratio of present species is probably representative of what was originally present. An additional problem is the fact that recent work has cast doubts on the Eemian age of this site. The dating evidence will be extensively discussed in this chapter. Nevertheless, the consensus view seems to be that the main assemblages from the site must be dated to MIS5e (*e.g.* Behm-Blancke 1960, Bratlund 1999, Gaudzinski 2004, Van Kolfschoten 2000, Roebroeks, Conard, and Van Kolfschoten 1992, Roebroeks and Speleers 2002, Wenzel 2002).

This chapter consists of an introduction to the site and a discussion of the debate surrounding its dating. An overview of the archaeological materials recovered at the site will then be provided, with emphasis on the bone assemblage. Moreover, the environment of the site will be reconstructed in order to provide an overview of the available resources at the time of occupation. This will be followed by a discussion on the information this site provides regarding the foraging strategies responsible for the accumulation of the bone assemblage.

6.2 The site

The travertine complex of Taubach represents a small travertine deposit, covering an area of about 0.2 km². It is located in the Bundesland of Thuringia in Germany, close to the city of Weimar. The travertines are located on a terrace bordering the Ilm river valley. The surface of the terrace is located about 7 metres above the valley floor. Archaeological finds were collected during commercial exploitation of the travertines (Bratlund 1999). Taubach was the first known German site that proved human presence in the *Diluvialzeit* (*e.g.* Eichhorn 1909) and became famous because of the large numbers of well-preserved mammal bones found at the location.

6.3 Dating

The traditional date assigned to the site was based on the composition of its mammal assemblage. The mammal species found at Taubach and also at the nearby site of Ehringsdorf, especially the lower travertines at the latter, were thought to be indicative of warm environments and were dated to the last interglacial. However, there are some problems with this date. The lower travertines of Ehringsdorf have been redated and now appear to be older than originally thought. They probably date to MIS 7 (Bratlund 1999, 74, 81). With regard to the large mammal fauna, the lower travertines of Ehringsdorf have yielded the most similar known faunal assemblage compared to that of Taubach (Bratlund 1999, 81). This has led to doubts as to whether the bone assemblage was actually formed during MIS 5e.

As pointed out, the travertine deposits at Taubach are distributed over a small area. Unfortunately, the totality of this area has now been built over, so most stratigraphic information must be obtained from profiles described around the turn of the previous century. One additional profile was described in 1972 (Bratlund 1999, 63-64). From the stratigraphic information and two direct dates obtained in recent years it appears that an Eemian date fits the stratigraphic column of the site *in toto*. However, all sources contemporaneous with the collecting of bones from the site state that the materials were collected from a layer in the lower part of the sequence, below the massive travertines

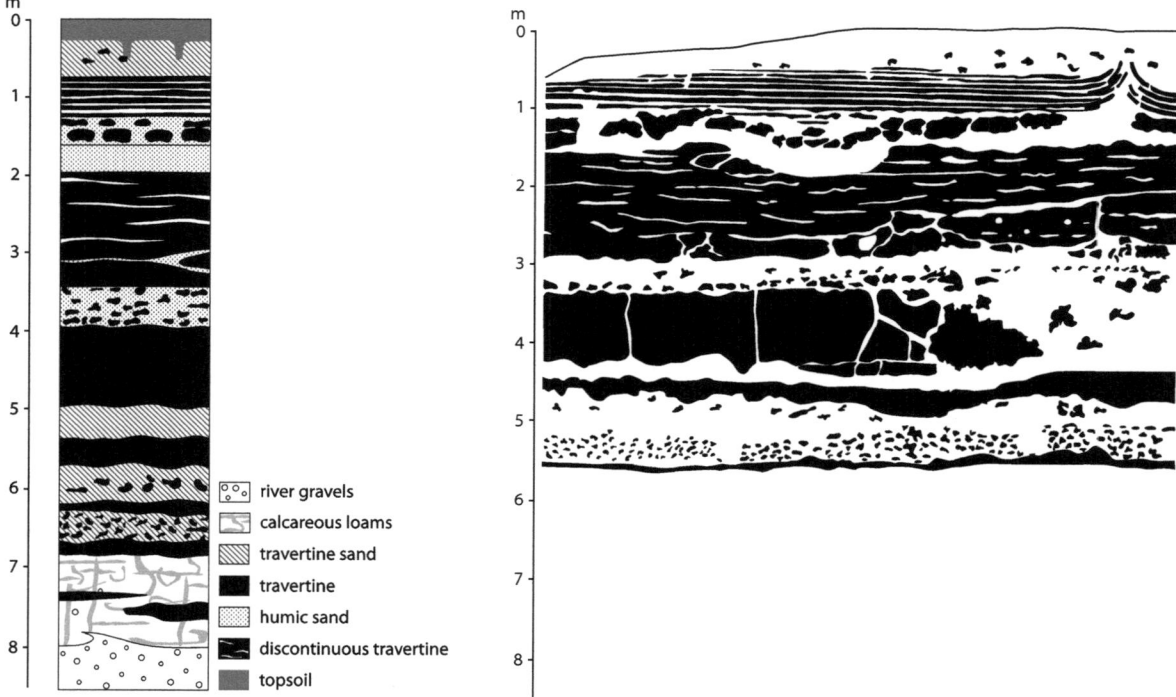

Figure 6.1: Idealised profile of the Taubach travertine deposits. Based on (Steiner 1977, 110).

Figure 6.2: Schematic drawing of the profile exposed in 1972 showing Travertine in black. Note the discontinuity in the large travertine bank between 3 and 4 metres. This indicates that the identification of the Werksteindtravertine as a marker horizon may be problematic. Based on (Steiner 1977, 93).

that were the object of exploitation (Bratlund 1999, 67, 69). The samples for the direct dates were taken from a higher part of the stratigraphy. Therefore, the available direct dates only provide a *terminus ante quem* for the formation of the large mammal assemblage. This shows that the Taubachian fossil assemblages do not necessarily represent an occupation during full interglacial conditions.

An idealised stratigraphic column, the Idealprofil, was constructed on the basis of the 1972 profile (See fig. 6.1). Problematic in this respect is the fact that the travertine stratigraphy of the site is very variable. There is no continuous marker horizon available that is present throughout the travertine deposit. Many authors use the thick beds of travertine that were the focus of exploitation (*Werksteintravertine*) the layer between 4 and 5 metres in fig. 6.1, called bed 11 in the literature, as a marker horizon (e.g. Bratlund 1999, Steiner 1977). However, even this layer is discontinuous and grades into travertine sands locally (See fig. 6.2). The descriptions from the time of exploitation describe a layer of sandy travertine, called the Knochensand (bone sand) that yielded the large mammal remains (Bratlund 1999, 67). This is invariably described as a sandy layer situated beneath the indurated travertines (Steiner 1977, 87, 89). Two important things must be noted with regard to the 1972 profile. Firstly, the layers beneath the solid travertine deposits did not yield any bones, so the precise stratigraphic position of the bone sand could not be clarified. On the other hand, a layer of humic sand above the exploited travertines did yield one molar belonging to fallow deer (Dama dama), as well as several bone fragments of longbones. The largest of these fragments was 14 centimetres in length (Steiner 1977, 99-100). This may indicate that there were at least two findlevels at Taubach (e.g. Bratlund 1999, 70). Secondly, the Mollusken sand, Mollusc sand, is described as a separate unit from the layers underlying it, and with good reason, as will be discussed later. However, at the time of bone collection, all layers beneath the *Werksteintravertine* were often collectively referred to as the bone sand (Bratlund 1999, 70).

The available direct dates are two 230Th/234U dates. One sample was taken from the *Werksteintravertine*, yielding a date of 116.000 ± 19.000 years. The other dated sample was obtained from bed 7, the indurated travertine between two and three metres in fig. 6.1, this sample yielded a date of 111.000 ± 12.000 years. Therefore, a date in the Eemian for the upper part of the sequence is well established (Bratlund 1999, 70).

As pointed out, these dates do not prove that underlying bone sand necessarily dates to the same period. We know that travertines in Germany were only formed during warm periods, and they are usually assumed to indicate interglacial conditions. However, their formation need not be restricted to interglacials. Travertine deposits from Stuttgart for example may date in part to MIS 5c (Wenzel 2002, 40). Therefore, some travertine formation could also have taken place during an intra-Saalian warm phase.

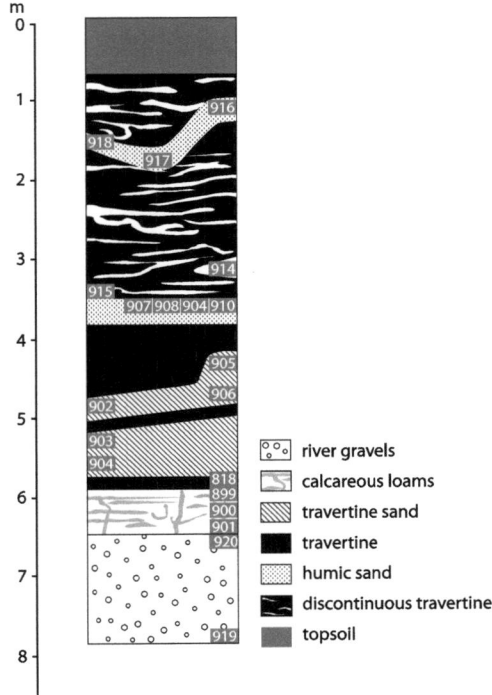

In 1972, the excavated profile was sampled for molluscs, among other things. Analysis of the molluscs from lower sandy layers of this profile seem to point to relatively cold environmental conditions. They have been termed a *reliktische Kaltzeitfauna*. This makes an Eemian date problematic (Bratlund 1999, 80). In fig. 6.3, the profile and locations of samples for the analysis of snails are shown. Of interest with regard to the bone sand are the layers between the *Ilmkies*, the river gravels underlying the travertine deposits, and the *Steinbank*, the exploited massive layer of travertine. The samples were studied by (Zeissler 1977). According to her, the samples from the lower part of the sequence in the Mergel represent species indicative of cold and steppic conditions. She interprets the assemblage as a transitional fauna, showing an environment that is getting warmer (samples 901-898, see fig. 6.3) (Zeissler 1977, 155). The same species are also

Figure 6.3: Schematic profile with locations of mollusc samples. Based on Zeissler, (1977, 141).

represented in the lower Travertine units, although in these units the number of dry species increases and also woodland species increase slightly (samples 903 & 904, see fig. 6.3) (Zeissler 1977, 155). However, from sample 902 upwards a full interglacial fauna is in evidence. According to Zeissler (1977), this must indicate a hiatus in the lower travertine deposits. Bratlund assumes that the bone collection comes from the layers beneath the mollusc sand and must therefore date to an early phase of the Eemian or a temperate phase of the Saalian (Bratlund 1999, 80-81). However, since often no distinction was made between these sediments at the time of exploitation, at least part of the bone assemblage may have been recovered from the mollusc sand.

The micromammal sample that has been used to date to the site, comes from the layer of humic sand above the *Werksteintravertine* in the Idealprofil, and is inferred to represent full interglacial conditions (Bratlund 1999, 71-72). Therefore the micromammals have been used to date the site to the Eemian (*e.g.* Van Kolfschoten 2000, 2002). However, since the sample comes from a different layer than the large mammal bones this date can only be used as a *terminus ante quem*. Since some tools were recovered from this layer, we can be certain that hominins were present in the area at this period in time. Unfortunately, in the 1972 research, only the river deposits at the base of the sequence and the mollusc sand yielded micromammal remains, not the lower layers of the lower part of the travertine deposits (Heinrich and Jánossy 1977, 401).

Evolutionary trends in large mammal species can also be used to date the site. In the case of Taubach, beaver (*Castor fiber*) and horse (*Equus taubachensis*) teeth have been examined. Unfortunately, this provides a less fine-grained resolution than examination of micromammal fossils would. In the case of the beaver remains they seem to be more advanced than the ones found at Ehringsdorf (Bratlund 1999, 72). The horse sample on the other hand is too small to draw definitive conclusions from, but the remains probably date to before 100 ka (Bratlund 1999, 72-73). A recent analysis of the remains of Merck's rhinoceros has shown that the Taubach fossils were distinctly more advanced than those of the lower Travertine from Ehringsdorf, supporting a younger date for Taubach (Made 2000). A similar point has been made for the giant deer (*Megaloceros giganteus*) remains. According to Van der Made (2003, 376-377) those at Ehringsdorf are significantly older than the Eemian remains, among which those of Taubach.

The large mammal fauna from the site has traditionally been interpreted as signifying warm interglacial circumstances. However, according to Bratlund (1999), a lot of winterhard species are present in the assemblage. She combines this with the indications from the molluscs from the *Mergel* and the lower travertine to date the site to the early Eemian. Because of the mollusc evidence, she theorises that the latest possible date for the assemblage would be during pollenzone 3 of the Eemian (Bratlund 1999). On the other hand, she upholds the possibility of the site dating to an intra-Saalian warm phase.

Unfortunately, accepting a date in the early Eemian is also problematic for the assemblage as a whole. First, there is the possibility that part of the assemblage comes from layers higher up in the sequence, like the mollusc sand. This is made more likely by the presence of Aesculapian snake (*Elaphe* aff. *longissima*) and European pond turtle (*Emys orbicularis*) in the museum collections (Mlynarski and Ullrich 1977). Both of these species need warm environments and are now restricted to more southern parts of Europe. More importantly, a similar argument can be advanced for one of the more important constituents of the assemblage, Merck's rhinoceros. This species shows features that suggest an adaptation to closed environments, especially in comparison to the other known rhinoceros species from this era. Its teeth have lower crowns than that of narrow-nosed rhinoceros (*Dicerorhinus hemitoechus*) and woolly rhinoceros (*Coelodonta antiquitatis*), suggesting more emphasis on browsing than on grazing. Moreover, its teeth have less cementum than these other species, likewise suggesting a specialisation for browsing. This impression is strengthened by the fact that its locomotion apparatus is more gracile than that of the other species suggesting an adaptation to a closed environment. In this respect it is also interesting to note that although the species is always found in interglacial contexts, it never entered Spain. This can be taken as an indication that it could not deal with open environments. The same is suggested by the fact that at those German sites where it occurs together with the smaller narrow-nosed rhinoceros, it is always present in higher numbers. Usually when two similar species co-occur, the smaller one is more abundant. This also suggests that in the vicinity of these sites, closed environments were more abundant than open ones (Van der Made in press, 44-46).

The debate surrounding the site's date is hard to resolve, since the stratigraphic descriptions from the time of exploitation are not very detailed and there was a lot of variation within the Taubach

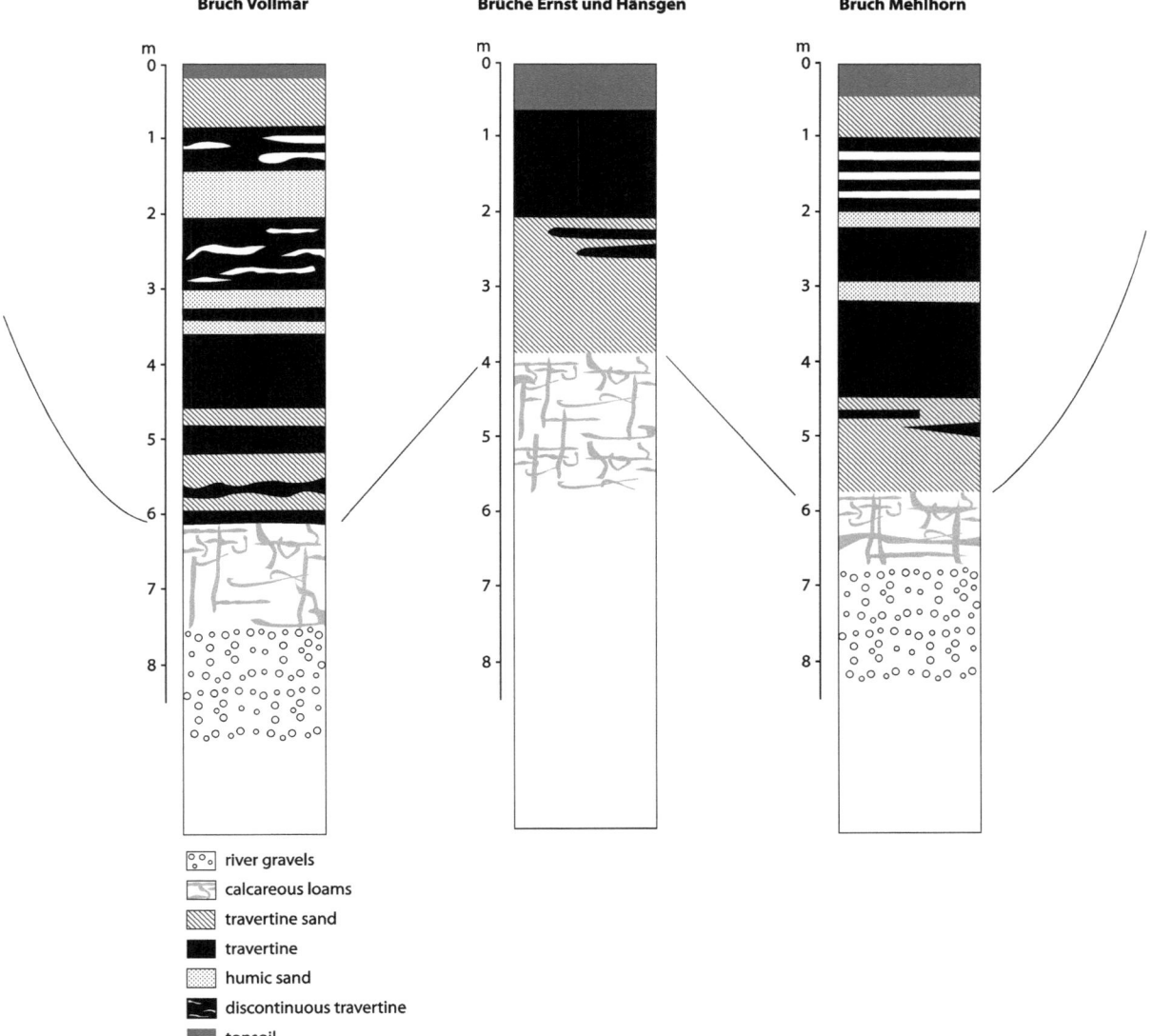

Figure 6.4: Cross section through the Taubach travertine deposits based on old descriptions and the 1972 profile. Note the high position of the bone sand in the Zentralbereich. Based on (Steiner 1977, 111).

deposits, as shown in Figure 6.4. To me, there seem to be three options. First, we can take Bratlund's estimates to be correct. Combined with the data on Merck's rhinoceros we might than assume that the large mammal assemblage dates to the third pollen phase of the Eemian, combining a transitional environment and moderately cold conditions with closed areas in the environment. Another possibility is to assume that most of the large mammal assemblage comes from the mollusc sand. Since this was sometimes grouped together with the bone sand at the time of exploitation this is a possibility. Furthermore, the reptiles in the assemblage do seem to point to the environment being warmer than at present. A combination of these two hypotheses is also a possibility. The warmth-loving species, especially the reptiles in all probability come from the mollusc sand. A large part of the bone assemblage could be from the lower travertine sands. These could date to the early Eemian, or a temperate phase within the later stages of MIS 6.

The third possibility is to assume that the surviving descriptions about the provenance of the bones from the time of exploitation are incorrect. The fauna might then come from the lower humic layer. This is the only layer that yielded stone tools and large mammal remains in 1972. Furthermore, due to the variability of the stratigraphy, as seen in the grading of the Werksteintravertin in travertine sand within a few metres in the 1972 profile (fig 6.2), this might actually fit some of the original descriptions, where the findlayer is described to be travertine sand, but quite high up in the deposit (cf. Ernst und Hänsgen in fig. 6.4).

I prefer the second possibility for the time being. I think that the combined data from the species that are present in the layers and the travertine deposits warrants dating of these layers within the Eemian rather than MIS 7. The exact position of the assemblage within the pollenzones is a topic to which I will return below when discussing the environment. First I will shortly present the archaeological finds from the site.

6.4 The archaeological finds

As pointed out, this was the first site to be discovered in Germany that yielded evidence of human presence in the *Diluvialzeit*, i.e. the Pleistocene. Indications of human presence were found in the form of *Brandschichten*, charred layers said to contain charcoal and ashes (Bratlund 1999, 67). They have been claimed to represent hearths that show many phases of use (Schäfer 1990, 54). Furthermore, the bone sand and the humic sand above the *Werksteintravertine*, yielded artefact assemblages (Bratlund 1999, 64, 67). Also, many of the bones collected at the site show cut-marks or are charred, testifying that hominins were involved in the accumulation of the bone assemblage (Behm-Blancke 1960, Bratlund 1999). Additionally, some publications report tools made of bone and antler (*e.g.* Behm-Blancke 1960, Valoch 1984). According to Bratlund (1999, 90-91) the ones present in the collection she studied were mistakenly identified as artefacts.

The finds show that hominins were present in the area and that their activities were at least partly responsible for the formation of the assemblages. However, natural factors probably also contributed to the formation of the bone assemblages. The travertine deposits provide an area of excellent preservation and therefore, animals that died of natural causes or were killed by carnivores in the area will also have been preserved (Bratlund 1999, 86-87). Besides, it is apparent that the site represents a palimpsest of many different occupational episodes. This is indicated by the large quantities of bone that were found at the site. Some collectors even described the bone sand as being saturated with fossils (Bratlund 1999, 67).

The artefact assemblage represents a selection made by collectors of these remains of repeated occupations. The character of the bone assemblage is uniform, suggesting that similar assemblages were left during the different occupational episodes. Furthermore, the kind of stone tool assemblage found at Taubach is thought to be analogous to the assemblages of a group of Eemian sites in Central Europe. This has led some researchers to name a culture after this site, the Taubachian (*e.g.* Valoch 1984, 193). All stages of flint-knapping are represented at the site. The amount of knapping debris and natural pieces on the other hand is underrepresented in the surviving collections. On the other hand, the fact that so-called *Trümmerstücken* and artefact made on non-flint materials are present at all suggests the collection methods were less biased than sometimes assumed (Schäfer 1990, 55-56).

The Taubachian has been characterised as a microlithic industry. The artefacts produced are small and there are few formal tools among the assemblages. Raw materials were mostly locally collected and this led to quite high percentages of non-flint artefacts. Moreover, reduction strategies were thought to be quite primitive and Levallois-reduction absent. The cores found at Taubach are of irregular form and of a non-Levalloisian character (see for example Valoch 1984).

This characterisation appears to be faulty and based on biased publications (Schäfer 1990, 61-63). The small size of the artefacts found at Taubach can be attributed to the raw materials used. Most artefacts were made from pebbles found in the gravels of the nearby Ilm River (Schäfer 1990, 57, Valoch 1984, 195). In general, the dimensions of these pebbles were limited. The average length of cores is only 36 mm. However, when comparing Taubach to similar assemblages, like the one found at Ehringsdorf, it does seem that hominins at Taubach were able knappers and managed to reach a higher *Längeneffizienz* than at other sites, i.e. they effectively maximised the length of flakes they produced (Schäfer 1990, 57-58). Furthermore, Taubach seems to show quite high "leptolithisation", meaning that flakes are on average very thin and elongated (Schäfer 1990, 58). Reduction strategies were not as primitive as sometimes proposed. According to Behm-Blancke (1960, 169), the reduction technique resembles the Levallois technique.

Bone working was also considered to be an important feature of the Taubachian. At other sites that have been classified as Taubachian, like Kůlna and Tata, many bone and ivory retouchoirs have been found. At Taubach, because of the collection methods and emphasis on complete and/or identifiable bones, these may have been missed. On the other hand, a piece of antler with engraved regular lines has been reported from the site. Similar pieces have been found at Kůlna (Valoch 1984, 198). Furthermore, purported antler digging sticks have been recovered at the site. It has been hypothesised that they were used in order to dig pitfalls for the hunting of the large animals found at the site (Behm-Blancke 1960, 205). However, during her study, Bratlund was unable to locate antlers that were convincing artefacts (Bratlund 1999, 90-91). Therefore, this aspect of the Taubachian has not been convincingly demonstrated at this site. Most likely, many of the "artefacts" were naturally damaged pieces of bone and antler that were mistaken for artefacts.

6.5 The bone collection

Since the bone assemblage was collected largely in the 19th century, an important concern is to determine to what degree the collection is representative of what was originally there. Furthermore, it is essential to ascertain the role that hominin activities played in the formation of the bone assemblage. One problematic aspect of the bone assemblage of this site is the fact that the remains are dispersed over many collections. This is because during the height of scientific interest in the site at the end of the 19th century, bones from this site were highly valued palaeontological collector's items (Bratlund 1999, 81). Moreover, before scientific interest in Taubach was stirred, exploitation of the travertine had already started and at the time large collections of bones were dumped in the Ilm River (Bratlund 1999 87, 82).

Still, located at the *Forschungsstation für Quartärpaläontologie* of the *Forschungsinstitut Senckenberg* in Weimar, the largest surviving collection has been surveyed by Bratlund (1999). This collection was accumulated by local scientists with direct access to the Taubach quarries. Therefore, the provenance of the finds in the collection is clear. This does not mean that the collection is unbiased. The collection shows a clear focus toward complete and identifiable bones. This has resulted in a dominance of cranial material and especially of isolated teeth, which make up 34.74% (n=1540) of the collection studied by Bratlund (1999, 85-86). Furthermore, collection choices may be partially responsible for the dominance of Merck's rhinoceros and brown bear in the surviving sample (Bratlund 1999, 82, 151). On the other hand, these species were also reported as being dominant in earlier publications (Behm-Blancke 1960, Bratlund 1999). Therefore, their abundance in these deposits is probably a real phenomenon. This can be taken as an indication that the list of species and their relative

Species	Total fragments	Cut-marked	MNI
Ursus arctos	1537	292	52
Stephanorhinus kirchbergensis (some Dicerorhinus hemitoechus)	1224	99	76
Bovids (Mainly Bison, some Bos)	533	25	18
Castor fiber	319	10	17
Cervus elaphus	207	2	not provided
Palaeoloxodon antiquus	182		not provided
Equus taubachensis	161	1?	not provided
Sus scrofa	96		not provided
Capreolus capreolus	58		not provided
Megaloceros giganteus	6		not provided
Ursus spelaeus	7		not provided
Panthera leo	5		not provided
Crocuta crocuta	1		not provided
Canis lupus	7		not provided
Panthera pardus	lost		
Lynx lynx	lost		
Meles meles	lost		
Lutra lutra	lost		
Unidentified carnivore	4		
Unidentified	86	3	

Table 6.1: Composition of the Taubach mammal assemblage. After (Bratlund 1999, 84, 86).

abundance in the collection may roughly reflect the original frequencies. If there was a collection bias against smaller, less interesting animals for example, we would expect a small and still extant animal like beaver to be only very poorly represented. Moreover, the pattern of recovery for this species is similar to that of Merck's rhinoceros, brown bear and large bovids. This has resulted in small bones of the hand and feet being very well represented, accounting for 18.2% (n=58) of the beaver material (Bratlund 1999, 130).

The faunal assemblage present at the Forschungsstation für Quartärpaläontologie numbers 4433 pieces. It comprises a very diverse fauna. An overview of the collection is provided in table 6.1. As stated, the dominant species are Merck's rhinoceros and brown bear. Other abundant species are large bovids and beaver. In addition to the species that are present in the collection presented by Bratlund, other species have in the past been reported as hailing from Taubach, these are also listed in table 6.1. Of these, it should be noted that the actual remains are now lost and only those belonging to leopard (*Panthera pardus*) have been published. Moreover, some remains of mammoth (*Mammuthus primigenius*) and reindeer (*Rangifer tarandus*) are present in museum collections that are said to come from the site. They are probably derived from different deposits though (Bratlund 1999, 84). Bratlund did not study the remains of small animals, like birds and reptiles, but they are rare (Bratlund 1999, 84). However, (large) mammals were the focus of collection activities, so the small animals present will have been severely biased against.

Since the spatial distribution of the archaeological finds cannot be studied anymore, the opportunities to conduct taphonomic studies in order to determine what natural processes may have contributed to the formation of the bone assemblage are severely limited. Furthermore, we do not know how the bones were distributed in relation to the artefacts and so-called Brandschichten. Therefore, we can only use modifications on the bones themselves to infer hominin activities (Bratlund 1999, 86-97). In the past, researchers have tried to reconstruct hominin hunting and transport behaviour, based on the bone-categories present in the samples. For example, it was thought that since ribs and vertebrae of Merck's rhinoceros were not represented at the site, they were killed at some distance of the site and brought in. However, this pattern seems to have been a product of the collection methods. Apparently ribs were not very valuable commercially for the quarry workers and thus were not collected. When people started looking for them, apparently ribs were found in abundant numbers (Behm-Blancke 1960, 207). Because of the collection bias, body part representation in the assemblage will not tell us much about Neanderthal hunting strategies, I will not go into this in detail here (for information see Bratlund 1999). Table 6.1 thus provides an insight into what prey species were available. In addition to the information we can glean from the species that were present, we must also keep in mind that plants were available, though we do not know their importance (Behm-Blancke 1960, Wenzel 2002).

The most abundant species present at the site also provide us with most indications for hominin activities. Brown bear (*Ursus arctos*), Merck's rhinoceros, bison (*Bison priscus*) and beaver account for 90% of the sample. Between 6 and 12% of the bones of these species were cut-marked, except for brown bear, which stands at 26% (Bratlund 1999, 91). Another bone modification that can be attributed to hominin influence is charring, which shows that the bone was in very close contact with fire. The charred bone sample is also dominated by Merck's rhinoceros and brown bear (Bratlund 1999, 87). Breakage of bones in order to exploit their marrow content cannot be studied in the assemblage, since collection focused on undamaged bones. However, Tafel XXXVI in (Eichhorn 1909) shows the distal ends of five broken metatarsi of bison, demonstrating that bones were broken for marrow at the site. How regular the behaviour was can unfortunately no longer be reconstructed.

Indications for hominin activities on bones of other species are rare. This is partly due to the collection methods though. Many species are mainly represented by teeth and cranial fragments. They are durable elements and allow for easy species determination. However, they do not yield much information on their role in hominin or carnivore subsistence strategies. Out of 207 red deer (*Cervus elaphus*) specimens in the collection, only 11 are postcranial bones, 67 are isolated teeth and another important group is antlers (n=106). Of the postcranial bones, two, a talus and a phalange, show cut-marks. This means that if we discount the isolated teeth and antler specimens in the collections, about 6% of red deer bones are cut-marked (Bratlund 1999, 91). The collections of bones of other ungulates are small; most species do not show any cut-marks. However, some boar jaw fragments show impact scars, which may indicate hominin involvement with the bones. Horse is also represented mainly by teeth. Of the bones that are present, the meaty parts of the skeleton are underrepresented. However, one phalange exhibits a possible cut-mark (Bratlund 1999, 92).

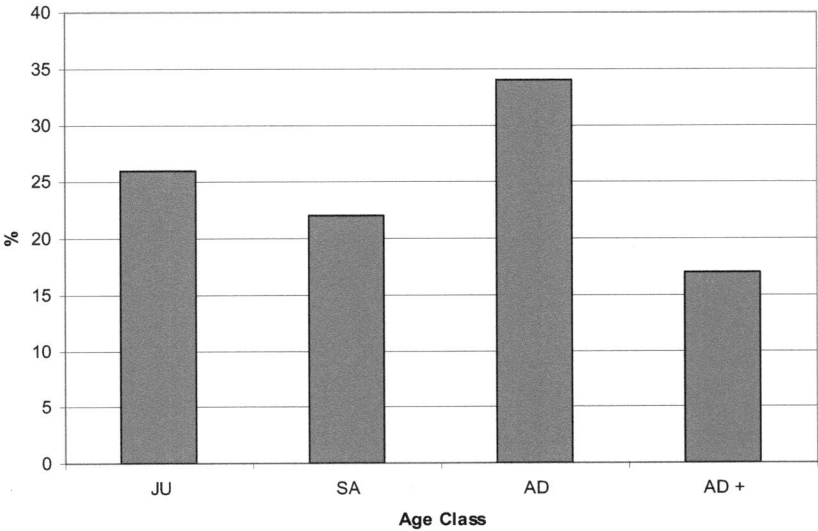

Figure 6.5: Age profile of straight-tusked elephant at Taubach. Data from (Bratlund 1999, 92). Ju: Juvenile; SA: subadult; AD: adult; AD+: Old adults.

Another indication that an assemblage is not a natural sample can be gleaned from the mortality profile of the species present, as discussed in chapter 3. The age-profile of the straight-tusked elephants from Taubach has been used to argue that elephants were hunted at the site despite the fact that cut-marks and impact scars are absent on the bones of the species. Figure 6.5 illustrates the age-structure of the population based on the examination of 99 elephant molars from Taubach. Unfortunately, some of the molars may have belonged to the same individual, affecting the reliability of the data (Guenther 1977, 282). However, it is immediately obvious that this age-distribution does not rerpresent a classic attritional profile, since adults are very well represented. The good representation of juveniles has been used as an argument supporting the fact that the assemblage was hunted (Guenther 1977, 283). Nevertheless, comparison of the Taubach age-profile with those of natural death assemblages shows that if anything juveniles are underrepresented in the Taubach assemblage (*e.g.* Haynes 1985, Haynes 1987). Assemblages with such a good representation of adults at Taubach are rare and it is this factor that in my opinion may be used in support of a hunting interpretation. A similar age-profile is known from the site of Ambrona though (Haynes 1987, 665-666). As discussed in chapter 3, at this site hominin involvement with the elephant assemblage appears to have been minimal. The mammoth site of Hot Springs in the United States provides another example of a natural death assemblage containing more adult and old individuals than would be expected (Haynes 1988, 665). Since a similar age-profile as that illustrated in figure 6.5 may arise in natural circumstances, the age-structure of the population of Taubach provides insufficient support for an interpretation of their remains in terms of hominin hunting.

Not only do the bones of the four most abundant species exhibit cut-marks, these occur patterned at specific locations, suggesting a systemised way of carcass exploitation. This would only be possible if hominins had the control over the carcass and could choose the parts they were exploiting, since already exploited carcasses would require ad hoc exploitation of the parts that were left. Therefore, scavenging is an untenable explanation for the formation of this assemblage.

The species that is represented by the largest number of bones is brown bear. Furthermore, this species exhibits the highest frequency of cut-marks. In terms of the Minimum Number of Individuals (MNI), 52 individuals are represented, making Merck's rhinoceros better represented in that respect. One of the reasons of the overrepresentation of this species in terms of NISP and cut-marks NISP is the abundance of hand and foot bones in the assemblage. As discussed in section 4.6, carnivores have 5 carpals, tarsals etc., while in herbivores these have been reduced in number. Moreover, these are very durable elements and therefore likely to survive in the archaeological record. This means that in terms of NISP, brown bear is overrepresented at this site. In bears, the cut-marks point to a standardised pattern of head removal and tongue extraction. The limbs were heavily filleted, even the paws (Bratlund 1999, 118). Cut-marks are present on 26% of

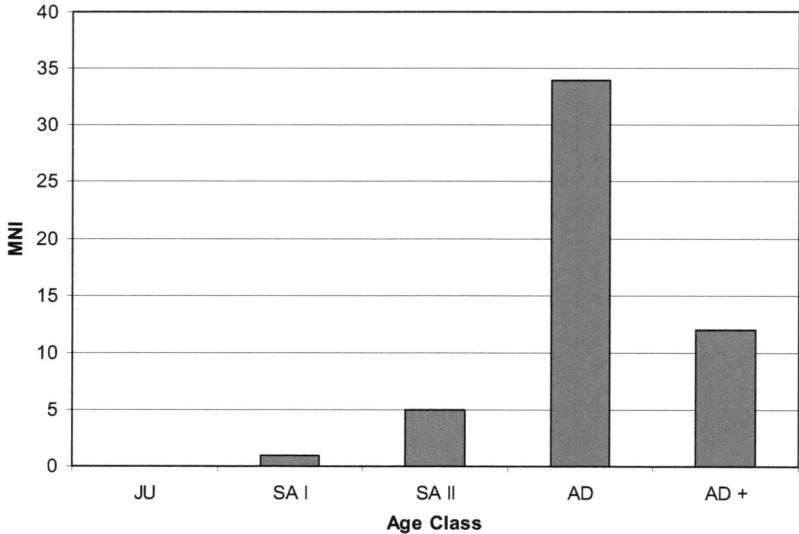

Figure 6.6: Age profile of brown bear from Taubach. Data from (Bratlund 1999, 113). Ju: Juvenile; SA: subadult; AD: adult; AD+: Old adults.

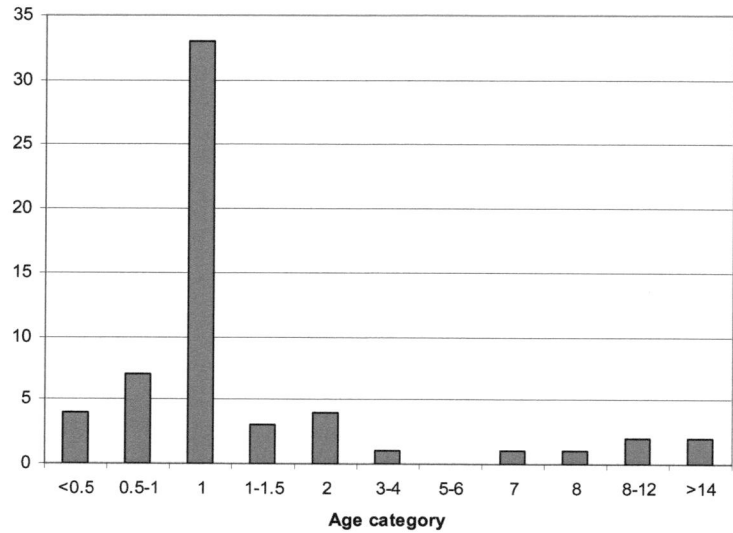

Figure 6.7: Age profile of Merck's rhinoceros from Taubach (N=65). Based on (Bratlund 1999, 100).

all bear bones, a percentage twice as high as in the other species; this is caused by the filleting of the paw bones. This pattern is consistent with fur exploitation of the animals (Auguste 1995a, 162). In contrast to the pattern seen in Merck's rhinoceros, in bears there is no concentration on young individuals, as shown in Figure 6.6 (Auguste 1995a, Bratlund 1999, 112-113). In this species therefore, prime-aged adults are the most heavily represented category.

The most abundant species, with respect to the MNI, represented in the assemblage is Merck's rhinoceros. However, a very small share of the bones classified as Merck's rhinoceros in the collections at the *Forschungsstation für Quartärpaläontologie* is considerably smaller than the rest of the rhinoceros bones (n=28). These probably represent narrow-nosed rhinoceros. As stated earlier, these two species often co-occur. Because the number of fragments is so small, they have been included in the Merck's rhinoceros sample (Bratlund 1999, 93-94). The species is represented by 1224 bones and the MNI has been estimated at 76 (Bratlund 1999, 93, 101). The exploitation of rhinoceros seems to have focused on separating the head from the body and removing the tongue, disarticulation of the carpal-metacarpal joints in the limbs, and filleting the longbones. Even the feet were skinned and filleted (Bratlund 1999, 107-108). Since the discovery of the site it has been apparent that young individuals dominate the rhinoceros assemblage (*e.g.* Behm-Blancke 1960, 201-203). Bratlund used the dentition of the assemblage to determine the age structure and in the collection studied by her, there were 44 calves, 7 subadult individuals and 25 adults (Bratlund 1999, 100). An age profile of this species is presented in figure 6.7 (Unfortunately Bratlund (1999) uses different age-categories than Louguet-Lefebvre (2005) applies to the Biache-Saint-Vaast assemblage).

The next best represented prey category comprises several species: the large bovids. The bones in the assemblage belong mainly to Bison, two subspecies of which were present: *Bison priscus priscus*, which predominated, and *Bison priscus mediator*. Furthermore, two or three postcranial bones belong to Bos primigenius. Concerning MNI's, adults are again in the majority, they are represented by at least 34 individuals. There are also at least 12 older individuals represented in the assemblage. Furthermore, one young animal and 5 older subadults are represented (Bratlund 1999, 123). The horncores at the site, as well as the majority of the bones belonged to males. Cut-marks are present mainly on carpals, tarsals and phalanges, but they are too small in number to make generalisations regarding the pattern of exploitation (Bratlund 1999).

The final species that shows traces of exploitation is beaver. Only 10 bones of this species show clear cut-marks, so as with the large bovids, a pattern of exploitation is hard to deduce (Bratlund 1999, 130). At least 17 individuals are present in the assemblage. Their age is hard to determine, however, it seems that most individuals represented were older subadults or adults (Bratlund 1999, 130-131).

The material studied by Bratlund and presented here forms only a small remnant of what must originally have been a huge assemblage. The good representation of a species like beaver in the bone assemblage, even with regard to its smaller bones, shows that collection bias with regard to species was not great. Only one species that was mentioned to be present in large numbers in early publications, the straight-tusked elephant, is not very well represented in the assemblage studied by Bratlund. The fauna was even originally named after this species and dubbed antiquus-fauna (*e.g.* Behm-Blancke 1960, Eichhorn 1909). In 1922, Soergel wrote that more than 100 rhinoceroses and more than 70 bears, as well as at least 64 elephants had been found at Taubach (in Behm-Blancke 1960, 204). However, I think this emphasis on elephant might in part be due to its size. If anything, the larger extinct species were specifically collected and should be overrepresented. Therefore, I deem it unlikely that straight-tusked elephant is underrepresented in the studied collection, but more likely that it was given an inordinate amount of attention in early publications.

According to Bratlund (1999, 150), the site may represent a salt lick that was of interest to rhinoceros. The fact that this was an area of higher salinity seems to be supported by the ostracod evidence. The enormous amount of material that was originally present shows that the site represents a palimpsest. As pointed out in chapter 4 this is advantageous with regard to the application of OFT to a site, because we can assume that short-term variations in prey availability have been averaged out.

6.6 The environment

Given the dating uncertainties surrounding this assemblage, reconstructing the environment of the site becomes slightly problematic because environmental differences between the late Saalian and early Eemian pollen phases may have been quite large. On the other hand, the large mammal assemblage also yields information about the nature of the environment. As argued in section 6.3, I will assume that the site dates to the early Eemian. In this section, I will summarise the environmental indicators we have for the site and the wider surroundings and propose a tentative scenario of what the environment of the site looked like at the time of the formation of the archaeological deposits.

The German travertines were formed during warm climatic phases. However, as stated above, some of the travertine build-up may have occurred during interstadials, as well as interglacials. At least we can therefore be certain that the climate was warm during the accumulation of the bone assemblage. The Taubach travertines were formed by warm water welling up at the edge of the Ilm river valley. From the valley's edge, it trickled down to the river. Because of the lowering temperature and pressure after surfacing, part of the calcium carbonate present in the water precipitated, forming the travertine deposits (Speleers 2000, Steiner 1977). The depositional circumstances varied drastically within the area of travertine build-up. Differential precipitation could change the local relief and change the direction in which the water flowed, which had consequences for later travertine formation. This resulted in differential deposition of travertines and in many horizontal and vertical facies changes (Steiner 1977,112). This means that sandy and indurated travertines were not necessarily deposited in different climatic conditions.

These warm water sources were probably an attractive location for Pleistocene hunter/gatherers. Moreover, these water sources would not freeze in winter. In contrast to most other German travertine deposits, leaf impressions are absent in the Taubach travertines. This suggests that the immediate environment of the area where the water welled up and deposited was open (Steiner 1977, 113). The travertine build-up took place in shallow bodies of water. However, the occurrence of ash-lenses or hearths and land snails in the bone sand suggests that the ponds dried up periodically (Bratlund 1999, 67). The immediate environment of the site was therefore a marshy area, a *Rieselfeld* with streams of water trickling down from the terrace edge to the river valley. The water formed streams and periodically ponds in which the travertine was deposited. The exact configuration of these was very variable and the travertine deposition influenced the shape of the area and bodies of water.

Unfortunately, plant remains and pollen are not known from the deposits. Furthermore, as mentioned, micromammals were not recovered from the bone sand sensu stricto, only from the overlying mollusc sand. Molluscs from the lower layers of the bone sand have been studied however (see fig. 6.3 for a schematic profile with the sampling locations). Their implications with regard to the dating of the site have already been discussed. In this section I will go into the evidence that the molluscs provide with regard to the environment of the site.

Sample numbers 901 upwards to 905 are of interest (see fig. 6.3). Sample 901 is quite small, only containing 35 molluscs, but the other samples under consideration contained several hundred specimens (Zeissler 1977). As discussed previously, the mollusc samples can be grouped in two categories. Firstly, samples 901 to 903 show species indicative of high mountains and continental steppes, indicating a climate that was colder than nowadays. In the other group, from sample 902 upward, warm species are very well represented (Zeissler 1977, 155). This indicates a hiatus in the stratigraphic sequence, since such transitions tend to take place gradually. Furthermore as molluscs have a low dispersal rate, it would take them time after a climatic improvement to establish themselves in the region. From sample 903 onwards they are clearly well established in the region.

Evidence regarding the vegetation of the site is absent. However, at a regional level, studies of pollen can yield important insights in the vegetation present. Cores have been analysed from the sites of Gröbern, Grabschütz and Neumark Nord, which are not too distant from the site. Other sites that were studied include Bispingen from Northern Germany, La Grande Pile in France and Dziewule in Poland (*e.g.* Binka and Nitychoruk 2003, Guiot *et al.* 1992, Kühl and Litt 2003, Litt 1990, Litt, Junge, and Böttger 1996). The pollen-sequence of the Eemian is quite well known and is uniform over large areas of western and central Europe (*e.g.* Kühl and Litt 2003, 206). Pollen cores have demonstrated the successive colonization of Europe by different tree species. The Eemian has been subdivided into pollen stages according to the dominant tree species. Reconstructions of the Eemian climate and environment can therefore be made with reasonable confidence. There is some discussion however, about the stability of the climate in the Eemian and the best method to reconstruct climate based on the pollen cores (Cheddadi *et al.* 1998, Kühl and Litt 2003, Litt, Junge, and Böttger 1996). Characteristic of full Eemian climatic circumstances is the spread of climatically sensitive species like Holly (*Ilex*), Ivy (*Hedera*), Mistletoe (*Viscum*), Box (*Buxus*) and honeysuckle (*Lonicera*) (Litt, Junge, and Böttger 1996, Wenzel 2002). In this study, the early pollen-phases of the Eemian are of relevance.

The following picture can be painted combining the known pollen sequences from central Germany and further afield. (See fig 5. for the pollen sequence found at Gröbern which offers an example of these developments.) The melting of the ice in the late Saalian signals a start of temperate conditions with reasonably high summer and winter temperatures. This warming up is interrupted by the Kattegat-stadial and a return to very cold and dry conditions. This stadial lasts for about 1000 years, after which temperatures rise rapidly (Beets, Beets, and Cleveringa 2006). The earliest phase of the Eemian is characterised by the expansion of pioneer species, most notably birch (*Betula*). Study of varve counts has shown that this phase has a short duration of about 100 years (Kühl and Litt 2003). The second phase of the Eemian is still dominated by pioneer species. In addition to birch, pine (*Pinus*) now becomes important, this phase is therefore known as the *Pinus-Betula* stage. It has a duration of about 200 years. In the third phase of the Eemian, deciduous trees start making their appearance in northwestern Europe. The most ubiquitous of these species is oak

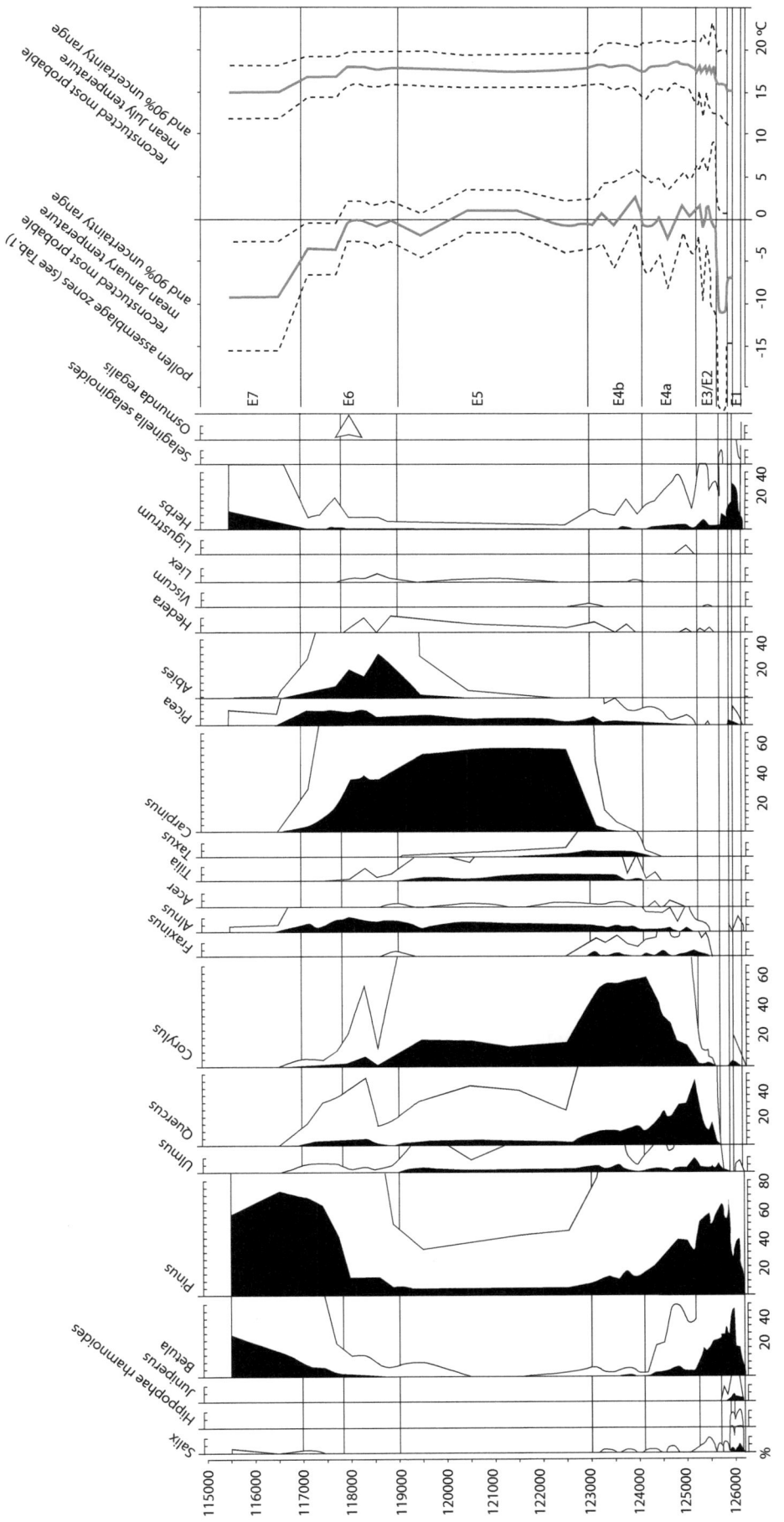

Figure 6.8 Simplified pollen diagram of Gröbern. Redrawn after (Kühl & Litt 2003, 207).

(*Quercus*), which is why this phase is dubbed *Pinus Quercetum mixtum*. Other species of tree present are ash (*Fraxinus*) and elm (*Ulmus*). This phase lasts for about 450 years (*e.g.* Kühl and Litt 2003, Litt, Junge, and Böttger 1996). The later phases show the subsequent expansion of dominance of hazel (*Corylus*), then hornbeam (*Carpinus*) and fir (*Abies*). These phases have a longer duration than the earlier pioneer phases. The *Corylus* phase lasts about 2200 years, the *Carpinus* phase about 4000. Then the climate cools somewhat in the later part of the Eemian. Fir and spruce (*Picea*) make their appearance in the sixth phase. This phase lasts about 2000 years. The seventh and final pollen stage of the Eemian also lasts about 2000 years and is again dominated by pine (Kühl and Litt 2003, Litt, Junge, and Böttger 1996).

As said, most archaeological finds at Taubach probably date to the earlier pollen phases. The combination of the mollusc evidence with the presence of species requiring relatively warm environments like the pond turtle might point to a date at the end of the pioneer phases, in phase three when deciduous trees already become important in the pollen-diagrams. However, reconstructions of the January and July temperatures show that temperatures increased very steeply in the first pollen phase with mean January temperatures already at 0 degrees for Bispingen and La Grande Pile. It is thought that the highest July temperatures of the interglacial were reached in the early stages of the Eemian. This is shown by the early appearance of many thermophilous taxa (*e.g.* Binka and Nitychoruk 2003, 164). In pollen phase three mean January temperatures were higher than today with an average of +2 °C at Gröbern and July temperatures of 17-18 °C (see right hand columns in figure 6.8 (Kühl and Litt 2003, 210)). It seems therefore that climatic circumstances improved drastically from the earliest phases of the Eemian onwards. Temperatures rose steeply already in the first phase of the Eemian and the highest temperatures were reached in the Quercus phase of the Eemian. The absence of a climax fauna in the mollusc remains can therefore be explained as the result of a lag effect due to low dispersal speeds.

With regard to the occupation of Eemian environment, it is important to know how closed the environment was, since it has been proposed that Neanderthals could not deal with a densely forested environment. An important indicator for the openness of the environment is the ratio between arboreal and non-arboreal pollen. Traditionally, values of non-arboreal pollen of 10% and lower are interpreted as evidence for closed forest. On the other hand, the relationship between the amount of non-arboreal pollen and environmental openness is not very straightforward and would ideally be supplemented by additional environmental data (*e.g.* Svenning 2002, 135). In the Gröbern diagram, during the first pollen phase of the Eemian, non-arboreal pollen represent over 20% of the pollen spectrum. This decreases during phase 1 reaches about 10% during phase 2, only to drop to very low levels during the last part of phase 2. From pollen phase three up until the end of pollen phase 7, non-arboreal pollen values are lower than 10% (Litt 1990). This suggests that the environment of Gröbern was covered with forest from at least phase 2 of the Eemian. The forest became ever more closed during this period and was definitely closed from phase 3 onward.

In recent years, there has been discussion about how closed European interglacial forests were before humans started to have an impact. Based on the proportions of arboreal and non-arboreal pollen in pollen cores they were thought to have been closed. However, based on some of the herbivores that were present during these periods, it has been proposed that the environment contained more open spaces than indicated by the pollen evidence. These open spaces were created and maintained by large herbivores. This would have resulted in a woodland pasture type of vegetation (*e.g.* Birks 2005, 154).

This discussion has been resolved by looking at the Holocene situation. In this period, oak and hazel were important constituents of the European flora. They need canopy openings in order to reproduce. The question is whether treefalls would provide enough openings in order for these species to regenerate. In the Holocene, this was the case because in Ireland and in Zealand in Denmark, large herbivores were absent, while proportions of oak and hazel in pollen cores were similar to those in the rest of Europe (Birks 2005, Svenning 2002). Therefore, for the Holocene, the discussion seems to be settled in favour of a more closed environment. The fact that hazel and oak remain present in reasonably large percentages in the pollen spectra suggests that treefalls and fire may have provided enough openings in the canopy for them to reproduce. Furthermore, there are some niches, like steep slopes for hazel and poor acidic soils for oak where they do better than the competition, so they may have maintained a presence in these niches that is reflected in the pollen cores (Svenning 2002, 139). Finally, beaver is a species of animal that was present in the Holocene and that produces open patches in the landscape along streams. This species feeds on trees and has been known to fell trees with diameters of up to 1 metre (Collen and Gibson 2000, 443). This species may therefore have created open spaces in Ireland and Denmark.

In the Eemian, we have a different situation because more large herbivores are present. At Taubach, we are dealing with elephants, two species of rhinoceros, giant deer and horses in addition to the traditional European herbivores like aurochs, bison and deer. A review of pollen research of interglacial sites in northwestern Europe shows that most lakes that sampled an upland environment show evidence of a closed environment. However, some areas, like river valleys show higher amounts of non-arboreal pollen, up to 40%. The same seems to be true for sites with poor soils such as calcareous uplands and sandy areas (Svenning 2002). Moreover, the composition of Eemian forests was slightly different from the Holocene ones. Most important is the fact that the role of the European beech (Fagus sylvatica) was smaller in the Eemian than in the Holocene. Beech is a plant that is particularly shade-loving: it grows in dark forests and young specimens do not grow well in light conditions. However, in the Eemian the main shade-producing trees seem to have been hornbeam and fir. These species need lighter conditions during their phase as young trees (Wenzel 2002, 48). Therefore, we can assume that the Eemian forests were closed, but that open spaces were present and to a larger degree than in the Holocene.

The presence of certain species of animal in the assemblage allows us to draw some conclusions about the specific environment at Taubach. First, there is the aforementioned European pond turtle; this species'presence at the site points to the summer temperatures being quite high (18° C in July) and winters being mild, and at least to winters without prolonged periods of severe frost (*e.g.* Van Kolfschoten 2000). Furthermore, the presence of wild boar may be significant. This species range limit is now on the northern European plain, which points to it being at least in part climatically restricted (Van Kolfschoten 1995, 78). The fact this species is present at Taubach suggests that it cannot have been much colder at the time of the deposition of the assemblage than it is nowadays.

Some species present require a forested environment. I already discussed Merck's rhinoceros as a forest indicator. Straight-tusked elephant is also usually found with forest indicators (Bratlund 1999, 78). Of the extant fauna, roe deer, wild boar, beaver, brown bear, lynx and badger are forest indicators (Bratlund 1999, Svenning 2002). On the other hand, some species present prefer open environments. Important among these are narrow-nosed rhinoceros and horse. Lion and hyena also avoid dense forests nowadays, although they do live in woodlands (Bratlund 1999, Svenning 2002). In this respect it is important to note that the traditional forest indicators are much better represented at the site than indicators of open environments. A quick inventory of the environment suggests mosaic vegetation near the site, with a dominance of woodland environment, but also open spaces.

A species that would have had enormous influence on the environment would have been the straight-tusked elephant. Elephants are nowadays considered keystone species that actively modify their environments and by these modifications also influence the actions of other species in the environment (*e.g.* Haynes 2006). Firstly, elephants feed in bulk: on average African elephants consume about 150 to 250 kg. every day. This would have a great impact on the vegetation. Furthermore, elephants actively influence the landscape by building mineral licks and maintaining waterholes (Haynes 2006, 27). At Taubach these activities may have been important for the direct environment of the site. Another species that would have an important influence on the area directly surrounding the site is beaver. The presence of beaver may have resulted in an absence or a decrease in the number of trees in the immediate vicinity. However, this species needs woody vegetation to feed and it rarely feeds further than 100 metres away from water (Collen and Gibson 2000, 443). Therefore we can conclude that, even though leaf impressions are absent at Taubach, in the wider environment forest was the dominant type of vegetation.

The immediate environment of the site has been described as savannah-like because of the absence of leaf impressions (Steiner 1977, Steiner and Wiefel 1977). However, we may assume that forest was the dominant vegetation type in the wider environment. From Eemian pollen phase 2 onwards, the environment at nearby sites seems to be quite closed. Nevertheless, the Eemian forests in general were of a slightly less dense character than in the Holocene. At Taubach this impression is reinforced by the presence of horse, some narrow-nosed rhinoceros and straight-tusked elephant.

6.7 Applying OFT to Taubach

After presenting an overview of the environment and the bone assemblage of the site we will analyse the data using the methodology of diet breadth described in chapter 4. At this site the interesting problem is to see how Neanderthals dealt with forested environments where biomass is mostly locked up in tree trunks and leaves (*e.g.* Binford 2001, 106). Actual mammal biomass is very low, less than 0.5 tonne per kilometre in European temperate forests. More open environments may offer much more herbivore biomass for human hunter/gatherers to exploit (Delpech 1999, 22). Biomass may have been slightly higher in the Eemian than in the Holocene, because the forests had a more open character, but the proportions of arboreal and non-arboreal pollen at nearby sites leave no doubt that the dominant vegetation type was forest.

An important factor we need to consider when analysing the diet breadth at the site is the site's function. As pointed out in chapters 3 & 4, transport decisions may have an important influence on which bones end up at which sites. Debates as to whether the animals were killed on site or were transported to the site from some distance have taken place in the past. The processing of all skeletal parts is strongly suggestive of a kill site. Furthermore, the presence of hearths at kill sites is not uncommon in the ethnographic record, so their presence need not be an indication of the site functioning as a central place (Bratlund 1999, 135).

As argued, because of the very large amounts of material recovered, the site probably represents a palimpsest formed over a long time. Another indication for this is the fact that bears and rhinoceros live solitarily nowadays. Many different episodes of exploitation must therefore be represented. According to (Bratlund 1999, 135), sustainable exploitation of both bears and rhinoceros would allow at most 4 or 5 kills per year. In view of the amount of material of these species recovered at the site, we can conclude that the assemblage reflects a long history of occupations. This is especially true since the collection Bratlund studied represents only a fraction of the original assemblage. Therefore we can assume that the site exhibits a time-averaged ranking of animals and short-term fluctuations in ranking will have been averaged out.

Based on animal weights, we would expect the heaviest species to be the most high-ranked one and the less the species weigh, the lower they would be ranked. Table 6.2 gives an overview of reconstructed body weights of the animals found at Taubach. If the ranking used by Neanderthals were based on body weight alone, we would expect Neanderthals to exploit a number of the heavier species. Since body weight is inversely related to population density (*e.g.* Silva, Brown, and Downing 1997), the heaviest species are expected to be quite rare. Therefore, a number of species would need to be exploited in order to lower encounter rates sufficiently to ensure a steady supply of food.

With regard to the currency used by the hominins responsible for the Taubach assemblage, a few things can be noted immediately. It is clear that this ranking does not explain all the exploitation patterns seen in the Taubach assemblage. As pointed out in chapter 4, this ranking based on animal weight alone is a simplification. Still, weight does seem to be an important criterion among hunter/gatherers when selecting prey. From this ranking it is clear that at Taubach the exploited species, except for beaver, were among the heaviest in the environment.

On the other hand, the heaviest species, straight-tusked elephant, may not have been exploited. The bone sample of the species does not show indications of hominin involvement, bar one charred piece (Bratlund 1999, 87). However, the species was apparently considered an important constituent of the site in early publications and its presence in the collections was interpreted as the result of hominin hunting (*e.g.* Behm-Blancke 1960). As stated above, it has been argued that the sample is dominated by young individuals, like the sample of Merck's rhinoceros (Bratlund 1999, 92). However as shown by Fig 6.5, this pattern is much less pronounced than in the Merck's rhinoceros sample. Although we do not see a "classic" attritional mortality profile in this species, it is based on a small sample. Moreover, since traces of exploitation are absent, I do not think this provides a convincing argument for the hunting of straight-tusked elephant.

Nevertheless, taking caloric value as currency they would be expected to be the highest ranked species and to have been exploited on encounter in traditional OFT models. Moreover, the species is represented by quite a large amount of material, while as the heaviest species it would be expected to be present in the lowest population densities. This can be partly explained by taphonomic factors. Their bones are the largest and collection was therefore probably biased in favour of their recovery. Furthermore as an exotic species they may have received even more attention than would be expected solely on the basis of their size.

Rank	Species	Weight	NISP
1	Palaeoloxodon antiquus	5495	182
2	Stephanorhinus kirchbergensis	2000	1224
3	Bison priscus	687[25]	533
4	Ursus spelaeus	500	7
5	Megaloceros giganteus	450[26]	6
6	Ursus arctos	400	1537
7	Equus caballus	335	161
8	Cervus elaphus	200[27]	207
9	Panthera spelaea	195	5
10	Crocuta crcocuta	69	1
11	Sus scrofa	89	96
12	Panthera pardus	60[28]	lost
13	Canis lupus	45	7
14	Capreolus capreolus	23[29]	58
15	Lynx lynx	20	lost
16	Castor fiber	18	319
17	Meles meles	10	lost
18	Lutra lutra	7	lost

Table 6.2: Reconstructed ranking of the species represented at Taubach, according to animal body weight.

Other heavy species whose bones do not show traces of exploitation are giant deer and cave bear (*Ursus spelaeus*). On the other hand, these species are rare in the assemblage, so we cannot be sure that they would not have been exploited when encountered. One of the explanations for the absence of these indications on their bones could be that they were very rare in the environment and were therefore almost never encountered. Therefore, their bones did not end up at the site in greater numbers. It seems that giant deer was a mixed feeder, browsing as well as grazing, but it is usually found in combination with indicators of an open environment (Bratlund 1999, 74). Furthermore, their big antlers would at least have prevented male giant deer from moving through dense woodland (Stuart *et al.* 2004, 684). Cave bear appears to be a species that can cope with a closed environment, so there is no reason to assume that it was rare in the area (Bocherens and Drucker 2003, 5). Therefore, its absence from the diet may have other causes.

Adopting weight as currency, the exploitation of Merck's rhinoceros is to be expected. It is the second heaviest species in the environment, weighing in at 2000 kilos,. Both hunting using traps and confrontational hunting have been documented ethnographically for rhinoceros (Bratlund 1999, 138-141). Merck's rhinoceros was slightly larger and heavier than the modern African white rhinoceros. Older calves, which form the majority of the MNI at Taubach, were probably independent of their mothers, if their life-histories resemble those of extant species of rhinoceros. They would be about two-thirds of the size of the adults (Bratlund 1999, 142-144). Since traps do not preferentially select for age classes (Bratlund 1999, 143), at least the rhinoceroses will have been captured by confrontational hunting. The behaviour of rhinoceroses has been subject of much discussion. They are often said to be dangerous, but with a view to modern African rhinoceros this seems exaggerated (Bratlund 1999, Despart-Estes 1991).

Bison is also among the heaviest species in the environment. Moreover, the focus of exploitation was on adult males (Bratlund 1999, 149), which are considerably heavier than the females. This species is thus among the highest ranked available prey species. Moreover, adult males are the individuals most likely to be encountered alone; therefore hunting them may not be as dangerous as hunting a herd of females (Bratlund 1999, 150).

The exploitation of brown bear, ranked as the 6th heaviest species, was intensive. It is represented by a large number of individuals and almost 300 brown bear bones exhibit cut-marks. Hunting brown bear is nowadays considered to be very dangerous. Ethnographically it is known that as soon as guns became available, traditional methods of bear hunting were usually rapidly abandoned in favour of hunting with and guns. Many of the traditional methods were focused on two specific things: keeping the bear from fleeing and preventing the bear from focusing on specific targets.

---

25 Estimate taken from Macdonald (2006). The weight provided by Brook and Bowman (2004) is quite low (523 kg.) Macdonald (2006) provides the following weights: for American bison (*Bison bison*) females: 545 kg., males 818 kg. For European bison (*Bison bonasus*) males: 800 kg. Since males were the focus of hunting at Taubach this estimate is used.

26 Estimate taken from Louguet-Lefebvre (2005). The estimate provided by Brook and Bowman (2004) (700 kg.) is higher than all other estimates I encountered, the estimate from Louguet-Lefebvre (2005) seems more reasonable, although Pushkina and Raia. (2008) provide a lower one (387 kg.).

27 Estimate taken from Pushkina and Raia. (2008), since Brook and Bowman (2004) provide a very high estimate (500 kg.).

28 Estimate taken from Pushkina and Raia.(2008), since Brook and Bowman (2004) provide a very high estimate (90 kg.).

29 Estimate taken from Pushkina and Raia. (2008), since Brook and Bowman (2004) provide a very high estimate (30 kg.).

Spears were then used to kill it (Bratlund 1999, 147). In addition to the danger of catching it, eating bear meat may also have been dangerous. Since bears scavenge a lot of meat, many of them are infected with the porkworm, a parasite that can cause prolonged illness and even death in humans (Bratlund 1999, 147). Bratlund hypothesizes that bears may have been hunted when they appeared at a kill site to scavenge the remains of previous hominin kills (Bratlund 1999, 150).

Brown bears have a yearly activity cycle that can point to the likely season of their exploitation. In winter, brown bears hibernate, in late winter and early spring they have exhausted their winter fat stores and are very lean. Therefore, from an OFT perspective their ranking in this season will be quite low and exploitation unlikely. In autumn however, they will be building up fat reserves in order to survive the winter. At this time, their caloric value will be at its highest. On the other hand, the ranking used by a predator is based on more than caloric yield. Killing these animals during hibernation would also be an interesting option, since this would considerably lower the risk and possibly the search time associated with the hunt. The problem with this possibility is the fact that I deem it unlikely that the bears hibernated in the travertine field itself. Therefore, their bones would have been transported to the site from the denning sites. It would seem more logical to process the animals on the spot instead of transporting them. In that case one would expect to see a clearer focus on meat-bearing parts at the site and fewer hand and foot bones. Since this did not happen, we may assume that the bears were hunted in the vicinity of the site.

In autumn, if bears are amassing fat reserves they are more likely to try and scavenge hominin kills as hypothesised by Bratlund. Moreover, it is likely that they would also be aggressive and were more likely to attack hominins themselves during this period (e.g. \Quammen, 2005, 305-306; http://www.mala.bc.ca/www/discover/rmot/project.htm). Therefore, encounter rate with this species will be elevated. In combination with their aggressive behaviour this may have led to Neanderthals preferentially killing them in this season.

The exploitation of red deer is problematic. It is present in reasonably large numbers in the assemblage and two of the remains bear cut-marks. This indicates that there was at least some interference of hominins with bones of this species. On the other hand, the species was not heavily exploited. This is quite strange, since it is a large herbivore that has been exploited at many sites during the Palaeolithic (*e.g.* Steele 2004). On the other hand, it is a lot lighter than the other exploited species, therefore in normal situations it was probably not in the set of exploited species.

The number of red deer bones found at the site is not only lower than that of the other exploited species, but it is also severely biased. 106 of the pieces are antlers, of which 11 were unshed and 57 were shed. Another 67 pieces were isolated teeth, which do not usually bear signs of exploitation. This makes the significance of red deer exploitation even harder to assess, since the bones that might reveal exploitation are underrepresented. The smaller species yield similar assemblages and their bones do not show uncontroversial signs of exploitation (Bratlund 1999, 91-92).

In the case of red deer we must assume that the species was not very important to hominins. The fact that a smaller species like beaver is better represented in the assemblage shows that we cannot attribute the paucity of red deer bones wholly to a collection bias. The shed antlers and many of the bone fragments may well be part of the natural background fauna, since for example male cervids apparently spend the winters in low lying areas rich in water sources where winter kills are often significant. Because many of these animals die near sources of water trampling of their remains was probably commonplace. This may be an additional factor why there is a dominance of cranial bones, teeth and antler fragments among the cervids (Barnosky 1985, 340, 343).

The exploitation of beaver, which is one of the smallest mammals present in the assemblage, is striking. Caloric value alone cannot explain the presence of large amount of beaver material in the assemblage. This intuitively seems to be a clear example of a species being exploited for nonfood yields, i.e. its fur. On the other hand, beaver meat is apparently of great nutritional value, due to high concentrations of proteins, minerals and poly-unsaturated fatty acids (Jankowska *et al.* 2005). Furthermore, in autumn, its nutritional value and thus its ranking increases because large amounts of fat are stored in the tails (Macdonald 2006, 144). Only ten cut-marks were found on beaver bones. Most of these seem to point to disarticulation and filleting. However, three cut-marks on mandibles seem to be the result of skinning of the animal (Bratlund 1999, 132).

In order to gain insight in the diet breadth that was practised at Taubach, we also need to calculate in the encounter rate and handling cost of the available species. As with Biache-Saint-Vaast, the encounter rate of the species will be modelled by reconstructing their population densities using the correlation between body size and population density provided by Silva, Brimacombe, and Downing

(2001). Handling cost will again be modelled by looking at whether species were carnivores or not, body size of species and whether species lived in groups or solitarily.

Population density determines what the encounter rate of a species was, but the encounter rate of a species cannot be used to predict its exploitation. The diet breadth model states that the most highly ranked species will always be exploited. When their encounter rate is low, species will be added to the optimal set, but highly ranked species will not be dropped from the set (MacArthur and Pianka 1966). Estimating population densities for a Pleistocene animal assemblage with extinct species is speculative. It appears that across mammals there is a significant correlation between body weight and population density (*e.g.* Eisenberg 1990, Silva, Brimacombe, and Downing 2001, Silva, Brown, and Downing 1997). This does not explain all variability in population densities, but does seem to be the major variable determining mammal population densities (Silva, Brimacombe, and Downing 2001, 475-477). A second important variable is the dietary specialisation of an animal species (Eisenberg 1990, Silva, Brimacombe, and Downing 2001). I have reconstructed the population densities for the species represented in the Taubach assemblage (table 6.3) using the equations provided by Silva, Brimacombe, and Downing (2001, 477)[30]. It must be realised though, that these are only rough estimates of average population densities. Population densities can vary tremendously between populations of a species, for example because of circumstances in the local habitat. The numbers here reflect the expected population density for a species with a specific body weight and diet, in their typical habitat. If Taubach was at the edge of a species' range, this may have had important consequences for its population density.

As can be seen all the exploited species, except beaver, have quite low population densities. Moreover, the extent of beaver habitat in the environment was limited, consisting of the Ilm River and the wetland area where the travertine was forming. Therefore the beaver population in the area that was exploited from this site may not have been very large. Furthermore, in the case of bison and rhinoceros a specific sex and age class of the population was targeted, further limiting the number of available prey animals. If we assume that Neanderthals exploited an area up to 10 kilometres away from the site, as modern day hunter/gatherers do (*e.g.* Vita-Finzi and Higgs 1970), this area would contain a rhinoceros population of about 48 animals in the 314 km² of territory available to them. As argued earlier, the territory was probably smaller due to locomotion costs being 30% higher in Neanderthals than in modern humans. If we assume an exploitation distance of maximally 7 kilometres from the site this would amount to a territory of 154 km². In that case the rhinoceros population in the territory would probably number around 23 or 24 animals. Because of their selectivity in age class, only a few animals would be available for exploitation. Bison, of which only the adult males were exploited, presents a similar situation.

Diet breadth was thus narrow and the species that were exploited were present in low population densities. This leads to the supposition that despite low population densities and dispersed resources (cf. Gamble 1999, 228-229), the hominins responsible for the Taubach assemblage were able to manipulate the encounter rates with suitable prey well. They were apparently able to predictably encounter and dispatch juvenile rhinoceros, adult male bison, adult bears and beaver, without having to add other more common species to the diet. In view of the reconstructed population densities, targeted exploitation of elephants becomes less likely. They are present at half the density of Merck's rhinoceros. Therefore, if

Species	Density (ind/km²)
Palaeoloxodon antiquus	0.075
Stephanorhinus kirchbergensis	0.15
Bison priscus	0.31
Ursus spelaeus	0.384
Megaloceros giganteus	0.413
Ursus arctos	0.19
Equus caballus	0.505
Cervus elaphus	0.717
Panthera spelaea	0.063
Crocuta crcocuta	0.04
Sus scrofa	1.243
Panthera pardus	0.045
Canis lupus	0.053
Capreolus capreolus	3.119
Lynx lynx	0.118
Castor fiber	3.685
Meles meles	0.331
Lutra lutra	0.616

Table 6.3: Reconstructed population densities for the species present in the Taubach assemblage.

---

30 The equations used are: Herbivores: Log D = 1.42 – 0.68(Log M); Carnivores: Log D = 1.41 – 1.83(Log M) – 0.34(Log M²) + 0.28(Log M³). Since no equation is provided for omnivores, I decided to treat brown bear as a carnivore and wild boar as a herbivore. I used the weights supplied by Brook and Bowman (2004).

they had been exploited one would have expected this species to be better represented in the assemblage.

In the case of rhinoceros and bears, 4-5 kills of a population per year is the maximum for sustainable exploitation of a population according to Bratlund (1999, 135). Given the fact that the collection Bratlund studied represents only a fraction of the original assemblage, the site must reflect a successful hunting strategy that was in use for a long period of time. The exploitation of this area was prolonged and represented an economically very efficient strategy of meat acquisition.

In addition to the encounter rate, another important consideration on whether to exploit animal species is their handling cost. As explained in chapter 4, this represents the combined effect of the hunting and processing skills of the hunter and the anti-predator skills of the prey. High handling cost lower the overall return rate. Therefore, handling cost may influence the ranking of prey species. In order to get an indication of handling cost I scored the animal species on the basis of a few characteristics. The modelling of handling cost using these characteristics aims to show whether they influenced a species' handling cost. If species that score positive for the characteristics are nevertheless exploited we can conclude that Neanderthals possessed strategies to deal effectively with their impact on a species' handling cost.

Very important in the handling cost is the risk associated with hunting dangerous animals. I designated carnivorous species to be extra risky. I assume that they are more dangerous to hunt than herbivores. I assigned cave bears to the carnivores since they fall within the order of carnivores and they did possess carnivore "weapons", like claws and large teeth. Another attribute that I correlate with hunting risk is the size of the animal. I also assume that larger animals are more dangerous than smaller ones. I took a weight of 300 kilo's as a threshold, above which animals get a "danger bonus". This is the weight of the expected maximum size of prey for a mammalian carnivore of the same weight as a Neanderthal. A third variable is whether animals are solitary or whether they live in groups. I assume that animals living in groups hold a greater advantage when faced with predators than solitary animals. This is because in a group chances of early perception of predators increases and because animals moving in a group will usually have to be isolated before a kill can be attempted. Table 6.4 summarises the scores.

Species	Size	Carnivore	In group	
			Male	Female
Palaeoloxodon antiquus	+	-	-	+
Dicerorhinus kirchbergensis	+	-	-	-
Bison priscus	+	-	-	+
Ursus spelaeus	+	+	-	+
Megaloceros giganteus	+	-	-	-
Ursus arctos	+	+	-	+
Equus caballus	+	-	-	-
Cervus elaphus	-	-	+	+
Panthera spelaea	-	+	+	+
Crocuta crocuta	-	+	-	-
Sus scrofa	-	-	-?	+
Panthera pardus	-	+	+	+
Canis lupus	-	+	+	+
Capreolus capreolus	-	-	-	+
Lynx lynx	-	+	-	-
Castor fiber	-	-	+	+
Meles meles	-	+	?	?
Lutra lutra	-	+	?	?

Table 6.4: Handling cost attributes. Species that are marked with + in categories are deemed to have increased handling cost due to their size, carnivorous "weapons" or social structure.

In this table, brown bear is ranked as dangerous because it is a carnivore. Since it is over 300 kilos it also qualifies for the "weight bonus". Cave bear also scores as dangerous because of its size and because it is a carnivore. However, since cave bear is even larger than brown bear it may have been more dangerous, even though this is not expressed in table 6.4. This can be a reason why it was left alone. Merck's rhinoceros and male bisons are both very large animals, but are also solitary. Furthermore, in the case of Merck's rhinoceros concentrating on juvenile individuals diminishes the danger of hunting them.

Male elephants only score positive for the "weight bonus". On the other hand, as they are more than twice as heavy as Merck's rhinoceros, we can hypothesize that these animals were simply too large and dangerous. The Neanderthals responsible for the bone assemblage focussed on juvenile rhinoceroces presumably to lower the risk to themselves. Juvenile elephants are found in the maternal herds and are therefore well protected. Full-grown solitary males are the largest and most dangerous individuals around and will probably have been left alone for that reason.

This does not apply to male giant deer however. They are ranked in between the exploited species of bison and brown bear. There are a few reasons why they may not have been as highly ranked by hominins as the ranking on the basis of weight suggests. Firstly, in the males, which presumably lived solitarily, 10% of the weight is represented by the antlers (Macdonald 2006, 725). Therefore the actual ranking on the basis of edible weight may have been lower. Furthermore, although the species was both a grazer and a browser, its presence traditionally taken as an indicator for an open environment (Bratlund 1999, 78). It may therefore not have coped well in the increasingly forested environments of the Eemian. The reconstructed population density may thus be an overestimation. If this species was comparatively rare it may not have been worthwhile to add to the Neanderthal repertoire the behaviours and strategies needed to predictably encounter and kill it.

The selection of brown bear over cave bear may be at least partly explained by the difference in size. Brown bear is highly ranked but a little smaller than the cave bear. Furthermore, in contrast to the more herbivorous cave bear, brown bear is a carnivore that is known to eat humans, even nowadays. This may have provided an extra incentive to hunting it. Cave bear may have been less aggressive to Neanderthals upon encounter, but more difficult to kill and therefore left alone. Moreover in the season when brown bear is at its most aggressive, autumn, its ranking may also be higher than normally since its fat content is very high at this time because it is accumulating fat for its hibernation. Another reason is the fact that bear may be a good candidate for non-food yields. The heavy processing of its paws in evidence at both Taubach and Biache-Saint-Vaast has been attributed to processing of the animal for its fur at both sites (Auguste 1992, Auguste 1995a). One would expect cave bears to be exploited during the early parts of their hibernation, since handling cost is low at that time. This has been observed at the Balver Höhle for instance (Kindler 2008). If this behaviour was practised, bones were not transported to the site of Taubach.

The exploitation of beaver is unexpected on the basis of its ranking. Arguments in favour of hunting them may be that they were also more highly ranked than one would anticipate on the basis of weight alone, since their ranking increases because of non-food yields. Another reason may be that they were probably present at the site itself, since the travertines were forming in a swampy area. Therefore, search time may have been reduced to almost zero, therefore enabling high post-encounter return rates.

Red deer remains a problematic species. Two bones exhibit cut-marks, showing hominin involvement at least on occasion. The traditional diet breadth model assumed that a species is either in the optimal set and exploited on encounter, or it is not and is always left alone. This does not seem to have been the case with red deer, which had higher population densities than the other exploited species and must therefore have been encountered with some regularity. More refined OFT models, like the contingency model (Bettinger 1987, 133), state that a species will only be exploited if the gain to be had from exploitation of this species will be higher than the expected cost of continued tracking for the highest ranked species (see chapter 4). If the hunters operated following the second rule than the exploitation of red deer may have been quite rare. Rhinoceros, bison and brown bear are heavier and more highly ranked than red deer, the expected cost of continued tracking may in many cases not have been too high and the expected gains from these species were (much) higher. In this scenario, red deer may only have been exploited on very unsuccessful hunting expeditions.

The diet breadth of the hominins responsible for the Taubach assemblage was thus quite narrow. Only four species were routinely exploited. For both rhinoceros and bison ranking on the basis of weight does seem to be a sufficient explanation for their inclusion in the diet. The exploitation of brown bear, beaver and the minor involvement with red deer are harder to explain. Peculiar too is the fact that cave bear and giant deer were not included in the optimal set. Especially male giant deer seem to have shared many characteristics with rhinoceros and bison. Its exclusion may have been caused its scarcity in the environment. It went extinct in the Holocene interglacial and may not have been able to deal well with interglacials. Furthermore during the autumn, the hypothesised season of occupation at Taubach, their ranking may have dropped due to weight loss during rut.

As said, brown bear does represent quite a large amount of meat, but is a dangerous species. In addition to weight, some arguments in favour of this species' exploitation may be brought forward. First, it provided an added bonus in the form of fur. Second, its ranking may have been higher seasonally because of a high fat content. The exploitation of beaver may also have been related to its fur. Furthermore, if it resided at the site in the ponds where the travertine was being formed, its search cost may have been very low, which may have increased its ranking.

6.8 Discussion

How can we interpret these patterns of exploitation in terms of hominin foraging strategies? First, because of the preponderance in the assemblage of species indicative of a forested environment, we can argue that Neanderthals were able to deal with Eemian forested environments characterised by dispersed animal resources (contra Gamble 1992, Gamble 1999). Moreover, they did so by exploiting a small set of species, suggesting that hunting of these species was done efficiently enough to meet the needs of Neanderthals.

There are some reasons to assume that life was different for Eemian hunter/gatherers than for groups living in colder conditions. The most striking thing about the animals exploited at Taubach is that the main focus is on very large, solitary animals. In the Weichselian, it appears that at many sites the dominant species were ungulates living in large herds (see for example the overview provided by Grayson and Delpech 2006). As proposed in chapter 4, this might be caused by the fact that hunter/gatherers in the Eemian operated in smaller bands than in periods when herbivore biomass was more readily available. When operating in small groups, concentrating on solitary animals is probably a more productive strategy than trying to deal with a large herd of animals.

Reducing group size is one of the possible solutions to dealing with conditions in which resources are dispersed and their location hard to predict. I think the situation in an interglacial would have provided a powerful feedback mechanism for restricting Neanderthal group size: Large herds moving predictably through the landscape were rarer than in colder conditions. Therefore, the potential for supporting larger aggregations of hunters was also diminished. In order to deal with this, residential mobility may have been increased. When residential moves are made before return rates in a certain area drop too far, larger groups may still be supported (*e.g.* Binford 2001, 239-241). Furthermore, again, because of locomotion costs the territory exploited from a central place was radically smaller than that of modern day hunter/gatherers. This increased the need for higher residential mobility. Decreasing group size will result in slower depletion of resources around a base camp. Furthermore, in forested environments the total amount of biomass available to human foragers is lower than in savannah or steppe like environments (Delpech 1999), so the Eemian landscape offered a lower carrying capacity for human groups than environments in colder periods did.

The narrow diet breadth, focused on very large animals at Taubach reflects a hunting strategy geared towards high yields. However, because of the low population densities that these animals have in general, it may also have been a high-risk strategy. These risks were apparently well buffered, otherwise diet breadth would have been greater. The buffering mechanism is unclear. It may be that females foraged for plant food at least during warm seasons. Plant foods certainly were available during the Eemian; at the site of Rabutz, some burnt hazelnet shells were found (Wenzel 2002). At the nearby site of Neumark Nord, charred plum seeds and acorns were recovered (Roebroeks pers comm.). They are unknown for Taubach though. Another possibility for women's foraging may have been concentrating on small animals, like the beavers found at the site.

However, manipulating the encounter rate with the animals probably also lowered the risk of this hunting strategy. Bratlund (1999) suggested that the site was a magnet-location for rhinoceros because it probably functioned as a salt lick. Furthermore, since it was on a terrace overlooking the Ilm-river valley it may have been a strategic place to observe movements of other animals, since river valleys were more open environments than most of the rest of the landscape during interglacials. The manipulation of encounter rates with prey is another domain in which females may have contributed to the foraging effort. As proposed by Kuhn and Stiner (2006), females may also have assisted males in the less dangerous aspects of hunting large mammals. In the Eemian environment, with its low prey visibility, female tracking may have been an important contribution to the manipulation of encounter rates with prey. It appears that female tracking skills may substantially influence male hunting success in modern day hunter/gatherers (*e.g.* Biesele and Barclay 2001). In a situation as at Taubach, where diet breadth is very narrow, ensuring a frequent enough encounter rate is very important, making the female contribution to tracking prey potentially essential.

Another way to buffer uncertain foraging returns would be by increasing diet breadth. However, smaller animals would also be dispersed and encounter rates would be unpredictable. Moreover, in comparison to larger animals, processing costs would be relatively high. Furthermore, in closed environments, herd size of social herbivores is lowered (*e.g.* Guthrie 1990, 155). Consequently whereas a focus on herd animals in colder periods might enable hunting parties to kill a significant number of animals in one encounter, this would be much less productive in the Eemian. Therefore, even though herds have a greater chance of spotting predators early and have a good defence mechanism because they are in a group, their maximum yield would have been drastically lowered in the Eemian. Finally, returns would drop faster than in contemporary hunter/gatherers because of higher locomotion costs for Neanderthals. Therefore, broadening the diet may have been counter-productive.

On the other hand, the diet was broadened at least occasionally, as evidenced by the cut-marks on red deer bones and the putative exploitation marks on horse and boar. If the hunting episodes represented at the site took place mostly in autumn, as hypothesised earlier, cervids, especially males may be ranked lower than expected on the basis of body weight. Apparently stags do not feed often during rut and by autumn will have lost significant amounts of weight. Thus hunting cervids like red and giant deer may not have been very profitable in autumn (*e.g.*, Barnosky 1985, Speth and Tchernov 2001). Therefore, during certain seasons broadening the diet may have been a more interesting proposition than during others. Still, the bulk of material suggests that only a narrow set of species provided the mainstay of the diet. Moreover, specific categories of these species were targeted, narrowing diet breadth even further.

This suggests that the Taubach assemblage must represent the activities of small groups of hominins over a long time. In reaction to the warm climate and more dispersed unpredictable resources, Neanderthals themselves probably became more dispersed as well. They skimmed off the largest animals in the landscape, making a few kills per episode and then moved on to a different territory. According to White (2006), if Neanderthals needed 3000 kcal/day, they needed to procure 1.85 kilos of fat rich meat per day. With a return rate of 60% a reindeer could feed a group of 10 for 3 days and a horse for 6 days. A reindeer weighs about 86 kilos according to Pushkina and Raia (2008). The animals on which Neanderthals focused at Taubach may have been rare, but one kill would supply them with food for a considerable period of time. Concentrating on smaller but still unpredictable resources would, in the long run, not yield a steady enough flow of food.

Of course hunters employ other considerations than animal weight alone in order to select their prey. In the exploited set, brown bear and beaver may have provided non-food benefits to hunters because of their fur. Both of these species also have elevated rankings in autumn, because they store fat for the winter at this time of year. Furthermore, in the case of brown bear, the killing of these animals may have had additional benefits because this eliminated direct competitors.

There is also another value that prey may have lent to its dispatcher that I have not yet treated extensively in this chapter: prestige. As pointed out in chapter 4, meat can be used as a socio-political currency in hunter/gatherer societies. Hunting large and dangerous animals may in this case be important in showing off ones good qualities. Bratlund (1999, 150-151) has indeed proposed this as a reason for the emphasis on Merck's rhinoceros and brown bear. There is one problem with this hypothesis however: if prestige was an important consideration, especially when hunting brown bear, one would expect cave bear to be well represented at the site as well, since it is much larger than brown bear. The fact that this species was not exploited suggests that prestige may not have been an important consideration in prey selection.

6.9 Conclusion

Interpreting a site like Taubach with a long history of research is complicated. First, it must be recognised that there is a clear bias towards complete and identifiable bones. However, since even small bones of a small species like beaver are well represented, the bias does not appear too severe. Furthermore, the preponderance of dental elements and cranial parts although certainly partly attributable to the collection preferences at the time of exploitation is probably also partly caused by trampling, an important process near contemporary waterholes and springs.

Unfortunately, the date of the site is not fully certain. Most of the faunal evidence points to this site being younger than Ehringsdorf. Furthermore, the site was accumulated over quite a long period of time, yet shows a narrow diet breadth, which points to a stable environment. In unstable environments, species would be added to and dropped from the optimal set regularly as encounter rates of the highest ranked species fluctuated. This leads me to hypothesize that the site was formed during a climatically stable period of time. Whether this is an intra-Saale warm phase or the Eemian does not make much difference for the interpretation of the foraging behaviour represented in the assemblage. A date in the Eemian, probably no earlier than phase three seems most logical.

The local environment of the site was open, as shown by the absence of leaf imprints at the site. However, the preponderance of species associated with forested environments and analysis of pollen cores from nearby sites suggest that the wider environment was dominated by forest. Again, because of the long period of time reflected in the assemblage we can safely conclude that Neanderthals were able to maintain a lasting occupation of the Eemian forests. This is underlined by the fact that a level dating to the climax phase of the Eemian was found to contain stone tools during research in 1977.

The focus on large solitary animals suggests that Neanderthals probably hunted in small groups. This may also explain why the very largest animals, elephants, and also adult rhinoceros were avoided. Group sizes may have been too small to tackle these prey. Lowering group size seems a logical reaction to the fact that there was less food available in the environment compared to colder periods. Furthermore, resources were dispersed, and less predictable. Three other Eemian sites are known, they are single carcass sites (Gaudzinski 2004). This seems to be a reflection of animals being randomly scattered in the environment. Only at a magnet location like Taubach could a palimpsest develop. The fact that large animals are well represented at the site seems to suggest they were not killed too far from the site. If the so-called *Brandschichten* represent hearths, this investment in "site-furniture" may point to longer occupations. Additionally, even while the collection methods were biased, a lot of production waste is present in the collections of artefacts (Schäfer 1990, 56). This suggests that the site functioned as a convenient campsite for hominins from which they exploited the nearby environment.

In terms of diet breadth, the exploitation of adult male bison and subadult rhinoceros seems logical. After elephant they represent the heaviest animals available. They are both solitary and therefore more easily hunted than for example female bison. Brown bear exploitation is dangerous, but it may have presented advantages in the form of fur and, in autumn, high fat content. Furthermore from ethnography it is clear that hunting large and dangerous animals brings status and therefore social advantages to hunters. In this case, these large animals are also direct competitors and even pose a threat to hominins, therefore hunting them may have brought hunters a significant amount of prestige. Females may have foraged for plant foods and also beaver, which does not seem such a dangerous adversary. Moreover, it may have been present directly on the site, which would ensure high return rates. This species may also have been hunted preferably in autumn, because of elevated fat contents.

In conclusion, this chapter has shown that Neanderthals were able to deal with forested interglacial environments. Moreover, they managed to subsist on a small set of species and only specific categories of individuals of these species for a prolonged period of time. This suggests that they had arrived at a stable foraging adaptation. It appears that in this case, they settled on the largest animals in the environment, with the exception of elephant. It is likely that this necessitated living in smaller social groups than in open environments and with a higher degree of residential mobility.

7 Hyena foraging

7.1 Introduction

After analysing Middle Palaeolithic sites guided by Optimal Foraging Theory (OFT), this chapter aims to provide an additional evaluation of the applicability of this reasoning to the Pleistocene by applying OFT reasoning to the foraging behaviour of the Pleistocene European cave hyena (*Crocuta spelaea*). The results of this analysis will be compared to the results of the analysis of Middle Palaeolithic sites. This species was chosen because of its important similarities to Neanderthals, most significantly the facts that both species are of roughly similar size and they are both social carnivores. It is proposed that in order for the application of OFT to Pleistocene foraging behaviour to be fruitful, the theory should be able to highlight the differences between the foraging niches of both species.

It is expected that Neanderthals and cave hyenas occupied different niches during the Middle and Late Pleistocene, since they co-existed in large areas, where both species left a rich record of their activities (*e.g.* Brugal, Fosse, and Guadelli 1997, Fosse *et al.* 1998). If both species occupied a similar niche, this would have resulted in the local extinction of one of the two. As this was patently not the case, we are presented with an opportunity to test whether applying OFT to cave hyenas results in a different modelled diet. Hence, this case-study provides a check of the validity of this kind of analysis. Hyenas are often seen as scavengers, which would be an important niche difference allowing them to co-exist with predators. However, this view is not correct in the case of spotted hyena (*Crocuta crocuta*), since this species is an accomplished hunter (*e.g.* Kruuk 1972). Genetically it is closely related to cave hyena (Rohland *et al.* 2005), suggesting that this species too was an important predator in its environment. Therefore cave hyena and Neanderthal niches were potentially very similar. It must be noted though, that the range of species consumed by a predator represents only one facet of its niche. The different niches of cave hyenas and hominins may have been defined by other adaptations than the range of species they exploited, like spatial segregation, or the use of different strategies (*e.g.* Stiner 1992, 446).

Studying hyena foraging has advantages over the study of foraging by other carnivores. Hyenas have long been recognised as an important taphonomic agent in the formation of bone deposits at archaeological sites, both in Plio-Pleistocene African and European studies. This has led to a great amount of actualistic and palaeontological research into the foraging strategies of hyenids and their palaeolontological residues, in order to see what their role in the archaeological record has been (*e.g.* Binford, Mills, and Stone 1988, Brugal, Fosse, and Guadelli 1997, Diedrich and Žák 2006, Horwitz 1998, Lam 1992, Stiner 1992, Villa *et al.* 2004).

Unfortunately, not all excavated hyena sites have been published in detail and the environmental conditions of many sites are not clarified at all in the publications that were at my disposal. I will present two case studies, for which sufficient data are available, namely the French sites of Lunel-Viel and Camiac. In the case of Lunel-Viel, the bone assemblage has been published in great detail, but unfortunately, not much information is available for environmental reconstruction. At Camiac we have information about the environment in which the cave hyenas foraged. However, details about the skeletal part representation and age-structure of the species represented are scant. The information that these sites yield will be combined and supplemented with information from other sites in order to arrive at a synthesized image of foraging strategies of Pleistocene cave hyenas that can be compared to our understanding of Neanderthal foraging.

Additionally, all extant hyena species employ scavenging as part of their foraging strategies. Spotted hyenas often employ scavenging as a secondary strategy, but in some populations this strategy contributes an important part of the total calories that are consumed. Modelling hyena foraging niches with OFT may therefore also produce insight in the viability of scavenging in hominin foraging strategies.

In order to be able to construct a diet breadth model for hyenas, I will first shortly present our knowledge of extant hyenid species, emphasising the spotted hyena, because it is anatomically and genetically very similar to the cave hyena. This will be followed by a discussion on the character of the bone accumulations that are produced by hyenas, which is crucial in order to be able to interpret Pleistocene hyena bone assemblages. After this I will present the sites used as case-studies. The knowledge on Pleistocene hyena behaviour gained from these case-studies will then be supplemented with knowledge gained from other Pleistocene sites and a scenario will be developed that interprets hyena foraging decisions and clarifies the separation between their niche and that of Neanderthals.

7.2 Hyena ecology

Hyenids are a group of feliform carnivores. They are a small Family in the class Mammalia, of which only four species are in existence today. These four species are the remnants of a much larger group. In the late Miocene, 24 species are known to have existed (Watts and Holekamp 2007, r657). The extant species show quite a wide range of adaptations. One of them, the aardwolf (*Proteles cristatus*), feeds mostly on termites and is only distantly related to the other three species. Due to the distant relationship and incongruous foraging pattern it will not be referred to in this chapter. The other three species feed mostly on meat of macrofauna, which is acquired by hunting and scavenging. These species are brown hyena (*Hyaena brunnea*) and striped hyena (*Hyaena hyaena*), which are closely related, and spotted hyena (Mills and Bearder 2006). Hyenas are distributed over a large area. Striped hyena is found in India, the Near East and areas in North and East Africa. Brown hyena is found mainly in southern Africa, while spotted hyena lives in most of Sub-Saharan Africa. (Mills and Bearder 2006, Watts and Holekamp 2007).

In Pleistocene Europe, several hyenids existed. In the late Pliocene and early Pleistocene, two forms occurred, the "gigantic" short-faced hyena (*Pachycrocuta brevirostris*) and the medium sized *Hyaena perrieri*. The latter species may be closely related to the brown hyena, the former species was probably distantly related to the modern spotted hyena. During the Middle and Late Pleistocene there is a species resembling the striped hyena, *Hyaena prisca*, and the cave hyena (Brugal, Fosse, and Guadelli 1997, Diedrich and Žák 2006).

The cave hyena will be the focus of this analysis, since its sites have been well researched and because it was the most common of the Late Pleistocene species. Anatomically it appears to be closely related to modern day spotted hyena. However, Cuvier found it sufficiently different from spotted hyena to define it as a separate species (Fosse 1997, 17). Modern genetic analysis, however, has shown that spotted hyena and cave hyena samples fall in the same group and can be regarded as belonging to a single species (Rohland *et al.* 2005, 2441). Spotted hyenas therefore present a suitable behavioural analogue. The close kinship of the Pleistocene and contemporary populations suggests that they may have been behaviourally similar. On the other hand, denning and bone accumulation occurs in all three contemporary hyena species, suggesting that it is an ancestral feature of this group. Therefore, reference to bone accumulations produced by other species will occasionally be made.

Hyenas are social carnivores living in clans. Among brown and striped hyenas, clans are small and they usually consist of related individuals. A brown hyena clan can comprise only a mother and her offspring. On the other hand, spotted hyena clans may number up to 80 individuals, but on average, clans number 25 individuals (Kruuk 1972, Mills and Bearder 2006, Watts and Holekamp 2007). These clans are multi-male, multi-female groups. Moreover, in-group relatedness in spotted hyena is low. This kind of social system is more reminiscent of that of primates than of carnivores (Watts and Holekamp 2007, r658). It contrasts sharply with the social system of the other two species.

As pointed out above, the cave hyena was closely related to the modern spotted hyena. This species has a remarkable social system in which females are the dominant sex (Watts and Holekamp 2007, 660). Females exhibit elevated levels of testosterone and the female reproductive organs in the species have been masculinised. Spotted hyena females have a penis-like clitoris, through which the females give birth (Drea and Frank 2003, 124). Furthermore, females are about 12 % larger than males. Males weigh between 45 and 62 kilos, whereas females weigh 55 to 82.5 kilos (Mills and Bearder 2006). The masculinization has important consequences for childbirth in this species. The first time a female gives birth, the clitoris has to tear, since it is too small to allow the fetal head to pass through it. The first period of labour is therefore prolonged and painful in spotted hyenas. This results in an elevated number of stillborn cubs from a female's first pregnancy and delivery. Moreover, it also leads to elevated mortality in female hyenas. As much as 36% of the female population may die during their first labour (Frank, Weldele, and Glickman 1995).

Pleistocene cave hyenas were larger than their modern day counterparts. This may be an expression of Bergman's rule (discussed in section 2.4 for Neanderthals) (Brugal, Fosse, and Guadelli 1997, 160). The body weight of Pleistocene hyenas was higher than that of Neanderthals, which is estimated by (Sorensen and Leonard 2001) as 55 kg. for females and 65 kg. for males. Moreover, female Pleistocene cave hyenas in Europe have also been described as being slightly larger than the males (Diedrich and Žák 2006, 252). This can be taken as an additional indication that Pleistocene cave hyenas had a similar social system as modern spotted hyenas.

Spotted hyenas have a very strict dominance hierarchy that regulates interactions within the group. Remarkably, the rank of a spotted hyena individual is not dependent on its size or strength, but is derived from its mother's rank. The rank of an individual in the group determines the timing of its access to food. This is very important, since competition for food seems to be more intense in spotted hyenas than in any other carnivore (Drea and Frank 2003, Watts and Holekamp 2007). In order to deal with the feeding competition, hyena individuals usually spend a lot of time in small subgroups that forage in a dispersed manner throughout the territory. They can therefore best be described as living in a fission fusion society (Watts and Holekamp 2007, r659).

All hyena species forage nocturnally. They are usually seen as obligate scavengers. This view is correct in the case of brown and striped hyenas that acquire most of their prey by scavenging. Yhe only hunting observed in these hyena species is hunting for small species like dogs and rodents (*e.g.* Horwitz 1998, Mills and Bearder 2006). In the case of spotted hyenas scavenging is a less important foraging strategy. They are known to scavenge, but often seem to prefer fresh kills above scavenged meat (Cooper, Holekamp, and Smale 1999, 159). However, spotted hyena behaviour nowadays varies and different feeding strategies will be employed depending upon the ecological circumstances. Despite the variation in foraging behaviour in different ecological settings, medium- to large-sized ungulates form the mainstay of hyena diets in most areas (Brugal, Fosse, and Guadelli 1997, Lam 1992, Mills and Bearder 2006).

Spotted hyenas often forage alone. As pointed out, a large portion of the hyena diet is obtained by hunting, although scavenging is quite important in many populations. In this respect, it should be noted that adult spotted hyenas can also kill prey as large as wildebeest (*Connochaetes taurinus*) on their own[31] (Mills 1985, Watts and Holekamp 2007). Solitary foraging is attractive for many individuals because of the intense competition for food in this species. This competition is more intense than in other social carnivores. Therefore it is often profitable for individuals, especially low-ranking ones, to forage alone. Additionally, while hunting success does improve when hunting in groups, this improvement is not dramatic, which may explain why 75% of successful hyena hunts were executed solitarily (Watts and Holekamp 2007, r659). After a successful hunt, group members often converge on the kill, competing for the food with the individual that obtained it (Watts and Holekamp 2007, r658). Still, group hunting does occur in this species. Furthermore, hunting in groups allows hyenas to target larger species than Wildebeest. Hyenas hunting in groups regularly kill animals like zebras (*Equus sp.*). Moreover, groups have been observed hunting buffalo (*Syncerus caffer*) and even giraffes (*Giraffa camelopardalis*). In very exceptional cases hunting of juvenile elephants (*Loxodonta africana*) has been observed (Fosse 1996, Watts and Holekamp 2007). The latter species are only attacked if the victim is very young, injured or pregnant (Cooper, Holekamp, and Smale 1999, 152).

In general therefore, spotted hyenas only hunt prey of up to about 250 kg. The preferred prey in many areas seems to consist of large antelopes like gemsbok (*Oryx gazella*) and wildebeest (Cooper, Holekamp, and Smale 1999, Kruuk 1972, Mills and Bearder 2006). Smaller species of antelope, like gazelles (*Gazella sp.*) are also exploited, but due to their smaller body size their caloric contribution to the diet is usually insignificant. During a study of a group of spotted hyenas in the Masai Mara for example, 297 instances of exploitation of a wildebeest carcass were witnessed and 240 instances of the exploitation of a Thomson's gazelle (*Gazella thomsoni*) carcass. Taking body size into account, wildebeest carcasses provided about 47.7% of the dietary biomass, while Thomson's gazelles provided an estimated 4.3% (Cooper, Holekamp, and Smale 1999, 153).

When hunting, spotted hyenas often preferentially target either young or old individuals. For example, in the Serengeti, 36% of wildebeest that are killed are under one year of age, and 30% are senile. With zebras in the same area, 48% of hunted individuals are under four years old and 17% are senile. In the Kalahari Desert, 31.7% of prey killed by hyenas are gemsbok younger than one year of age, while 11.5% of the killed animals are wildebeest of similar age (Fosse 1996, Fosse 1999).

---

31   This species weighs up to 230 kg. according to Mills and Bearder (2006).

In addition to hunting, spotted hyenas scavenge. However, the contribution of scavenging can be unimportant in the diet of spotted hyenas. It is thought that the amount of food procured by scavenging is dependent on the ecological situation. In areas rich in biomass, scavenging is relatively unimportant. This is the case for both the populations on the Masai Mara plains in Kenya and in the Ngorongoro crater in Tanzania. Here hunted food constitutes 95% and 82% of the consumed food respectively. In the Serengeti and other areas in southern Africa, this percentage is generally 70% or lower. In Kruger park for example, the amount of hunted and scavenged meat both account for about 50% of the consumed diet (Cooper, Holekamp, and Smale 1999, Mills and Bearder 2006).

On the richer plains of East Africa, small and medium-sized ungulates are more abundant than in southern Africa. In the latter area, megaherbivores form a much larger proportion of the herbivore guild. Therefore, larger amounts of carrion are available in southern Africa than in eastern Africa (Cooper, Holekamp, and Smale 1999, 158). At least in eastern Africa the low predictability of available carrion, as well as the low patch quality of carrion, results in spotted hyenas in a preference for hunted food (Cooper, Holekamp, and Smale 1999, 159).

In conclusion we have seen that spotted hyenas adapt their foraging behaviours to the ecological setting. For example, close to aquatic resources, they have been shown to be capable of fishing for example, and at least one population routinely hunts small Nile crocodiles (*Crocodilus niloticus*) (Lam 1992, 398). At least some of the variability in the prey categories can be explained in terms of ecological variation. In more closed areas, where group size is smaller, generally smaller species are hunted than in open areas. Moreover, the focus on young animals seems to be more important in more closed areas (Brugal, Fosse, and Guadelli 1997, 174). Most importantly, the amount of scavenged food in the diet seems to vary according to the ecological circumstances in which a hyena population finds itself (Cooper, Holekamp, and Smale 1999). However, not all the variation in the diet of spotted hyenas has a straightforward ecological explanation (Lam 1992, 404).

7.3 Hyena sites

Most important for our purpose is the fact that hyenas leave a material record of their activities. Much of their life is organised around denning sites which can be divided into two types. Natal dens are isolated sites, used by a usually low-ranking mother to give birth and nurse her cubs. More high ranking mothers usually give birth in the "communal den", which is used by all individuals of a group (Boydston, Kapheim, and Holekamp 2006). In addition to dens, there are also places where food is cached (Diedrich and Žák 2006, Pokines and Peterhans 2007). This means that we potentially have sites that provide a glimpse of the totality of hyena foraging strategies, something that is harder to come by for other carnivores.

In spotted hyenas, the den is an important focus of the life of a clan. Cubs are raised here and the den plays an important role in social learning, because the young learn their place in the dominance hierarchy and corresponding role in group life at these sites (Drea and Frank 2003, Watts and Holekamp 2007, r658). Remains of prey are transported to these sites, sometimes over large distances (*e.g.* Brugal, Fosse, and Guadelli 1997, Diedrich and Žák 2006, Lam 1992, Mills and Bearder 2006).[32] In contrast to striped and brown hyena, spotted hyenas do not provision their offspring with transported food. Until the young leave the den, they subsist solely on milk (*e.g.* Pokines and Peterhans 2007, 1915). The bones transported to communal dens are thus usually transported by adults to feed themselves. The function of this behaviour seems to be to decrease the chance of theft by other predators or by group members (Pokines and Peterhans 2007). The bone assemblages therefore reflect the diet of adult hyenas.

The location of the communal den may be relocated frequently throughout the territory of the clan. In one 10-year study, this happened once a month on average. Most denning sites were only used once, although some popular locations were re-occupied periodically (Boydston, Kapheim, and Holekamp 2006). Den moves can be prompted by several factors, like increases in ectoparasite populations, or a disturbance at the den, for example by lions. In other cases, the reasons for moves remained unclear (Boydston, Kapheim, and Holekamp 2006). Increases in foraging efficiency can be cited as reasons for den moves in areas with migratory prey. However, den moves are often made over short distances, averaging about 1.5 kilometre (Boydston, Kapheim, and Holekamp 2006). Still,

---

32   Unfortunately, exact minimal transport distances are only rarely specified in the literature. A minimum of 4.6 km can be given for dens analysed by Lam (1992). Here crocodiles hunted at Lake Turkana were excavated in a den 4.6 kilometres from the shore.

in areas with a lot of standing prey, the den may be moved regularly may happen in response to changing prey densities

Like foraging behaviour, denning and bone accumulating behaviour in modern hyenas is varied. In southern Africa, spotted hyenas do not seem to accumulate significant quantities of bones in their dens, in contrast to eastern Africa, where this has been observed (Sutcliffe 1970, 1111, Pokines and Peterhans 2007). The evidence from the European Pleistocene record will be discussed at a later stage, but it is clear that cave hyenas did accumulate large quantities of bone materials in their dens. In contrast to the Pleistocene situation, the number of hyena remains present in excavated modern dens is small (cf. Fosse 1997, 16), even though high juvenile mortality has been recorded for modern spotted hyena (*e.g.* Drea and Frank 2003, Mills and Bearder 2006).

A number of bone assemblages of Pleistocene age that were at least mostly accumulated by hyenas have been excavated in western and Central Europe. A much larger number of sites is known where cave-use seems to have alternated between hominins and hyenas. Furthermore, even cave sites that show a clear hyena signature sometimes contain small numbers of hominin tools (*e.g.* Villa and Soressi 2000). Bone assemblages associated with hyena activities can be divided into different categories. One type of assemblage points to the use of a site as a denning site, while other assemblage types demonstrate the existence of prey deposit and consumption sites (*e.g.* Diedrich and Žák 2006). In addition some sites contain bone accumulations that appear to reflect activities of multiple, competing carnivores (*e.g.* Fosse *et al.* 1998, 54). We must therefore exercise caution when analysing sites in terms of hyena foraging strategies. It appears that denning sites will show the best signature of hyena foraging activities, since these reflect the results of foraging by a group over a period of time.

Some clear characteristics have been proposed to determine whether hyenas were the principal accumulators of a bone assemblage or not. Important indicators of hyena sites are the presence of large numbers of coprolites, sometimes concentrated in "latrines" (Stiner and Kuhn 1992, 437). A high ratio of carnivores to herbivores when compared to hominin accumulation is also common. Moreover, within the carnivore group hyenas themselves are often important. This is because hyenas interact frequently with other carnivores, while in general carnivores tend to avoid each other (Cruz-Uribe 1991). Moreover, the fierce intra-specific competition results in high infant mortality in dens, explaining the abundance of hyena fossils. Furthermore, the presence of abundant gnaw marks on the bones is an important characteristic (Brugal, Fosse, and Guadelli 1997, Stiner 1992). The species of hyena that accumulated the bones is usually determined by the remains of hyenas present in the accumulations, especially in the case of den sites where juveniles die inside the den. In most cases in Pleistocene Europe, the accumulating species was cave hyena.

Large numbers of coprolites and an abundance of hyenid remains are associated with denning sites. These sites can be re-used for long periods of time, especially when these are located in caves (Pokines and Peterhans 2007). This enables us to analyse large time averaged assemblages. Denning sites can be considered comparable to a "Central Place" in hominins in that they are the focal point of the activities of all individuals in a clan. Cubs are born at these sites and they remain there. Spotted hyena infants wage an important struggle for dominance with their siblings very rapidly after they are born. During these struggles 25% of all cubs that are born are killed by their siblings. In addition to cubs being killed soon after birth, in areas where food is scarce, the dominant cub may prevent a subordinate cub from feeding, resulting in death by starvation (Frank, Glickman, and Licht 1991). This results in high numbers of juvenile bones at hyena dens (Drea and Frank 2003). The use of denning sites is spatially organised. Young are raised in small niches of the cave, while food remains are concentrated in larger rooms. The clearest indication of spatial organisation is tends to be concentration of large numbers of coprolites in latrines (*e.g.* Horwitz 1998, Stiner 1992, Sutcliffe 1970).

However, not all bone assemblages that appear to have been accumulated by hyenas resemble denning sites. In some sites, for example, the hyena age profile is not dominated by juveniles, but by adults (Fosse *et al.* 1998, 53-54). These assemblages appear to reflect competition for prey with other carnivores or conspecifics, for example from a different clan. Another type of site is the prey deposit site, where carcasses have been deposited. This behaviour has also been observed in modern hyenas (Diedrich and Žák 2006, 250). In European contexts, the cool environments of caves provided hyenas with ideal areas for prey storage. Moreover, in some cases, vertical cave systems were available. These were difficult to access and therefore provided well protected storage sites. This analysis will be restricted to denning sites whose hyena population contains predominantly juvenile individuals. It is hoped that this selection will result in the analysis of assemblages showing minimal influence from other carnivores as opposed to analysing assemblages in which adult hyenas are abundant.

It is hoped that bone assemblages from such sites, provide a more reliable image of cave hyena foraging strategies than sites with "mixed" assemblages. Nevertheless, the nature of hyena den assemblages already implies some biases with regard to the bone collection deposited at the site. The most important factor is the fact that cave hyenas, like modern spotted hyenas, were adapted to destroy large bones. This adaptation enables them to scavenge carcasses without much meat, because they can still exploit greasy bones and marrow, in contrast to for example felids (*e.g.* Blumenschine 1987). This behaviour results in the preferential destruction of certain categories of bone. Especially small species will be underrepresented in the Number of Identified Specimens (NISP) of a site: usually only the cranial skeleton of small ungulates is present at Pleistocene dens (*e.g.* Brugal, Fosse, and Guadelli 1997, Diedrich and Žák 2006, Fosse 1996, Lam 1992). In larger species, whose bones are more difficult to destroy, the overrepresentation of cranial remains decreases. Since more identifiable skeletal parts have survived, larger species will therefore be overrepresented in hyena den assemblages.

Another important point concerns hyena transport behaviour. Hyenas transport remains of prey animals to their dens. This transport can take place over quite great distances. Sometimes two animals even cooperate. Lam (1992, 392) for example, describes a spoor consisting of two sets of spotted hyena tracks, with the drag mark of a crocodile tail between them. The transport behaviour may introduce a bias in the species that are represented at den sites. Large species may be transported less often, as is also the case in hominin sites (see chapter 3). On the other hand, if a small animal is captured and multiple hyenas feed on it, there may be few remains left to transport to the den. Therefore, counterintuitively, small animals may be underrepresented at den sites, since they provide too small a package to share with multiple individuals.

In modern hyena sites, on the other hand, it has been observed that the ratio of represented species strongly resembles the actual ratios in which the species are present in the environment (Stiner 1992, 446). This suggests that the biases influencing the survival of bones in hyena dens sites may not be too drastic.

7.4 Expectations for the study of Pleistocene hyenas

The foregoing discussion of modern spotted hyenas enables us to model the likely behaviour of the closely related cave hyena. We will assume that cave hyenas were as large as Neanderthals, which means that 300 kilograms would be the expected upper limit of the size of their prey. In the case of group foraging, larger species may have been taken, however spotted hyenas appear to prefer foraging alone in many cases.

Therefore, we expect Pleistocene European hyenas, like modern day spotted hyenas, to focus on medium-sized ungulates, for example red deer or reindeer. These could be hunted solitarily and in groups. They are therefore expected to be well-represented in hyena bone assemblages. Larger prey species, like horses or bovids are expected to be rarer, since they had to be taken in groups. Because of the versatility of foraging strategies in spotted hyenas, consisting of solitary hunting, group hunting and scavenging, we expect that hyenas will have had a broad diet. Since scavenging is practised frequently and hunting is focussed on the weak individuals, we expect the age profiles of prey animals at cave hyena sites to be biased in favour of juvenile and senile individuals.

7.5 Case-studies

I will analyse cave hyena foraging strategies on the basis of two French sites that have been published in reasonable detail. Firstly, I will discuss Lunel-Viel, an early site. On the basis of faunal remains, this site can be dated to the Middle Pleistocene. Secondly I will discuss the site of Camiac, which is dated to MIS 3.

7.5.1 Lunel-Viel

Near the village of Lunel-Viel, located between Nîmes and Montpellier, in the Hérault département, a system of four caves has been discovered. The cave designated Lunel-Viel 1 was found to contain Pleistocene faunal remains in the 19th century. In the 20th century, a team led by Bonifay carried out excavations in this cave, which yielded a large bone assemblage (over 8000 pieces identified to anatomical and/or species level), and a small stone artefact assemblage (Fosse 1996, 47). Based on the recovered faunal remains, the site has been dated to the middle part of the Middle Pleistocene, to about 350 ka. During the excavation, 11 *couches* were recognised. These have been grouped into two assemblages, a lower (inf.) assemblage, containing *couches* 6-11 and an upper (sup.) assemblage containing *couches* 1-5 (Fosse 1996). These two assemblages differ slightly in character. The site provides us with a large and time-averaged assemblage to which OFT can be applied.

Several lines of evidence suggest that the bones recovered were accumulated by cave hyenas. Firstly, hyena remains (mostly cave hyena, but also small numbers of *Hyaena prisca*) were found in the excavations. Additionally, numerous hyena coprolites were recovered. Moreover, gnaw marks are visible on the "quasi-totality" of recovered herbivore bone materials (Fosse 1996, 55). Indexes of the manner of fracturation of the bone have been compared to reference collections of both hunter/gatherer and hyena bone collections, compiled by Bunn (Bunn 1983). These comparisons show that the manner of bone breakage is comparable to that seen in modern hyena dens (Fosse 1996, 51-52).

However, there are some differences between the upper and lower assemblages. First, the number of bones in the Upper Assemblage is smaller than in the Lower one. Conversely the Upper Assemblage contains more stone artefacts than the Lower Assemblage. In the upper level, the identified bones outnumber artefacts by a ratio of 2.7, while in the lower level this ratio is 10.6 (Fosse 1996, 73). Refitting studies have shown that the association of the stone artefacts with the bone assemblage accumulated by hyenas is the result of post-depositional processes. The artefacts were probably displaced from the cave entrance downslope into the interior of the cave where the hyena bone assemblage was accumulated (Villa and Soressi 2000, 209). Another difference between the Upper and the Lower Assemblage is the hyena population itself. In the Upper Assemblage, the hyena sample is dominated by adults, while in the lower assemblage it is dominated by juveniles (Fosse 1996, 70). The Lower Assemblage thus shows a stronger hyena signature. The fact that very young animals dominate the hyena population suggests that it was a denning site. Hence, during the formation of the Lower Assemblage, hyenas used this cave for long periods of time rearing their vulnerable cubs. We can therefore be certain that hominin use of the cave was ephemeral during this time. The analysis is thus limited to this assemblage.

The NISP counts of the recovered bone material from Lunel-Viel are listed in table 7.1. The lower assemblage is heavily dominated by cervids, with aurochs (*Bos primigenius*) being second in importance and cave hyenas themselves in third place. For the aurochs sample, the ratio between the sexes could be determined because of their sexual dimorphism. In the lower assemblage, it appeared that 33% of the assemblage was male, while 67% was female (Fosse 1996, 78).

Cranial elements are overrepresented in the cervid sample. This corresponds to the observations about small ungulates at other Pleistocene dens mentioned in the previous paragraph. The dominance of these elements is reduced in the equids and they are quite rare compared to postcranial bones in the bovid sample (Fosse 1996, 50). With regard to the longbones, especially humerus and tibia, the distal ends are overrepresented. This is to be expected, because the proximal ends are more spongy and contain more marrow. They were therefore preferentially consumed. Moreover, cylinders, longbones missing both diaphyses, which are characteristic of hyena dens have also been recovered (Fosse 1996, 50). It appears that just like in modern spotted hy-

	NISP	
Species	Lower	Upper
Cervids (*Cervus elaphus* + *Euctenoceros mediterraneus*)	2707	523
Bos primigenius trocheros	893	324
Crocuta spelaea intermedia	562	223
Equus mosbachensis palustris	373	152
Canis lupus lunellensis	99	28
Equus hydruntinus	53	24
Sus sp.	46	14
Dicerorhinus etruscus	39	13
Hyaena prisca	16	3
Cuon priscus	7	1
Panthera spelaea[33]	5	6
Felis (Lynx) spelaea	5	2
Ursus cf. *deningeri*	5	-
Capreolus cf. *süssenbornensis*	4	-
Panthera pardus[34]	4	2
Bison cf. *schoetensacki*	2	-
Meles thorali spelaeus	1	1
Vulpes vulpes	1	11
Felis (Lynx) cf. *pardina*	1	-
Felis monspessulana	1	-
Mustela palerminea	1	
Lutra sp.	-	2
Total	4825	1329

Table 7.1: The faunal assemblage from Lunel-Viel. Based on (Fosse 1996, 71).

---

[33] Multiple species are listed as Felis spelaea. This species was listed under class A Carnivores. Moreover, Fosse (1996) refers to lions in his text.

[34] Referred to as Felis (Panthera) lunellensis by Fosse 1996). Testu (2006) determines it to be Panthera pardus.

ena dens, distal appendicular bones and cranial elements are overrepresented (compare Fosse 1996, 74-76, Pokines and Peterhans 2007).

For some groups, the age structure of the represented animals could be estimated, based on the wear of their teeth. The age structure of the largest group, the cervids, is illustrated in graph 1. Age-classes I and II represent juvenile animals, while age classes X and above represent old individuals. It is clear that in the lower level, juveniles are best represented. Next to these two age-classes, young adults from age-class IV and V were present in relatively large quantities. The age structure of the horses is illustrated in graph 2. The equid sample is dominated by individuals from the 5-6 year-old and 3-4 year-old categories. However, the age categories from 7 to 10 are also quite well represented (Fosse 1996, 53, 68). Prime-age in horse is generally considered to be the age category between 6 and 9 years old (*e.g.* Fernandez, Guadelli, and Fosse 2006).

In the bovid sample it must be noted that dental remains are rare. However, combining dental remains with the stages of fusion of postcranial bones, some indication of the age of the animals represented at the site is listed by Fosse (1996, 53). According to him, the bovid sample from the lower assemblage contained five young animals and 28 adults. In hyenas, as discussed above, the lower assemblage is dominated by juvenile animals. In wolves, the sample consisted of ten young

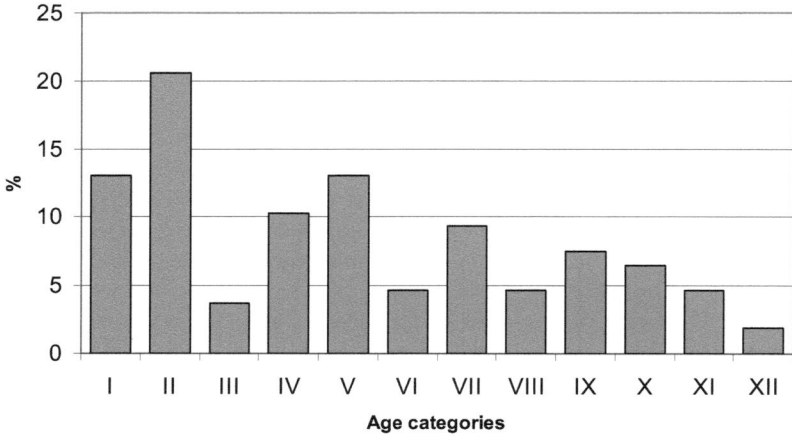

Figure 7.1: Age structure of the cervids represented in the lower assemblage.
Adapted from (Fosse 1996, 68).

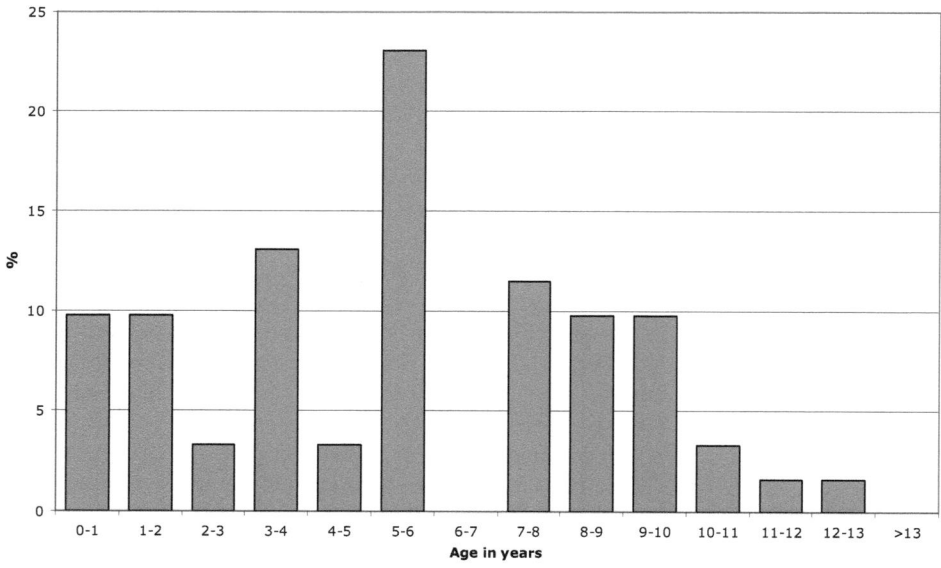

Figure 7.2: Age structure of the horses represented in the lower assemblage.
Adapted from (Fosse 1996, 68).

Species	MNI Young	MNI Adult
Bos primigenius	5	28
Equus hydruntinus	3	3
Sus sp.	2	3
Dicerorhinus etruscus	3	2

Table 7.2: Age categories of the less common species represented in Lunel-Viel in terms of MNI. Based on (Fosse 1996, 54).

Rank	Species	Weight	NISP
1	Dicerorhinus etruscus	1250[35]	39
2	Bison cf. schoetensacki	650	2
3	Bos primigenius trocheros	600	893
4	Ursus cf. deningeri	560	5
5	Equus mosbachensis	335	373
6	Cervus elaphus	200	2707
7	Panthere spelaea	195	5
8	Equus hydruntinus	188	53
9	Panthera pardus	90	4
10	Sus sp.	89	46
11	Crocuta crocuta	70	562
12	Canis lupus lunellensis	45	99
13	Hyaena prisca	40[36]	16
14	Capreolus cf. süssenbornensis	32[37]	4
15	Felis (Lynx) spelaea	20	5
17	Cuon priscus	15	7
18	Felis (Lynx) cf. pardina	10	1
19	Meles thorali spelaeus	10	1
20	Felis monspessulana	5	1
21	Mustela palerminea	<1	1

Table 7.3: Ranking of the animals present in the Lunel-Viel assemblage. Weights from: (Brook and Bowman 2004, Louguet-Lefebvre 2005).

adults and two adults (Fosse 1996, 54). With regard to other animals, present in smaller numbers, it appears that the small equid (*Equus hydruntinus*) is represented in the lower assemblage by three young and three adult animals. Boar (*Sus* sp.) is represented by at least two young animals, one young adult, one prime-aged individual and one very old animal. Lastly, the rhinoceros (*Dicerorhinus etruscus*), is represented by three young and two adults in the lower assemblage (Fosse 1996, 54).

Unfortunately, there is no pollen data that can be used to reconstruct the environment; hence reconstruction must be attempted on the basis of the species that are present in the assemblage. The large mammal fauna of the Lower Assemblage is indicative of a temperate climate. In the uppermost layer belonging to the lower assemblage, bird and tortoise remains indicate climatic warming (Fosse 1996, 48). This layer only contained about 10% of the bone assemblage from the lower assemblage. We can therefore assume that this assemblage was largely formed during a period of temperate conditions. The dominance of cervids is interpreted by Fosse (1996) as reflecting the importance of forested areas in the environment, while equids provide evidence of the existence of open areas in the surroundings of the site. Of course, the foraging preferences of hyenas may influence the data on which the environmental reconstruction is based. Fortunately, birds were also found at the site. It is unlikely that they constituted an important part of the hyena diet. These animals therefore provide us with information on the environment that is independent of hyena preferences. Three groups of bird species are important. Species preferring wooded areas are best represented, followed by species preferring rocky and open terrains (Fosse 1996, 48).

As for the hominin sites discussed in the previous chapters, I constructed a ranking of the species present based on their body weight, listed in table 7.3. A comparison of the ranking with the table listing the identified bones at species level shows that the most highly ranked species, rhinoceros, was not exploited heavily. The same is true for Bison and Deninger's bear, both of which are even rarer in the assemblage. The next most highly ranked ungulates are present in large numbers. The smallest, cervids were exploited most intensively, but horse and aurochs are also present in large numbers. Wolves are also present in reasonably large numbers, even though they are not very highly ranked. However, many studies indicate that aggression between different carnivore species is a common phenomenon. In addition to trying to steal carcasses from carnivores of other species, carnivores often kill other carnivores (see overview in Van Valkenburgh 2001, 104-105). Usually, the killed carnivores are not consumed, though. However, since the wolves were probably transported to the site, this may have been the case here.

The hyenas responsible for the accumulation of this bone assemblage thus preferentially targeted medium to large sized ungulates. The smaller species may be underrepresented due to differential bone destruction. Moreover, smaller species may have been completely devoured at the kill site and therefore transported to the den site less often.

---

35 According to Louguet-Lefebvre (2005), this is a small species, with a shoulder height of 1.5 m., while for Dicerorhinus kirchbergensis a shoulder height of 2.5m is given. She did not provide an estimate for Dicerorhinus hemitoechus but does state that it is of medium height. I therefore estimated this species at 60% of D. kirchbergensis as listed by Brook and Bowman (2004).

36 I used the estimates provided by Brook and Bowman (2004) for Hyaena hyeana and Hyaena brunnea, since they are probably closely related to Hyaena prisca, for which no estimate was provided.

37 I used the estimate provided by Brook and Bowman (2004) for Capreolus capreolus.

Species	Density (ind/km²)
Cervus elaphus	0.7166
Bos primigenius trocheros	0.3395
Crocuta crocuta	0.0431
Equus mosbachensis	0.5046
Canis lupus	0.0525
Equus hydruntinus	0.7474
Sus scrofa	1.2428
Dicerorhinus etruscus	0.2119

Table 7.4: Reconstructed population densities of the most important species at Lunel Viel. For methodology see previous chapters.

The abundance of cervids in the assemblage can be attributed to their encounter rate. This can be approximated by reconstructing their population density. As pointed out in the previous chapters, population density is dependent on body weight. In table 7.4, the population densities for the most common species in the Lower Assemblage are listed. Based on reconstructed population density alone, we would expect equids to be better represented than bovids. The fact that this is not the case may be caused by the environment. If wooded areas predominated in the surroundings of Lunel-Viel, there would be less suitable habitat for equids than for aurochs, which are more at home in wooded areas. Modern equids spend between 80 and 99% of their time in the grassland zones of their range. Wooded areas are only sought out for shelter during storms etc. (Burke *et al.* 2008, 897). If forest was the dominant vegetation type, the area was probably more suitable for cervids and aurochs than for equids and bison. However, the near-absence of bison is striking. They are more adapted to open areas than aurochs, but since equids were also present in large numbers, suitable habitat was probably available to them. They may have been at a disadvantage because they had to compete both with aurochs and horse in parts of their niche. These species may have been better adapted to the specific environmental facets of the area, leaving the bison that has an intermediate adaptation little forage. An alternative explanation is that its rarity is due to identification bias. *Bos* and *Bison* bones resemble each other, so bones belonging to bisons may have been erroneously classified as Aurochs.

With regard to cervids there is a clear focus on the exploitation of juvenile individuals; senile individuals are rare. I assume that most of the remains that have been recovered were obtained by hunting instead of scavenging. This is hard to prove however, since high juvenile mortality also occurs naturally. The fact that old individuals are less common than adults suggests that hunting cervids may have been preferred to their scavenging. In horses the focus is not on juvenile animals, but on young adults. However, mature individuals are also well represented. The age structure of the horses suggests that they were not obtained by scavenging, since adults are very well represented. They were thus probably hunted by hyenas. The same seems true for the bovid sample, although the data provided on the age structure are less detailed. However, juveniles form about 15% of the assemblage, while the rest of the animals represented were adults. Unfortunately, data on whether senile individuals were present in the assemblage is not presented. Still on the basis of the age-class data that show a majority of adult individuals, we can assume that hunting was the main strategy for the exploitation of aurochs.

In addition to the three dominant ungulates, a few species represent between two to just under one percent of the assemblage each. In the case of wolves, young adults are largely dominant, and the only other age-group represented is that of the mature adults. Their presence should probably be explained as being the result of aggression by cave hyenas to competing carnivores. We must assume that wolves were probably hunted on encounter. The presence of equal numbers of young and adult animals for *Equus hydruntinus* appears to be the result of hunting, although again, we cannot be certain. The pattern presented for wild boar is difficult to interpret. In addition to the two juveniles, one senile individual is present, while one young adult and one mature adult are also represented. Scavenging can account for the presence of these weak categories, but the number of represented individuals is too small to draw conclusions from.

The exploitation of rhinoceros at Lunel Viel may be explained as the result of scavenging, since this very large animal is quite difficult to hunt. Modern-day hyenas rarely hunt animals larger than 250 kg.[38] Moreover, pachyderms provide the best scavenging opportunities in actualistic studies in East Africa (cf. Blumenschine 1987). The fact that more young are present in the assemblage can be cited in support of this assumption, but the pattern is not conclusive. Another factor that can be cited in favour of a scavenging strategy in this case is the encounter rate. Based on reconstructed population densities cervids should be encountered 3.3 times more often than rhinoceros. In the assemblage, rhinoceros is far rarer than one would expect if it were hunted on encounter. This sug-

---

38 Less than 1% in a study covering 801 cases (Cooper, Holekamp and Smale 1999).

gests that exploitation of rhinoceros was quite a rare event. Presumably, the number of scavengeable carcasses in the landscape was not very high and competition was often intense (cf. Blumenschine 1987). Therefore, not too many remains may have been available to transport back to the site.

At this site hunting of medium and large sized ungulates provided the mainstay of the diet of cave hyenas. This is apparent even though smaller species may be underrepresented because they will not have been transported to the site as frequently. Still, red deer is also in the size category that is expected to suffer a large degree of bone destruction (*e.g.* Brugal, Fosse, and Guadelli 1997, Fosse *et al.* 1998, Villa *et al.* 2004). Therefore, the rarity of boar, *Equus hydruntinus*, roe deer and other small species must at least partly reflect hyena foraging strategies. The importance of scavenging is hard to ascertain, but is expected to be relatively insignificant in terms of its caloric contribution to the diet. This is thought to be the case in view of the age profiles of the species that are represented at the site. Still, the forested environment indicated by the faunal assemblage must have provided hyenas more scavenging opportunities than their modern savannah habitat, because visibility of carcasses is lower in wooded environments. It has been shown that in East Africa carcasses remain available to scavengers longest in wooded zones of the landscape (cf. Blumenschine 1987). The effect of the forested environment on scavenging opportunities may be augmented by the temperate climate in which decay processes are slowed compared to modern day Africa (Fosse *et al.* 2004).

7.5.2 Camiac

Camiac is another example of a cave site with a bone assemblage accumulated by hyenas (Guadelli *et al.* 1988, Guadelli 1989). It is located in the southwest of France, and is situated at the edge of calcareous terrace, overlooking the valley of tributary of the Canodonne river. This valley is connected to the Dordogne valley (Guadelli *et al.* 1988, Guadelli 1989). This site was strategically situated near the confluence of different river valleys and provided an excellent location to monitor prey. The site has been dated using ^{14}C of a bone fragment, yielding an age of 35.100 +2000/-1500 bp. (Guadelli *et al.* 1988, Guadelli 1989).

The site consists of a small cave and an area of plateau in front of it, from which a large collection of bone materials was recovered. The excavation also yielded a small stone assemblage, which shows that the site was used by both hominins and hyenas. There are convincing arguments to interpret the bone assemblage as reflecting hyena foraging strategies though. First, the concentration of bones was excavated in the southern part of the excavated area, while the majority of artefacts was recovered in the northern part of the excavation. Second, there are no hominin traces of exploitation on the bones, while hyena traces are abundant. Gnaw marks are very common, on most longbones, the epiphyses have been destroyed and many bones show signs of having been ingested by hyenas (Guadelli *et al.* 1988, 61). Moreover, hyena coprolites were also common in the excavated area. Unfortunately, no age profile is available for the hyena remains, but the fact that they are relatively numerous may also be cited in support of the interpretation of this assemblage as having been accumulated by hyenas.

The faunal assemblage of Camiac is presented in table 7.5. It is quite a diverse assemblage, especially in view of the number of bones that was identified (compare the number of species with Taubach or Biache-Saint-Vaast for example). The assemblage is dominated by horse (*Equus caballus*), bovids (mostly bison (*Bison priscus*)) and woolly rhinoceros. If we assume that the bones determined as "bovid" represent both bison and aurochs in the same proportions as the bones that could be determined to species level, 260 of the bovid bones would have belonged to bison. I will therefore assume that 299 bison bones are represented in the assemblage and 38 aurochs bones. Following this line of reasoning, bison would be the second best represented species at the site, while aurochs would be fifth best represented, falling between cave hyena and mammoth.

Some data about the age-structure of the taxa present in the assemblage is reported by Fosse (1996). He bases his report on a

Species	NISP	MNI
Equus caballus gallicus	337	12
Bovines indet.	293	
Coelodonta antiquitatis	200	26
Crocuta crocuta spelaea	76	9
Bison priscus	39	10
Mammuthus primigenius	22	5
Megaloceros giganteus	19	4
Cervus elaphus	12	1
Equus hydruntinus	8	2
Panthera spelaea	5	2
Bos primigenius	5	1
Vulpes vulpes	5	1
Ursus spelaeus	4	2
Canis lupus	2	2
Panthera spelaea var. *cloueti?*	2	1
Alopex lagopus	2	1
Sus scrofa	2	1
Rangifer tarandus	2	1
Total	1035	81

Table 7.5: The faunal assemblage recovered at Camiac. From (Guadelli et al. 1988, 62).

	NISP	
Group	Young	Adult
Cervids	-	12
Equids	19	326
Bovids	3	327
Rhinocerotids	11	182
Proboscideans	4	15

Table 7.6: The age structure of the main taxa present in the faunal assemblage, as reported in (Fosse 1996, 78).

personal communication by the lead author of the paper on Camiac that was available to me. Unfortunately, the age structure is not given in MNI counts based on dentition, but in NISP (nombre de restes). This data is reproduced in table 7.6. These counts do not seem very reliable to me, since all the identified bones are incorporated in the age structure. Not every skeletal part is very suitable for age-determinations however. Different types of bone fuse at different moments in time, etc. Moreover, juvenile bones will also be preferentially destroyed. Bones of adults have a much better chance of survival, therefore juveniles may be underrepresented using this method.

Only small percentages of the bones identified to species show indications of belonging to juvenile individuals. For the best represented group, equids this is about 5.5%, in rhinocerotids this is about 5.7%. In bovids, the percentage is lowest, at 0.9%, while in mammoths, it is 21%. Regarding the latter species, it has to be realised of course that the sample is very small. The same is true for cervids, in whose sample none of the bones belonged to a juvenile individual.

The environment of the site at the time of occupation can be reconstructed from the faunal assemblage and from pollen recovered from the coprolites found at the site. The species list reveals a number of cold adapted species, like reindeer (*Rangifer tarandus*), polar fox (*Alopex lagopus*), mammoth (*Mammuthus primigenius*) and woolly rhinoceros (*Coelodonta antiquitatis*). In addition, the large number of horse remains and the dominance of bison over aurochs bones suggest that the environment was quite open. The presence of red deer and especially wild boar (*Sus scrofa*) shows that forested areas were also present in the surroundings of the site.

The environmental reconstruction based on the species that are present in the assemblage is corroborated by analysis of pollen present in the hyena coprolites that were recovered at the site. 48% of the pollen in the coprolites is arboreal. Pine (*Pinus*) makes up 46.8% of the pollen, while one percent belonged to birch (*Betula*) (Guadelli *et al.* 1988, 63). The sediments of the site were also analysed for pollen, yet these yielded a Mediterranean flora. These pollen must be intrusive in the sediments, since both the bone assemblage and the coprolites point to radically different environmental circumstances.

A ranking of the species present in the assemblage has been compiled in table 7.7. It is clear instantly, that apart from mammoth, the heaviest groups of species present, woolly rhinoceros and bovids are intensively exploited. The most heavily exploited species, horse (*Equus caballus*), is ranked lower, but is still a large species. Other species are represented less strongly in the assemblage.

It is striking that the represented prey species are mainly large herbivores and in the case of woolly rhinoceros even a megaherbivore. As has been pointed out, it is likely that smaller species are underrepresented in hyena den assemblages. Therefore, it can be hypothesised that cervids like red deer and reindeer were probably more important in cave hyena foraging strategies practised at this site than their representation in terms of NISP suggests. On the basis of this assemblage it seems clear that the focus of hyenas was probably geared towards the larger species that were present in the environment. Moreover, cranial remains of smaller ungulates preferentially survive the hyenas' destruction, if these species were important in hyena foraging strategies, at least cranial remains would have been well represented at this site, yielding a higher MNI. The importance of cervids and other smaller species like boar was therefore limited.

Since only very imperfect information on the age structure has been published for this site we cannot draw too many conclusions about the age classes exploited by cave hyenas here. Adult bones are dominant in all taxa except for the proboscideans. Based on this data, for most cases, we would expect the represented animal species to have been exploited by hunting adults. Juvenile bones are more prone to destruction by hyenas however, so that juvenile individuals are probably underrepresented in the bone assemblage. Therefore the importance of scavenging may be underestimated slightly.

This site shows that hyenas preferentially exploited very large species. Equids seem to have been the most heavily exploited species, closely followed by bison. Most striking is the fact that woolly rhinoceros accounts for almost 20% of the assemblage. Considering that it would probably have been present in low population densities (See table 7.8) compared to the smaller species, we can conclude

Rank	Species	Weight	NISP
1	Mammuthus primigenius	5000	22
2	Coelodonta antiquitatis	2900	200
3	Bison priscus	650[39]	39[40]
4	Bos primigenius	600[41]	5[42]
5	Ursus spelaeus	500	4
6	Megaloceros giganteus	450	19
7	Equus caballus	335	337
8	Cervus elaphus	200[43]	12
9	Panthera spelaea	195[44]	5
10	Equus hydruntinus	188	8
11	Sus scrofa	89	2
12	Rangifer tarandus	86[45]	2
13	Crocuta crocuta	70	76
14	Canis lupus	45	2
15	Alopex lagopus	5	2
16	Vulpes vulpes	5	5

Table 7.7: Ranking of the animals represented in the assemblage of Camiac. Weights based on (Brook and Bowman 2004, Louguet-Lefebvre 2005).

Species	Density (ind/km^2)
Equus caballus	0.5046
Bison priscus	0.3216
Coelodonta antiquitatis	0.1163
Crocuta crocuta	0.0431
Bos primigenius	0.3395
Mammuthus primigenius	0.0803

Table 7.8: Reconstructed population densities for the most important species at Camiac.

that woolly rhinoceros was preferentially targeted by hyenas. The low number of juvenile bones in the sample may even point to them being hunted with a focus on adults. On the other hand, it is unclear how many of the adult bones in the sample actually belonged to old individuals. In view of this species' body size I prefer to regardscavenging or hunting of weak individuals as the explanation for their presence at the site.

7.6 Discussion

The two case-studies have shown that foraging behaviours in Pleistocene European cave hyenas deviate from the expectations that were formulated on the basis of comparative studies of spotted hyenas. The focus on cervids in Lunel-Viel is in keeping with what would be expected on the basis of spotted hyena behaviour in Africa. However, the importance of bovids at both Lunel-Viel and Camiac is remarkable. Animals of that size are only rarely hunted by spotted hyenas. The largest prey species they take down regularly is zebra (Cooper, Holekamp, and Smale 1999). The presence of large numbers of aurochs at Lunel-Viel and bison at Camiac shows that the Pleistocene European hyenas were capable of routinely killing much larger prey.

The presence of woolly rhinoceros at Camiac is even more surprising. This species is more than three times larger than the large bovids that were present. Woolly rhinoceros is present at other hyena sites in France, but usually contributes small percentages of the NISP. Nevertheless at a number of sites in the Bohemian Karst, in accumulations produced by hyenas, quite a large number of woolly rhinoceros remains have been found, sometimes accounting for more than 20% of the NISP. In these cases hunting of juvenile animals up to about one year of age seems to have been practised,

---

[39] My estimate since I deem the estimates provided by both Brook and Bowman (2004) and Louguet-Lefebvre (2005) to be unrealistically low.

[40] A large number of the bones identified as "bovines indet." can be assumed to have belonged to this species

[41] My estimate, since I deem the estimates provided by both Brook and Bowman (2004) and Louguet-Lefebvre (2005) to be unrealistically low.

[42] Some of the bones identified as "bovines indet." must be added to this figure

[43] My estimate, since the estimates provided by both Brook and Bowman (2004) and Louguet-Lefebvre (2005) are unrealistically high.

[44] Panthera spelaea var. cloueti is assumed to be equal in rank to Panthera spelaea.

[45] I used the estimate provided by Pushkina and Raia (2008) since the estimate provided by Brook and Bowman (2004) is very low (60 kg.).

while adults were probably scavenged (Diedrich and Žák 2006, 258). Whether scavenging or hunting provided the bulk of woolly rhinoceros at the site, it is clear that this species was preferentially targeted by cave hyenas. We would expect this species to be present in low population densities, therefore encounter rate with this species would have been low; much lower at least than encounter rates with cervids, bovids and equids would have been. Even though this species is overrepresented because its bones are very hard to destroy (*e.g.* Diedrich and Žák 2006, 264), the importance of this heavy species must have been high in caloric terms.

As pointed out, the scavenging opportunities provided by pachyderms are good, since meat is available for a long time and large amounts of it are available. Their availability will have lasted longer in MIS 3, compared to the modern day African ecosystems in which actualistic studies are executed (*e.g.* Blumenschine 1987). Therefore scavenging of pachyderms may have been a productive foraging strategy. However, if this was practised by hyenas, we would also expect a greater number of proboscideans at hyena den sites. These are rare at both Camiac and the Bohemian Karst (Diedrich and Žák 2006). I deem it possible that hunting woolly rhinoceros was practised by hyenas. They would probably have focused on juvenile or weakened individuals. In this regard a detailed study of the remains from Camiac would be helpful.

There is another possible explanation though. Actualistic research suggests that not even hyenas are able to exploit pachyderm carcasses fully, since the skin is difficult to penetrate. When hyenas leave these carcasses, food would still have been available. If Neanderthals had primary access to megaherbivores, their activities may thus have opened up new scavenging opportunities to hyenas. Since scavenging is a well-established foraging strategy in hyenas and the large amounts of food provided by pachyderms will probably not have been exploited fully by Neanderthals, ravaging megaherbivores exploited by Neanderthals may be a likely scenario.

This brings us to the important methodological problem of identifying the accumulating agent of the assemblages under consideration. Both sites that were analysed contain stone artefact assemblages in addition to the bone assemblages. This is not uncommon in the case of hyena dens (Villa and Soressi 2000), however it does open up the possibility that the bone assemblages were not solely accumulated by hyenas. At Lunel-Viel the association of artefacts with the bone assemblage was probably the result of post-depositional processes (Villa and Soressi 2000, 209). This view is strengthened by the strong presence of juvenile hyenas. Hyenas were able to raise their vulnerable cubs in this cave, which suggests that there was minimal disturbance by hominins. Unfortunately, the case is not as clear-cut at Camiac. The bone assemblage has all the characteristics of a hyena assemblage. Moreover, an abundance of coprolites and the important presence of hyena itself all suggest use as a den. This is strengthened by the absence of hominin inflicted marks on the bones. Yet hominin influence cannot be totally ruled out. The case for the interpretation of Camiac as a den may be boosted by the publication of the age-structure of the hyenas. If juveniles are an important category this would show that cubs were raised there and hominin influence was minimal.

Few well published age-profiles are available for the prey species represented in hyena dens. The age profiles for the lower assemblage from Lunel-Viel suggest that in cervids the emphasis was on juveniles, although the other age classes are by no means absent. The highest peaks in the graph showing the age-profile for horses concern young adults, but mature adults are well represented. In bovids, the emphasis may have been on adults, but the data are insufficient to be certain. The available data on the age categories of the species represented at Camiac are even poorer, but except for mammoth, the number of juvenile bones seems to be small.

Most authors expect hyenas to focus on weak individuals in populations. It is generally assumed that only hominins consistently hunt prime-aged prey (*e.g.* Steele 2002, 307). In many studies of modern spotted hyenas, a preference for juvenile and senile individuals is apparent. The age profiles for Pleistocene hyena dens do not always conform to this pattern. The pattern for equids at Lunel-Viel for example shows that adults are well represented. A recently published study shows even more clearly that cave hyena strategies may also have focussed on adult animals. At Fouvent, located in the Haute-Saône, a large faunal assemblage was recovered. Only a study of the horse remains found at the site has been published. With 41.2% of the NISP, they were the dominant species represented at the site though, followed by cave hyena with 34.7% (Fosse 1997, 17). The age profile of the equids present at the site is indistinguishable from that of equids at the Middle Palaeolithic sites of Bau de l'Aubesier and Combe Grenal, showing a dominance of horses aged 6-9, or prime-aged individuals (Fernandez, Guadelli, and Fosse 2006, 180).

However, there is a lot of variation in the age profiles of prey animals found in hyena dens. At some sites, young animals do make up an important part of the ungulate animals, and in some cases even represent a majority (Brugal, Fosse, and Guadelli 1997, Fosse 1999). However, some sites show that they were definitely capable of hunting primarily adults of large species like horse.

The fact that cave hyenas hunted larger species of prey than spotted hyenas do, can at least in part be explained by the fact that they were larger than their modern-day counterparts. In general there seems to be a relationship between predator size and prey size, with prey size increasing disproportionally in relation to predator size (see formula in section 4.5) (Radloff and Toit 2004, 410). On the other hand, the estimated weight of the largest common spotted hyena prey, zebra, is about 288 kilos. (Brook and Bowman 2004, Cooper, Holekamp, and Smale 1999). Buffalo is only rarely hunted and according to Cooper Holekamp and Smale (1999, 152-153), only when weakened. This species weighs between 500 to 600 kilos. Bison is heavier than buffalo and was exploited regularly at Camiac, but also at other excavated hyena dens, like Bois Roche (Villa *et al.* 2004). This suggests that in some Pleistocene cave hyena populations, hunting in groups may have been more important than it was to modern-day spotted hyenas, allowing them to take larger prey more often.

A final remark concerns an interesting category of finds amidst hyena bone accumulations, namely antler material. Especially red deer (*Cervus elaphus*) antlers were collected by hyenas. These antlers had nutritional value, since hyenas could chew them and digest the bone collagen. Many of the antlers that are found in these deposits are shed. For example, at Guattari, 56 shed antlers were found, against 13 unshed ones (Fosse *et al.* 1998, 55). This shows that we need to be careful when interpreting collections of shed antlers as the results of hominin activities, since hominins are clearly not the only agents that can be responsible for the accumulation of these items. Whether antler material was collected by hominins or hyenas is often easily distinguished, however. Hyenas are thought to have collected antlers in order to exploit their fat content and they will therefore be gnawed (Fosse *et al.* 1998, 55).

7.7 Conclusion

This chapter has shown that using OFT to differentiate between cave hyena and Neanderthal foraging strategies is difficult. European hyena dens and Middle Palaeolithic bone assemblages show a large overlap in the categories of prey that are present. Both hyenas and Neanderthals were apparently able to systematically target large ungulates, such as horses and bovids. Still, both cave hyena and Neanderthals appear to have been successful in Pleistocene Europe. This suggests that they were both able to monopolise large amounts of biomass. Therefore some differentiation in niches must have existed, otherwise both species would not have been able to co-exist. The results of the analysis do indeed point to a number of differences in the foraging niches of both species which will be listed and discussed below.

The most important difference is in the greater variation in species and age-categories of prey present in hyena dens. This is not unexpected. In modern-day Africa there is a lot of competition among different species of carnivore for similar species of prey. The composition of the carnivore guild in a region is shaped by this competition. In many areas of Africa, the presence of small species of carnivores like cheetah or wild dog is severely limited by the fact that larger predators like lion and spotted hyena consume most of the available biomass and moreover frequently kill smaller predators. In addition, in some areas, the number of hyenas seems to be limited by lions, while in other areas it is the other way round (Owen-Smith and Mills 2008, Van Valkenburgh 2001).

Studies of contemporary predators suggest that overlapping prey choice is a common phenomenon in the predator guild. Differentiation of niches may not be effectuated in the range of species that is taken, but can be effectuated in another field. For example in the timing, with some predators taking certain species at other times than others, *i.e.* differences in seasonality (*e.g.* Stiner 1992, 433). This kind of niche separation may have been present in the exploitation of bears for example. It appears that in many areas hyenas exploit caves in which bears hibernate, scavenging on the remains of bears that died during hibernation (Diedrich and Žák 2006, 260-262). Neanderthals, as shown by both Taubach and Biache-Saint-Vaast assemblages, actively hunted these large predators.

Another obvious difference between the Neanderthal and hyena niche lies in the mode of acquisition and exploitation of prey species. Hyenas practise a significant amount of scavenging in addition to hunting. The amount of scavenging practised may be quite minor in some spotted hyena populations, but it is practised in all populations and in many it does play an important role with regard to subsistence. Scavenging is such an important strategy in hyenas, that they evolved adaptations geared toward a scavenging way of life, including an acute sense of smell that is used to locate carcasses, a gastro-intestinal tract that can cope with decaying meat, teeth that can crush bones in order to be able to profit from carcasses with little or no meat, etc. (*e.g.* Tooby and DeVore 1987). Hominins probably had different adaptations in order to intercept prey. Instead of an acute sense of smell, they may have used their increased intelligence to predict locations where prey would be and will have ambushed or hunted them at strategic locations. This is shown by the consistent use of sites like Biache-Saint-Vaast and Taubach to kill fixed species of prey.

Subtle niche differences between Neanderthals and cave hyenas may be found in the categories of prey that were taken by both species. Many recent analyses show that Neanderthals most often focussed specifically on prime-aged individuals in ungulates (see examples in chapter 3). Hyenas were able to target prime-aged ungulates, as shown by the equids represented in Fouvent, but it appears that the focus on prime-aged individuals is less clear-cut than in Neanderthals. At present, a focus on prime aged individuals has been demonstrated for some species at some sites, but this focus is less obvious in other den sites and other prey species (*e.g.* Brugal, Fosse, and Guadelli 1997, 174, Fosse, 1999 #696, 82). This suggests that hunting strategies practised by hyenas may have been more variable and more opportunistic than those practised by Neanderthals. This impression is reinforced by the fact that bone assemblages recovered from hyena dens are usually more diverse than those from hominin sites (Fosse 1997, 18).

Both species largely focussed on the same range of prey species. In similar circumstances, Neanderthals would probably focus on a narrower set of species and age categories of prey. Cave hyenas accumulations show more variety, in the form of a larger diversity of species and in represented age-categories.

Another important difference between their niches may be the fact that hyenas are adapted to nocturnal foraging. We assume that Neanderthals, like modern humans and apes were diurnal foragers. Temporal partitioning of resources by adapting activity cycles is a mechanism of niche differentiation that has been observed in nature (Kronfeld-Schor and Dayan 2003, Richards 2002).

Moreover, Neanderthals may have routinely hunted categories of prey slightly higher up in the "spectrum of danger". In the case of woolly rhinoceros in the Bohemian Karst, cave hyenas seem to have preferentially hunted animals under the age of one. When we compare this with hunting of rhinoceros at Taubach and Biache-Saint-Vaast, Neanderthals seem to have focussed on slightly older individuals. In the case of bears, Neanderthals apparently hunted bears at some sites, while hyenas seem to have profited mostly from individuals that died during hibernation.

As discussed earlier, there is a significant relationship in most predators between predator size and prey size (Radloff and Toit 2004). Hyenas and hominins being in the roughly the same range of weight, would naturally also select the same range of prey categories. Therefore this small difference in focus of hunting may point to a difference in strategies.

One of the ways in which the relationship between predator and prey size can be circumvented is by hunting in groups. Wild dogs in Africa are able to bring down much larger prey relative to their size than most other predators in the same environment. This is because they always hunt in packs (Radloff and Toit 2004, 416). As I have argued, pack hunting was probably more important in cave hyena than it is in modern day spotted hyena. However, if social structure and feeding competition in cave hyena were anything like they are in spotted hyena, hunting large prey in large groups may not have been as profitable for individual cave hyenas. Sharing of food from kills does not seem to be important in spotted hyenas (Mills 1985, Watts and Holekamp 2007), so lower-ranked individuals may not have had much to gain from cooperative hunting.

At Lunel-Viel where the forested environment may have limited visibility and speed of movement when compared to more open areas, individual hunting of cervids may have been a very profitable strategy for solitary individuals, since other group members would have converged on kills and carcasses more slowly than in open areas. Moreover, prey will have been more dispersed through the landscape than in open areas, where animals prefer to concentrate in large herds for safety. This means that carcasses and kills would haveoccurred more dispersed through the environment, and so presumably would foraging cave hyenas.

Sharing of meat seems more important in both modern humans and our primate cousins, chimpanzees (*e.g.* Hawkes 1993, Stanford 2001a, Stanford 2001b). In chimpanzees for example, meat is available to low-ranking individuals. If they capture prey, they can divide it, even if high-ranking individuals arrive on the scene (De Waal 2005, 197). Given the behaviour of their closest relatives it is predicted that division of meat was also common among Neanderthals. Therefore they had more incentive to form larger groups of hunters, able to hunt larger species than cave hyenas. Cave hyenas probably preferred to forage in smaller groups or solitarily if circumstances permitted. At Lunel-Viel for example, the closed environment may have led to the occurrence of many cervids in small groups. The hyenas were probably able to exploit them in a solitary fashion. At Camiac, in more open environments, hyena groups were probably more attuned to hunting in groups. Cervids were less important for the diet here. They probably occurred in larger groups due to the open environment, necessitating exploitation by hyenas hunting in packs. In these circumstances hunting cervids became less important in favour of larger species offering larger "packages" of meat.

Scavenging is another foraging activity that can be done solitarily. Scavenging opportunities were also probably more abundant in Pleistocene Europe than in modern African savannahs where most actualistic work on scavenging as a subsistence strategy has been done (Fosse *et al.* 2004). In colder periods with animals concentrated in herds, this may have been an interesting strategy. However, in this period, the open landscape would also have improved visibility. In East Africa, it appears that scavenging opportunities are most abundant in riparian zones in the landscape (Blumenschine 1987). Therefore more scavenging opportunities may have been available to hyenas in the forested environments at Lunel-Viel than around Camiac.

In this case OFT can be invoked to explain why this role of scavenging is not expected to be important in Neanderthals. Since Neanderthals presumably had a different social organisation, with less intra-group competition for meat, scavenging ungulates was probably not rewarding for them. If food-sharing was practised, it would be more rewarding for individual Neanderthals to cooperate and concentrate on hunting large prey. This has the advantage of safe-guarding a more reliable, steady supply of food is procured. Moreover return rates for the cooperative hunting of herbivores would be higher than the return rates that could be achieved by scavenging their carcasses. Only scavenging of very large animals like rhinoceros or proboscideans is predicted to have been profitable for Neanderthals.

Another facet of the explanation of the signalled pattern may lie in spotted hyena social structure. Hyenas live in multi-male, multi-female groups, much like primates do. Females are solitarily burdened with the raising of their cubs. Alloparental care is unknown in spotted hyenas (Mills 1985, Watts and Holekamp 2007). Females therefore need to hunt in order to feed their offspring. Hunting dangerous prey would result in losing reproductively active females, and their dependent offspring from a pack. Losing reproductively active females from a population has much greater negative consequences than losing reproductively active males. The rate of reproduction of a population does not hinge on the available amount of sperm, since one male has much more sperm than needed to fertilise a female. The amount of available uteri is much more important for the reproductive rate of a population and these can be fertilised by a small number of males.

Males are thus more expendable than females in a population. If hunting was done by male Neanderthals, they could afford to hunt dangerously. Moreover, if reproductive success was linked to success in hunting, something that is seen in both hunter/gatherers and chimpanzees, it may have been profitable for males to pursue dangerous categories of game. If successful this probably provided them with better mating opportunities than the hunting of smaller less dangerous prey would have. In hyenas, where no division of labour was in place, hunting the most dangerous prey species would result in potentially losing both females and their offspring and was therefore probably avoided. On the other hand, this applied only to large carnivores like bears and megaherbivores like rhinoceros. The horse age-profile at Fouvent shows that when confronted with ungulates living in herds they were able to focus on the prime-aged, and thus most dangerous, individuals.

Application of OFT to hyenas and comparing the results of the analysis with the results of analyses of Neanderthal foraging produces better understanding of both species' foraging behaviour. This shows that OFT is a productive approach to studying Pleistocene foraging strategies. Moreover, the information available for both the hyena and the Middle Palaeolithic sites that were used in this thesis was not ideal. This suggests that the results of similar analyses may be improved in the future.

8 Discussion

This study has tested whether the diet breadth model from the domain of Optimal Foraging Theory (OFT) can be used to analyse Pleistocene foraging strategies. In this chapter I will synthesize the results of this study. As pointed out in chapter 1, understanding the Neanderthal dietary niche is very important with regard to testing a multitude of theories on hominin life-histories, group size, language abilities and the function and cause of increases in Middle and Late Pleistocene brain sizes. The use of ecological theory can greatly contribute to our insight into Neanderthal foraging niche. However, before the diet breadth model could be applied to the Pleistocene, some obstacles had to be overcome. First, I will discuss the problems that are encountered when applying the diet breadth model to Pleistocene foraging and the solutions I arrived at in this study. This will be followed by a section that deals with the specific problems that were encountered when trying to apply the model to the selected archaeological and palaeontological sites that were analysed. Finally I will summarise the results of this study with regard to our understanding of the Neanderthal foraging niche and place these results within their wider archaeological context.

8.1 Application of the diet breadth model to archaeological data

Before OFT can be used to analyse foraging strategies evidenced by the archaeological record, a number of methodological issues need to be addressed. The diet breadth model has been developed in behavioural ecology for situations where one can observe which prey is taken at what frequency. In order to apply OFT to the archaeological record we must try to distil that information from a time-averaged and biased archaeological record. This study has highlighted some of the problems of applying OFT to archaeology but also proposed solutions, which will be discussed shortly here.

In order to estimate which prey is taken at what frequency, I have chosen to analyse the Number of Identified Specimens (NISP) of the represented species as a measure of the frequency of their exploitation. As discussed in chapter 4, this measure is not unproblematic. A possible solution to the problems is to use a different index to analyse the bone assemblages. A useful measurement could be the MNI of a species present in the assemblage. This would negate the problems stemming from the different composition of skeletons and at least partly overcome biases from differential processing and transport of different species. However, there are different ways of calculating MNI, leading to different possible outcomes (*e.g.* Reitz and Wing 1999). Therefore, using MNI when comparing sites whose primary analysis has been done by different archaeozoologists may be problematic. Moreover, not all authors publish MNI's. Hence, in order to compare different bone assemblages published by different authors, NISP is the only measure that can be used for the sites studied in this thesis. Because of our awareness of the problems associated with this variable, we may be able to correct the representation of different species based on the number of skeletal elements they possess. Moreover, behaviours like transport and processing can be modelled using measures for skeletal part representation.

The problems associated with transport behaviour are part of a larger set of problems concerning the various biases in the studied assemblages. As discussed in chapters 3 and 4, hunter/gatherers characteristically exploit their territories using some form of mobility, exploiting part of their territory until resources become scarcer and then moving on to a different area. Moreover, hunter/gatherers produce several types of sites; some sites are only occupied for specific activities, while others function as a home base or central place. This has obvious and important repercussions for this study. The archaeological sites from different areas and time periods analysed cannot be taken as representative of the full array of foraging strategies of the occupants. The analysis can only illuminate the foraging behaviour reflected at Taubach and Biache-Saint-Vaast themselves. Season-specific activities due to seasonal changes in ranking of prey species cannot be studied in this way.

Nevertheless, at both Biache-Saint-Vaast and Taubach, large amounts of material were found, which suggests that these sites occupied an important position in the foraging strategies of the groups occupying them. Also, hunting was not focussed on a single species, but multiple exploited species are present at both sites. This suggests that we are not dealing with specialised hunting camps. Moreover, at least at Biache-Saint-Vaast stone tool production was important, suggesting the juxtaposition of several activities. Investment in site furniture may have taken place at Taubach if we accept reports of hearths being present at the site. Therefore we can assume with reasonable certainty that the sites represent an important proportion of the foraging activities practised by the groups occupying them.

With regard to the selection of assemblages formed by cave hyenas (*Crocuta spelaea*), similar problems are encountered. Studies show that the communal den of a spotted hyena (*Crocuta crocuta*) clan is moved regularly, on average once a month according to one 10-year study. Many sites are not re-used, but some dens are re-used periodically over long periods of time (Boydston, Kapheim, and Holekamp 2006, Pokines and Peterhans 2007) . Moreover, next to communal dens, other types of sites are also produced. For example some females (often low-ranking ones) rear their young in an isolated natal den for the first month of their life (Boydston, Kapheim, and Holekamp 2006). Furthermore, hyenas have also been alleged to produce caches (Diedrich and Žák 2006).

With regard to the hyena accumulations analysed in this study, the sheer amount of material found precludes the idea that the sites functioned as natal dens. The age-distribution of the hyena population of the analysed accumulation at Lunel-Viel suggests that the site functioned as a communal den. No information was available on the age-structure of the hyenas at Camiac, but at least the abundance of coprolites can be taken as an indication that hyenas were present at the site for a prolonged period of time, suggesting that the site did not function as a cache, but as a communal den. If den use of cave hyenas is comparable to that of spotted hyenas, the analysis of hyena sites may give more insight in the total spectrum of foraging behaviours exhibited by these species than the analysis of Neanderthal sites. This is the case because the hyena accumulations are the result of multiple occupations that took place during different seasons. If we take modern human foraging strategies as an analogue for Neanderthals, the use of specific sites may have been tied to a specific season in Neanderthals. Therefore, occupation of Neanderthal sites may habitually have taken place in the same season.

The application of the diet breadth model can be improved by selection of sites of which the Central-Place character can be more securely ascertained. This kind of site is rare in the archaeological record however. A site like Kebara in Israel, might qualify. Here the occupied space was organised in the same way over a long time, long enough to accumulate several meters of sediment, suggesting very intensive use (*e.g.* Bar-Yosef *et al.* 1992, Meignen *et al.* 1998, Shea 2003, 181). In northwest Europe, this calibre of site is unknown though.

Another improvement in the application of OFT to the Pleistocene archaeological record would be to study several sites in a micro-region that functioned in the same settlement system. This would enable studying the full scale of foraging activities practised over the course of a year. The execution of such a research design is made impossible by the fact that there are huge gaps in preservation, and therefore in some contexts almost no securely dated sites with bone assemblages can be recovered. Moreover, the uncertainties associated with the direct dating methods for this period of time are so large that it is very hard to define a set of sites that would have functioned within the same system.

Finally, when applying this method to archaeological sites, one must carefully consider the argumentation one uses. If the excavated assemblage is taken to represent the optimal diet breadth, one must then explain why some species are not included in it. This can be done by simply positing that the return rates of these species were low. Such a manoeuvre does not explain anything however, unless one can specify why the return rate was lower than that of the exploited species. Moreover this does not take into account the possibility that the assumptions of the model, i.e. the currency that was maximised, may be incorrect and therefore the model that is used can easily be perpetuated. This means that if species that are expected to be included in the optimal set were left unexploited, one must scrutinise the assumptions underlying the model carefully in order to gauge whether for example the ranking that is used may be incorrect simply because an irrelevant currency was chosen.

8.2 Reconstructing the model's variables

In behavioural ecology, much information needed to successfully apply the diet breadth model can be collected in the field. Such data had to be estimated for Pleistocene applications, which presented an important challenge for the successful application of the model to Neanderthal foraging behaviours. Estimating these data proved more complicated than I had initially expected. The amount of variation of estimates, even for basic attributes like animal body weight is considerable. With regard to Pleistocene applications, these problems are exacerbated by the fact that some of the available prey species are extinct nowadays.

More importantly, taphonomy precludes a full analysis of foraging strategies, since some categories of remains are only very poorly preserved. The most obvious categories of these consists of plant foods. As discussed in chapter 3, virtually nothing is known about the vegetal component of the Neanderthal diet and what little information we have is mostly from the Mediterranean. This study focuses on the faunal component of the foraging niche. However, both analysed archaeological assemblages are from periods with a "temperate" climate. Therefore, we cannot dismiss a potential vegetal component of the diet of the occupants of the sites. In terms of caloric contribution, I assume that the faunal component was much more important however. This is corroborated by the isotopic evidence of one individual from Sclayn, dating to MIS 5c or 5e, which shows a "carnivore signature" even in a warm climatic phase (Bocherens and Biliou 1998). Other sources of food may also be underrepresented in the archaeological record. As discussed in chapter 3, ichtyological remains in particular are often underrepresented in the archaeological record. But again, isotopic evidence seems to demonstrate that aquatic resources did not play an important role in Neanderthal diets.

Ethnographic data support the idea that plant foods would not have provided the mainstay of a hunter/gatherer diet at temperate latitudes (*e.g.* Kelly 1995, 67-69). Binford has extrapolated the data on extant hunter/gatherer diets to the environment of Pleistocene Europe and concludes that animal foods must have provided the mainstay of the diet, except in some areas in the Mediterranean (Binford 2001, 193, fig. 6.07). Moreover, he suggests that during glacials, the boundary of the areas where animals provided 50% or more of the diet may have moved southward to North Africa (Binford 2007, 193). Still, we must take into account that plants may have provided a highly ranked source of food at temperate latitudes at least seasonally. The role played by aquatic foods in contemporary hunter/gatherers is large at temperate latitudes. The exploitation of aquatic resources, or rather its rarity, in Middle Palaeolithic contexts is therefore an important research topic. For this study, it seemed most productive to focus on the mammal component of Neanderthal subsistence, since the available information unambiguously shows that this was the most important source of calories.

In order to construct a ranking of the available mammal species, I used body weight estimates from the literature. As pointed out in the previous chapters, many widely differing estimates for the same species can be found in the literature (Brook and Bowman 2004, Louguet-Lefebvre 2005, Pushkina and Raia 2008). The weights used can therefore not be considered anything more than "educated guesses". In addition, other attributes could influence the ranking of species. Some of these have been discussed in chapter 4. With regard to the application of OFT to Pleistocene archaeology, especially fur may have been a factor that influenced the ranking of certain prey species. In general, the fur of larger animal species is thicker than that of smaller species, which might give large fur-bearing species a bonus in the ranking. This applies especially to brown bear, whose fur has better insulating qualities than that of for example polar bear. Another interesting case is that of polar fox, which has very thick fur with good insulative qualities (Scholander *et al.* 1950, 230). This may be a valuable attribute that could be incorporated in future rankings, especially for sites situated in cold environments.

Other factors are even more difficult to reconstruct, most notably for extinct animals. Especially environmental preference and population density, both important variables, posed problems. In order to reconstruct the environmental preference of extinct animals, we can use anatomical features like dentition and manner of locomotion. This can be combined with chemical evidence on the isotopic signature of fossil remains. This reflects an animal's dietary habits and therefore to a certain degree its environment. The outcomes of these analyses can be ambiguous though. Isotopic studies of cave bears (*Ursus spelaeus*) for example have been used to argue for both a vegetarian diet (Bocherens, Fizet, and Mariotti 1994) and an omnivorous diet (Richards *et al.* 2008a). We must therefore take into account that a species' habitat may have been variable and cannot always be easily characterised.

In the case of extant species, the habitat preferences of modern populations can be observed and used to model the preferences of their Pleistocene counterparts. Therefore our knowledge of the biotope of these species is more reliable. On the other hand, some problems do exist in this domain. First, a species' adaptation needs not have remained unchanged since the Middle or Late

Pleistocene, since it has been under evolutionary selection and may have adapted to different habitats. Second, in modern-day Europe, many large mammal species have been relegated to living in marginal areas, since most of the prime land in the continent has been developed for human activities. Furthermore, due to the extinction of some animals that played an important role in the ecological structure of the landscape, like proboscideans and large carnivores, the modern guilds of animals are very different from those of the Pleistocene.

We know from the excavated assemblages that animal communities of the Pleistocene were non-analogous to those of the present (*e.g.* Stewart 2004, Stewart 2005). This is often attributed to the environment in the Pleistocene being more "mosaic" than nowadays (*e.g.* Gamble 1999, 112). In this study the problem is most clearly illustrated by the representation of horses at an interglacial site like Taubach. Pollen records indicate the environment was densely forested. Equids are adapted to grazing in open areas and are therefore not expected to be present at interglacial sites in forested environments. The environment must therefore have been more varied than nowadays. As pointed out above, elephants and mammoths were probably keystone species, with a big impact on the environment, thereby promoting open spaces and diversity of vegetation (*e.g.* Haynes 2006, Shoshani 1998). Moreover the presence of more species of predators may also have affected the opportunities of different herbivores, possible enabling more species to co-exist (Leibold 1996, Quammen 2005).

These problems seriously affect the accuracy of predictions based on habitat preferences, such as estimates of the population densities of the different species that were available. This compounds the problem of estimating population density, in turn making the encounter rate with species difficult to predict. In this study I have chosen to use simple body weight based formulas to get an idea of the population density of species in ideal circumstances. Combined with the indications about the environment we can therefore gauge the likely encounter rate with the species at stake. In the future, this formula may be improved by more precise environmental reconstructions. This will not erase this problem completely, since the analytical techniques like pollen analysis still yield information that, for example in the case of Taubach, is to some degree at odds with the excavated mammal communities. Another interesting option is to take the abundance of species in the palaeontological record as a measure of their population density. However, this may be problematic, because some species will be underrepresented in the fossil record because their ecological niche is unfavourable for fossilization. These species would not normally be encountered in areas where their bones might be preserved, something that has been proposed for Merck's rhinoceros (Billia 2008, 35).

Even more difficult is the reconstruction of the handling costs of the various species. This variable depends on the capabilities of the predator and the anti-predator behaviours of a prey species. I have chosen to use simple attributes of the available species to get an indication of the level of difficulty hunting the species in question may have entailed. The effects of using different kinds of stone tool technology and different strategies for intercepting, killing and processing certain species is hard to estimate. I assume that no specialized tools were needed in order to butcher the different species, since all species concerned were mammals. However, one might hypothesize that skinning pachyderms may have been more costly than skinning other mammals and that this activity may thus have required specialised tools. This has not been incorporated in the handling costs of species in this study however. I do assume that the cost of butchery becomes relatively higher in smaller species since they possess similar skeletons to larger species, resulting in a similar procedure of butchery. The amount of meat that they yield is much smaller though. Especially in small mammals, handling costs may thus become prohibitively high (*e.g.* Ugan 2005).

In reconstructing handling costs, great improvements could be realised if archaeological information on hunting strategies and the killing power of the weapons used could be incorporated in the handling costs of prey species. This is hard to realise though. Information on the weaponry used is rare. Wooden spears are known from Schöningen, and Clacton, but it is uncertain how widespread their use was. Moreover there is controversy over whether these spears were thrown (Rieder 2003) or thrusted (Churchill 2002). Moreover, stone-tipped spears may also have been used in the Middle Palaeolithic (*e.g.* Shea 2006, Villa and Lenoir 2006). However, it is unsure what tool forms can be classified as spear points in Middle Palaeolithic assemblages and what percentage of points was actually used as a spear point. Strategies using traps are even even harder to model, although a site like La Cotte de Saint-Brelade shows that Neanderthals were certainly capable of organising an ambush. Reconstructing handling costs in this kind of detail would be interesting in order to refine Pleistocene applications of OFT, but as some of the attributes to be modelled are very difficult to approximate, this may do little to improve the fit of the model. It was therefore thought that for the scope of this study it would be more productive to focus on simple proxies to gain insight in the handling costs.

Finally, we must realise that the variables on which the models are based have been defined not by Neanderthals, but by researchers. Identification of prey categories, for example is done based on the biological species concept. Neanderthal foragers may not have recognised all species we identify as separate categories of prey. One could hypothesise that the difference between Merck's rhinoceros (*Stephanorhinus kirchbergensis*) and narrow-nosed rhinoceros (*Dicerorhinus hemitoechus*) was not very important to Neanderthals. They are very similar animals, both falling into the heaviest category of species, leading solitary lives etcetera. Therefore, Neanderthals may have adpoted a single "rhinoceros" category in their foraging decisions. I assume that the categorizations used by Neanderthals will at least be approximated by the biological species concept used in this study. Moreover in the absence of any sources of information on "emic" categorizations used by Neanderthals, no real solution can be found for this problem.

8.3 Modelling Neanderthals

Besides the problems surrounding the reconstruction of the variables described above, reconstructing the characteristics of the predator for which the model is supposed to operate is not unproblematic either. As discussed in chapter 2, Neanderthal energetics and life histories were probably different from ours and these biological factors may have affected foraging behaviour. However, in many areas, there is little or no consensus as to how much Neanderthals differed from the modern pattern.

First, Neanderthals may have had an elevated BMR. It is thought that this trait was an adaptation to the cold, also present in modern-day hunter/gatherers in cold climates. Moreover, the increase in Neanderthal BMR may have been greater than in modern human groups according to some (e.g Churchill 2007), because they were less able to fashion insulating clothes. This in itself has no repercussions for the working of the diet breadth model, since it does not alter encounter rates or return rates. Therefore, an optimal set will still be exploited consiting of the species for which the combined encounter rate and handling cost yields the highest composite return rate. On the other hand, it does have repercussions for Neanderthal behaviour. Because of their higher energetic requirements, Neanderthals needed to realise a very high return rate (Churchill 2007, Sorensen and Leonard). This may have proven problematic in some circumstances, for example if the optimal return rate decreased, for instance because of a drop in herbivore biomass in the landscape. In such cases Neanderthals may be forced to adapt, for example by increasing their mobility rates or by changing their group size or migrating to other areas, sooner than a modern human group would.

Cold adaptations have also been used to explain the fact that Neanderthals seem to exemplify Allen's and Bergman's rule see (chapter 2). They are quite heavy for their length and have relatively short limbs. Both these factors decrease their surface area relative to their volume, thereby reducing the amount of heat loss. As discussed in chapter 2 and 4, their relatively short lower limbs have other consequences, besides minimising heat loss. They are thought to significantly increase their cost of locomotion (Steudel-Numbers and Tilkens 2004, Weaver and Steudel-Numbers 2005). This has consequences for their diet breadth, since it influences handling cost. It is predicted to favour a smaller diet breadth in Neanderthals than in modern humans in comparable circumstances. It is expected that return rates for Neanderthals would drop faster in response to higher tracking and pursuit costs, thus leading to a lower optimal diet breadth.

Recent work suggests that they may also have exhibited different activity patterns. Results of analyses of skeletal correlates of activity patterns are not always conclusive though. In a recent study, Pearson, Cordero, and Busby (2007, 150-151) argue that Neanderthal activity patterns may have been comparable to those of modern human foragers living in rugged terrain, like Epigravettians from Italy. It has been proposed though that Neanderthals were characterised by more intensive subsistence practices than their modern human contemporaries (Pearson, Cordero, and Busby 2007, 151). In light of their proposed high energetic needs, this is a logical hypothesis.

Another interesting factor is the fact that Neanderthals seem to have matured faster than modern humans. Studies into the formation of teeth have yielded conflicting results so far (Ramirez-Rozzi and Bermúdez de Castro 2004, Smith *et al.* 2007) contra (Guatelli-Steinberg *et al.* 2005). If Neanderthals did mature faster than modern humans, this would have placed a great energetic demand on the adults providing for the child. Again, this does not impact upon behaviour according to the diet breadth model, but on the other hand may have made poorer areas unfeasible for Neanderthal occupation, while a species with lower energetic needs, like *Homo sapiens sapiens*, may have been able to colonise the area.

8.4 This study

In order to apply the diet breadth model, two important Middle Palaeolithic sites are analysed in this study: Taubach and Biache-Saint-Vaast. They are compared with two Pleistocene hyena dens, Lunel-Viel and Camiac. The archaeological sites were chosen because both sites yielded large bone assemblages that have been published. These assemblages are unambiguously associated with hominin activities, since cut-marks are abundant and the occurrence of carnivore marks is minimal. Moreover, carnivore remains at the sites are rare and no other indications of their presence, like coprolites, were reported. The selected sites therefore provide a good opportunity to study hominin foraging strategies.

With regard to the comparison between the archaeological materials and the hyena sites, there is certainly much room for improvement. Ideally, one would use hyena dens without any indications for hominin activity, while the sites used in this study both yielded small stone artefact assemblages. Unfortunately, almost all published Pleistocene hyena dens harbour stone tools. Because of the character of the bone assemblage, the presence of hyena traces on the bones and the absence of traces of hominin activities on the bones I have assumed that the accumulation of the bone assemblages can be attributed mainly to hyena activities. Moreover, the hyena dens used in such a comparison should ideally be located in the same region and dated to the same period as the archaeological sites that are being analysed. Unfortunately, no well-published hyena dens in the vicinity of Taubach and Biache-Saint-Vaast were available for analysis. Therefore, the choice of sites used in the present study, although far from ideal is the best available at present.

With regard to the archaeological sites, other sites from the same latitude containing well preserved and well published bone assemblages are uncommon. Although for future applications, analysis of some other sites may be very useful, many of the sites that are available provide little information. One well-published site with regard to Neanderthal hunting strategies is the site of Wallertheim. This site, which has been analysed by Gaudzinski (1995, 1996) might be expected to be included in this study. It has been left out of this analysis for two important reasons. First, two excavations at the site have yielded very different results. The assemblage that was analysed by Gaudzinski was excavated in the early 20th century and points to specialised hunting of bison. However, excavations in the vicinity of the early excavations in the nineties by Conard *et al.* (*e.g.* Conard *et al.* 1995, Conard and Prindiville 2000, Conard, Prindiville, and Adler 1998) failed to replicate the results reported by Gaudzinski. Multiple find levels were identified, some containing bone assemblages and stone tools, but it could not always be ascertained that the artefacts were associated with the bone assemblages. None of the findlevels yielded a bone collection comparable to the one studied by Gaudzinski (Conard and Prindiville 2000, 295). Second, the assemblage analysed by Gaudzinski provides indications for exploitation of only one species, namely bison (*Bison priscus*). The site may therefore have functioned as a special-purpose site and analysis would probably not yield insight in the full suite of Neanderthal foraging strategies and the set of species that they exploited. This is underscored by the large variety of species that is represented in the layers that were researched in the nineties. The possibility of a site not yielding a representative picture of Neanderthal foraging strategies is also the reason for the exclusion of other sites, like Salzgitter-Lebenstedt, which show focussed exploitation of one animal species only.

For other sites that contain large bone assemblages in which multiple species of animal are present, the association of the species with hominin activities was not unambiguous. At Buhlen for example, mammoth, woolly rhinoceros and horse remains are present in large numbers. The number of cut-marks on the other hand is quite small and gnaw marks have also been observed (*e.g.* Prins 2005). Other sites like the caves of Scladina (Pathou-Mathis 1998), that yielded both hominin remains and lithic artefacts, seem to have functioned as a carnivore den as well, making it difficult to separate hominin from carnivore activities. The number of sites suitable for the application of OFT therefore proved to be quite limited.

In the end, the sites of Taubach and Biache-Saint-Vaast appeared to be the only sites in northwestern Europe that satisfied most of the requirements for the application of the diet breadth model. This does not mean that they were wholly unproblematic. The amount of information about the bone assemblage was not ideal, most obviously in the case of Biache-Saint-Vaast, but to a lesser degree in the case of Taubach as well. Furthermore, the amount of environmental information could be improved for both sites.

In the case of Biache-Saint-Vaast, the publication of a second monograph, which was announced in 1988, might resolve some of the issues that currently hamper the application of OFT to the site. With regard to Taubach, some of the information needed is now lost forever, since bones have been destroyed or lost and the stratigraphic provenance of the old collections may be hard to reconstruct. If the location of the supposed *Knochensand* can be ascertained, the application of radiometric dating methods may at least resolve the issues surrounding the date of the assemblage. With a solution to this problem, the certainty with which the environment can be reconstructed increases. Some of the information needed for Taubach may yet be gained. Further studies may clarify exactly how many narrow-nosed rhinoceros (*Dicerorhinus hemitoechus*) bones are present in the rhinoceros sample and how many aurochs (*Bos primigenius*) bones are included in the bison sample.

8.5 Application of OFT to Biache-Saint-Vaast and Taubach

The analysis of Biache-Saint-Vaast and Taubach has shown that applying the principles from the diet breadth model on archaeological assemblages is a valuable approach in order to interpret excavated bone assemblages. On the other hand, it is abundantly clear that the ranking that was used, based on the weight of the animals represented, does not in itself fully explain the set of species that was exploited. In some cases a high handling cost could be used to explain the patterns, but for some species the fact that they were apparently left unexploited cannot be explained satisfactorily using the diet breadth model.

As argued in chapter 4, using a ranking based on caloric values, or in this case animal body weights as a proxy of caloric value, the diet breadth model predicts that the heaviest species present in the environment would be exploited. Because of the fact that they are usually present in quite low population densities, it would predict that several species would be exploited on encounter in order to ensure a high enough encounter rate to guarantee a steady food supply. As shown in the previous chapters, these predictions have been proven to be correct. Diet breadth at both analysed Neanderthal sites proved to be narrow. Moreover, the species that were exploited consisted of very heavy species, with one notable exception, namely the beaver exploited at Taubach.

However, some exceptions to the predictions are also obvious. At both analysed Middle Palaeolithic sites, the most highly ranked species, straight-tusked elephant (*Palaeoloxodon antiquus*) was not or only rarely exploited. On the other hand, since this was by far the heaviest species present in the environment, the encounter rate for this species was low. Therefore, the poor representation of this species at sites does not necessarily mean that it was not exploited on encounter, but might signal that is was simply not encountered very often. However, if we use the reconstructed population densities and compare the projected densities of elephants with the projected densities of the rhinoceros species, the proboscidean population density is about half as high as that of rhinoceros. Since rhinoceros were heavily exploited at both analysed Palaeolithic sites, it is proposed that if exploiting elephants was an important activity of the occupants of both Biache-Saint-Vaast and Taubach, it would have left a more visible signature.

In the case of elephants, invoking handling cost does seem reasonable. As predators usually hunt species of up to about twice their own size (*e.g.* Owen-Smith and Mills 2008), hunting a species about 80 times as heavy as themselves may have simply been too dangerous for Neanderthals. This problem is exacerbated by the fact that the smaller females and young, the categories that one might overcome more easily than adult males, live in herds, making their exploitation potentially even more difficult than that of lone males.

Another large species that was not exploited at either site is giant deer (*Megaloceros giganteus*). The average weight of this species and thus its rank is hard to ascertain, with estimates ranging from 388 to 700 kilo's (Brook and Bowman 2004, Pushkina and Raia 2008). A weight of 450 kg. as posited by Louguet-Lefebvre (2005) seems reasonable though. If this estimate is correct, the only species that weighs less but is regularly exploited is brown bear (*Ursus arctos*). It seems therefore that this species is close to the lower limit of species that would be exploited by the occupants of Biache-Saint-Vaast and Taubach. On the other hand, at Biache-Saint-Vaast smaller species are said to have been exploited at least occasionally. At Taubach, red deer (*Cervus elaphus*) bones and possibly a horse bone (*Equus taubachensis*) have been cut-marked; if these smaller species were exploited ephemerally, it is hard to understand why this kind of exploitation would not have focused on the larger giant deer. An alternative explanation may be that distinguishing between remains of giant deer and large specimens of red deer can be difficult. Therefore, the amount of red deer may be overrepresented relative to giant deer.

If we assume that the poor representation of giant deer was not the result of misidentification of their remains, the explanation of their poor representation at the studied sites is not straightforward. For females and young, we may envisage high handling costs, since they presumably lived in herds, but males lived solitarily for most of the year, except during rut. It is proposed that the species was too small to form part of the optimal set at the analysed sites. The inclusion of smaller bears in the diet may be related to other factors, which will be dealt with later. Signs of occasional hunting as exhibited for red deer at Taubach are less likely to be found in this species since it was present at lower population densities. Biache-Saint-Vaast on the other hand does seem to be located in an ideal environment for this species. It would be interesting to see whether it is represented among the species showing occasional cut-marks.

Falling under the optimal set of species at both sites are Merck's rhinoceros (*Stephanorhinus kirchbergensis*) and narrow-nosed rhinoceros. Both weigh in excess of two tons and are only outranked by the proboscideans (and in cold periods by woolly rhinoceros (*Coelodonta antiquitatis*). At Biache-Saint-Vaast, narrow-nosed rhinoceros dominates, while at Taubach Merck's rhinoceros is the most abundant. As argued in the previous chapters, this difference in representation is dependent on the environmental circumstances at both sites and not on Neanderthal preferences.

Another difference in the selection of rhinoceros does seem to reflect different hominin hunting behaviour, namely the age-classes of the animals represented at the different sites. At Biache-Saint-Vaast young adult animals were preferentially targeted, while at Taubach, juveniles are the best represented age-category. The dominant age-category at Taubach, determined using stages of tooth eruption is that of individuals of about 1 year of age (Bratlund 1999, 100). At Biache-Saint-Vaast animals between 6 and 9 (see chapter 5) years of age predominate. It is thought that rhinoceros reach their largest size at about 9 years of age. The animals exploited at Biache-Saint-Vaast are thus much larger than at Taubach. They were probably harder to exploit because of their size, but also because they were older and more experienced. Since the MNI of rhinoceros at both sites is high this pattern is unlikely to be coincidental. It is proposed that the difference may lie in the fact that the hominins responsible for the accumulation of the bone assemblage at Biache-Saint-Vaast lived in open environments, with higher animal biomass densities. They therefore probably lived in larger groups and were able to more efficiently pursue and kill mature animals.

Bovids are the next highest ranked category of prey. They were also exploited at both analysed sites. At Biache-Saint-Vaast aurochs is the exploited species; it is hard to ascertain from the literature whether bison was also present. At Taubach, bison is the best represented species, but some aurochs bones have also been identified. The relative importance of bovids is very different at the sites. At Biache-Saint-Vaast, aurochs accounts for almost half of the NISP of the site. At Taubach, the importance of bovids is much less, they represent about 12% of the total NISP for the site. At both sites, adults are clearly in the majority with regard to the other age-classes. At Biache-Saint-Vaast, with an MNI of 196, 145 individuals were adults (Auguste and Patou-Mathis 1994, 22). At Taubach, the MNI is much smaller, but adults still account for more than half of the MNI (Bratlund 1999, 128). At both sites, males predominate. At Taubach, analysis of the horn cores shows that they are all derived from males, although the rest of the bone sample suggests that a small proportion of the animals represented at the site must have been female. At Biache-Saint-Vaast, the sex of 83 individuals could be determined, among which were 49 males and 34 females. This suggests that the emphasis on males was stronger at Taubach than at Biache-Saint-Vaast.

It is proposed that the hunting of adult male bovids again indicates a strategy geared toward exploiting the largest solitary species present in the environment. The emphasis on solitary species may have been less stringent at Biache-Saint-Vaast, since it is thought that the occupants at this site lived in larger social groups, thus making it more feasible to deal with animals living in herds. This might be reflected in the larger ratio of female animals at the site. It would be interesting to see whether the emphasis on males over females changes in the different layers sampled at this site. It is proposed that in more open environments, Neanderthals were able to live in larger groups, due to the fact that more secondary biomass would be available to them. Therefore in these circumstances, the hunting of animals living in herds can be predicted to have occurred more frequently.

8 Discussion

The final important category of prey at both sites is bears. Brown bear (*Ursus arctos*) is present at both sites. Moreover, at Taubach, cave bear is present, while at Biache-Saint-Vaast its predecessor, Deninger's bear (*Ursus deningerii*) has been found. At both sites, emphasis was on the smaller brown bear. This species accounts for about 15% of the NISP at Biache-Saint-Vaast and about 35% at Taubach. Deninger's bear accounts for about 3% of the total NISP at Biache-Saint-Vaast and at least some of the bones show traces of exploitation similar to those present on brown bear bones at the site (Auguste 2003, 138). Moreover, as shown in chapter 5, its age distribution is not a natural one as it is dominated by adults. Cave bear is very rare at Taubach and does not show traces of exploitation. The near-absence of these animals at both sites is hard to explain in terms of environmental circumstances. When we look at their reconstructed population densities, it appears that cave bear was present in larger numbers than brown bear. Even when reconstructing their population density as carnivores, their population density is estimated to have been slightly lower at 0.315 individuals per km^2 instead of 0.356, which is still much higher than the population density of brown bear.[46] It has been proposed that cave bears were better suited to closed environments than to open environments. This could explain why they are rare at Biache-Saint-Vaast. The environment here was open and a competitor like brown bear might have been able to realise high population densities in this environment, marginalising the potential for cave bears to live there. We would expect the opposite pattern at Taubach, since this site was situated in a closed environment. Yet here brown bear is again dominant and there are no traces of exploitation on the cave bear remains. Therefore, the species would be more highly ranked than brown bear and would have a higher encounter rate, especially in the case of Taubach. This suggests that the lack of signs of exploitation must be explained in terms of hominin activities instead of a very low encounter rate with this species.

In this case, the interpretation is proposed to lie in the realm of handling costs. Both species of bear fall in the order of Carnivora and even though cave bears may have been largely herbivorous (but see Richards *et al.* 2008a), they were certainly equipped with dangerous attributes, like claws and canines. In addition, cave bears were about 30% larger than brown bears. For the latter species it is suggested that hunting is best carried out using a "large calibre gun" and even then multiple shots are usually required to dispatch it (Charles 1997). An even larger species may have been even harder to hunt. This may have led Neanderthals to prefer the exploitation of brown bear, which may have been less dangerous to them. Again, this problem may have been more serious in the case of Taubach when group size is thought to have been smaller. Some caution is necessary with regard to this interpretation. It is also possible that my reconstruction of their population densities is incorrect. Even though the vegetation was suitable for this species, the surroundings of the analysed sites did not provide other important aspects of their niche. It has been proposed that cave bears decline when humans compete with them for caves as living space (*e.g.* Grayson and Delpech 2003). Since the sites that are analysed are in areas devoid of caves, cave bears may simply not have found denning sites in these areas and therefore may never have been present in large numbers. Nevertheless, since both species of bear hibernate, one would expect both species to be rare if this were a problem.

The incorporation of brown bear in the diet is quite peculiar, since it weighs roughly the same as the unexploited giant deer, maybe even less. Its ranking may have been elevated for two reasons however. First, its ranking may have been higher shortly before it started hibernation, since it would have built up large energy reserves. Some ethnographically known groups considered this the only time that the species was "fit" for eating (Charles 1997, 256-257). Second, this species may have been valued for other attributes, like its fur. Cut-marks on their bones at both Biache-Saint-Vaast and Taubach indeed suggest that they were skinned.

At Biache-Saint-Vaast, bears are the second most common species in the assemblage as a whole. Strikingly, they disappear during the formation of the upper levels as has been discussed in chapter 5. Since bears are thought to be cold-tolerant species and species indicative of temperate environments like red deer are still present in the assemblages, it is thought that this cannot be explained in terms of climatic deterioration. When the climate cooled, hunting herd animals became ever more important. In this circumstance a dangerous species like brown bear, also the lowest ranked exploited species, would be the first to be dropped from the exploited set in favour of ungulates that could be "mass-collected".

---

[46] The function for carnivores has a parabolic shape, resulting in higher population densities for the largest carnivores compared to medium-sized species (Silva, Brimacombe and Downing 2001).

This interpretation must also be treated with caution though. First, the bone assemblages of the upper levels are much smaller than of the lower levels and most notably of level II A. We can therefore not be certain that these levels reflect Neanderthal exploitation strategies over long periods of time. Exceptions to the normal pattern may also be reflected in these levels and will not be "averaged out" in these smaller assemblages. Second, the bone surfaces of the D-levels are weathered; therefore traces of exploitation could not be studied. It is therefore uncertain to what extent hominins interfered with the bones.

At Taubach, one small species was regularly exploited, namely beaver (*Castor fiber*). This species is not highly ranked, weighing less than 20 kilo's on average. On the other hand, the exploitation of this species may be explained at least in part by the fact that it could be exploited very close to the site, dramatically lowering search cost. Moreover, the caloric value of this species was seasonally elevated because in autumn, beavers build up important fat reserves in their tail (Jankowska *et al.* 2005).

The rare traces of exploitation on the bones of quite small species at both sites seem problematic at first. In the original model an optimal set was defined of highly ranked species that would be exploited on encounter and all species outside this set would not be exploited upon encounter. Using the reconstructed population densities of equids and cervids it is clear that they must have been encountered much more frequently than some of the exploited species. The number of bones of these species bearing cut-marks is very small however. This indicates that they were not automatically exploited on encounter. It does show on the other hand that they were at least occasionally exploited.

This may be explained by the fact that both analysed sites represent palimpsests that were formed over long periods of time. The composition of the optimal set of species exploited by a predator may change over very short periods of time, however. Predators respond to fluctuations in the density of prey species that are highly ranked. If the most highly ranked species are present in large numbers, the diet breadth will become narrower. If the highly ranked species are rare, diet breadth will widen. The exploitation of smaller species at both sites may therefore be a reflection of responses to periods of shortage of the preferred prey.

The foregoing shows that there is a reasonable fit in terms of species exploited between the predictions made by the diet breadth model and foraging strategies practised at the analysed sites. The number of exploited species is small and the exploited species are among the largest species available with the exception of proboscideans. This suggests that using body weight as currency approximates the currency Neanderthals used in ranking the available prey species well.

There is one additional factor that may have played a role in the ranking of species at both sites. This is the value of the fur of a prey species. This is illustrated by the exploitation of brown bear at both sites and of beaver at Taubach. Brown bear is the smallest exploited species, it is about as large as giant deer, which is left unexploited. Its ranking and also that of beaver may have been boosted by the value of their fur, which is of high quality (*e.g.* Scholander *et al.* 1950). The exploitation of beaver cannot be easily explained using its weight or caloric value as currency. As argued, its search cost may have been lowered significantly for hominins occupying Taubach, thus increasing the return rate. In addition, it possessed high quality fur that again could have significantly increased return rates, when compared to the returns from exploiting its meat alone.

One argument against the importance of this factor in the ranking of species is the fact that ursids disappear from the layers in Biache-Saint-Vaast that were formed during the coldest climate. This is hard to account for. The exploitation of bears had clearly been geared towards the fur (*e.g.* Auguste 1995a, Auguste 2003), yet just when hominins would have most need for insulative furs they disappeared from the record. It is possible that the season of the last occupations was different from the season of occupation during which the other levels were accumulated. It may be that fur was either not needed (summer) or not available (winter), yet this proposition is very hard to test.

Another factor that plays an important role in the ranking of foodstuffs by both modern humans and chimpanzees is the political gain that it can bring. Meat is a valued resource and in the case of modern humans the meat of some animals is valued more than that of others. Hunting of specific species may thus have provided benefits to the hunter, increasing their return rate beyond the caloric value alone. This is another attribute that may have elevated the ranking of brown bear. Since cave bear is rare, and I expect it to have been a more prestigious prey because of its size, I assume that prestige did not play a large role in the ranking of prey species.

Both sites thus show a focus on rhinoceros, ursids and bovids. The differences in importance of the groups between the sites are difficult to account for using the diet breadth model. The original model predicts that animals that are in the optimal set will be exploited upon encounter. This would lead us to expect the species with the highest population density to be the best represented species. The representation of species at Biache-Saint-Vaast follows this expectation reasonably well.[47] This is not the case at Taubach though, where rhinoceros and brown bear are dominant over bison, which, based on its reconstructed population density, would have been expected to be more common.

An important factor that can explain this pattern is the emphasis on the males of bison at Taubach. This has been interpreted as being the result of a preference for solitary animals. Female bison live in herds, while males are either solitary or live in bachelor groups, except during the mating season. If only male bison were included in the optimal set, the population density of the individuals of the species that would be exploited on encounter would be drastically lowered when compared to the population density of the species as a whole.

The application of OFT to these sites has thus provided interesting insights in the foraging decisions that were made by the occupants of the sites. It does not provide perfect predictions or explanations of the foraging behaviours that were practised though. Its function is mostly as a starting point of analysis, especially since many of the interpretations that were put forward still need to be tested. This is the case for example with proposed differences in Neanderthal group size and their implications for foraging behaviour. All in all, the application of the diet breadth model does allow us to gain more insight into why which species were exploited.

As an additional test to see how useful the model is in interpreting past foraging strategies, it was applied to foraging by cave hyenas in Pleistocene Europe. As argued in chapter 7, Neanderthals and cave hyenas share a lot of characteristics. Moreover, although hyenas are slightly larger, the difference in size between the two is quite small. One would therefore expect both species to concentrate on prey of similar size. On the other hand, both species have left a rich record of their activities in Middle and Late Pleistocene Europe. Moreover many archaeological sites contain evidence of hyena presence, for example in the form of gnaw-marks on bones and most known hyena dens contain at least a few archaeological artefacts (*e.g.* Villa and Soressi 2000). This suggests that the species occupied different niches, since otherwise one or the other would have gone extinct. This presents an excellent opportunity to see whether interpreting bone assemblages using OFT enables us to define a niche difference between the species.

The analysis of the dens of Lunel-Viel and Camiac showed that there is considerable overlap in the species that were exploited by hyenas and hominins. At both sites, bovids are well represented. In addition, at Camiac, woolly rhinoceros is one of the best represented species. Moreover, looking at the age-distribution of the equids at Lunel-Viel, we see that a large proportion of the bones present at the site belonged to adult animals. The recent analysis of the equids of the hyena den of Fouvent shows that an even more pronounced focus on prime-aged individuals is visible there (Fernandez, Guadelli, and Fosse 2006). This suggests that cave hyenas and Neanderthals often competed for similar resources.

Some differences in their respective niches can also be pointed out, though. First, the number of species that were present in the analysed hyena dens was greater than at the archaeological sites, even though at Camiac, the total assemblage is much smaller than at Taubach, while the assemblage at Lunel-Viel is roughly similar in size to Taubach. This can be attributed in part to the fact that hyenas scavenge. Since scavenging eliminates the need to hunt the prey, the handling cost of a carcass that is encountered may be very low and this may lead to the consumption of small species that would not be hunted. Another factor that may play a role is the fact that solitary hunting expeditions by hyenas may have targeted other species than group hunting episodes. Therefore, the fact that hyenas used a greater number of strategies in order to exploit the animal biomass that was available led to a wider diet breadth. The den in most cases represents a palimpsest of the results of all these strategies and therefore contains a larger number of prey categories. A similar pattern can be observed with regard to the age-categories of the prey species that were hunted by hyenas. As pointed out, at some sites hyenas focus on prime-aged adults of certain species. This is not the case for all sites and all prey

---

47   If we take the optimal set to comprise narrow-nosed rhinoceros, aurochs and brown bear. Adding up the modeled population densities of the species yields a total population density of 0.732 individuals of animals inside the set per km^2. The proportion of aurochs in this number is about 50%, brown bear about 26% and narrow-nosed rhinoceros 24%.

species though. This may also be related to varied foraging tactics, scavenging and solitary hunting may lead to the exploitation of a larger amount of young and old individuals, while group hunts may lead to the killing of large numbers of prime-aged individuals.

The greater variation in the number of prey species and vulnerable age categories represented at hyena dens is likely to be underestimated by looking at NISP-counts. This is caused by the fact that hyenas are able to destroy bones, and the bones of smaller species and especially young individuals are more likely to have been removed from the assemblages.

When looking at the totality of hyena dens that were surveyed in chapter 7 it also appears that hyenas may have focussed on less dangerous prey categories than Neanderthals did. The sites where a focus on ursids is exhibited seem mostly to represent scavenged animals that died during hibernation. Moreover, in the rhinocerotids, the focus of exploitation seems to have been on very young animals. However, at some of their sites, carnivores are quite common, as is the case with wolves at Lunel-Viel, which is unexpected if dangerous prey was avoided. On the other hand, as mentioned before, carnivores often interact aggressively, sometimes even killing individuals of different species (Van Valkenburgh 2001). This behaviour must therefore be placed at least partly outside the foraging domain, since such aggression probably takes place for different reasons than for the direct procurement of food only. Moreover, outside of the probably scavenged bears, large carnivores are rare at the sites.

It is proposed that this difference may be caused by a difference in social structure between hyenas and Neanderthals. In hyenas, the male's role in reproduction is limited to copulation. Males play no part in provisioning of offspring. This task is carried out solely by the mother, also without assistance from relatives. The loss of a female is therefore evolutionarily damaging. The loss of a male less so, since there are usually enough males to ensure successful reproduction.

Because hunting in hominins is thought to have been a mainly male activity, especially the dangerous tasks, the death of one of the hunting party may have been more acceptable to Neanderthals than to hyenas. Of course, in the case of Neanderthals, such risky activity would only have been undertaken if the payoff was high enough. In the case of hunting bears, this latter factor shows that some prestige or privileged access to females might still be associated with hunting larger prey. As argued above, this is not in evidence however, so possibly the payoff of the selected prey in terms of calories and fur was high enough to entice Neanderthals to hunt adult bears and rhinoceroces.

The comparison with hyenas thus shows that the niche of Neanderthals and hyenas overlapped. This is also the case with contemporary predators in many areas, like the African savannah. However, important differences have also been observed. Hyenas exhibit a more variable, opportunistic kind of prey selection. This is thought to reflect the practice of quite different activities while foraging: scavenging, hunting solitarily and hunting in groups. These activities in part yielded different kinds of prey.

These differences can also be explained in terms of their social structure. Because of the strict dominance hierarchy in hyenas and the fierce competition for food, solitary foraging becomes a very productive strategy, especially for low-ranked individuals. Therefore scavenging and hunting solitarily are probably practised extensively. When the dominance hierarchy is not as strict and some form of food-sharing is in place, as is thought to be the case in Neanderthals, hunting in groups for very specific high-ranked prey may become more rewarding.

8.6 The analysis in context

The analysis of the bone assemblages of sites studied in this thesis has ignored other sources of evidence. First, we can also study the artefacts that are found and try to tie them in with our interpretations of Neanderthal foraging tactics. Second, more Middle Palaeolithic bone assemblages are known that show that the strategies deployed at Taubach and Biache-Saint-Vaast were part of a wider repertoire of subsistence strategies. This is to be expected since OFT predicts that different circumstances will have led to the adoption of different foraging strategies by Neanderthals. These sources of evidence have been discussed in chapter 3, so here it suffices to make some general points that are important to contxtualise the results of this study.

With regard to the stone tools we know that Middle Palaeolithic sites are in most cases characterised by a Mode 3 technology. The tool types at most sites are dominated by scraper types and weapons are generally considered to be rare. This view needs to be modified in some respects. First, a lot of variability exists in Middle Palaeolithic assemblages. The bandwidth of this variability is generally regarded as quite small, but this view needs revision. For example, a large number of sites is known in the Late Pleistocene where the reduction strategy is based on blade production. Second, weapons may not be as rare as often thought. For example, analysis of convergent scrapers has shown that they may have functioned as spear points of thrusted spears (Villa and Lenoir 2006). With regard to these findings it is interesting to point out that the majority of Biache-Saint-Vaast "scrapers" were apparently hafted (Beyries 1988). Moreover, we can assume that the use of wooden weapons as known from Clacton, Schöningen and Lehringen was widespread.

After the Middle Palaeolithic, "transitional industries" have been found over large areas of Europe. At least in the case of the French Châtelperronian, Neanderthal fossils have been found associated with these industries. In these assemblages artefacts have been found with dimensions that, based on ethnographic evidence, point to a use as projectile points (Shea 2006). This may indicate that in the latest phase of their existence, Neanderthals used spearthrowers.

The Middle Palaeolithic weapons, thrusted spears but also Schöningen spears that may have been thrown (*e.g.* Rieder 2003) are suitable only for "close encounter hunting". This suggests that Neanderthals must have deployed strategic behaviour, like driving animals into ambushes. First to get close enough to the prey to use their spears. Second, because ethnographic studies suggest that hunting with these types of weapons is usually practised only when animals are first put at a disadvantage (*e.g.*Binford 2007).

With regard to the osseous evidence, it is important to realise that even though proboscideans were not exploited at the sites in this study, their exploitation is not unknown from the archaeological record, as discussed in chapter 3. A number of sites is known where artefacts and proboscidean remains occur together. At many of these the manner of exploitation remains unclear, but hunting can certainly not be excluded for sites like La-Cotte-de-Saint-Brelade and Lehringen. In the context of this analysis of Taubach, the sites of Lehringen and Gröbern are very interesting. They date to the Eemian, like Taubach. Gröbern is even situated very close to Taubach, and can therefore be expected to be environmentally similar. Both these sites contain the carcass of a single old male elephant and a small collection of artefacts. At Lehringen a spear was found in association with the remains as well. For Gröbern it has been proposed that the carcass was scavenged. The spear at Lehringen suggests that here hunting may have been practised. These sites demonstrate the exploitation of elephants in contrast to Taubach. However, the fact that weakened, solitary individuals were exploited shows that this exploitation was limited to cases in which handling cost was significantly lowered. These cases therefore do not contradict the interpretation put forward in this study.

La Cotte-de-Saint-Brelade is slightly younger than Biache-Saint-Vaast, dated to a cold phase in MIS 6. Here, on two occasions a group of mammoths and woolly rhinoceros died at the base of a cliff. It has been proposed that they were driven off the cliff (Scott 1980, Scott 1986). This suggests that during cold phases in the open landscapes hominins were capable of living in large enough groups to organise this activity. This conforms to the interpretations put forward here. It suggests that when hominin groups were large enough, even mammoth fell within the range of prey that could be captured. This could only be accomplished through lowering handling costs by driving them into a natural trap. If the landscape lacked such opportunities handling cost may not have been lowered enough to allow these animals to be exploited.

Hominin involvement with bears has long been a controversial topic. Because many caves show the juxtaposition of Mousterian artefacts with bear remains, in the early 20th century a "cave bear cult" was proposed to have been practised by Neanderthals. This hypothesis came under fierce attack in the second half of the previous century. It is now thought that many ursid bones found in caves belonged to animals that died during hibernation (Auguste 2003, Pacher 2002, 244). The caves were later occupied by hominins, resulting in the co-occurrence of bones and Middle Palaeolithic artefacts. On the other hand, some sites do show unambiguous evidence for the exploitation of cave bear by Neanderthals. The most well-known example is the Grotte du Renne at Arcy-sur-Cure. At this site, layer Xc has yielded cave bear bones showing clear hominin exploitation traces (David 2002). The German site of Balver Höhle also harbours evidence for the intensive exploitation of cave bear by Neanderthals (Kindler 2008).

The exploitation of brown bear is also rare in the Middle Palaeolithic archaeological record and it must be realised that Biache-Saint-Vaast and Taubach are exceptions with regard to the large amounts of brown bear materials that were exploited at these sites. At other sites in Italy and France cut-marked bones of this species have been found though (Auguste 2003).

The largest contrast with the studied assemblages are the many sites where the focus of exploitation was clearly on medium-sized ungulates. Most of these sites are situated in cold and open environments, and the faunal assemblages are dominated by reindeer (*Rangifer tarandus*), like Salzgitter-Lebenstedt in Germany or equids, as at Zwoleń in Poland. These do not contradict the predictions made in this study but represent groups operating on the mammoth steppe, focussing on large groups of ungulates that were in more or less predictable locations. These herds probably formed predictable patches, whose exploitation yielded high payoffs.

On the other hand, many assemblages dominated by cervids, most importantly red deer are known, especially in more southern areas (see for an overview of French sites Grayson and Delpech 2006). Exploitation of this species was minimal at the sites analysed in this study. Moreover it was predicted that when faced with closed environments, hominins would focus on very large and solitary prey species. These sites therefore contradict the deductions arrived at in this study, since one would expect exploitation at these sites to focus on megafauna like rhinoceros or aurochs. This suggests that when faced with a more or less closed environment, some populations may have adopted a strategy in which diet breadth was widened significantly and in which a focus on medium-sized ungulates was adopted.

Some comments need to be made in relation to the patterns observed at these sites however. First, many of the assemblages dominated by cervids listed in (Grayson and Delpech 2006) also contain quite large amounts of horse (*Equus caballus*)[48] suggesting open environments. Some of these sites even contain reindeer remains, pointing to a setting in cold, possibly "Mammoth-steppic" environments.[49] These sites may therefore be grouped with sites in open areas where the focus was on herd animals whose movements were more or less predictable. Second, many of the sites are located in more southern, Mediterranean areas. In these areas, broadening the diet may have been a more suitable response, since growing seasons are longer and the density of suitable resources may have been higher (Roebroeks 2003). Here, broadening the diet may have led to more drastic decreases in search costs than in the northern sites that were analysed, which would have made this a more profitable strategy. A third point of interest is the fact that many of the sites listed by Grayson and Delpech (2006) are located in rockshelters. These may represent sites to which animal remains were transported by hominins. This may have led to an overrepresentation of the smaller species. This may also be the reason why the sites in (Grayson and Delpech 2006) contain very few remains of rhinoceros.

This suggests that the focus on the heaviest species present in the environment as supported by the sites analysed in this study was by no means universal in Neanderthals, especially in the Late Pleistocene. It may be that the strategies proposed to have been responsible for the accumulation of the analysed bone assemblages were mostly adaptive in the more northern areas. Still, isotope analysis of Neanderthals at Arcy-sur-Cure suggests that they did maintain a focus on the heavier animals (Bocherens *et al.* 2005). Therefore the results of this study should be thoroughly tested against more southerly sites in the future.

---

48 *e.g.* Canalettes 2, 3; Pech de l'Azé 4B4
49 *e.g.* Combe-Grenal 9, 34, 35; Regourdou 3, 4; Grotte XVI C.

9 Conclusion

Using the archaeological record to gain insight in the "knowledge-intensity" of foraging strategies remains a difficult undertaking. However, this study has shown that it is helpful to adopt theories from behavioural ecology, as an aid in the interpretation of archaeological bone assemblages. Using ecological theory as a framework when interpreting clues about past foraging behaviour has yielded more plausible interpretations on why certain species were exploited, while others were left untouched. This type of research is therefore a valuable addition to the study of Pleistocene subsistence strategies. By improving behavioural ecological models we can create a basis from which the radically changing ideas surrounding the evolution of foraging strategies and their implications for the evolution of hominin life-histories, group size, intelligence, and the like. can be evaluated.

The application of OFT models still needs to be improved though. Refining the variables used in the model may improve its "fit" to the archaeological data. In order to gain insight in the decisions made during Neanderthal foraging activities it seems most important to refine our prey ranking. Estimating the added value of animal fur may further clarify why brown bear was hunted while giant deer was not. This is also the case for a more difficult variable, namely prestige value of foraging products. With regard to the knowledge intensity of foraging strategies, reconstructing the handling cost of the available prey seems productive. More refined understanding of the anti-predator behaviours of prey species may clarify whether species that were difficult to hunt were avoided or whether they were regularly exploited for example.

However, by reconstructing the handling cost, even using the simplest of variables we gained some insight in the "knowledge-intensity" of Neanderthal foraging. This analysis has therefore added depth to current zooarchaeological studies that have provided a very high-quality baseline by proving *that* Neanderthals indeed hunted at certain archaeological sites. Now we can also interpret *why* they avoided specific species and focussed on others.

For instance, we can convincingly argue that during interglacial circumstances, a focus on large and solitary species was adopted. This suggests that caloric value was a very important consideration in Neanderthal foraging strategies, as the diet breadth model predicts. We can also see that the handling cost of herd animals resulted in a low ranking and that these species were thus not exploited. Moreover we know that even in interglacial conditions, while hunting in small groups, some animals were still killed regularly. Brown bear, even nowadays considered dangerous prey for hunters with firearms was routinely hunted at both sites for example.

In contrast we can also explain why specialised hunting of ungulates was adopted in "mammoth-steppic" environments. When the environment becomes more open as in the upper levels of Biache-Saint-Vaast, dangerous species like bear are dropped from the set of exploited species, and herd animals become more important. In a full-fledged mammoth steppe, hunting of herd animals becomes even more important and the large, solitary species are probably not exploited at all. In these environments, Neanderthals were able to increase their group size and were able to drive herds of species into an ambush. This suggests that Neanderthals were able to very well coordinate their action in order to deal with hunting animals living in large herds.

In the future this kind of analysis has to be drastically refined. Some recommendations as to how we can go about this have already been made in the previous sections. Moreover, the interpretations that we arrive at using this kind of analysis have to be tested against future excavated sites, such as the rich assemblage very recently excavated at Neumark Nord in Germany. This can help to overcome problems of equifinality of different hypotheses.

The scenarios developed here and to be tested are quite simple. First, Neanderthals invested in simple versatile technology, but they were able to dispatchprime-aged individuals of species much larger than themselves. The upper boundary of species that they considered prey is much higher than would be expected for a predator, which usually does not regularly hunt species much more than twice its size. This shows that Neanderthals must have successfully applied refined strategies, using knowledge of the landscape and the animal species to ambush and kill these dangerous species of prey.

Second, Neanderthal population densities varied with the amount of animal biomass that was available in the landscape, like in modern hunter/gatherers. They may have been more severely affected by drops in available biomass, because of their high energetic needs and may have been forced to abandon territories that modern humans could colonize. Another factor that may have influenced Neanderthals' ability to successfully exploit landscapes is the character of the landscape. Because of the close-encounter character of Neanderthal hunting strategies, the possibilities in the landscape to prepare ambushes may have made up a significant part of animals handling costs. Moreover, their population density will have been significantly lower than that of modern humans hunter/gatherers would have been. This had consequences for their group size and social structure. It is proposed that adjustments to group size and social structure may have been an important way to deal with fluctuations in available biomass. This is thought to have important repercussions for the focus of their hunting activities. They seemingly preferred solitary prey in more closed environments. This suggests that hunting behaviour in Neanderthals was a collective enterprise. From this, it follows that a well-developed system of food distribution must have been in place. Had this not been the case, solitary foraging strategies like we see in hyenas would have been more profitable for many individuals.

Evidence for "mass-collecting" of cervids and smaller ungulates is mostly derived from the last glacial. This is caused in part by taphonomic factors. We simply know more sites from this period than from preceding times. On the other hand, this is also thought to be related to changes in the ecological structure of the environment. The rich mammoth-steppe environment will have allowed for Neanderthals to exploit the landscape in larger groups and this will have enabled more refined hunting tactics, like animal drives and ambushes, making large groups of herbivores available for exploitation.

Finally, the changes in the ecological structure of the environment during MIS 3 may have had severe consequences for the viability of the Neanderthal's way of life. They needed to realise very high return rates and because of the added costs of locomotion, their foraging radii will have been smaller than those of anatomically modern humans. When changes in the available biomass were combined with a change in the predator guild (like the appearance of modern humans) this may have put Neanderthals under severe stress, ultimately leading to their demise.

10 References

Adler, D. S., G. Bar-Oz, A. Belfer-Cohen, and O. Bar-Yosef. 2006. Ahead of the game, Middle and Upper Palaeolithic hunting behaviors in the Southern Caucasus. *Current Anthropology* 47:89-118.

Ahern, J. C. M., J. D. Hawks, and S.-H. Lee. 2005. Neandertal taxonomy reconsidered...again: a response to. *Journal of Human Evolution* 48:647-652.

Aiello, L., and P. Wheeler. 1995. The expensive-tissue hypothesis, The brain and digestive system in human and primate evolution. *Current Anthropology* 36:199-221.

—. 2003. "Neanderthal thermoregulation and the glacial climate," in *Neanderthals and modern humans in the European landscape during the last glaciation*. Edited by T. H. van Andel and W. Davies, pp. 147-166. Cambridge: MacDonald institute for Archaeological Research.

Albert, R. M., S. Weiner, O. Bar-Yosef, and L. Meignen. 2000. Phytoliths in the Middle Palaeolithic depostits of Kebara Cave, Mt. Carmel Israel: Study of plant materials for fuel and other purposes. *Journal of Archaeological Science* 27:931-947.

Ameloot-Van der Heijden, N. 1989. "Les séries des niveaux E de la couche D0 du gisement paléolithique moyen de Biache-Saint-Vaast (Pas-de-Calais)," in *Paléolithique et Mésolithique du Nord de la France, Nouvelles recherches*, vol. 1. Edited by A. Tuffreau, pp. 43-50. Lille: Centre d'Études et de Recherches Préhistoriques, Université des Sciences et Techniques de Lille Flandres Artois.

Andel, T. H. van 2003. "Glacial environments I: The Weichselian climate in Europe between the end of the OIS-5 interglacial and the last glacial maximum," in *Neanderthals and modern humans in the European landscape during the last glaciation : Archaeological results of the Stage 3 project*. Edited by T. H. van Andel and W. Davies. Cambridge: MacDonald Institute for Archaeological Research.

Andersen, K. K., N. Azuma, J.-M. Barnola, M. Bigler, P. Biscaye, N. Caillon, J. Chappellaz, H. B. Clausen, D. Dahl-Jensen, H. Fischer, J. Flükiger, D. Fritzsche, Y. Fuyii, K. Goto-Azuma, K. Grønvold, N. S. Gundestrup, M. Hansson, C. Huber, C. S. Hvidberg, S. J. Johnsen, U. Jonsell, J. Jouzel, S. Kipfstuhl, A. Landais, M. Leuenberger, R. Lorrain, V. Masson-Delmotte, H. Miller, H. Motoyama, H. Narita, T. Popp, S. O. Rasmussen, D. Raynaud, R. Rothlisberger, U. Ruth, D. Samyn, J. Schwander, H. Shoji, M.-L. Siggard-Andersen, J. P. Steffensen, T. Stocker, A. E. Sveinbjörnsdóttir, A. Svensson, M. Takata, J.-L. Tison, T. Thorsteinsson, O. Wantanabe, F. Wilhelms, and J. W. C. White. 2004. High-resolution record of Northern Hemisphere climate extending into the last interglacial period. *Nature* 431:147-151.

Antoine, P., N. Limondin-Lozouet, P. Auguste, J.-L. Locht, B. Galheb, J.-L. Reyss, E. Escude, P. Carbonel, N. Mercier, J.-J. Bahain, C. Falgueres, and P. Voinchet. 2006. Le tuf de Caours (Somme, France): Mise en évidence d'une séquence Eemienne et d'un site Paléolithique associé. *Quaternaire* 17:281-320.

Arsuaga, J.-L., C. Lorenzo, J.-M. Carretero, A. Gracia, I. Martinez, N. Garcia, J.-M. Bermúdez de Castro, and E. Carbonell. 1999. A complete human pelvis from the Middle Pleistocene of Spain. *Nature* 399:255-258.

Arsuaga, J. L., I. Martinez, A. Gracia, and C. Lorenzo. 1997. The Sima de los Huesos crania (Sierra de Atapuerca, Spain). A comparative study. *Journal of Human Evolution* 33:219-281.

Arts, N., and J. Deeben. 1981. *Prehistorische jagers en verzamelaars te Vessem: Een model*. Vol. 20. *Bijdragen tot de studie van het Brabantse Heem*. Eindhoven: Stichting Brabants Heem.

Auguste, P. 1988a. Apports paléontologiques et archéozoologiques de l'étude de la faune des grands mammifères de Biache-Saint-Vaast (Pas-de-Calais). *Revue Archéologique de Picardie*:63-68.

—. 1988b. "Etude des restes osseux des grands mammifères des niveaux D, D1, II base," in *Le gisement Paléolithique Moyen de Biache-Saint-Vaast (Pas-de-Calais) Volume I*, vol. 21, *Mémoires de la Société Préhistorique Française*. Edited by A. Tuffreau and J. Sommé, pp. 133-169. Chalons-sur-Marne: Paquez et fils.

—. 1992. Étude archéozoologique des grands mammifères du site pleistocène moyen de Biache-Saint-Vaast (Pas-De-Calais, France): Apports biostratigraphiques et palethnographiques. *L'Anthropologie* 96:49-70.

—. 1993. "Acquisition et exploitation du gibier au Paléolithique moyen dans le nord de la France. Perspectives paléo-écologiques et palethnographiques," in *Exploitation des animaux sauvages à travers le temps*. Edited by J. Desse and F. Audoin-Rouzeau, pp. 49-62. Juan-les-Pins: APDCA.

—. 1995a. Chasse et charognage au Paléolithique moyen: L'apport du gisement de Biache-Saint-Vaast (Pas-De-Calais). *Bulletin de la Société Préhistorique Française* 92:155-167.

—. 1995b. De la taphocenose a la paleobiocenose: Reconstitution des paleo-environnements pleistocenes de la France septentrionale a l'aide des mammiferes. *Geobios* 28:9-16.

—. 2003. "La chasse à l'ours au Paléolithique moyen: Mythes, réalités et état de la question," in *Le rôle de l'environnement dans les comportements des chasseurs-cueilleurs préhistoriques*, vol. 1105. Edited by M. Pathou-Mathis and H. Bocherens, pp. 135-142. Oxford: Archeopress.

Auguste, P., M. H. Moncel, and M. Patou-Mathis. 1998. "Chasse ou "charognage": Acquisition et traitement des rhinocéros au Paléolithique moyen en Europe occidentale," in *Économie préhistorique: les comportements de subsistance au paléolithique actes des rencontres 23-24-25 octobre 1997*. Edited by J.-P. Brugal, L. Meignen, and M. Patou-Mathis, pp. 133-151. Sophia Antipolis: APDCA.

Auguste, P., and M. Patou-Mathis. 1994. "L'aurochs au Paléolithique," in *Aurochs, le retour, Aurochs, vaches & autres bovins de la préhistoire à nos jours* pp. 13-26. Lons le Saunier: Centre Jurassien du patrimoine.

Bar-Yosef, O. 1995. "The origins of modern humans," in *The Archaeology of society in the holy land*. Edited by T. E. Levy, pp. 112-123. New York: Facts on file.

—. 2004. Eat what is there: Hunting and gathering in the world of Neanderthals and their neighbours. *International Journal of Osteoarchaeology* 14:333-342.

Bar-Yosef, O., B. Vandermeersch, B. Arensburg, A. Belfer-Cohen, P. Goldberg, H. Laville, L. Meignen, Y. Rak, J. D. Speth, E. Tchernov, A.-M. Tillier, and S. Weiner. 1992. The excavations in Kebara Cave, Mt. Carmel. *Current Anthropology* 33:497-550.

Barnard, C. 2004. *Animal Behaviour, Mechanism, development, function and evolution*. Harlow: Pearson education.

Barnosky, A. D. 1985. Taphonomy and hers structure of the extinct Irish Elk, *Megaloceros giganteus*. *Science* 228:340-344.

Barrett, L., R. Dunbar, and J. Lycett. 2002. *Human evolutionary ecology*. Basingstoke: Palgrave.

Barton, N. 2000. "Mousterian hearths and shellfish: Late Neanderthal activities on Gibraltar.," in *Neanderthals on the edge, Papers from a conference marking the 150th anniversary of the Forbes' Quarry discovery, Gibraltar*. Edited by C. B. stringer, R. N. E. Barton, and J. C. Finlayson, pp. 211-220. Oxford: Oxbow Books.

Barton, R. N. E., A. P. Currant, Y. Fernandez-Jalvo, J. C. Finlayson, P. Goldberg, R. Macphail, P. B. Pettitt, and C. B. Stringer. 1999. Gibraltar Neanderthals and results of recent excavations in Gorham's, Vanguard and Ibex caves. *Antiquity* 73:13-23.

Bate, D. M. A. 1937. "Part II Palaeontology: The fossil fauna of the Wady El-Mughara caves," in *The Stone Age of Mount Carmel, Volume I*. Edited by D. A. E. Garrod and D. M. A. Bate. Oxford: Clarendon Press.

10 REFERENCES

Beauval, C., B. Maureille, F. Lacrampe-Cuyaubère, D. Serre, D. Peressinotto, J.-G. Bordes, D. Cochard, I. Couchoud, D. Dubrasquet, V. Laroulandie, A. Lenoble, J.-B. Mallye, S. Pasty, J. Primault, N. Rohland, S. Pääbo, and E. Trinkaus. 2005. A late Neandertal femur from Les Rochers-de-Villeneve, France. *Proceedings of the National Academy of Sciences* 102:7085-7090.

Beerenhout, B. 2001. "Vissen," in *Archeologie in de Betuweroute: Hardinxvel-Giessendam Polderweg, Een mesolithisch jachtkamp in het rivierengebied (5500-5000 v. Chr)*, vol. 83, *Rapportage Archeologische Monumentenzorg*. Edited by L. P. L. Kooijmans, pp. 243-276. Amersfoort: Rijksdienst voor het oudheidkundig bodemonderzoek.

Beets, D. J., C. J. Beets, and P. Cleveringa. 2006. Age and climate of the late Saalian and early Eemian in the type-area, Amsterdam basin, The Netherlands. *Quaternary Science Reviews* 25:876-885.

Behm-Blancke, G. 1960. Altsteinzeitliche Rastplätze im Travertingebiet von Taubach, Weimar, Ehringsdorf. *Alt-Thüringen* 4:201-246.

Bellomo, R. V. 1994. Methods of determining early hominid behavioral activities associated with the controlled use of fire at FxJj 20 Main, Koobi Fora, Kenya. *Journal of Human Evolution* 27:173-195.

Berger, T. D., and E. Trinkaus. 1995. Patterns of trauma among Neanderthals. *Journal of Archaeological Science* 22:841-852.

Bermúdez de Castro, J. M., J. L. Arsuaga, E. Carbonell, A. Rosas, I. Martínez, and M. Mosquera. 1997. A hominid from the Lower Pleistocene of Atapuerca (Spain): Possible ancestor to Neandertals and modern humans. *Science* 276:1392-1395.

Bermúdez de Castro, J. M., M. Martinón-Torres, E. Carbonell, S. Sarmiento, A. Rosas, J. van der Made, and M. Lozano. 2004a. The Atapuerca sites and their contribution to the knowledge of human evolution in Europe. *Evolutionary Anthropology* 13:25-41.

Bermúdez de Castro, J. M., M. Martinón-Torres, S. Sarmiento, and M. Lozano. 2004b. Gran Dolina-TD6 versus Sima de los Huesos dental samples from Atapuerca: evidence of discontinuity in the European Pleistocene population? *Journal of Archaeological Science* 30:1421-1428.

Bettinger, R. L. 1987. Archaeological Approaches To Hunter-Gatherers. *Annual Review of Anthropology* 16:121-142.

—. 1991. *Hunter-Gatherers, Archaeological and evolutionary theory. Interdisciplinary contributions to Archaeology*. New York/London: Plenum Press.

Beyries, S. 1988. "Etude tracéologique des racloirs du niveau IIA," in *Le gisement Paléolithique Moyen de Biache-Saint-Vaast (Pas-de-Calais) Volume I, Stratigraphie environnement études archéologiques*, vol. 21, *Mémoires de la Société Préhistorique Française*. Edited by A. Tuffreau and J. Sommé, pp. 215-230. Paris: Sociéte Préhistorique Française.

Biesele, M., and S. Barclay. 2001. Ju/'Hoan women's tracking knowledge and its contribution to their husband's hunting success. *African Study Monographs Supplementary* 26:67-84.

Billia, E. M. E. 2008. Revision of the fossil material attributed to Stephanorhinus kirchbergensis (Jäger 1839) (Mammalia, Rhinocerotidae) preserved in the museum collections of the Russian Federation. *Quaternary International* 179:25-37.

Binford, L. R. 1980. Willow smoke and dogs' tails: Hunter-gatherer settlement systems and archaeological site formation. *American Antiquity* 45:4-20.

—. 1981. *Bones, Ancient men and modern myths. Studies in Archaeology*. New York: Academic Press.

—. 1982. The archaeology of place. *Journal of Anthropological Archaeology* 1:5-31.

—. 1984. *Faunal remains from Klasies River Mouth*. New York: Academic Press.

—. 1985. Human ancestors: Changing views of their behavior. *Journal of Anthropological Archaeology* 4:292-327.

—. 1987. "Were there elephant hunters at Torralba?," in *The evolution of human hunting*. Edited by M. H. Nitecki and D. V. Nitecki, pp. 47-105. New York: Plenum Press.

—. 1988. "Étude taphonomique des restes fauniques de la grotte Vaufrey, couche VIII," in *La grotte Vaufrey, Paléoenvironnement, chronologie, activités humaines*, vol. XIX, *Mémoires de la Société Préhistorique Française*. Edited by J.-P. Rigaud, pp. 525-563. Chalons-sur-Marne: Paquez et fils.

—. 2001. *Constructing frames of reference, An analytical method for Archaeological theory building using ethnographic and environmental data sets*. Berkely/Los Angeles/London: University of California Press.

—. 2007. "The diet of early hominids: Some things we need to know before "Reading" the menu from the archaeological record," in *Guts and Brains: An integrative approach to the hominin record*. Edited by W. Roebroeks, pp. 185-222. Leiden: Leiden University press.

Binford, L. R., M. G. L. Mills, and N. M. Stone. 1988. Hyena scavenging behavior and its implications for the interpretation of faunal assemblages from FLK 22 (the zinj floor) at olduvai gorge. *Journal of Anthropological Archaeology* 7:99-135.

Binka, K., and J. Nitychoruk. 2003. The Late Saalian, Eemian and Early Vistulian pollen sequence at Dziewule, eastern Poland. *Geological Quarterly* 47:155-168.

Bird, R. 1999. Cooperation and conflict: The behavioral ecology of the sexual division of labor. *Evolutionary Anthropology: Issues, News, and Reviews* 8:65-75.

Birks, H. J. B. 2005. Mind the gap: How open were European primeval forests. *Trends in Ecology & Evolution* 20:154-156.

Bischoff, J. L., R. W. Williams, R. J. Rosenbauer, A. Aramburu, J. L. Arsuaga, N. Garcia, and G. Cuenca-Bescos. 2007. High-resolution U-series dates from the Sima de los Huesos hominids yields 600 kyrs: implications for the evolution of the early Neanderthal lineage. *Journal of Archaeological Science* 34:763-770.

Bisson, M. S. 2001. Interview with a Neanderthal: An experimental approach for reconstructing scraper production rules and their implications for imposed form in Middle Palaeolithic tools. *Cambridge Archaeological Journal* 11:165-184.

Blades, B. S. 2001. *Aurignacian lithic economy, Ecological perspectives from Southwestern France. Interdisciplinary contributions to Archaeology*. New York: Plenum Press.

Blasco, R. 2008. Human consumption of tortoises at Level IV of Bolomor Cave (Valencia, Spain). *Journal of Archaeological Science* 35:2839-2848.

Bleed, P. 1986. The optimal design of hunting weapons: Maintainability and reliability. *American Antiquity* 51:737-747.

Bliege Bird, R., and E. A. Smith. 2005. Signaling theory, strategic interaction and symbolic capital. *Current Anthropology* 46:221-248.

Blumenschine, R. J. 1987. Characteristics of an early hominid scavenging niche. *Current Anthropology* 28:383-407.

Bocherens, H., and D. Biliou. 1998. "Implications paléoenvironmentales et paléoalimentaires de l'étude isotopique du Néandertalien de la couche 4," in *Récherches aux grottes de Sclayn, Volume 2: l'Archéologie*, vol. 79. Edited by M. Otte, M. Pathou-Mathis, and D. Bonjean, pp. 311-328. Liège: Université de Liège.

Bocherens, H., and D. Drucker. 2003. "Reconstructing Neandertal diet from 120,000 to 30,000 bp. Using carbon and nitrogen isotopic abundances," in *Le rôle de l'environnement dans les comportements des chasseurs-cueilleurs préhistoriques*, vol. 1105, *BAR International Series*. Edited by M. Pathou-Mathis and H. Bocherens, pp. 1-8. Oxford: Archeopress.

Bocherens, H., D. G. Drucker, D. Biliou, M. Pathou-Mathis, and B. Vandermeersch. 2005. Isotopic evidence for the diet and subsistence pattern of the Saint-Césaire Neanderthal: Review and use of a multi-source mixing model. *Journal of Human Evolution* 49:71-87.

10 REFERENCES

Bocherens, H., M. Fizet, and A. Mariotti. 1994. Diet, physiology and ecology of fossil mammals as inferred from stable carbon and nitrogen isotope biogeochemistry: implications for Pleistocene bears. *Palaeogeography, Palaeoclimatology, Palaeoecology* 107:213-225.

Boëda, E. 1988. "Analyse technologique du débitage du niveau IIA," in *Le gisement Paléolithique Moyen de Biache-Saint-Vaast (Pas-de-Calais) Volume I*, vol. 21. Edited by J. Sommé and A. Tuffreau, pp. 185-214. Chalons-sur-Marne: Chalons-sur-Marne.

Boëda, E., J. M. Geneste, C. Griggo, N. Mercier, S. Muhesen, J. L. Reyss, A. Taha, and H. Valladas. 1999. A Levallois point embedded in the vertebra of a wild ass (Equus africanus): Hafting, projectiles and Mousterian hunting. *Antiquity* 73:394-402.

Boesch, C. 2003. "Complex cooperation among Taï Chimpanzees," in *Animal social complexity, intelligence, culture and individualized societies*. Edited by F. B. M. de Waal and P. L. Tyack, pp. 93-110. Cambridge: Harvard University Press.

Boesch, C., and M. Tomasello. 1998. Chimpanzee and human cultures. *Current Anthropology* 39:591-614.

Boone, Y. 1976. "Le rammassage des coquillages," in *La préhistoire Française, Tome I: Les civilisations paléolithiques et mesolithiques de la France*. Edited by H. d. Lumley. Paris: Éditions du Centre National de la Recherche Scientifique.

Boydston, E. E., K. M. Kapheim, and K. E. Holekamp. 2006. Patterns of den occupation by the spotted hyaena (Crocuta crocuta). *African Journal of Ecology* 44:77-86.

Brain, C. K. 1981. *The hunters or the hunted? An introduction to African cave taphonomy*. Chicago: University of Chicago Press.

Brain, C. K., and A. Sillent. 1988. Evidence from the Swartkrans cave for the earliest use of fire. *Nature* 336:464-466.

Bratlund, B. 1999. Taubach revisited. *Jahrbuch des Römisch-Germanischen Zentralmuseums Mainz* 46:61-174.

Brook, B. W., and D. M. J. S. Bowman. 2004. The uncertain blitzkrieg of Pleistocene megafauna. *Journal of Biogeography* 31:517-523.

Brugal, J.-P., P. Fosse, and J.-L. Guadelli. 1997. "Comparative study of bone assemblages made by recent and Pleistocene hyenids," in *Proceedings of the 1993 bone conference Hot Springs, South Dakota*, vol. 1, *Occasional Publication*. Edited by L. A. Hannus, L. Rossum, and R. P. Winham, pp. 158-187. Sioux Falls: Archaeology Laboratory Augustana Collega.

Bunn, H. T. 1983. "Comparative analysis of modern bone assemblages from a San hunter-gatherer camp in the Kalahari Desert, Botswana and from a spotted hyena den near Nairobi Kenya," in *Animals and archaeology: 1. Hunters and their prey*, vol. 163, *BAR International Series*. Edited by J. Clutton-Brock and C. Grigson, pp. 143-148. Oxford.

Bunn, H. T., and E. M. Kroll. 1986. Systematic butchery by Plio/Pleistocene hominids at Olduvai Gorge, Tanzania. *Current Anthropology* 27:431-452.

Burke, A., D. Ebert, J. Cardille, and D. Dauth. 2008. Paleoethology as a tool for the development of archaeological models of land-use: the Crimean Middle Palaeolithic. *Journal of Archaeological Science* 35:894-904.

Cannel, A. 2002. Throwing behaviour and the mass distribution of geological hand samples, hand grenades and Oldowan manuports. *Journal of Archaeological Science* 29:335-339.

Carbonell, E., J. M. J.-M. Bermúdez de Castro, J. M. Pares, A. Perez-Gonzalez, G. Cuenca-Bescos, A. Olle, M. Mosquera, R. Huguet, J. van der Made, A. Rosas, R. Sala, J. Vallverdu, N. Garcia, D. E. Granger, M. Martinon-Torres, X. P. Rodriguez, G. M. Stock, J. M. Verges, A. Allue, F. Burjachs, I. Caceres, A. Canals, A. Benito, C. Diez, M. Lozano, A. Mateos, M. Navazo, J. Rodriguez, J. Rosell, and J. L. Arsuaga. 2008. The first hominin of Europe. *Nature* 452:465-469.

Charles, R. 1997. The Exploitation of Carnivores and Other Fur-bearing Mammals during the North-western European Late and Upper Paleolithic and Mesolithic. *Oxford Journal of Archaeology* 16:253-277.

Chatters, J. C. 1987. Hunter-gatherer adaptations and assemblage structure. *Journal of Anthropological Archaeology* 6:336-375.

Cheddadi, R., K. Mamakowa, J. Guiot, J.-L. d. Beaulieu, M. Reille, V. Andrieu, W. Granoszewski, and O. Peyron. 1998. Was the climate of the Eemian stable? A quantitative climate reconstruction from seven European pollen records. *Palaeogeography, Palaeoclimatology, Palaeoecology* 143:73-85.

Churchill, S. E. 1998. Cold adaptation heterochony and Neanderthals. *Evolutionary Anthropology* 7:46-61.

—. 2002. Of assegais and bayonets: Reconstructing prehistoric spear use. *Evolutionary Anthropology* 11:185-186.

—. 2007. "Bioenergetic perspectives on Neanderthal thermoregulatory and activity budgets," in *Neanderthals revisited: New approaches and perspectives, Vertebrate Paleobiology and Paleoanthropology*. Edited by K. Harvati and T. Harrison, pp. 113-134. Dordrecht: Springer.

Collen, P., and R. J. Gibson. 2000. The general ecology of beavers (Castor spp.), as related to their influence on stream ecosystems and riparian habitats, and the subsequent effects on fish – a review. *Reviews in Fish Biology and Fisheries* 10:439-461.

Conard, N. J., P. M. Grootes, and F. H. Smith. 2004. Unexpectedly recent dates for human remains from Vogelherd. *Nature* 430:198-201.

Conard, N. J., J. Preuss, R. Langohr, P. Haesaerts, T. van Kolfschoten, J. Becze-Deak, and A. Rebholz. 1995. New geological research at the Middle Palaeolithic locality of Wallertheim in Rheinhessen. *Archäologisches Korrespondenzblatt* 25:1-12.

Conard, N. J., and T. J. Prindiville. 2000. Middle Palaeolithic hunting economies in the Rhineland. *International Journal of Osteoarchaeology* 10:286-309.

Conard, N. J., T. J. Prindiville, and D. S. Adler. 1998. "Refitting bones and stones as a means of reconstructing Middle Palaeolithic subsistence in the Rhineland," in *Économie préhistorique: les comportements de subsistance au paléolithique actes des rencontres 23-24-25 octobre 1997*. Edited by J.-P. Brugal, L. Meignen, and M. Patou-Mathis, pp. 273-290. Sophia Antipolis: APDCA.

Cooper, S. M., K. E. Holekamp, and L. Smale. 1999. A seasonal feast: long-term analysis of feeding behaviour in the spotted hyaena (Crocuta crocuta). *African Journal of Ecology* 37:149-160.

Coqueugniot, H., J.-J. Hublin, F. Veillon, F. Houët, and T. Jacob. 2004. Early brain growth in *Homo erectus* and implications for cognitive ability. *Nature* 431:299-302.

Costamagno, S., and V. Laroulandie. 2004. "L'exploitation des petits vertébrés dans les Pyrénées françaises du Paléolithique au Mésolithique: un inventaire taphnomique et archéozoologique," in *Petits animaux et sociétés humaines : Du complément alimentaire aux ressources utilitaires : actes des rencontres, 23-25 octobre 2003* Edited by J.-P. Brugal and J. Desse, pp. 403-416. Antibes: APDCA.

Costamagno, S., L. Meignen, C. Beauval, B. Vandermeersch, and B. Maureille. 2006. Les Pradelles (Marillac-de-Franc, France): A Mousterian reindeer hunting camp? *Journal of Anthropological Archaeology* 25:466-484.

Crevecoeur, I., and E. Trinkaus. 2004. From the Nile to the Danube: A comparison of the Nazlet Khater and Oase I early modern human mandibles. *Anthropologie* 42:203-213.

Cruz-Uribe, K. 1991. Distinguishing Hyena from Hominid Bone Accumulations. *Journal of Field Archaeology* 18:467-486.

d'Errico, F., and M. F. S. Goñi. 2003. Neanderthal extinction and the millennial scale climatic variability of OIS 3. *Quaternary Science Reviews* 22:7690788.

d'Errico, F., J. Zilhão, M. Julien, D. Baffier, and J. Pelegrin. 1998. Neanderthal acculturation in Western Europe. *Current Anthropology* 39:s1-s44.

Dahlberg, F. Editor. 1981. *Woman the gatherer*. New Haven: Yale University Press.

Daniel, I. R. J. 2001. Stone raw material availability and Early Archaic settlement in the southern United States. *American Antiquity* 66:237-265.

David, F. 2002. "Les ours du Châtelperronien de la Grotte du Renne à Arcy-sur-Cure (Yonne)," in *L'ours et l'homme*, vol. 100. Edited by T. Tillet and L. R. Binford, pp. 185-192. Liège: Université de Liège.

Dean, D., J.-J. Hublin, R. Holloway, and R. Ziegler. 1998. On the phylogenetic position of the pre-Neandertal specimen from Reilingen, Germany. *Journal of Human Evolution* 34:485-508.

Dean, M. C. 2006. Tooth microstructure tracks the pace of human life-history evolution. *Proceedings of the Royal Society, Series B: Biological Sciences* 273:2799-2808.

Delpech, F. 1999. Biomasse d'ongulés au Paléolithique et inférences sur la demographie. *Paleo* 11:19-42.

Despart-Estes, R. 1991. *The behavior guide to African mammals, Including hoofed mammals, carnivores, primates*. Berkeley/Los Angeles/London: The University of California Press.

Desse, G., and J. Desse. 1976. "La pêche," in *La préhistoire Française, Tome I: Les civilisations paléolithiques et mesolithiques de la France*. Edited by H. d. Lumley, pp. 697-702. Paris: Éditions du Centre National de la Recherche Scientifique.

Dibble, H. L. 1995. Middle Palaeolithic scraper reduction: Background clarification and review of the evidence to date. *Journal of Archaeological Method and Theory* 2:299-368.

DiClemente, D. F., and D. A. Hantula. 2003. Optimal foraging online: Increasing sensitivity to delay. *Psychology and Marketing* 20:785-809.

Diedrich, C. J., and K. Žák. 2006. Prey deposits and den sites of the Upper Pleistocene hyena *Crocuta crocuta spelaea* (Goldfuss, 1823) in horizontal and vertical caves of the Bohemian Karst (Czech Republic). *Bulletin of Geosciences* 81:237-276.

Domínguez-Rodrigo, M. 2002. Hunting and scavenging by early humans, The state of the debate. *Journal of World Prehistory* 16:1-54.

Domínguez-Rodrigo, M., T. R. Pickering, S. Semaw, and M. J. Rogers. 2005. Cutmarked bones from Pliocene archaeological sites at Gona, Afar, Ethiopia: Implications for the function of the world's oldest stone tools. *Journal of Human Evolution* 48:109-121.

Dorn, M. W. 1997. Mesoscale fishing patterns of factory trawlers in the Pacific Hake (*Merluccius productus*) fishery. *California Cooperative Oceanic Fisheries Investigations Reports* 38:69-76.

Drea, C. M., and L. G. Frank. 2003. "The social complexity of spotted hyenas," in *93*. Edited by F. B. M. de Waal and P. L. Tyack, pp. 121 - 148. Cambridge: Harvard University Press.

Duarte, C., J. Maurício, P. B. Pettitt, P. Soutro, E. Trinkaus, H. v. d. Plicht, and J. Zilhão. 1999. The early Upper Palaeolithic human skeleton from the Abrigo do Lagar Velho (Portugal) and modern human emergence in Iberia. *Proceedings of the National Academy of Sciences* 96:7604-7609.

Dunbar, R. I. M. 1992. Neocortex size as a constraint on group size in primates. *Journal of Human Evolution* 22:469-493.

—. 2001. "Brains on two legs: Group size and the evolution of intelligence," in *Tree of origin, What primate behaviour can tell us about Human social evolution*. Edited by F. B. M. de Waal. Cambridge: Harvard University Press.

Eichhorn, G. 1909. *Die paläolithischen Funde von Taubach in den Museen zu Jena und Weimar, Festschrift zum 350-jährigen Jubiläum der Universität Jena*. Jena: Verlag von Gustav Fischer.

Eisenberg, J. F. 1990. "The behavioral/ecological significance of body size in the mammalia," in *Body size in mammalian paleobiology, Estimation and biological implications*. Edited by J. Damuth and B. Macfadden, pp. 25-37. Cambridge: Cambridge University Press.

Eisenmann, V. 1991. Les chevaux Quaternaires Européens (mammalia, perissodactyla). Taille, typologie, biostratigraphie et taxonomie. *Geobios* 24:747-759.

Farizy, C., F. David, J. Jaubert, and J. Leclerc. 1994. "Fonctionnement du site: Hommes et bisons," in *Hommes et bisons du paléolithique moyen à Mauran (Haute-Garonne), vol. XXX, Supplément à Gallia Préhistoire*. Edited by C. Farizy, F. David, and J. Jaubert, pp. 239-245. Paris: CNRS Éditions.

Féblot-Augustins, J. 1993. Mobility strategies in the Late Middle Palaeolithic of Central Europe and Western Europe: Elements of stability and variability. *Journal of Anthropological Archaeology* 12:211-265.

—. 1997. *La circulation des matières premières au Paléolithique*. Vol. 75. *ERAUL*. Liège: Université de Liège.

Fernandez, P., J.-L. Guadelli, and P. Fosse. 2006. Applying dynamics and comparing life tables for Pleistocene Equidae in anthropic (Bau de l'Aubesier, Combe-Grenal) and carnivore (Fouvent) contexts with modern feral horse populations (Akagera, Pryor Mountain). *Journal of Archaeological Science* 33:176-184.

Fernandez-Jalvo, Y., P. Andrews, and C. Denys. 1999. Cut marks on small mammals at Olduvai Gorge Bed-I. *Journal of Human Evolution* 36:587-589.

Finlayson, C. 2005. Biogeography and the evolution of the genus *Homo*. *Trends in Ecology & Evolution* 20:457-463.

Finlayson, C., F. G. Pacheco, J. Rodriguez-Vidal, D. A. Fa, J. M. G. Lopez, A. S. Perez, G. Finlayson, E. Allue, J. B. Preysler, I. Caceres, J. S. Carrion, Y. F. Jalvo, C. P. Gleed-Owen, F. J. J. Espejo, P. Lopez, J. A. L. Saez, J. A. R. Cantal, A. S. Marco, F. G. Guzman, K. Brown, N. Fuentes, C. A. Valarino, A. Villalpando, C. B. Stringer, F. M. Ruiz, and T. Sakamoto. 2006. Late survival of Neanderthals at the southernmost extreme of Europe. advanced online publication.

Finlayson, J. C., and G. Pacheco. 2000. "The southern Iberian peninsula in the late Pleistocene: Geography, ecology and human occupation," in *Neanderthals on the edge, Papers from a conference marking the 150th anniversary of the Forbes' Quarry discovery, Gibraltar*. Edited by C. B. Stringer, R. N. E. Barton, and J. C. Finlayson, pp. 139-154. Oxford: Oxbow Books.

Fosse, P. 1996. La grotte n°1 de Lunel-Viel (Hérault, France): Repaire d'hyènes du Pleistocène Moyen. *Paléo* 8:47-81.

—. 1997. Variabilité des assemblages osseux créés par l'hyène des cavernes. *Paléo* 9:15-54.

—. 1999. "Cave occupation during Palaeolithic times: Man and/or Hyena?," in *The Role of Early Humans in the accumulation if European Lower and Middle Palaeolithic bone assemblages, Ergebnisse eines Kolloquiums*, vol. 42, *Monographien*. Edited by S. Gaudzinski and E. Turner, pp. 73-88. Bonn: Verlag des Römisch-Germanischen Zentralmuseums.

Fosse, P., J.-P. Brugal, J.-L. Guadelli, P. Michel, and J.-F. Tournepiche. 1998. "Les repaires d'hyènes des cavernes en Europe occidentale: presentation et comparaison de quelques assemblages osseux," in *Économie préhistorique: les comportements de subsistance au paléolithique actes des rencontres 23-24-25 octobre 1997*. Edited by J. P. Brugal, L. Meignen, and M. Pathou-Mathis, pp. 43-61. Sophia Antipolis: APDCA.

Fosse, P., F. Laudet, N. Selva, and A. Wajrak. 2004. Premières observations néotaphonomiques sur des assemblages osseux de Bialowieza (N.-E. Pologne): intérêts pour les gisements Pleistocènes d'Europe. *Paleo* 16:91-116.

Frank, L. G., S. E. Glickman, and P. Licht. 1991. Fatal sibling aggression, precocial development, and androgens in neonatal spotted hyenas. *Science* 252:702-704.

Frank, L. G., M. L. Weldele, and S. E. Glickman. 1995. Maculinization costs in hyaenas. *Nature* 377:584-585.

Frison, G. C. 1989. Experimental use of Clovis weaponry and tools on African elephants. *American Antiquity* 54:766-784.

Gamble, C. 1986. *The Palaeolithic settlement of Europe. Cambridge World Archaeology.* Cambridge: Cambridge University Press.

—. 1987. "Man the shoveler: Alternative models for Middle Pleistocene colonization and occupation in Northern Latitudes," in *The Pleistocene Old World, Interdisciplinary Contributions to Archaeology.* Edited by O. Soffer, pp. 81-98. New York/London: Plenum Press.

—. 1992. Reply to Roebroeks *et al. Current Anthropology* 33:569-571.

—. 1999. *The Palaeolithic societies of Europe. Cambridge World Archaeology.* Cambridge: Cambridge University Press.

Gamble, C., W. Davies, P. Pettitt, and M. Richards. 2004. Climate change and evolving human diversity in Europe during the last glacial. *Philosophical Transactions of the Royal Society of London Series B: Biological sciences* 359:243-254.

Gaudzinski, S. 1995. Wallertheim revisited: A re-analysis of the fauna from the Middle Palaeolithic site of Wallertheim. *Journal of Archaeological Science* 22:51-66.

—. 1996. On bovid assemblages and their consequences for the knowledge of subsistence patterns in the Middle Palaeolithic. *Proceedings of the Prehistoric Society* 62:19-39.

—. 1999. "The faunal record of the Lower and Middle Palaeolithic of Europe: Remarks on human interference," in *The Middle Paleolithic occupation of Europe.* Edited by W. Roebroeks and C. Gamble. Leiden: Leiden University Press.

—. 2004. A matter of high resolution? The Eemian interglacial (OIS 5e) in North Central Europe and Middle Palaeolithic subsistence. *International Journal of Osteoarchaeology* 14:201-211.

Gaudzinski, S., and W. Roebroeks. 2000. Adults only. Reindeer hunting at the Middle Palaeolithic site of Salzgitter-Lebenstedt. *Journal of Human Evolution* 38:497-521.

—. 2003. Profile analysis at Salzgitter-Lebestendt. A reply to Munson & Marean. *Journal of Human Evolution* 44:275-281.

Geist, V. 1978. *Life strategies, Human evolution, Environmental design, Toward a biological theory of Health.* New York: Springer Verlag.

Geneste, J. M. 1989. "Économie des ressources lithiques dans le moustérien du Sud-Ouest de la France," in *L' Homme Neandertal, Actes du colloque international de Liège (4-7) décembre 1986), volume 6: La subsistance,* vol. 33, *ERAUL.* Edited by M. Patou and L. G. Freeman. Liège: Université de Liège.

Gibbons, A. 1998. Solving the brain's energy crisis. *Science* 280:1345-1347.

Gijn, A. v. 1992. A funtional analysis of the Belvédère flints. *Analecta Prehistorica Leidensia* 21:151-157.

Gravina, B., P. Mellars, and C. B. Ramsey. 2005. Radiocarbon dating of interstratified Neanderthal and early modern human occupations at the Chatelperronian type-site. *Nature* 438:51-56.

Grayson, D. K., and F. Delpech. 1994. The evidence for Middle Palaeolithic scavenging from stratum VIII, Grotte Vaufrey (Dordogne, France). *Journal of Archaeological Science* 21:359-376.

—. 1998. Changing Diet Breadth in the Early Upper Palaeolithic of Southwestern France. *Journal of Archaeological Science* 25:1119-1129.

—. 2003. Ungulates and the Middle-to-Upper Paleolithic transition at Grotte XVI (Dordogne, France). *Journal of Archaeological Science* 30:1633-1648.

—. 2006. "Was there increasing dietary specialization across the Middle-to-Upper Palaeolithic transition in France?," in *When Neanderthals and Modern Humans met, Tübingen Publications in Prehistory.* Edited by N. J. Conard. Tübingen: Kerns Verlag.

—. 2008. The large mammals of Roc de Combe (Lot, France): The Châtelperronian and Aurignacian assemblages. *Journal of Anthropological Archaeology* 27:338-362.

Green, R. E., A.-S. Malaspinas, J. Krause, A. W. Briggs, P. L. F. Johnson, C. Uhler, M. Meyer, J. M. Good, T. Maricic, U. Stenzel, K. Prüfer, M. Siebauer, H. A. Burbano, M. Ronan, J. M. Rothberg, M. Egholm, P. Rudan, D. Brajkovic, Z. Kucan, I. Gusic, M. Wikström, L. Laakkonen, J. Kelso, M. Slatkin, and S. Pääbo. 2008. A complete Neandertal mitochondrial genome sequence determined by high-throughput sequencing. *Cell* 134:416-426.

Guadelli, J. L. 1989. Étude taphonomique du repaire d'hyènes de Camiac (Gironde, France), Éléments de comparaison entre un site naturel et un gisement préhistorique. *Bulletin de l'Association Française pour l'Étude du quaternaire* 2:91-100.

Guadelli, J.-L., M. Lenoir, L. Marambat, and M.-M. Paquero. 1988. "Un gisement de l'interstade Würmien en Gironde: Le gisement de Camiac à Camiac et Saint-Denis," in *L'Homme de Neandertal, actes de la colloque International de Liège (4-7 Décembre 1986), Volume 4: La Technique*, vol. 31, *Études et recherches archéologiques de l'Université de Liège*. Edited by L. Binford and J.-P. Rigaud, pp. 59-60. Liège: Université de Liège.

Guatelli-Steinberg, D., C. S. Larsen, and D. L. Huchinson. 2004. Prevalence and the duration of linear enamel hypoplasia: A comparative study of Neandertals and Inuit foragers. *Journal of Human Evolution* 47:65-84.

Guatelli-Steinberg, D., D. J. Reid, T. A. Bishop, and C. S. Larsen. 2005. Anterior tooth growth periods in Neandertals were comparable to those of modern humans. *Proceedings of the National Academy of Sciences* 102:14197-14202.

Guenther, E. W. 1977. "Die Backenzähne der Elefanten von Taubach bei Weimar," in *Das Pleistozän von Taubach bei Weimar*, vol. 2. Edited by H.-D. Kahlke, pp. 265-304. Berlin: Akademie Verlag.

Guiot, J., M. Reille, J. L. d. Beaulieu, and A. Pons. 1992. Calibration of the climatic signal in a new pollen sequence from La Grande Pile. *Climate Dynamics* 6:259-264.

Guitierrez, G., D. Sánchez, and A. Marín. 2002. A reanalysis of the ancient mitochondrial DNA sequences recovered from Neanderthal bones. *Molecular Biology and Evolution* 19:1359-1366.

Gurven, M., H. Kaplan, and M. Guitierrez. 2006. How long does ik take to become a proficient hunter? Implications for the evolution of extended development and long life span. *Journal of Human Evolution* 51:454-470.

Guthrie, D. R. 2001. Origin and causes of the mammoth steppe: a story of cloud cover, woolly mammal tooth pits, buckles, and inside-out Beringia. *Quaternary Science Reviews* 20:549-574.

Guthrie, R. D. 1990. *Frozen fauna of the mammoth steppe, The story of Blue Babe*. Chicago: The University of Chicago Press.

—. 2006. On the pleistocene extinctions of Alaskan mammoths and horses. *Nature* 441:207-209.

Hardy, B. L. 2004. Neanderthal behaviour and stone tool function at the Middle Palaeolithic sites of La Quina, France. *Antiquity* 78:547-565.

Hardy, B. L., M. Kay, A. E. Marks, and K. Monigal. 2001. Stone tool function at the paleolithic sites of Starosele and Buran Kaya III, Crimea: Behavioral implciations. *Proceedings of the National Academy of Sciences* 98:10972-10977.

Harvati, K., S. R. Frost, and K. P. McNulty. 2004. Neanderthal taxonomy reconsidered: Implications of 3D primate models of intra- and interspecific differences. *Proceedings of the National Academy of Sciences of the United States of America* 101:1147-1152.

Harvati, K., E. Panagopoulou, and P. Karkanas. 2003. First Neanderthal remains from Greece: The evidence from Lakonis. *Journal of Human Evolution* 45:465-473.

Hawkes, K. 1993. Why hunter-gatherers work, An ancient version of the problem of public goods. *Current Anthropology* 34:341-361.

Hawkes, K., J. F. O'Connell, N. G. Blurton-Jones, H. Alvarez, and E. L. Charnov. 1998. Grandmothering, menopause and the evolution of human life histories. *Proceedings of the National Academy of Sciences* 95:1336-1339.

10 REFERENCES

Haynes, G. 1985. Age profiles in elephant and mammoth bone assemblages. *Quaternary Research* 24:333-345.

—. 1987. Proboscidean die-offs and die-outs: Age profiles in fossil collections. *Journal of Archaeological Science* 14:659-688.

—. 2002. *The early settlement of North America, The Clovis era.* Cambridge: Cambridge University Press.

—. 2006. Mammoth landscapes: good country for hunter-gatherers. *Quaternary International* 142-143:20-29.

Heinrich, W.-D., and D. Jánossy. 1977. "Insektivoren und Rodentier aus dem Travertin von Taubach bei Weimar," in *Das Pleistozän von Taubach bei Weimar*, vol. 2, *Qartärpaläontologie, Abhandlungen und Berichte des Instituts für Quartärpaläontologie Weimar*. Edited by H.-D. Kahlke, pp. 401-411. Berlin: Akademie Verlag.

Henrich, J. 2004. Demography and cultural evolution: how adaptive cultural processes can produce maladaptive losses - The Tasmanian case. *American Antiquity* 69:197-214.

Hockett, B., and J. Haws. 2003. Nutritional ecology and diachronic trends in Palaeolithic diet and health. *Evolutionary Anthropology* 12:211-216.

Hockett, B., and J. A. Haws. 2002. Taphonomic and methodological perspectives of leporid hunting during the Upper Palaeolithic of the Western Mediterranean Basin. *Journal of Archaeological Method and Theory* 9:269-302.

—. 2005. Nutritional ecology and the human demography of Neandertal extinction. *Quaternary International*.

Hofreiter, M., D. Serre, H. N. Poinar, M. Kuch, and S. Pääbo. 2001. Ancient DNA. *Nature Reviews Genetics* 2:353-359.

Holliday, T. W. 1997. Postcranial evidence of cold adaptation in European Neanderthals. *American Journal of Physical Anthropology* 104:245-258.

Horwitz, L. K. 1998. "The influence of prey body size on patterns of bone distribution and representation in a striped hyena den," in *Économie préhistorique: les comportements de subsistance au paléolithique actes des rencontres 23-24-25 octobre 1997*. Edited by J. P. Brugal, L. Meignen, and M. Pathou-Mathis, pp. 31-42. Sophia Antipolis: APDCA.

Höss, M. 2000. Neanderthal population genetics. *Nature* 404:453-454.

Hublin, J.-J. 1998. "Climatic changes, paleogeography, and the evolution of the Neandertals," in *Neandertals and modern humans in Western Asia*. Edited by K. Aoki, T. Akazawa, and O. Bar-Yosef, pp. 295-310. New York/London: Plenum Press.

Hublin, J.-J., F. Spoor, M. Braun, F. Zonneveld, and S. Condemi. 1996. A late Neanderthal associated with Upper Palaeolithic artefacts. *Nature* 381:224-226.

Husseman, J. S. D. L. M. G. P. C. M. C. R. W. H. Q. 2003. Assessing differential prey selection patterns between two sympatric large carnivores. *OIKOS* 101:591-901.

Ingold, T. 1992. Foraging for data, camping with theories: Hunter-gatherers and nomadic pastoralists in archaeology and anthropology. *Antiquity* 66:790-803.

—. 2000. "The optimal forager and the economic man," in *The perception of the environment : Essays on livelihood, dwelling and skill*. Edited by T. Ingold, pp. 27-39. London: Routledge.

Isaac, B. 1987. Throwing and human evolution. *The African Archaeological Review* 5:3-17.

Isaac, G. L. 1978. The food-sharing behavior of protohuman hominids. *Scientific American* 238:90-108.

—. 1983. "Bones in contention: Competing explanantions for the juxtaposition of early Pleistocene artifacts and faunal remains," in *Animals and archaeology: 1. Hunters and their prey*, vol. 163, *BAR International Series*. Edited by J. Clutton-Brock and C. Grigson, pp. 1-19. Oxford.

Jankowska, B., T. Żmijewski, A. Kwiatkowska, and W. Korzeniowski. 2005. The composition and properties of beaver (Castor fiber) meat. *European Journal of Wildlife Research* 51:283-286.

Jaubert, J., M. Lorblanchet, H. Laville, R. Slot-Moller, A.Turq, and J.-P. Brugal. 1990. *Les chasseurs d'Aurochs de La Borde. Documents d'Archéologie Française*. Paris: Editions de la maison des sciences de l'homme.

Jochim, M. A. 1988. Optimal foraging and the division of labour. *American Anthropologist* 90:130-136.

Johansen, L., and D. Stapert. 1995/1996. Handaxes from Denmark: Neandertal tools or 'vicious flints'. *Palaeohistoria* 37/38:1-28.

Jones, E. L. 2004. Dietary evenness, prey choice and human-environment interactions. *Journal of Archaeological Science* 31:307-317.

Jöris, O. 2003. Zur chronostratigraphischen Stellung der spätmittelpaläolithischen Keilmessergruppen, Der versuch einer kulturgeographischen Abgrenzung einer mittelpaläolithischen Formengruppe. *Bericht der Römisch-Germanischen Kommission* 84:50-153.

Jöris, O., and M. Street. 2008. At the end of the 14C timescale - The Middle to Upper Palaeolithic record of Western Eurasia. *Journal of Human Evolution* 55:782-802.

Kaplan, H., and K. Hill. 1985. Hunting ability and reproductive success among Ache male foragers: preliminary results. *Current Anthropology* 26:131-133.

Kaplan, H., K. Hill, J. Lancaster, and A. M. Hurtado. 2000. A theory of human life-history evolution: Diet intelligence and longevity. *Evolutionary Anthropology* 9:156-185.

Kaplan, H. S., and A. J. Robson. 2002. The emergence of humans: The coevolution of intelligence and longevity with intergenerational transfers. *Proceedings of the National Academy of Sciences of the United States of America* 99:10221-10226.

Kelly, R. L. 1992. Mobility/sedentism: Concepts, archaeological measures and effects. *Annual Review of Anthropology* 21:43-66.

—. 1995. *The foraging spectrum: Diversity in hunter-gatherer lifeways*. Washington: Smithsonian Institution Press.

—. 2001. *Prehistory of the Carson desert and Stillwater mountains, Environment, mobility and subsistence in a Great Basin wetland*. Vol. 123. *University of Utah Anthropological papers*. Salt Lake City: University of Utah Press.

Kelly, R. L., and L. C. Todd. 1988. Coming into the country: Early paleoindian hunting and mobility. *American Antiquity* 53:231-244.

Kindler, L. 2008. "Late Pleistocene Neanderthal land-use and territoriality in central Europe: A faunal perspective from the Balve Cave, Germany," in *Palaeolithic Mesolithic Conference*. British Museum.

Klein, R. G. 2003. Whither the Neanderthals. *Science* 299:1525-1527.

Kolen, J. 1999. "Hominids without homes: On the nature of Middle Palaeolithic settlement in Europe," in *The Middle Palaeolithic of Europe*. Edited by W. Roebroeks and C. Gamble, pp. 139-175. Leiden: University of Leiden.

Kolfschoten, T. van 1995. On the application of fossil mammals to the reconstruction of the palaeoenvironment of northwestern Europe. *Acta Zoologica Cracoviensia* 38:73-84.

—. 2000. The Eemian mammal fauna of central Europe. *Geologie en Mijnbouw* 79:269-281.

—. 2002. "The Eemian mammal fauna of the northwestern and central european continent," in *Le dernier interglaciare et les occupations humaines du Paléolithique moyen*, vol. 8. Edited by A. Tuffreau and W. Roebroeks, pp. 21-30. Lille: Université des Sciences et Technologies de Lille.

Koller, J., U. Baumer, and D. Mania. 2001. High tech in the Middle Palaeolithic: Neandertal-manufactured pitch identified. *European Journal of Archaeology* 4:385-397.

Krause, J., L. Orlando, D. Serre, B. Viola, K. Prufer, M. P. Richards, J.-J. Hublin, C. Hanni, A. P. Derevianko, and S. Paabo. 2007. Neanderthals in central Asia and Siberia. *Nature* 449:902-904.

Krebs, J. R., and N. B. Davies. 1997. "The evolution of behavioural ecology," in *Behavioural ecology, An evolutionary approach, Fourth edition*. Edited by J. R. Krebs and N. B. Davies, pp. 3-12. Oxford: Blackwell Science.

Krings, M., H. Geisert, R. W. Schmitz, H. Kranitzki, and S. Pääbo. 1999. DNA sequence of the Mitochondrial hypervariable region II from the Neanderthal type specimen. *Proceedings of the National Academy of Sciences* 96:5581-5585.

Kronfeld-Schor, N., and T. Dayan. 2003. Partitioning of time as an ecological resource. *Annual Review of Ecology, Evolution, and Systematics* 34:153-181.

Kruuk, H. 1972. *The spotted hyena: A study of predation and social behavior. Wildlife behavior and ecology*. Chicaga: University of Chicaga Press.

Kühl, N., and T. Litt. 2003. Quantitative time series reconstruction of Eemian temperature at three European sites using pollen. *Vegetation History and Archaeobotany* 12:205-214.

Kuhn, S. L. 1995. *Mousterian lithic technology: An ecological perspective*. Princeton: Princeton University Press.

—. 1998. "The economy of lithic raw materials and the economy of food procurement," in *Économie préhistorique: les comportements de subsistance au paléolithique actes des rencontres 23-24-25 octobre 1997*. Edited by J. P. Brugal, L. Meignen, and M. Pathou-Mathis, pp. 215-225. Sophia Antipolis: APDCA.

Kuhn, S. L., and M. C. Stiner. 2006. What's a mother to do? The division of labor among Neanderthals and Modern Humans in Eurasia. *Current Anthropology* 47:953-980.

Lahr, M. M., and R. A. Foley. 1998. Towards a theory of modern human origins: Geography, demography and diversity in recent human evolution. *Yearbook of Physical Anthropology* 41:137-176.

Lalueza, C., A. Péréz-Perez, and D. Turbón. 1996. Dietary inferences through buccal microwear analysis of Middle and Upper Pleistocene human fossils. *American Journal of Physical Anthropology* 100:367-387.

Lam, Y. M. 1992. Variability in the behaviour of spotted hyaenas as taphonomic agents. *Journal of Archaeological Science* 19:389-406.

Langbroek, M. 2003. Out of Africa, A study into the earliest occupation of the Old world. PhD, Leiden University.

Langejans, G. H. J. 2006. "Residue analysis on Earlier Stone Age tools; from reconstructing the past to an honest methodology." *African Genesis: A symposium on Hominid evolution in Africa, University of the Witwatersrand, South Africa, 2006*, pp. 73-74. Abstracts of contributions to the African Genesis Conference.

—. 2007. PIXE and residues; Examples from Sterkfontein and Sibudu, South Africa. *South African Archaeological Bulletin* 62:71-73.

Le Gall, O. 1988. "Analyse palethnologique de l'Ichtyofaune de la Grotte Vaufrey," in *La grotte Vaufrey, Paléoenvironnement, chrologie, activités humaines*, vol. XIX, *Mémoires de la Société Préhistorique Française*. Edited by J.-P. Rigaud, pp. 566-568. Chalons-sur-Marne: Paquez et fils.

Lebel, S., E. Trinkaus, M. Faure, P. Fernandez, C. Guérin, D. Richter, N. Mercier, H. Valladas, and G. A. Wagner. 2001. Comparative morphology and paleobiology of Middle Pleistocene human remains from the Bau de l'Aubesier, Vaucluse, France. *Proceedings of the National Academy of Sciences* 98:11097-11102.

Leibold, M. A. 1996. A graphical model of keystone predators in food webs: Trophic regulation of abundance, incidence and diversity patterns in communities. *The American Naturalist* 147:784-812.

Lemorini, C. 1992. Variabilité ou spécialisation fonctionelle? Une révision du rapport entre forme et fonction au Moustérien. *Analecta Prehistorica Leidensia* 25:17-24.

Levi-Sala, I. 1986. Use-wear and post-depositional surface modification: A word of caution. *Journal of Archaeological Science* 13:229-244.

Liobine, V. P. 2002. *L'Acheuléen du Caucase. ERAUL*. Liège: Université de Liège.

Litt, T. 1990. "Sttratigraphie und Ökologie des eeminterglazialen Waldelefanten-Slachtplatzes von Gröbern, Kreis Gräfenhainichen," in *Neumark - Gröbern. Beiträge zur Jagd des mittelpaläolithischen Menschen*, vol. 43, *Veröffentlichungen des Landesmuseums für Vorgeschichte in Halle*. Edited by D. Mania, M. Thomae, T. Litt, and T. Weber, pp. 193-208. Berlin: Deutscher Verlag der Wissenschaften.

Litt, T., F. W. Junge, and T. Böttger. 1996. Climate during the Eemian in north-central Europe - a critical review of the palaeobotanical and stable isotope data from central Germany. *Vegetation history and Archaeobotany* 5:247-256.

Livingston, S. 2001. "Avian faunal remains," in *Prehistory of the Carson desert and Stillwater mountains, Environment, mobility and subsistence in a Great Basin wetland*, vol. 123, *University of Utah Anthropological papers*. Edited by R. L. Kelly, pp. 280-288. Salt Lake City: University of Utah Press.

Lloveras, L., M. Moreno-García, and J. Nadal. 2008. Taphonomic analysis of leporid remains obtained from modern Iberian lynx (Lynx pardinus) scats. *Journal of Archaeological Science* 35:1-13.

Locht, J.-L. 2005. Le paléolithique moyen en Picardie: État de la recherche. *Revue Archéologique de Picardie*:27-35.

Lombard, M. 2005. Evidence of hunting and hafting during the Middle Stone Age at Sibudu cave, KwaZulu-Natal, South Africa: A multinanalitycal approach. *Journal of Human Evolution* 48:279-300.

Lombard, M., and L. Wadley. 2007. The morphological identification of micro-residues on stone tools using light microscopy: progress and difficulties based on blind tests. *Journal of Archaeological Science* 34:155-165.

Lorblanchet, M. 1999. *La naissance de l'art : genèse de l'art préhistorique dans le monde*. Paris: Éditions Errance.

Louguet-Lefebvre, S. 2005. *Les mégaherbivores (Élephantidés et Rhinocerotidés) au Paléolithique moyen en Europe du Nord-Ouest*. Vol. 1451. *BAR International Series*. Oxford: Archeopress.

Ludvico, L. R., I. M. Bennett, and S. Beckerman. 1991. Risk sensitive foraging behaviour among the Barí. *Human ecology* 19:509-516.

Lummaa, V. T. C.-B. 2002. Early development, survival and reproduction in humans. *Trends in Ecology & Evolution* 17:141-147.

Lyman, R. L. 1994. *Vertebrate taphonomy. Cambridge Manuals in Archaeology*. Cambridge: Cambridge University Press.

—. 2003. The influence of time anveraging and space averaging on the application of foraging theory in zooarchaeology. *Journal of Archaeological Science* 30:595-610.

MacArthur, R. H., and E. R. Pianka. 1966. On optimal use of a patchy environment. *American Naturalist* 100:603-609.

Macdonald, D. W. Editor. 2006. *The Encyclopedia of Mammals, New edition*. Oxford: Oxford University Press.

Macphail, E. M. 1982. *Brain and intelligence in vertebrates*. Oxford: Oxford University Press.

Made, J. van der 2000. A preliminary note on the rhino's from Bilzingsleben. *Praehistorica Thuringia* 4:41-64.

—. 2003. "*Megaloceros giganteus* from the Middle Pleistocene of Neumark Nord," in *Erkenntnisjäger, Kultur und Umwelt des frühen Menschen*, vol. 57. Edited by J. M. Burdukiewicz, L. Fiedler, W.-D. Heinrich, A. Justus, and E. Brühl, pp. 373-378. Halle (Saale): Landesamt für Archäologie Sachsen Anhalt - Landesmuseum für Vorgeschichte.

—. in press. The rhino's from the Middle Pleistocene of Neumark Nord (Germany).

Madella, M., M. K. Jones, P. Goldberg, Y. Goren, and E. Hovers. 2002. The exploitation of plant resources by Neanderthals in Amud Cave (Israel). *Journal of Archaeological Science* 29:703-719.

Madsen, D. B., and D. N. Schmitt. 1998. Mass collecting and the diet breadth model: A Great Basin example. *Journal of Archaeological Science* 25:445-455.

Marcy, J.-L., and A. Tuffreau. 1988a. "Le niveau D," in *Le gisement Paléolithique Moyen de Biache-Saint-Vaast (Pas-de-Calais) Volume I, Mémoires de la Société Préhistorique Française*. Edited by J. Sommé and A. Tuffreau, pp. 291-299. Chalons-sur-Marne: Paquez et fils.

—. 1988b. "Le niveau D1," in *Le gisement Paléolithique Moyen de Biache-Saint-Vaast (Pas-de-Calais) Volume I*, vol. 21, *Mémoires de la Société Préhistorique Française*. Edited by J. Sommé and A. Tuffreau, pp. 263-289. Chalons-sur-Marne: Paquez et fils.

Marks, A. E., H. J. Hietala, and J. K. Williams. 2001. Tool standardization in the Middle and Upper Palaeolithic: A closer look. *Cambridge Archaeological Journal* 11:17-44.

Martínez, I., J. L. Arsuaga, R. Quam, J. M. Carretero, A. Gracia, and L. Rodríguez. 2008. Human hyoid bones from the middle Pleistocene site of the Sima de los Huesos (Sierra de Atapuerca, Spain). *Journal of Human Evolution* 54:118-124.

Martinez, I., L. Rosa, J.-L. Arsuaga, P. Jarabo, R. Quam, C. Lorenzo, A. Gracia, J.-M. Carretero, J. M. J.-M. Bermúdez de Castro, and E. Carbonell. 2004. Auditory capacities in Middle Pleistocene humans from the Sierra de Atapuerca in Spain. *Proceedings of the National Academy of Sciences* 101:9976-9981.

Mazza, P. P. A., F. Martini, B. Sala, M. Magi, M. P. Colombini, G. Giachi, F. Landucci, C. Lemorini, F. Modugno, and E. Ribechini. 2006. A new Palaeolithic discovery: tar-hafted stone tools in a European Mid-Pleistocene bone-bearing bed. *Journal of Archaeological Science* In Press, Corrected Proof:1310-1318.

McComb, K., C. Moss, S. M. Durant, L. Baker, and S. Sayialel. 2001. Matriarchs as repositories of social knowledge in Elephants. *Science* 292:491-494.

McDougall, I., F. H. Brown, and J. G. Fleagle. 2005. Stratigraphic placement and age of modern humans from Kibish, Ethiopia. *Nature* 433:733-736.

McLaren, F. S. 1998. "Douara Cave, Syria: The botanical evidence from a Palaeolithic site in an arid zone," in *Life on the edge: Human settlement and marginality*, vol. 100, *Oxbow Monograph*. Edited by C. M. Mills and G. Coles, pp. 179-187. Oxford: Oxbow Books.

Meignen, L., S. Beyries, J. Speth, and O. Bar-Yosef. 1998. "Acquisition, traitement des matières animales et fonction du site au Paléolithique moyen dans la grotte de Kébara (Israël): Approche interdisciplinaire," in *Économie préhistorique: les comportements de subsistance au paléolithique actes des rencontres 23-24-25 octobre 1997*. Edited by J.-P. Brugal, L. Meignen, and M. Patou-Mathis, pp. 227-241. Sophia Antipolis: APDCA.

Meijer, T., and R. C. Preece. 2000. A review of the occurrence of *Corbicula* in the Pleistocene of North-West Europe. *Geologie & Mijnbouw* 79:241-255.

Mellars, P. 1996. *The Neanderthal legacy : an archaeological perspective from western Europe*. Princeton: Princeton University Press.

—. 2006. A new radiocarbon revolution and the dispersal of modern humans in Eurasia. *Nature* 439:931-935.

Mellars, P., B. Gravina, and C. B. Ramsey. 2007. Confirmation of Neanderthal/modern human interstratification at the Chatelperronian type-site. *Proceedings of the National Academy of Sciences* 104:3657-3662.

Mellars, P. A. 2004. Reindeer specialization in the early Upper Palaeolithic: the evidence from south west France. *Journal of Archaeological Science* 31:613-617.

Mercier, N., H. Valladas, O. Bar-Yosef, B. Vandermeersch, C. Stringer, and J.-L. Joron. 1993. Thermoluminescence Date for the Mousterian Burial Site of Es-Skhul, Mt. Carmel. *Journal of Archaeological Science* 20:169-174.

Mercier, N., H. Valladas, J.-L. Joron, J.-L. Reyss, F. Lévêque, and B. Vandermeersch. 1991. Thermoluminescence dating of the late Neanderthal remains from Saint-Césaire. *Nature* 351:737-739.

Mercier, N., H. Valladas, G. Valladas, J.-L. Reyss, A. Jelinek, L. Meignen, and J.-L. Joron. 1995. TL Dates of Burnt Flints from Jelinek's Excavations at Tabun and their Implications. *Journal of Archaeological Science* 22:495-509.

Mills, M. G. L. 1985. Related spotted hyenas forage together but do not cooperatie in rearing young. *Nature* 316:61-62.

Mills, M. G. L., and S. K. Bearder. 2006. "Hyena Family," in *The encyclopedia of mammals, New edition*. Edited by D. W. MacDonald, pp. 620-625. Oxford: Oxford University Press.

Milton, K. 1993. Diet and primate evolution. *Scientific American* 169:70-77.

—. 2003. The Critical Role Played by Animal Source Foods in Human (*Homo*) Evolution. *J. Nutr.* 133:3886S-3892.

Mithen, S. J. 1988. Modeling hunter-gatherer decision making: complementing optimal foraging theory. *Human Ecology* 17:59-83.

Mlynarski, M., and H. Ullrich. 1977. "Amphibien und Reptilienreste aus dem Pleistozän von Taubach," in *Das Pleistozän von Taubach bei Weimar*, vol. 2, *Qartärpaläontologie, Abhandlungen und Berichte des Instituts für Quartärpaläontologie Weimar*. Edited by H.-D. Kahlke, pp. 167-170. Berlin: Akademie Verlag.

Monahan, C. M. 1998. The Hadza carcass transport debate revisited and its archaeological implications. *Journal of Archaeological Science* 25:405-424.

Moncel, M.-H., C. Daujeard, E. Cregut-Bonnoure, P. Fernandez, M. Faure, and C. Guerin. 2004. L'occupation de la grotte de Saint-Marcel (Ardèche, France) au Paléolithique moyen: stratégie d'exploitation de l'environnement et type d'occupation de la grotte. L'exemple des couches i, j et j'. *Bulletin de la Société préhistorique française* 101:257-304.

Moncel, M.-H., A.-M. Moigne, and J. Combier. 2005. Pre-Neandertal behaviour during isotopic stage 9 and the beginning of stage 8. New data concerning fauna and lithics in the different occupation levels of Orgnac 3 (Ardèche, South-East France), occupation types. *Journal of Archaeological Science* 32:1283-1301.

Munaut, A. V. 1988. "Étude palynologique," in *Le gisement Paléolithique Moyen de Biache-Saint-Vaast (Pas-de-Calais) Volume I*, vol. 21, *Mémoires de la Société Préhistorique Française*. Edited by A. Tuffreau and J. Sommé, pp. 77-88. Chalons-sur-Marne: Paquez et fils.

Mussi, M. 1999. "The Neanderthals in Italy: a tale of many caves," in *The Middle Palaeolithic occupation of Europe*. Edited by W. Roebroeks and C. Gamble, pp. 49-80. Leiden: Leiden University Press.

Mussi, M., and P. Villa. 2008. Single carcass of Mammuthus primigenius with lithic artifacts in the Upper Pleistocene of northern Italy. *Journal of Archaeological Science* 35:2606-2613.

Neer, W. van. 1986. "La faune Saalienne du site Paléolithique Moyen du Mesvin IV (Hainaut, Belgique)," in *Chronostratigraphie et faciès culturels du Paléolithique Inférieur et Moyen dans l'Europe du Nord-Ouest*, vol. 26, *Supplement au Bulletin de l'Association Française pour l'Étude du Quaternaire*. Edited by A. Tuffreau and J. Sommé, pp. 103-111. Paris: Société Préhistorique Française.

Nishimura, T., A. Mikami, J. Suzuki, and T. Matsuzawa. 2006. Descent of the hyoid in chimpanzees: evolution of face flattening and speech. *Journal of Human Evolution* 51:244-254.

O'Connell, J. F., K. Hawkes, and N. G. Blurton-Jones. 1999. Grandmothering and the evolution of *Homo erectus*. *Journal of Human Evolution* 36:461-485.

O'Connell, J. F., K. Hawkes, K. D. Lupo, and N. G. Blurton-Jones. 2002. Male strategies and Plio-Pleistocene archaeology. *Journal of Human Evolution* 43:831-872.

Ovchinikov, I. V., A. Göterström, G. P. Romanova, V. M. Kharitonov, K. Lidén, and W. Goodwin. 2000. Molecular analysis of Neanderthal DNA from the Northern Caucasus. *Nature* 404:490-493.

Owen-Smith, N., and M. G. L. Mills. 2008. Predator-prey size relationships in an African large-mammal food web. *Journal of Animal Ecology* 77:173-183.

Owen-Smith, R. N. 1988 (1992). *Megaherbivores: The influence of very large body size on ecology. Cambridge Studies in Ecology*. Cambridge: Cambridge University Press.

Pacher, M. 2002. "Polémique autour d'un culte de l'ours des cavernes," in *L'ours et l'homme*, vol. 100, *ERAUL*. Edited by T. Tillet and L. R. Binford, pp. 235-246. Liège: Université de Liège.

Packer, C., M. Tatar, and A. Collins. 1998. Reproductive cessation in mammals. *Nature* 392:807-811.

Palombo, M. L. Filippi, P. Iacumin, A. Longinelli, M. Barbieri, and A. Maras. 2005. Coupling tooth microwear and stable isotope analyses for palaeodiet reconstruction: the case study of Late Middle Pleistocene Elephas (Palaeoloxodon) antiquus teeth from Central Italy (Rome area). *Quaternary International* 126-128:153-170.

Parfitt, S. A., R. W. Barendregt, M. Breda, I. Candy, M. J. Collins, G. R. Coope, P. Durbridge, M. H. Field, J. R. Lee, A. M. Lister, R. Mutch, C. R. Penkman, R. C. Preece, J. Rose, C. B. Stringer, R. Symmons, J. E. Whittaker, J. J. Wymer, and A. J. Stuart. 2005. The earliest record of human activity in northern Europe. *Nature* 438:1008-1012.

Pathou-Mathis, M. 1998. "Les espèces chassées et consommées par l'homme en couche 5," in *Récherches aux grottes de Sclayn, Volume 2: l'Archéologie*, vol. 79. Edited by M. Otte, M. Pathou-Mathis, and D. Bonjean, pp. 297-310. Liège: Université de Liège.

Pavlov, P., W. Roebroeks, and J. I. Svendsen. 2004. The Pleistocene colonization of northeastern Europe: A report on recent research. *Journal of Human Evolution* 47:3-17.

Pearson, O. M., R. M. Cordero, and A. M. Busby. 2007. "How different were Neanderthals habitual activities? A comparative analysis with diverse groups of recent humans," in *Neanderthals revisited: New approaches and perspectives, Vertebrate Paleobiology and Paleoanthropology*. Edited by K. Harvati and T. Harrison, pp. 135-156. Dordrecht: Springer.

Petit, J. R., J. Jouzel, D. Raynaud, N. I. Barkov, J.-M. Barnola, I. Basile, M. Bender, J. Chappellaz, M. Davis, G. Delaygue, M. Delmotte, V. M. Kotlyakov, M. Legrand, V. Y. Lipenkov, C. Lorius, L. Pepin, C. Ritz, E. Saltzman, and M. Stievenard. 1999. Climate and atmospheric history of the past 420,000 years from the Vostok ice core, Antarctica. *Nature* 399:429-436.

Pettitt, P. B., and A. W. G. Pike. 2001. Blind in a cloud of data: problems with the chronology of Neanderthal extinction and anatomically modern human expansion. *Antiquity* 75:415-420.

Pitts, M., and M. Roberts. 1997. *Fairweather Eden, Life in Britain half a million years ago as revealed by the excavations at Boxgrove*. London: Random House.

Plagnes, B., C. Causse, D. Genty, M. Paterne, and D. Blamart. 2002. A discontinuous climatic record from 187 to 74 ka from a speleothem of the Clamouse Cave (south of France). *Earth and Planetary Science Letters* 201:87-103.

Plisson, H., and S. Beyries. 1998. Pointes ou outils triangulaires? Données fonctionelles dans le Moustérien levantin. *Paléorient* 24:5-16.

Plug, C., and I. Plug. 1990. MNI Counts as Estimates of Species Abundance. *The South African Archaeological Bulletin* 45:53-57.

Pokines, J. T., and J. C. K. Peterhans. 2007. Spotted hyena (Crocuta crocuta) den use and taphonomy in the Masai Mara National Reserve, Kenya. *Journal of Archaeological Science* 34:1914-1931.

Ponce de León, M. S., L. Golovanova, V. Doronichev, G. Romanova, T. Akazawa, O. Kondo, H. Ishida, and C. P. E. Zollikofer. 2008. Neanderthal brain size at birth provides insights into the evolution of human life history. *Proceedings of the National Academy of Sciences* 105:13764-13768.

Porter, A. W. M. 1999. Modern human, early modern human and Neanderthal limb proportions. *International Journal of Osteoarchaeology* 9:54-67.

Potts, R. 1983. "Foraging for faunal reources by early hominids at Olduvai Gorge, Tanzania," in *Animals and Archaeology 1. Hunters and their prey*, vol. 163, *BAR International series*. Edited by J. Clutton-Brock and C. Grigson, pp. 51-62. Oxford: BAR.

—. 1998. Variability selection in hominid evolution. *Evolutionary Anthropology* 7:81-96.

Prins, N. 2005. Buhlen, lower site, The mammalian record MA-thesis, Leiden University.

Pushkina, D., and P. Raia. 2008. Human influence on distribution and extinctions of the late Pleistocene Eurasian megafauna. *Journal of Human Evolution* 54:769-782.

Quammen, D. 2005. *Monster of God: The man-eating predator in the jungles of history and the mind.* London: Pimlico.

Rabinovich, R. 1990. "Taphonomic research of the faunal assemblage from the Quneitra site," in *Quneitra: A Mousterian site on the Golan Heights*, vol. 31, *QEDEM Monographs of the Institute of Archaeology*. Edited by N. Goren-Inbar, pp. 189-219. Jerusalem: The Hebrew University of Jerusalem.

Rabinovich, R., and E. Hovers. 2004. Faunal analysis from Amud cave: Preliminary results and interpretations. *International Journal of Osteoarchaeology* 14:287-306.

Radloff, F. G. T., and J. T. d. Toit. 2004. Large predators and their prey in a southern African savanna: a predator's size determines its prey size range. *Journal of Animal Ecology* 73:410-423.

Ramirez-Rozzi, F. V., and J. M. J.-M. Bermúdez de Castro. 2004. Surprisingly rapid growth in Neanderthals. *Nature* 428:936-939.

Rapport, D. J., and J. E. Turner. 1977. Economic Models in Ecology. *Science* 195:367-373.

Reader, S. M., and K. N. Laland. 2002. Social intelligence, innovation and enhanced brain size in primates. *Proceedings of the National Academy of Sciences* 99:4436-4441.

Reille, M., V. Andrieu, J.-L. d. Beaulieu, P. Guenet, and C. Goeury. 1998. A long pollen record from Lac du Bouchet, Massif Central, France: For the period ca. 325 to 100 ka BP (OIS 9c to OIS 5e). *Quaternary Science Reviews* 17:1107-1123.

Reitz, E. J., and E. S. Wing. 1999. *Zooarchaeology. Cambridge Manuals in Archaeology*. Cambridge: Cambridge University Press.

Rendell, L., and H. Whitehead. 2001. Culture in whales and dolphins. *Behavioral and Brain Sciences* 24:309-382.

Richards, M. P., M. Pacher, M. Stiller, J. Quiles, M. Hofreiter, S. Constantin, J. Zilhao, and E. Trinkaus. 2008a. Isotopic evidence for omnivory among European cave bears: Late Pleistocene Ursus spelaeus from the Pestera cu Oase, Romania. *Proceedings of the National Academy of Sciences* 105:600-604.

Richards, M. P., P. B. Pettitt, M. C. Stiner, and E. Trinkaus. 2001. Stable isotope evidence for increasing dietary breadth in the European mid-Upper Palaeolithic. *Proceedings of the National Academy of Sciences* 98:6528-6532.

Richards, M. P., P. B. Pettitt, E. Trinkaus, F. H. Smith, M. Paunovic, and I. Karavanic. 2000. Neanderthal diet at Vindija and Neanderthal predation: The evidence from stable isotopes. *Proceedings of the National Academy of Sciences* 97:7663-7666.

Richards, M. P., and R. W. Schmitz. 2008. Isotope evidence for the diet of the Neanderthal type specimen. *Antiquity* 82:553-559.

Richards, M. P., G. Taylor, T. Steele, P. McPherron, M. Soressi, J. Jaubert, J. Orschiedt, J. B. Mallye, W. Rendu, and J. J. Hublin. 2008b. Isotopic dietary analysis of a Neanderthal and associated fauna from the site of Jonzac (Charente-Maritime), France. *Journal of Human Evolution* 55:179-185.

Richards, S. A. 2002. Temporal partitioning and aggression among foragers: modeling the effects of stochasticity and individual state. *Behav. Ecol.* 13:427-438.

Rieder, H. 2003. Der große Wurf der frühen Jäger, Nachbau altsteinzeitlicher Speere. *Biologie Unserer Zeit* 33:156-160.

Roberts, M. B. 1999. "Quarry 2 GTP 17," in *Boxgrove, A Middle Pleistocene hominid site at Earthham Quarry, Boxgrove, West Sussex*, vol. 17, *English Heritage Archaeological Reports*. Edited by M. B. Roberts and S. A. Parfitt, pp. 372-378. London: English Heritage.

Roberts, M. B., C. S. Gamble, and D. R. Bridgland. 1995. "The earliest occupation of the British isles," in *The earliest occupation of Europe*. Edited by W. Roebroeks and T. van Kolfschoten. Leiden: Leiden University Press.

Roche, H., A. Delagnes, J.-P. Brugal, C. Feibel, M. Kibunjia, V. Mourre, and P.-J. Texier. 1999. Early hominid stone tool production and technical skill 2.34 Myr ago in West Turkana, Kenya. *Nature* 399:57-60.

Roebroeks, W. 1986. "Archaeology and Middle Pleistocene stratigraphy: The case of Maastricht Belvédère (NL)," in *Chronostratigraphie et faciès culturels du Paléolithique Inférieur et Moyen dans l'Europe du Nord-Ouest*, vol. 26, *Supplement au Bulletin de l'Association Française pour l'Étude du Quaternaire*. Edited by A. Tuffreau and J. Sommé, pp. 81-88. Paris: Société Préhistorique Française.

—. 2003. "Landscape learning and the earliest occupation of Europe," in *Colonization of unfamiliar landscapes, The archaeology of adaptation*. Edited by M. Rockman and J. Steele. London/New York: Routledge.

—. 2005. Life on the Costa del Cromer. *Nature* 438:921-922.

—. 2008. Time for the Middle to Upper Paleolithic transition in Europe. *Journal of Human Evolution* 55:918-926.

Roebroeks, W., N. J. Conard, and T. van Kolfschoten. 1992. Dense forests, cold steppes and the Palaeolithic settlement of Northern Europe. *Current Anthropology* 33:551-586.

Roebroeks, W., J. Kolen, and E. Rensink. 1988. Planning depth, anticipation and the organization of Middle-Palaeolithic technology: The "archaic natives" meet Eve's descendants. *Helinium* 28:17-34.

Roebroeks, W., and T. van Kolfschoten. 1995. The earliest occupation of Europe: A reappraisal of the evidence. *Analecta Prehistorica Leidensia* 27:297-315.

Roebroeks, W., and B. Speleers. 2002. "Last interglacial (Eemian) occupation of the North European plain and adjacent areas," in *Le dernier interglaciare et les occupations humaines du Paléolithique moyen*, vol. 8, *Publications du CERP*. Edited by A. Tuffreau and W. Roebroeks, pp. 31-39. Lille: Université des Sciences et Technologies de Lille.

Roebroeks, W., and A. Tuffreau. 1999. "Palaeoenvironment and settlement patterns of the Northwest European Middle Palaeolithic," in *The Middle Palaeolithic occupation of Europe*. Edited by W. Roebroeks and C. Gamble. Leiden: Leiden University Press.

Rogers, A. R., and J. M. Broughton. 2001. Selective Transport of Animal Parts by Ancient Hunters: A New Statistical Method and an Application to the Emeryville Shellmound Fauna. *Journal of Archaeological Science* 28:763-773.

Rohland, N., J. L. Pollack, D. Nagel, C. Beauval, J. Airvaux, S. Paabo, and M. Hofreiter. 2005. The Population History of Extant and Extinct Hyenas. *Molecular Biology and Evolution* 22:2435-2443.

Rosenberg, K., and W. Trevathan. 2002. Birth, obstetrics and human evolution. *BJOG: An International Journal of Obstetrics and Gynaecology* 109:1199-1206.

Rosenberg, K. R., and W. Trevathan. 1996. Bipedalism and human birth: The obstetrical dilemma revisited. *Evolutionary Anthropology* 4:161-168.

Rougier, H. 2003. Étude descriptive et comparative de Biache-Saint-Vaast 1 (Biache-Saint-Vaast, Pas-de-Calais, France). PhD-Thesis, Université de Bordeaux 1.

Rougier, H., Ş. Milota, R. Rodrigo, M. Gherase, L. Sarcină, O. Moldovan, J. Zilhao, S. Constantin, R. G. Franciscus, C. P. E. Zollikofer, M. P. d. León, and E. Trinkaus. 2007. Peştera cu Oase 2 and the cranial morphology of early modern humans. *Proceedings of the National Academy of Sciences* 104:1165-1170.

Rousseau, D.-D., and J.-J. Puissegur. 1988. "Analyse de la malacofaune continentale," in *Le gisement Paléolithique Moyen de Biache-Saint-Vaast (Pas-de-Calais) Volume I*, vol. 21. Edited by A. Tuffreau and J. Sommé, pp. 89-102. Chalons-sur-Marne: Paquez et fils.

Santonja, M., A. Pérez-Gonzalez, P. Villa, E. Soto, and C. Sesé. 2001. "Elephants in the archaeological sites of Aridos (Jarama valley, Madrid Spain)," in *The world of elephants, Proceedings of the 1st international congress*. Edited by G. Cavaretta, P. Gioia, M. Mussi, and M. R. Palombo, pp. 602-606. Rome: Consiglio Nazionale delle Ricerche.

Schäfer, D. 1990. Merkmalanalyse mittelpaläolithischer Steinartefakte. *Ethnographisch-Archäologische Zeitschrift* 31:54-64.

Schiffer, M. B. 1972. Archaeological context and systemic context. *American Antiquity* 37:156-165.

Schild, R., A. J. Tomaszewski, Z. Sulgostowska, A. Gautier, A. Bluszcz, B. Bratlund, A. M. Burke, H. J. Jensen, H. Królik, A. Nadachowski, E. Stworzewicz, J. Butrym, H. Maruszczak, and J. E. Mojski. 2000. "The Middle Palaeolithic kill-butchery site of Zwolen, Poland," in *Toward modern humans : the Yabrudian and Micoquian, 400-50 k-years ago : proceedings of a congress held at the University of Haifa, November 3-9, 1996*, vol. S850, *BAR International Series*. Edited by A. Ronen and M. Weinstein-Evron, pp. 189-207. Oxford: Archeopress.

Schoener, T. W. 1971. Theory of Feeding Strategies. *Annual Review of Ecology and Systematics* 2:369-404.

Scholander, P. F., V. Walters, R. Hock, and L. Irving. 1950. Body insulation of some arctic and tropical mammals and birds. *The Biological Bulletin* 99:225-236.

Schreve, D. C. 2006. The taphonomy of a Middle Devensian (MIS 3) vertebrate assemblage from Lynford, Norfolk, UK, and its implications for Middle Palaeolithic subsistence strategies. *Journal of Quaternary Science* 21:543-556.

Schuurman, E. 2004. The large mammal remains of Buhlen (Lower site), Excavation 1982, 1985,1986. Ma-Thesis, Leiden University.

Schwartz, J. H., and I. Tattersall. 2000. The human chin revisited: what is it and who has it? *Journal of Human Evolution* 38:367-409.

—. 2002. *Terminology and craniodental morphology of the genus Homo (Europe)*. Vol. I. *The human fossil record*. New York: Wiley-Liss.

Scott, K. 1980. Two hunting episodes of Middle Palaeolithic age at La Cotte de Saint-Brelade, Jersey (Channel Islands). *World Archaeology* 12:137-152.

—. 1986. "The large mammal fauna," in *La Cotte de St. Brelade 1961-1978, Excavations by C.B.M. McBurney*. Edited by P. Callow and J. M. Cornford, pp. 109-137. Norwich: Geo Books.

Sept, J. 1992. Archaeological evidence and ecological perspectives for reconstructing early hominid subsistence behaviour. *Archaeological Method and Theory* 4:1-56.

Shea, J. J. 1993. "Lithic use–wear evidence for hunting in the Levantine Middle Paleolithic.," in *Traces et fonction: Les gestes retrouvés*, vol. 50, *ERAUL*. Edited by P. Anderson, S. Beyries, M. Otte, and H. Plisson, pp. 21-30. Liège: Université de Liège.

—. 2003. Neandertals, competition and the origin of modern human behaviour in the Levant. *Evolutionary Anthropology* 12:173-187.

—. 2006. The origins of lithic projectile point technology: evidence from Africa, the Levant, and Europe. *Journal of Archaeological Science* 33:823-846.

Sheehan, M. S. 2004. "Ethnographic models, archaeological data and the applicability of modern foraging theory," in *Hunter-gatherers in history, archaeology and anthropology*. Edited by A. Barnard, pp. 163-173. Oxford/New York: Berg.

Shennan, S. 2002. Archaeology and evolutionary ecology. *World Archaeology* 34:1-5.

Sherman, P. W. 1998. The evolution of the menopause. *Nature* 392:759-760.

Shoshani, J. 1998. Understanding proboscidean evolution: a formidable task. *Trends in Ecology & Evolution* 13:480-487.

Shott, M. 1986. Technological organization and settlement mobility: An ethnographic examination. *Journal of Anthropological Research* 42:15-51.

Sih, A., and K. A. Milton. 1985. Should the !Kung eat mongongos? *American Anthropologist* 87:395-402.

Silva, M., M. Brimacombe, and J. A. Downing. 2001. Effects of body mass, climate, geography and census area on population density of terrestrial mammals. *Global Ecology and Biogeography* 10:469-485.

Silva, M., J. H. Brown, and J. A. Downing. 1997. Differences in population density and energy use between birds and mammals: A macroecological perspective. *Journal of Animal Ecology* 66:327-340.

Skinner, M. 1997. Dental wear in immature Late Pleistocene European hominines. *Journal of Archaeological Science* 24:677-700.

Slimak, L., and Y. Giraud. 2007. Circulations sur plusieurs centaines de kilomètres durant le Paléolithique moyen. Contribution à la connaissance des sociétés néandertaliennes. *Comptes Rendus Palevol* 6:359-368.

Slott-Moller, R. 1990. "La Faune," in *Les chasseurs d'aurochs de La Borde, Un site de Paléolithique Moyen (Livernon, Lot), Documents d'Archéologie Française 27*. Edited by J. Jaubert, M. Lorblanchet, H. Laville, R. Slot-Moller, A. Turq, and J.-P. Brugal. Paris: Editions de la Maison des Sciences de l'Homme.

Smith, E. A. 1983. Anthropological applications of optimal foraging theory: A critical review. *Current Anthropology* 24:625-651.

—. 2004. Why do good hunters have higher reproductive success. *Human Nature* 15:343-364.

Smith, E. A., R. Bliege Bird, and D. W. Bird. 2003. The benefits of costly signalling: Meriam turtle hunters. *Behavioral Ecology* 14:116-126.

Smith, P. 1995. "People of the holy land from prehistory to the recent past," in *The Archaeology of society in the holy land*. Edited by T. E. Levy, pp. 58-74. New York: Facts on file.

Smith, T. M., M. Toussaint, D. J. Reid, A. J. Olejniczak, and J.-J. Hublin. 2007. Rapid dental development in a Middle Paleolithic Belgian Neanderthal. *Proceedings of the National Academy of Sciences* 104:20220-20225.

Sommé, J. 1988. "Géomorphologie et stratigraphie," in *Le gisement Paléolithique Moyen de Biache-Saint-Vaast (Pas-de-Calais) Volume I*, vol. 21, *Mémoires de la Société Préhistorique Française*. Edited by A. Tuffreau and J. Sommé, pp. 27-45. Chalons-sur-Marne: Paquez et fils.

Sommé, J., A. V. Munaut, J. J. Puisségur, and N. Cunat. 1986. "Stratigraphie et signification climatique du gisement Paléolithique de Biache-Saint-Vaast (Pas-de-Calais, France)," in *Chronostratigraphie et faciès culturels du Paléolithique Inférieur et Moyen dans l'Europe du Nord-Ouest*, vol. 26, *Supplement au Bulletin de l'Association Française pour l'Étude du Quaternaire*. Edited by A. Tuffreau and J. Sommé, pp. 186-196. Paris: Société Préhistorique Française.

Sommé, J., A. Tuffreau, M. J. Aitken, P. Auguste, J. Chaline, J.-P. Colbeaux, N. Cunat-Bogé, P. Geeraerts, J. Hus, J. Huxtable, E. Juvigné, A. V. Munaut, S. Occhietti, P. Pichet, J.-J. Puisségur, D.-D. Rousseau, and B. van Vliet-Lanoe. 1988. "Chronostratigraphie, climats et environnements," in *Le gisement Paléolithique Moyen de Biache-Saint-Vaast (Pas-de-Calais) Volume I*, vol. 21, *Mémoires de la Société Préhistorique Française*. Edited by A. Tuffreau and J. Sommé, pp. 115-119. Chalons-sur-Marne: Paquez et fils.

Sorensen, M. V., and W. R. Leonard. 2001. Neandertal energetics and foraging efficiency. *Journal of Human Evolution* 40:483-495.

Speleers, B. 2000. The relevance of the Eemian for the study of the Palaeolithic occupation of Europe. *Geologie en Mijnbouw* 79:283-291.

Speth, J. D. 2004. "Hunting pressure, subsistence intensification and demographic change in the Levantine Late Middle Palaeolithic," in *Human paleoecology in the Levantine Corridor*. Edited by N. Goren-Inbar and J. D. Speth, pp. 149-166. Oxford: Oxbow Books.

Speth, J. D., and K. A. Spielmann. 1983. Energy source, protein metabolism, and hunter-gatherer subsistence strategies. *Journal of Anthropological Archaeology* 2:1-31.

Speth, J. D., and E. Tchernov. 1998. "The role of hunting and scavenging in Neandertal procurement strategies, New evidence from Kebara," in *Neandertals and modern humans in Western Asia*. Edited by K. Aoki, T. Akazawa, and O. Bar-Yosef, pp. 223-240. New York/London: Plenum press.

—. 2001. "Neandertal hunting and meat processing in the Near East, Evidence from Kebara cave (Israel)," in *Meat-eating and Human evolution*. Edited by C. B. Stanford and H. T. Bunn, pp. 52-72. Oxford: Oxford University Press.

—. 2002. Middle Palaeolithic tortoise use at Kebara Cave (Israel). *Journal of Archaeological Science* 29:471-483.

—. 2003. "Paleoclimatic and behavioral implications of Middle Palaeolithic tortoise use at Kebara Cave (Israel)," in *Le rôle de l'environnement dans les comportements des chasseurs-cueilleurs préhistoriques, Bar International Series*. Edited by M. Pathou-Mathis and H. Bocherens, pp. 9-21. Oxford: Archeopress.

Sponnheimer, M., and J. A. Lee-Thorp. 1999. Isotopic evidence for the diet of an early hominid, Australopithecus africanus. *Science* 283:368-370.

Stanford, C. B. 1999. *The hunting apes: Meat eating and the origins of human behaviour*. Princeton: Princeton University Press.

—. 2001a. "A comparison of social meat-foraging by chimpanzees and human foragers," in *Meat-eating and human evolution*. Edited by C. B. Stanford and H. T. Bunn, pp. 122-140. Oxford: Oxford University Press.

—. 2001b. "The ape's gift: Meat-eating, meat-sharing and human evolution," in *Tree of origin: What primate behaviour can tell us about human social evolution*. Edited by F. B. M. de Waal. Cambridge/London: Harvard University Press.

Steegman, A. T. J., F. J. Cerny, and T. W. Holliday. 2002. Neandertal cold adaptation: Physiological and energetic factors. *American Journal of Human Biology* 14:566-583.

Steele, J. 2002. The modified triangular graph: A refined method for comparing mortality profiles in archaeological samples. *Journal of Archaeological Science* 29:317-322.

Steele, T. E. 2004. Variation in mortality profiles of Red deer (*Cervus elaphus*) in Middle Palaeolithic assemblages from Western Europe. *International Journal of Osteoarchaeology* 14:307-320.

Steiner. 1977. "Das geologische Profil des Travertin-Komplexes von Taubach bei Weimar," in *Das Pleistozän von Taubach bei Weimar*, vol. 2, *Qartärpaläontologie, Abhandlungen und Berichte des Instituts für Quartärpaläontologie Weimar*. Edited by H.-D. Kahlke, pp. 83-118. Berlin: Akademie Verlag.

Steiner, W., and H. Wiefel. 1977. "Zur Geschichte der geologischen Erforschung des Travertins von Taubach bei Weimar," in *Das Pleistozän von Taubach bei Weimar*, vol. 2, *Qartärpaläontologie, Abhandlungen und Berichte des Instituts für Quartärpaläontologie Weimar*. Edited by H.-D. Kahlke, pp. 9-81. Berlin: Akademie Verlag.

Steudel-Numbers, K. L., and M. J. Tilkens. 2004. The effect of lower limb length on the energetic cost of locomotion: Implications for fossil hominins. *Journal of Human Evolution* 47:95-109.

Stewart, J. R. 2004. Neanderthal-Modern human competition? A comparison between the mammals associated with Middle and Upper Palaeolithic industries in Europe during OIS 3. *International Journal of Osteoarchaeology* 14:178-189.

—. 2005. The ecology and adaptation of Neanderthals during the non-analogue environment of Oxygen Isotope Stage 3. *Quaternary International* 137:35-46.

Stiner, M. C. 1992. Overlapping species "Choice" by Italian Upper Pleistocene predators. *Current Anthropology* 33:433-451.

—. 1994. *Honor among thieves, A zooarchaeological study of Neandertal ecology*. Princeton: Princeton University Press.

—. 2001. Thirty years on the "Broad spectrum revolution" and Palaeolithic demography. *Proceedings of the National Academy of Sciences* 98:6993-6996.

—. 2002. Carnivory, coevolution and the geographic spread of the genus *Homo*. *Journal of Archaeological Research* 10:1-63.

—. 2005. *The faunas of Hayonim Cave, Israel: A 200,000-year record of Paleolithic diet, demography and society. American School of Prehistoric Research Bulletin*. Cambridge: Peabody Museum of Archaeology and Ethnology, Harvard University.

Stiner, M. C., and S. L. Kuhn. 1992. Subsistence, technology and adaptive variation in Middle Paleolithic Italy. *American Anthropologist* 94:306-339.

Stiner, M. C., N. D. Munro, and T. A. Surovell. 2000. The tortoise and the hare: Small game use, the broad-spectrum revolution and Paleolithic demography. *Current Anthropology* 41:39-73.

Stiner, M. C., N. D. Munro, T. A. Surovell, E. Tchernov, and O. Bar-Yosef. 1999. Paleolithic population growth pulses evidenced by small animal exploitation. *Science* 283:190-194.

Stiner, M. C., and E. Tchernov. 1998. "Pleistocene species trends at Hayonim cave, Changes in climate versus human behaviour," in *Neandertals and modern humans in Western Asia*. Edited by T. Akazawa, K. Aoki, and O. Bar-Yosef, pp. 241-262. New York: Plenum Press.

Stringer, C. 2002. Modern human origins: Progress and prospects. *Philosophical Transactions of the Royal Society of London Series B: Biological sciences* 357:563-579.

—. 2003. Out of Ethiopia. *Nature* 423:692-694.

Stringer, C., and C. Gamble. 1993. *In search of the Neanderthals*. London: Thames & Hudson.

Stringer, C. B., J. C. Finlayson, R. N. E. Barton, Y. Fernández-Jalvo, I. Cáceres, R. C. Sabin, E. J. Rhodes, A. P. Currant, J. Rodríguez-Vidal, F. Giles-Pacheco, and J. A. Riquelme-Cantal. 2008. Neanderthal exploitation of marine mammals in Gibraltar. *Proceedings of the National Academy of Sciences* 105:14319-14324.

Stringer, C. B., and J.-J. Hublin. 1999. New age estimates for the Swanscombe hominid, and their significance for human evolution. *Journal of Human Evolution* 37:873-877.

Stringer, C. B., E. Trinkaus, M. B. Roberts, S. A. Parfitt, and R. I. Macphail. 1998. The Middle Pleistocene human tibia from Boxgrove. *Journal of Human Evolution* 34:509-547.

Stuart, A. J. 2005. The extinction of woolly mammoth (Mammuthus primigenius) and straight-tusked elephant (Palaeoloxodon antiquus) in Europe. *Quaternary International* 126-128:171-177.

Stuart, A. J., P. A. Kosintev, T. F. G. Higham, and A. M. Lister. 2004. Pleistocene to Holocene extinction dynamics in giant deer and woolly mammoth. *Nature* 431:684-689.

Sutcliffe, A. J. 1970. Spotted hyaena: Crusher, gnawer, digester and collector of bones. *Nature* 227:1110-1113.

Svenning, J.-C. 2002. A review of natural vegetation openness in north-western Europe. *Biological Conservation* 104:133-148.

Tattersall, I. 1999. *The last Neanderthal, The rise, success and mysterious extinction of our closest human relatives, Revised edition*. Oxford: Westview Press.

Templeton, A. R. 2002. Out of Africa again and again. *Nature* 416:45-51.

Testu, A. 2006. Etude paléontologique et biostratigraphique des Felidae et Hyaenidae pléistocènes de l'Europe méditerranéenne, Université de Perpignan.

Thieme, H. 1997. Lower Palaeolithic hunting spears from Germany. *Nature* 385:807-810.

Thieme, H., and S. Veil. 1985. Neue Untersuchungen zum eemzeitlichen Elefanten-Jagdplats Leheringen, Ldkr. Verder. *Die Kunde* 36:11-58.

Thun Hohenstein, U. 2006. "Stratgie di sussistenza adottate dai Neandertaliani nel sito di Ripari Tagliente (Prealpi Venete)," in *Archeozoological studies in honor of Alfredo Riedel*, pp. 31-38. Bolzano.

Tinbergen, N. 1963. On aims and methods of ethology. *Zeischrift für Tierpsychologie* 20:410-433.

Todd, P. M. 2000. The Ecological Rationality of Mechanisms Evolved to make up Minds. *American Behavioral Scientist* 43:940-956.

Tooby, J., and I. DeVore. 1987. "The reconstruction of hominid behavioural evolution through strategic modelling," in *The evolution of human behavior: Primate models*. Edited by W. G. Kinzey, pp. 183-238. Albany: State University of New York Press.

Tortosa, J. E. A., V. V. Bonilla, M. P. Ripoll, R. M. Valle, and P. G. Calatayud. 2002. Big Game and Small Prey: Paleolithic and Epipaleolithic Economy from Valencia (Spain). *Journal of Archaeological Method and Theory* 9:215-268.

Trinkaus, E. 1995. Neanderthal mortality patterns. *Journal of Archaeological Science* 22:121-142.

Trinkaus, E., and C. E. Hilton. 1996. Neandertal pedal proximal phalanges: diaphyseal loading patterns. *Journal of Human Evolution* 30:399-425.

Trinkaus, E., O. Moldovan, S. Milota, A. Bilgar, L. Sarcina, S. Athreya, S. E. Bailey, R. Rodrigo, G. Mircea, T. Higham, C. B. Ramsey, and J. v. d. Plicht. 2003. An early modern human from the Pestera cu Oase, Romania. *Proceedings of the National Academy of Sciences* 100:11231-11236.

Tuffreau, A. 1988a. "Historique de fouilles effectuées à Biache-Saint-Vaast," in *Le gisement Paléolithique Moyen de Biache-Saint-Vaast (Pas-de-Calais) Volume I*, vol. 21, *Mémoires de la Société Préhistorique Française*. Edited by A. Tuffreau and J. Sommé, pp. 15-24. Chalons-sur-Marne: Paquez et fils.

—. 1988b. "L'industrie lithique du Niveau IIA," in *Le gisement Paléolithique Moyen de Biache-Saint-Vaast (Pas-de-Calais) Volume I*, vol. 21, *Mémoires de la Société Préhistorique Française*. Edited by J. Sommé and A. Tuffreau, pp. 171-183. Chalons-sur-Marne: Paquez et fils.

—. 1988c. "Stratigraphie de la séquence archéologique," in *Le gisement Paléolithique Moyen de Biache-Saint-Vaast (Pas-de-Calais) Volume I*, vol. 21. Edited by J. Sommé and A. Tuffreau, pp. 123-131. Chalons-sur-Marne: Paques et fils.

—. 1992. "Middle Palaeolithic settlement in Northern France," in *The Middle Palaeolithic: Adaptation, behavior and variability*, vol. 72, *University Museum Monograph*. Edited by H. L. Dibble and P. Mellars, pp. 59-73. Philadelphia: The University Museum of Archaeology and Anthropology.

Tuffreau, A., A. Lamotte, and J.-L. Marcy. 1997. Land-use and site function in Acheulean complexes of the Somme Valley. *World Archaeology* 29:225-241.

Tuffreau, A., and J.-L. Marcy. 1988a. "Le niveau II base," in *Le gisement Paléolithique Moyen de Biache-Saint-Vaast (Pas-de-Calais) Volume I*, vol. 21, *Mémoires de la Société Préhistorique Française*. Edited by J. Sommé and A. Tuffreau, pp. 231-261. Chalons-sur-Marne: Paquez et fils.

—. 1988b. "Synthèse des données archéologiques," in *Le gisement Paléolithique Moyen de Biache-Saint-Vaast (Pas-de-Calais) Volume I*, vol. 21, *Mémoires de la Société Préhistorique Française*`. Edited by A. Tuffreau and J. Sommé, pp. 301-307. Chalons-sur-Marne: Paquez et fils.

Tuffreau, A., and J. Sommé. 1988a. "Conclusion," in *Le gisement Paléolithique Moyen de Biache-Saint-Vaast (Pas-de-Calais) Volume I*, vol. 21, *Mémoires de la Société Préhistorique Française*. Edited by A. Tuffreau and J. Sommé, pp. 311-313. Chalons-sur-Marne: Paquez et fils.

—. Editors. 1988b. *Le gisement Paléolithique Moyen de Biache-Saint-Vaast (Pas-de-Calais) Volume I*. Vol. 21. *Mémoires de la Société Préhistorique Française*. Chalons-sur-Marne: Paquez et fils.

Ugan, A. 2005. Does size matter? Body size, mass collecting and their implications for understanding prehistoric foraging behaviour. *American Antiquity* 70:75-89.

Ugan, A., J. Bright, and A. Rogers. 2003. When is technology worth the trouble? *Journal of Archaeological Science* 30:1315-1329.

Ungar, P., K. J. Fennell, K. Gordon, and E. Trinkaus. 1997. Neandertal incisor beveling. *Journal of Human Evolution* 32:407-421.

Valensi, P., and K. E. Guennouni. 2004. "Comportements de subsistance et structures d'habitat sur le site de plein air de Terra Amata (Paléolithique inférieur, France)," in *Actes du XIVème Comgrès UISPP, Université de Liège, Belgique 2-8 Septembre 2001, Sessions générales et posters, Section 4 premiers hommes et Paléolithique Inférieur*, vol. 1272, *BAR International Series*. Edited by L. s. d. Congrès, pp. 75-85. Oxford: Archeopress.

Valensi, P., and E. Psathi. 2004. Faunal exploitation during the Middle Palaeolithic in south-eastern France and north-western Italy. *International Journal of Osteoarchaeology* 14:256-272.

Valkenburgh, B. van. 2001. "The dog eat dog world of carnivores, A review of past and present carnivore community dynamics," in *Meat eating and human evolution*. Edited by C. B. Stanford and H. T. Bunn, pp. 101-121. Oxford: Oxford University Press.

Vallverdú, J., E. Allue, J. L. Bischoff, I. Caceres, E. Carbonell, A. Cebria, D. Garcia-Anton, R. Huguet, N. Ibanez, K. Martinez, I. Pasto, J. Rosell, P. Saladie, and M. Vaquero. 2005. Short human occupations in the Middle Palaeolithic level i of the Abric Romani rock-shelter (Capellades, Barcelona, Spain). *Journal of Human Evolution* 48:157-174.

Valoch, K. 1984. Le Taubachien, sa géochronologie, paléoécologie et paléoethnologie. *L'Anthropologie* 88:193-208.

Vaquero, M., J. Vallverdú, J. Rosell, I. Pastó, and E. Allué. 2001. Neandertal behaviour at the Middle Palaeolithic site of of Abric Romaní, Cappellades, Spain. *Journal of Field Archaeology* 28:93-114.

Villa, P. 1990. Torralba and Aridos: Elephant exploitation in Middle Pleistocene Spain. *Journal of Human Evolution* 19:299-309.

Villa, P., P. Boscato, F. Ranaldo, and A. Ronchitelli. 2009. Stone tools for the hunt: points with impact scars from a Middle Paleolithic site in southern Italy. *Journal of Archaeological Science* 36:850-859.

Villa, P., J.-C. Castel, C. Beauval, V. Bourdillat, and P. Goldberg. 2004. Human and carnivore sites in the European Middle Palaeolithic: Similarities and differences inthe bone modification and fragmentation. *Revue de Paléobiologie, Genève* 23:705-730.

Villa, P., and M. Lenoir. 2006. Hunting weapons of the Middle Stone Age and the Middle Palaeolithic: Spear points from Sibudu, Rose Cattage and Bouheben. *Southern African Humanities* 18:89-122.

Villa, P., and M. Soressi. 2000. Stone tools at carnivore sites, the case of Bois Roche. *Journal of Anthropological Research* 56:187-215.

Villa, P., E. Soto, M. Santonja, A. Pérez-González, R. Mora, J. Parcerisas, and C. Sesé. 2005. New data from Ambrona, closing the hunting *versus* scavenging debate. *Quaternary International* 126-128:223-250.

Vita-Finzi, C., and E. S. Higgs. 1970. Prehistoric economy in the Mount Carmel area of Palestine: Site catchment analysis. *Proceedings of the Prehistoric Society* 36:1-37.

Vliet-Lanoe, B. van. 1988. "Etude pédologique et micromorphologique," in *Le gisement Paléolithique Moyen de Biache-Saint-Vaast (Pas-de-Calais) Volume I*, vol. 21, *Mémoires de la Société Préhistorique Française*. Edited by A. Tuffreau and J. Sommé, pp. 69-75. Chalons-sur-Marne: Paquez et fils.

Voormolen, B. 2008. Ancient hunters, modern butchers : Schöningen 13II -4, a kill-butchery site dating from the northwest European Lower Palaeolithic. PhD, Leiden University.

Vuure, C. van 2003. *De Oeros, Het spoor terug*. Vol. 186. *Raport*. Wageningen: Wageningen UR.

Waal, F. B. M. de 2005. *Our inner ape, The best and worst of human nature*. London: Granta Books.

Waguespack, N. M., and T. A. Surovell. 2003. Clovis Hunting Strategies, or How to Make out on Plentiful Resources. *American Antiquity* 68:333-352.

Waite, T. A., and R. C. Ydenberg. 1996. Foraging currencies and the load-size decision of scatter-hoarding grey jays. *Animal Behaviour* 51:903-916.

Waldbauer, G. P., and S. Friedman. 1991. Self-Selection of Optimal Diets by Insects. *Annual Review of Entomology* 36:43-63.

Walker, R., K. Hill, and G. McMillan. 2002. Age-dependency in hunting ability among the Ache of Eastern Paraguay. *2002* 42:639-657.

Wallace, I. J., and J. J. Shea. 2006. Mobility patterns and core technologies in the Middle Paleolithic of the Levant. *Journal of Archaeological Science* 33:1293-1309.

Watts, H. E., and K. E. Holekamp. 2007. Hyena societies. *Current Biology* 17:R657-R660.

Weaver, T. D., and K. Steudel-Numbers. 2005. Does climate or mobility explain the differences in body proportions between Neandertals and their Upper Palaeolithic successors. *Evolutionary Anthropology* 14:218-213.

Webb, R. E. 1989. "A reassessment of the faunal evidence for Neandertal diet based on some Western European collections," in *L'homme de Néandertal, actes de la colloque International de Liège (4-7 Décembre 1986), Volume 6: La subsistance*, vol. 33, *Études et recherches archéologiques de l'Université de Liège*. Edited by M. Patou and L. G. Freeman, pp. 155-178. Liège: Université de Liège.

Wenban-Smith, F. F., P. Allen, M. R. Bates, S. A. Parfitt, R. C. Preece, J. R. Stewart, C. Turner, and J. E. Whittaker. 2006. The Clactonian elephant butchery site at Southfleet Road, Ebbsfield, UK. *Journal of Quaternary Science* 21:471-483.

Wenzel, S. 2002. Leben im Wald - die Archäologie der letzten Warmzeit vor 125000 Jahren. *Mitteilungen der Gesellschaft für Urgeschichte* 11:35-63.

Whitbridge, P. 2001. Zen fish: A consideration of the discordance between artifactual and zooarchaeological indicators of Thule Inuit fish use. *Journal of Anthropological Archaeology* 20:3-72.

White, M., and N. Ashton. 2003. Lower Palaeolithic core technology and the origins of the Levallois method in North-Western Europe. *Current Anthropology* 44:598-609.

White, M. J. 2006. Things to do in Doggerland when you're dead: Surviving OIS3 at the northwestern-most fringe of Middle Palaeolithic Europe. *World Archaeology* 38:547-575.

White, T. D., B. Asfaw, D. DeGusta, H. Gilbert, G. D. Richards, G. Suwa, and F. C. Howell. 2003. Pleistocene *Homo sapiens* from Middle Awash, Ethiopia. *Nature* 423:742-747.

Wild, E. M., M. Teschler-Nicola, W. Kutschera, P. Steier, E. Trinkaus, and W. Wanek. 2005. Direct dating of Early Upper Palaeolithic human remains from Mladec. 435:332-335.

Winterhalder, B. 1987. "The analysis of hunter-gatherer diets: Stalking an optimal foraging model," in *Food and evolution, Toward a theory of human food habits*. Edited by M. Harris and E. B. Ross, pp. 311-341. Philadelphia: Temple University Press.

—. 2001. "The behavioural ecology of hunter-gatherers," in *Hunter-gatherers, An interdisciplinary perspective*, vol. 13, *Biological symposium series*. Edited by C. Panter-Brick, R. H. Layton, and P. Rowley-Conwy, pp. 12-38. Cambridge: Cambridge University Press.

Winterhalder, B., and E. A. Smith. 1992. "Evolutionary ecology and the social sciences," in *Evolutionary ecology and human behaviour, Foundations of human behaviour*. Edited by B. Winterhalder and E. A. Smith, pp. 3-23. New York: Aldine de Gruyter.

Wong, K. 2000. Paleolithic pit stop. *Scientific American* 283:13-14.

Wood, B., and M. Collard. 1999. The human genus. *Science* 284:65-71.

Wood, B., and D. Strait. 2004. Patterns of resource use in early *Homo* and *Paranthropus*. *Journal of Human Evolution* 46:119-162.

Wrangham, R. W., J. H. Jones, G. Laden, D. Pilbeam, and N. Conklin-Brittain. 1999. The raw and the stolen, Cooking and the evolution of human origins. *Current Anthropology* 40:567-577.

Wroe, S., J. Field, R. Fullagar, and L. S. Jermin. 2004. Megafaunal extinction in the late Quaternary. *Alcheringa* 28:291-331.

Zeissler, H. 1977. "Konchylien aus dem Pleistozän von Taubach, Grube Vollmar," in *Das Pleistozän von Taubach bei Weimar*, vol. 2, *Qartärpaläontologie, Abhandlungen und Berichte des Instituts für Quartärpaläontologie Weimar*. Edited by H.-D. Kahlke, pp. 139-160. Berlin: Akademie Verlag.

Ziaei, M., H. P. Schwarcz, C. M. Hall, and R. Grün. 1990. "Radiometric dating of the Mousterian site of Quneitra," in *Quneitra: A mousterian site on the Golan heights*, vol. 31, *QEDEM Monographs of the Institute of Archaeology*. Edited by N. Goren-Inbar, pp. 232-235. Jeruzalem: The Hebrew University of Jeruzalem.

Zilhão, J. 2001. *Anatomically archaic, behaviorally modern: the last Neanderthals and their destiny, 23e Kroonvoordracht gehouden voor de Stichting Nederlands Museum voor Anthropologie en Praehistorie te Amsterdam op 23 maart 2001*. Vol. 23. Amsterdam: Stichting Nederlands museum voor Antropologie en Prehistorie.

—. 2007. The emergence of ornaments and art: An archaeological perspective on the origins of "Behavioural Modernity". *Journal of Archaeological Research* 15:1-54.

Zilhão, J., F. d'Errico, J.-G. Bordes, A. Lenoble, J.-P. Texier, and J.-P. Rigaud. 2006. Analysis of Aurignacian interstratification at the Châtelperronian-type site and implications for the behavioral modernity of Neandertals. *Proceedings of the National Academy of Sciences* 103:12643-12648.

Zilhão, J., and P. Pettitt. 2006. On the new dates for Gorham's cave and the late survival of Iberian Neanderthals. *Before Farming*:Article 3.11.

Dutch Summary

Dit proefschrift doet verslag van een analyse van het foerageergedrag van Neanderthalers (*Homo neanderthalensis*). De vraagstelling die aan het onderzoek ten grondslag lag is tweeledig. Een eerste vraag is gebaseerd op etnografisch en primatologisch onderzoek waaruit blijkt dat bij moderne mensen en primaten jacht de meest kennisintensieve bezigheid is die uitgevoerd wordt. Daarom hebben een aantal onderzoekers geopperd dat de evolutie van onze grote hersenen gestimuleerd is door het toenemende belang van jacht tijdens onze evolutie De hieruit voortvloeiende onderzoeksvraag is hoe kennisintensief het foerageergedrag van Neanderthalers was. Neanderthalers hadden namelijk, net als de moderne mens (*Homo sapiens sapiens*), erg grote hersenen. Daarbij komt dat DNA-analyse aantoont dat de Neanderthaler een aparte soort was die niet aan de genenpoule van de moderne mens bijgedragen heeft. De Neanderthaler vormt dus een voorbeeld van parallelle evolutie van grote hersenen. Inzicht in de kennisintensiteit van het foerageergedrag van Neanderthalers kan daardoor gebruikt worden om de algemene geldigheid van de hypothese dat jacht de evolutie van onze hersenen stimuleerde te evalueren.

Om dit te onderzoeken is besloten een model dat bij ecologisch onderzoek ontwikkeld is toe te passen, namelijk het *Diet Breadth* model. Het doel hiervan was om in tegenstelling tot veel voorgaand onderzoek niet *a priori* aannames over de cognitieve capaciteiten van Neanderthalers ten grondslag te laten liggen aan de onderzoeksstrategie. Hieruit vloeit de tweede, methodologische, vraag voort. Namelijk de vraag of ecologische modellen die opgesteld zijn om foerageergedrag in de actualiteit te onderzoeken toe te passen zijn op Pleistocene situaties.

Om ecologische modellen toe te passen moet eerst een goed beeld opgebouwd worden van de soort waarop het model toegepast wordt. In hoofdstukken twee en drie wordt de beschikbare informatie over de biologie en de archeologische informatie over het gedrag van de Neanderthaler geanalyseerd. Op basis van deze hoofdstukken wordt een model van de Neanderthaler als carnivoor opgesteld dat gebruikt zal worden als invoerdata voor het toe te passen model dat in hoofdstuk vier besproken wordt. Het model is toegepast op twee Midden-Paleolithische vindplaatsen, hiervan wordt verslag gedaan in hoofdstukken vijf en zes. In hoofdstuk zeven wordt het model dan toegepast op twee vindplaatsen die het resultaat zijn van de activiteiten van grottenhyena's (*Crocuta spelaea*). Dit is bedoeld als extra toets van de zeggingskracht van het *Diet Breadth* model bij toepassingen op het verleden. Het doel is om te zien of de toepassing van het model inzicht geeft in de differentiatie van de niches van verschillende samen voorkomende en concurrerende roofdieren.

Op basis van de in hoofdstuk twee gepresenteerde biologische gegevens kan het volgende beeld van de Neanderthaler geschetst worden: De Neanderthaler was een succesvolle hominine die een opeenvolging van ijstijden en tussenijstijden in Eurazië overleefde. Het verspreidingsgebied van de Neanderthaler omvatte een groot gebied, resten zijn gevonden van West Europa tot in Zuid Siberië, de zuidelijke limiet van hun verspreiding was het Midden-Oosten.

De hersenen van Neanderthalers waren tenminste even groot als die van de moderne mens. Hun ledematen waren relatief kort, wat als een aanpassing aan een koud klimaat geïnterpreteerd kan worden. Een gevolg hiervan was dat lopen energetisch gezien 30 % duurder was voor Neanderthalers dan voor moderne mensen. Een andere aanpassing aan de koude was het feit dat ze groter en zwaarder waren dan moderne mensen (waardoor hun lichaamsoppervlakte relatief kleiner was dan dat van de moderne mens). Verder hadden ze waarschijnlijk een sneller metabolisme dan moderne mensen, waardoor ze meer warmte produceerden.

Door het feit dat ze grote hersenen hadden werden Neanderthalers, net als moderne mensen, geboren lang voordat hun hersenen volgroeid waren. Hierdoor kwamen baby's onvolgroeid en volkomen afhankelijk van de zorgen van hun ouders ter wereld. Het groeiproces bij Neanderthalers verliep op zijn minst even snel als bij moderne mensen en misschien zelfs sneller. Hierdoor moesten de ouders grote hoeveelheden voedsel verkrijgen om het groeiproces van hun kinderen te bekostigen. Verder is het aannemelijk dat om de toename in hersengrootte te bekostigen het maag-darmkanaal in Neanderthalers verkort was. Eenzelfde ontwikkeling is in onze eigen soort gepostuleerd. Hierdoor hadden Neanderthalers net als moderne mensen voedsel van hoge kwaliteit nodig, zoals fruit of vlees. Voedsel van lage kwaliteit kon simpelweg niet efficiënt genoeg verteerd worden en zou niet genoeg energie opleveren. Op basis van deze factoren kunnen we ervan uitgaan dat Neanderthalermoeders werden bijgestaan door mannen (vaders) voor de verzorging van hun kinderen.

In hoofdstuk drie wordt het archeologische bewijs voor het gedrag van Neanderthalers besproken, waarbij de nadruk ligt op de botassemblages die door activiteiten van Neanderthalers zijn gevormd. Aan de hand van de botassemblages in het Midden-Paleolithicum ontstaat het volgende beeld: Neanderthalers waren gespecialiseerde jagers op middelgrote en grote herbivoren. Er zijn vindplaatsen bekend waar gespecialiseerd jacht is gemaakt op bijvoorbeeld paarden, rendieren, bizons enzovoorts. Verder blijkt dat de jacht op veel vindplaatsen geconcentreerd was op volwassen dieren in de kracht van hun leven, de zogenaamde *prime-age* individuen. Dit zijn de meest aantrekkelijke prooidieren, maar ze zijn ook het meest moeilijk te bejagen. Op sommige vindplaatsen is bewijs gevonden voor de jacht op gevaarlijkere dieren, zoals roofdieren en neushoorns. Aanwijzingen voor de structurele exploitatie van kleine, snelle prooidieren, zoals vogels, kleine zoogdieren en vissen, zijn schaars. De exploitatie van planten is moeilijk te bestuderen omdat plantenresten onder de meeste omstandigheden niet bewaard blijven. Rond de Middellandse Zee zijn echter een aantal vindplaatsen bekend met aanwijzingen voor de exploitatie van plantaardig materiaal. Het lijkt er op basis van de schaarse aanwijzingen op dat dit in warme omgevingen een belangrijke voedselbron voor Neanderthalers kon zijn.

Ook wordt ingegaan op de werktuigfabricage en het gebruik van werktuigen door Neanderthalers. De nadruk ligt op de zeggingskracht die werktuigen hebben met betrekking tot foerageerstrategieën. Neanderthalers gebruikten een beperkt repertoire aan werktuigtypen. De dominante typen op de meeste vindplaatsen zijn schrabbers en *denticulées*. Hun werktuigen behielden vele tienduizenden jaren lang over een zeer groot gebied eenzelfde karakter. Hieruit volgt dat het beperkte aantal werktuigtypen waarschijnlijk voor een groot aantal taken werd gebruikt. Gespecialiseerde werktuigvormen waren zeldzaam of afwezig. Werktuigen die als wapens te interpreteren zijn, zijn ook zeldzaam. Recent is echter bewijs gevonden voor het gebruik van puntige werktuigvormen, die vroeger soms als schrabbers geïnterpreteerd werden, als speerpunten. Verder worden op sommige werktuigen gebruikssporen of zelfs residuen gevonden die duiden op een gebruik in de voedselvoorziening. In uitzonderlijke omstandigheden worden werktuigen van andere materialen dan steen gevonden. Een belangrijke vindplaats is Schöningen in Duitsland, waar verschillende houten speren gevonden zijn. Wapens zoals een speerwerper, of pijl en boog, die het doden van prooi op afstand mogelijk zouden maken zijn echter niet bekend.

In hoofdstuk vier wordt ingegaan op het *Diet Breadth* model dat toegepast zal worden op Pleistocene vindplaatsen. Het model is evolutionair van aard. Er wordt aangenomen dat het foerageergedrag van een individu directe consequenties heeft voor zijn evolutionaire *fitness*. Dit wordt ondersteund door etnografisch en primatologisch onderzoek, waarin is vastgesteld succes bij foerageren de *fitness* van de foerageerder in positieve zin beïnvloedt. Door het directe verband tussen *fitness* en foerageergedrag is onderzoek naar dit gedrag bij uitstek geschikt om inzicht te krijgen in de complexiteit van het gedrag van Neanderthalers.

Het *Diet Breadth* model is geconstrueerd om te voorspellen welke prooi een dier zal bejagen en welke met rust gelaten zal worden onder gegeven omstandigheden. Er wordt aangenomen dat een dier zal proberen zo efficiënt mogelijk te foerageren. Hierdoor zal een carnivoor zich concentreren op de meest aantrekkelijke prooidieren. Dit zijn over het algemeen de grootste prooidieren die hij kan doden, die leveren immers het meeste vlees op. Kleine prooidieren zullen niet geëxploiteerd worden, tenzij zonder de exploitatie van kleinere prooien niet voldoende voedseltoevoer gerealiseerd kan worden. Als grote prooidieren zeldzaam zijn of zeer moeilijk te bejagen zal men zich dus op kleinere dieren toeleggen.

Voor een archeologische toepassing is de methode aangepast. Bij archeologische analyses is het aantal geëxploiteerde prooidieren bekend, maar niet de factoren die ertoe leiden dat de breedte van het dieet de gestalte kreeg die wij waarnemen. In dit proefschrift wordt dus teruggeredeneerd. De "optimale dieetbreedte" van de Neanderthaler op de onderzochte vindplaats is bekend. De aanname is dat Neanderthalers zich bij voorkeur op grote prooidieren zullen richten tenzij andere factoren het rendement van deze prooidieren verlagen. Deze factoren worden in het model de *handling cost* genoemd. De factoren die invloed hebben op de *handling cost* kunnen uiteenlopen van het feit dat dieren gevaarlijk zijn tot de noodzaak om ingewikkelde of tijdrovende werktuigen te maken voor de exploitatie van bepaalde dieren (bijv. visnetten voor vis).

Dutch Summary

De door Neanderthalers bejaagde prooidieren worden ten eerste vergeleken met de andere beschikbare prooidieren. De beschikbare prooidieren worden gerangschikt op volgorde gewicht. Op basis daarvan wordt bekeken of de aanname dat Neanderthalers zich richtten op de zwaarst aanwezige soorten correct is. Als dit niet het geval is wordt onderzocht welke factoren geleid kunnen hebben tot de exploitatie van de teruggevonden prooidieren.

Eerst moet worden onderzocht of sommige prooien zeldzaam waren en daardoor weinig voorkomen in de opgegraven botassemblage. Daarom worden de bevolkingsdichtheden van de aanwezige diersoorten gereconstrueerd, gebruik makend van de correlatie tussen lichaamsgewicht en bevolkingsdichtheid. Verder wordt de omgeving van de vindplaats ten tijde van de bewoning gereconstrueerd. Dan wordt gekeken in hoeverre de beschikbare prooidieren aan de omgeving aangepast waren. Als diersoorten buiten hun voorkeurshabitat voorkomen dan is dat namelijk in lagere bevolkingsdichtheden dan binnen hun voorkeurshabitat.

Als zeldzaamheid van een soort in de omgeving van de vindplaats niet de verklaring kan zijn voor zeldzaamheid of afwezigheid in de botassemblage, kunnen andere verklaringen voor het gebrek aan exploitatie van de soort onderzocht worden, die liggen meestal in de *handling cost*. Daarom worden verschillende elementen van de beschikbare prooidieren bekeken. Ten eerste wordt gekeken naar de grootte van het dier, want hoe groter een prooi hoe gevaarlijker het is om de soort te bejagen. Ten tweede of het roofdieren betreft, want roofdieren zijn gevaarlijker om te jagen dan herbivoren. Ten derde wordt gekeken of dieren solitair leven of in groepen. In groepen levende dieren zijn moeilijker te bejagen doordat meer individuen aanwezig zijn, dus de kans groter is dat een der individuen een naderende jager opmerkt en de rest van de groep kan waarschuwen. Ook is het moeilijker een groep dieren aan te vallen en individuen te isoleren en te doden dan bij solitaire dieren. Verder wordt gekeken naar aanvullende redenen naast de calorische waarde van prooidieren waarom ze interessante prooi kunnen zijn. Deze redenen kunnen erg uiteenlopen, van waardering van prooidieren vanwege zeldzame voedingsstoffen of bont, tot prestige dat het doden van bijvoorbeeld gevaarlijke dieren een jager op kan leveren. Analyse van deze factoren geeft inzicht in de *handling cost* van prooidieren en vooral inzicht in de mate waarin Neanderthalers in staat waren sommige factoren in die *handling cost* te overwinnen om prooidieren alsnog te bejagen.

In hoofdstuk vijf wordt de vindplaats Biache-Saint-Vaast geanalyseerd. Deze site is gedateerd tijdens de overgang van *Marine Isotope Stage* (MIS) 7 naar MIS 6, circa 200.000 jaar geleden. Sporen van de bezigheden van Neanderthalers zijn in verschillende opeenvolgende afzettingen gevonden. Deze sporen documenteren het gedrag van Neanderthalers in uiteenlopende omgevingen, van gematigd en open tot een koude steppe tijdens het begin van een ijstijd. De opgegraven botten vertonen vele slachtsporen en zijn ondubbelzinnig een afspiegeling van foerageeractiviteiten van Neanderthalers. De vroegste afzettingen op de vindplaats, aan het einde van de warme periode MIS 7, bevatten de meeste botten. De botassemblage van deze lagen bestaat voor bijna de helft (48 %) uit botten van oeros (*Bos primigenius*), 34 % uit botten van beren, vooral bruine beer (*Ursus arctos*) en 15 % uit botten van neushoorns, vooral steppeneushoorn (*Dicerorhinus hemitoechus*), de grotere Merck's neushoorn (*Dicerorhinus kirchbergensis*) was zeldzaam. De nadruk ligt in alle drie categorieën op volwassen individuen. Vergelijking met de beschikbare prooidieren laat zien dat de zwaarst beschikbare prooi, de bosolifant (*Palaeoloxodon antiquus*) niet geëxploiteerd werd. Neushoorn en oeros waren daarna de zwaarst beschikbare prooidieren. Bruine beer was een stuk lichter, twee diersoorten die ook beschikbaar waren, reuzenhert (*Megaloceros giganteus*) en de beer van Deninger (*Ursus deningeri*) waren zwaarder dan bruine beer. Deze soorten zijn echter zeldzaam in de assemblage. Verder waren een grote hoeveelheid andere dieren aanwezig, zoals twee soorten paarden, edelhert, ree, wild zwijn en roofdieren zoals leeuw en wolf, deze dieren werden echter niet geëxploiteerd.

Tijdens de vorming van de vroegste afzetting op deze vindplaats werden vrijwel uitsluitend dieren die alleen leefden bejaagd. Beer en neushoorns leven alleen, terwijl bij de oeros de mannetjes solitair waren en de vrouwtjes in kuddes leefden. Voor 83 oerossen (er zijn resten van tenminste 196 individuen opgegraven op de vindplaats) kon het geslacht vastgesteld worden, hierbij ging het om 49 mannetjes en 34 vrouwtjes. Ook bij deze soort hadden de alleen levende mannetjes dus de voorkeur boven de in groepen voorkomende vrouwtjes.

Herten en paardachtigen waren in hogere bevolkingsdichtheden beschikbaar dan oeros en zeker dan neushoorn. De bewoners van de vindplaats konden dus het gedrag van zeldzame prooidieren zoals neushoorn en oeros goed genoeg voorspellen om geen kleinere diersoorten te hoeven exploiteren. Verder waren ze in staat om om te gaan met de hoge *handling cost* die het exploiteren van gevaarlijke grote dieren zoals neushoorn en beren met zich meebracht te omzeilen. De schaarste van de beer van Deninger en Merck's neushoorn wordt veroorzaakt doordat zij aan beboste omgevingen aangepast waren en dus zeldzaam waren in de omgeving van de vindplaats. Als de gelegenheid zich voordeed werden deze diersoorten bejaagd, dat laten snijsporen op hun botten zien.

Alleen de zeldzaamheid van reuzenhert kan niet aldus verklaard worden. De omgeving lijkt geschikt te zijn voor deze soort. Het feit dat de soort niet geëxploiteerd is terwijl hij toch zwaarder is dan de wel geëxploiteerde bruine beer is op het eerste gezicht raadselachtig. De volgende verklaringen worden geopperd. Ten eerste werden bruine beren structureel gevild op deze vindplaats. Deze prooi werd dus niet alleen om zijn vlees gewaardeerd, maar ook om zijn vacht. Verder is door de opgravers van de vindplaats gesuggereerd dat bewoning plaatsvond in de herfst. In dit seizoen bouwen bruine beren een vetreserve op voor hun winterslaap en zijn daardoor dus extra aantrekkelijk als prooi. Bij reuzenhertenmannetjes is het omgekeerde het geval. In de herfst waren reuzenhertenmannetjes ernstig vermagerd door het feit dat ze net de bronsttijd achter de rug hadden, waarin ze vrijwel niets eten. De vrouwtjes leefden net als bij oerossen waarschijnlijk in groepen en waren dus een lastigere prooi voor Neanderthalers.

De bewoningssporen in de jongere afzettingen van de vindplaats zijn armer, de botassemblages zijn kleiner en moeilijker in verband te brengen met het foerageergedrag van Neanderthalers. De samenstelling van de botassemblages verandert in deze periode, doordat het klimaat kouder werd. Steppeneushoorn en Merck's neushoorn verdwijnen, in deze lagen komt wolharige neushoorn (*Coelodonta antiquitatis*) voor. Ook verdwijnen de beren uit de botassemblages en worden paardachtigen belangrijker. Gezien het feit dat soorten als edelhert (*Cervus elaphus*) en oeros nog wel voorkomen is het onwaarschijnlijk dat bruine beer verdwijnt omdat het te koud voor deze soort is. Deze verandering is een gevolg van veranderende foerageerstrategieën van Neanderthalers. De omgeving wordt opener en kuddedieren leven dan vaak in grotere groepen. De locaties van die kuddes zijn ook beter te voorspellen dan in beboste omgevingen. Verder zijn in open omgevingen herbivoren en grotere dichtheden aanwezig, waardoor er voor Neanderthalers genoeg prooi beschikbaar was om zelf ook in grotere groepen te kunnen leven. Hierdoor konden Neanderthalers waarschijnlijk beter op in kuddes levende dieren jagen. Beren zijn weliswaar solitair, maar zeer gevaarlijke dieren, die ook tegenwoordig nog mensen doden. In de veranderende omstandigheden werd deze soort waarschijnlijk minder aantrekkelijk voor Neanderthalers en dus komt hij niet meer voor in de botassemblages.

Hoofdstuk 6 behandelt een andere archeologische site, Taubach in Thüringen. Deze vindplaats is gedateerd in het Eemien (MIS 5^e; 128.000 116.000 jaar voor heden). De site is ontdekt tijdens de exploitatie van een travertijngroeve. Bij de exploitatie van deze kalksteen in de late 19^e en de vroege 20^e eeuw werden er vele vondsten uit het Midden Paleolithicum gedaan. De botten die bewaard gebleven zijn (slechts een klein gedeelte van de originele assemblage, gezien het feit dat er veel weggegooid en verkocht zijn) zijn in 1999 nauwkeurig bestudeerd en gepubliceerd. Het blijkt dat er veel snijsporen op de botten aanwezig zijn. De botassemblage stelt ons dus in staat om het foerageergedrag van Neanderthalers in deze periode te bestuderen.

Tijdens het Eemien was het ongeveer even warm als tegenwoordig. West Europa was bedekt door dichte bossen. Warme beboste omgevingen worden gezien als omgevingen die ongeschikt zijn voor Neanderthalers. De meeste biomassa is immers opgeslagen in moeilijk te verteren plantaardig materiaal en herbivoren zijn hier een stuk zeldzamer dan in open steppes. Veel onderzoekers vermoeden dat Neanderthalers vooral aangepast waren aan de zogenaamde "mammoetsteppe" die zich over grote delen van Europa uitstrekte tijdens koudere periodes. Warme periodes zijn zelfs gekarakteriseerd als door Neanderthalers onbewoonde *green deserts*. Deze vindplaats is dus interessant omdat hij ons inzicht het aanpassingsvermogen van Neanderthalers kan geven.

De botassemblage van de vindplaats wordt gedomineerd door bruine beer (26%) en Merck's neushoorn (21%), gevolgd door bizon (*Bison priscus*) (9%) en bever (*Castor fiber*) (5%). Andere beschikbare prooidieren waren bosolifant, edelhert, reuzenhert, ree, paard, wild zwijn en roofdieren zoals leeuw, grottenbeer, hyena, lynx en luipaard.

Ook op deze vindplaats worden zeer grote prooidieren gejaagd. Alleen de grootste prooi, bosolifant lijkt niet bejaagd te zijn door de bewoners van de vindplaats. De interpretatie van de resten van bosolifant is echter problematisch, de botten van deze soort maken namelijk 4 % van de botassemblage uit. Er zijn geen snijsporen op de botten aangetroffen, maar snijsporen op olifantenbotten zijn erg zeldzaam omdat deze botten erg poreus zijn. Uiteindelijk leidt de combinatie van de afwezigheid van snijsporen en het feit dat de leeftijdsopbouw van de dieren niet wijst op jacht tot de hypothese dat bosolifanten niet geëxploiteerd werden op deze vindplaats.

In het geval van de één na grootste prooi, Merck's neushoorn, heeft men zich hier op jonge individuen, die net hun moeder verlaten hadden, gericht. Dit was waarschijnlijk een relatief makkelijke prooi. Dat geldt niet voor bruine beer, waar de jacht geconcentreerd was op volwassen individuen. Dat was ook het geval bij de exploitatie van bizons. Verder waren alle bizons waarvan het geslacht vastgesteld kon worden mannetjes. Bever is veel kleiner dan alle andere geëxploiteerde soorten. De exploitatie van dit dier kan niet verklaard worden op basis van zijn gewicht. Omdat de vindplaats naast een bron lag, hoefde men niet op zoek naar bevers, maar kwam men ze tegen in de naaste omgeving van de site. Hierdoor was de tijd die men kwijt was om deze prooi te zoeken verwaarloosbaar. Verder heeft bever een goede vacht, die misschien ook meespeelde bij de beslissing om het dier te bejagen.

Holenbeer (*Ursus spelaeus*) en reuzenhert werden ook niet geëxploiteerd al kwamen ze wel voor in de omgeving. Beide soorten zijn groter dan bruine beer. Reuzenhert is echter niet aangepast aan een beboste omgeving en was dus zeldzaam ten tijde van de bewoning van de vindplaats. De holenbeer was echter wel aangepast aan een beboste omgeving. De afwezigheid van exploitatie van deze soort kan worden geweten aan het feit dat het dier nog groter was dan bruine beer en dus nog gevaarlijker om te bejagen. De bruine beer werd, net als in Biache-Saint-Vaast gevild, wat erop duidt dat het deze bewoners van de site ook deels om de vacht van deze dieren te doen was.

Op deze vindplaats is de voorkeur voor alleen levende dieren nog sterker dan bij Biache-Saint-Vaast het geval was. Hier zijn namelijk helemaal geen vrouwelijke bizons aangetroffen. Ook lijkt in het geval van Merck's neushoorn het gevaar van de jacht bestreden te zijn door jonge dieren te bejagen. Dit wijst erop dat in de arme beboste omgevingen van het Eemien Neanderthalers in kleinere groepen leefden dan in koudere, open omgevingen. Hierdoor was jacht op grote dieren gevaarlijker dan op bijvoorbeeld Biache-Saint-Vaast, wat leidde tot een verandering in de prooidieren die bejaagd werden.

Hoofdstuk 7 gaat in op het forageergedrag van een van de belangrijkste concurrenten van de Neanderthaler in de strijd om voedsel: de holenhyena. Deze hyena is genetisch gezien niet te onderscheiden van de tegenwoordige gevlekte hyena (*Crocuta crocuta*) uit Afrika. Dit dier is een sociaal roofdier dat slechts een klein deel van zijn voeding verkrijgt door aaseten. De gevlekte hyena vervoert vaak resten van prooidieren naar een gemeenschappelijk hol. Hierdoor ontstaan botassemblages die we op dezelfde manier kunnen bestuderen als assemblages die op archeologische vindplaatsen opgegraven worden. In dit hoofdstuk worden twee opgegraven hyenavindplaatsen geanalyseerd: Lunel-Viel in het Zuidoosten van Frankrijk, afgezet in een warme periode rond 350.000 jaar geleden en Camiac bij Bordeaux, gevormd tijdens de laatste ijstijd. Deze vindplaatsen laten zien hoe hyena's zich gedroegen in omstandigheden die eender zijn aan die waarmee Neanderthalers geconfronteerd werden op de sites Biache-Saint-Vaast en Taubach.

In Lunel-Viel concentreren hyena's zich vooral op herten, die 56 % van de assemblage uitmaken. Ook oeros (19%) en paard (*Equus mosbachensis*) (7%) zijn belangrijke prooidieren. De leeftijd van de prooi is gevarieerd. Bij herten zijn jonge dieren goed vertegenwoordigd, maar ook volwassenen zijn aanwezig. Bij de paarden zijn volwassen dieren zelfs erg belangrijk. Hyena's waren dus in staat om niet alleen de jonge, oude of verzwakte individuen te bejagen, maar ook volwassen prooidieren. Alleen de grootste prooi, de etruskische neushoorn (*Dicerorhinus etruscus*), is zeldzaam. Herten waren de meest bejaagde prooi, dit geeft aan dat hyena's zich niet specifiek op grotere paarden of oerossen richtten, maar ze wel bejaagden als de mogelijkheid zich voordeed.

De assemblage die in Camiac opgegraven werd laat een ander patroon zien. Hier waren runderachtigen (bizon en oeros) en paard (beiden maken ongeveer 32% van de assemblage uit) de meest geëxploiteerde dieren, gevolgd door en wolharige neushoorn (19%). Botten van kleinere soorten zijn zeldzaam in deze assemblage. Doordat grote dieren in lagere bevolkingsdichtheden voorkomen dan kleine suggereert deze assemblage dat deze grote diersoorten gericht uitgezocht en bejaagd werden.

We kunnen de verschillen in forageergedrag tussen de beide hyena-vindplaatsen als volgt verklaren. Hyena's forageren bij voorkeur alleen. De intense en gewelddadige concurrentie om voedsel binnen deze soort zorgt ervoor dat het voor veel individuen zeer riskant is om mee te werken aan groepsjacht. Dominante individuen eigenen zich immers vaak het leeuwendeel van de buit toe. In warme, beboste omgevingen komen prooidieren verspreid over de omgeving in kleine groepen voor. Verder is het zicht beperkt en kan een individu dat alleen jaagt dieren doden of karkassen exploiteren buiten het zicht van anderen. In open omgevingen zoals op de mammoetsteppe komen veel dieren in grote kuddes voor. Verder zijn karkassen beter zichtbaar en die worden dus ook sneller geëxploiteerd. Om op dieren in grote groepen te jagen wordt groepsjacht belangrijker. Daardoor neemt ook de maximale grootte van prooidieren toe, in een groep kan nu eenmaal makkelijker een groot dier zoals een oeros gedood worden. Het is dus aannemelijk dat in Lunel-Viel hyena's vooral alleen foerageerden volgens *encounter hunting*. In de open omgeving van Camiac was deze strategie minder succesvol en werd meer in groepen gejaagd, ondanks het feit dat hyena's dan dus om moesten gaan met een hoge mate van concurrentie van groepsgenoten.

Neanderthalers jaagden waarschijnlijk altijd in groepen. Primatologisch en etnografisch onderzoek laat zien dat in onze familie voedsel harmonieuzer verdeeld wordt dan bij hyena's. Zo is bij chimpansees de jager van een prooi de eigenaar. Zelfs al is de eigenaar geen dominant individu, dit individu bepaalt wie meedeelt van de prooi. In mensen is voedselverdeling vaak aan uitgebreide regels gebonden. Hierdoor profiteert iedereen mee van een succesvolle jacht. Door het ontbreken van agressieve concurrentie was het voor Neanderthalers aantrekkelijker om in groepen te jagen dan voor hyena's. In warme perioden zullen zij zich meer dan hyena's op de grotere prooidieren gericht hebben. In koude perioden overlapt de prooikeuze van hyena's en Neanderthalers sterker. Neanderthalers lijken zich echter altijd op volwassen individuen gericht te hebben, terwijl hyena's minder sterk een concentratie op een bepaalde leeftijdscategorie laten zien. Neanderthalers jaagden waarschijnlijk gespecialiseerd op bepaalde prooidieren, terwijl hyena's meer variatie in hun foerageergedrag toonden. Zo combineerden zij aaseten, groepsjacht en solitair foerageren. Deze grotere variatie in strategieën vergeleken met de gespecialiseerde jacht bij Neanderthalers is wat hun niches differentieerde. Daarbij zijn hyena's meestal 's-nachts actief, terwijl primaten en mensen over het algemeen overdag actief zijn. Eenzelfde patroon kan bij hyena's en Neanderthalers in het Pleistoceen van kracht geweest zijn. Een differentiatie van niches in een temporele dimensie is een strategie die vooral vaak voorkomt in omgevingen die overvloedig in biomassa zijn, zoals de mammoetsteppe tijdens de laatste ijstijd ook was.

In hoofdstuk 8 worden de bevindingen van de analyse gesynthetiseerd. Ten eerste kan geconcludeerd worden dat de toepassing van de *Diet Breadth* model een waardevolle bijdrage kan leveren aan ons begrip van de ecologie tijdens het Pleistoceen. De verschillende niches van Neanderthalers en hyena's die door hun vrijwel gelijke grootte veel overlap hadden konden goed bestudeerd worden. Verder biedt deze methode ons de mogelijkheid om onderzoek te doen naar de redenen voor de aan- of afwezigheid van bepaalde prooidieren op archeologische vindplaatsen. In het verleden werd de aan- of afwezigheid van prooi op vindplaatsen vaak *ad hoc* geïnterpreteerd, terwijl door de een aantal factoren te modelleren, zoals *encounter rate*, *handling cost* en opbrengst een veel beter onderbouwd beeld van het foerageergedrag van Pleistocene carnivoren ontstaat.

Ten tweede wordt duidelijk dat Neanderthalers zeer geraffineerde jagers waren. Op basis van de geanalyseerde vindplaatsen kan gesteld worden dat buiten olifanten, Neanderthalers zich concentreerden op de grootst aanwezige dieren. Daarbij wordt ook de zeer gevaarlijke bruine beer geexploiteerd. Tegenwoordig wordt bij jacht op deze soort bijvoorbeeld aangeraden om een geweer met een zo groot mogelijk kaliber te gebruiken en meerdere schoten te lossen. De *handling cost* die de jacht op deze grote en gevaarlijke dieren met zich meebracht kon dus overwonnen worden door Neanderthalers.

Jacht op dieren die in groepen leven wordt minder gepraktiseerd op de vindplaatsen die bestudeerd zijn. Dit wordt geweten aan de *carrying capacity* van de omgeving. In beboste omgevingen zijn prooidieren in lage dichtheden aanwezig. Hierdoor waren Neanderthalers gedwongen om in kleinere groepen te leven en in deze omstandigheden heeft jacht op alleen levende dieren duidelijk voorkeur. In meer open omgevingen werd wel op in groepen levende dieren gejaagd. Dit werd al duidelijk bij Biache-Saint-Vaast, waar vrouwelijke oerossen ook bejaagd werden, zij het minder vaak dan de alleen levende mannetjes. Ook werd jacht op in kuddes levende soorten belangrijker in de latere perioden van bewoning van deze vindplaats. Toen was de omgeving minder bebost en was er dus meer prooi beschikbaar. Doordat er meer voedsel beschikbaar kwam konden er ook meer Neanderthalers in de omgeving overleven. Hierdoor nam hun groepsgrootte toe en kon met meer succes op dieren die in groepen leven gejaagd worden. In deze omstandigheden verdwijnt de gevaarlijke en vrij kleine bruine beer uit het dieet. Deze soort is relatief klein in vergelijking tot runderachtigen en neushoorns. Succesvolle jacht op kuddedieren maak het mogelijk om meerdere individuen uit die kudde te doden en dit leverde in de koudere omstandigheden waarschijnlijk meer op dan jacht op bruine beer.

Deze uitkomsten laten zien dat Neanderthalers als er voldoende voedsel was om grote groepen te voeden ook in staat waren om de problemen die jacht op kuddedieren met zich meebracht te overwinnen. Neanderthalers slaagden er dus in om in arme beboste omgevingen succesvol op verspreid levende zeldzame prooidieren te jagen en in rijkere omgevingen waren ze in staat kuddes grote herbivoren zoals oerossen en paarden te bejagen. Hieruit volgt dat ze een grote kennis hadden van het gedrag van hun prooi. Daardoor konden ze hun *encounter rate* zo manipuleren dat ze de grote, zeldzame prooidieren vaak genoeg tegenkwamen om niet voor hun voedselvoorziening ook nog kleinere minder interessante prooi te bejagen. Verder blijkt dat ze in groepen succesvol jacht op gevaarlijke en in groepen levende dieren konden coördineren. Dit wijst op een grote mate van vooruitzicht binnen Neanderthalers om hinderlagen te kunnen organiseren. Daarbij komt dat het wijst op een goede communicatie binnen groepen Neanderthalers waardoor ze als groep succesvol konden opereren.

Acknowledgements

First, I would like to mention my *promotores* Wil Roebroeks and Raymond Corbey, for rescuing me from a dire time of employment in commercial archaeology in the province of Zeeland and their patience during the process of writing this thesis.

The research reported in this thesis was funded by the Dutch Organisation for Scientific Research (NWO) as part of the research project "Thoughtful Hunters? The archaeology of Neanderthal communication and cognition". This work benefited greatly from discussions with the other project members, Najma Anwar and Kathy MacDonald.

The people active in the section "Human Origins" of the Faculty of Archaeology of Leiden University, Alexander Verpoorte, Adam Jagich and Mark Sier also provided important support and critically read large parts and in some cases all of this thesis. Wei Chu also read parts of the thesis and was forced to talk over stuff related to the writing of during long sessions in de Bontekoe.

Discussions, lunches, borrels and other interactions with colleagues Dianne van der Zande, Daan Isendoorn, Jimmy Mans, Welmoed Out, Ellis Grootveld and Stijn Arnoldussen provided me with inspiration and the essential distractions needed in order to complete a thesis. Erik van Rossenberg is thanked for the enormous amount of valuable literature he pointed out as well as being at the Faculty every weekend and drinking litres of coffee with me. Special thanks are due to colleagues Arne Wossink, Eva Kaptijn and Luc Amkreutz who were continually pestered over a period of five years for help with software problems, to supply translations, to download scientific papers while I was on holiday and unable to access digital journals, they solved many of the problems I encountered while writing this thesis. Alistair Bright not only took part in the foregoing activities but also expertly read the whole thesis. Els Koeneman provided invaluable support, in ordering books, lending unlendable books over weekends etc. Medy Oberendorff patiently drew the figures in this thesis.

Outside the department, much support was drawn from Nijland and Tuin who sacrificed many hours of their valuable time drinking coffee with me. Yearformation Orion is to be thanked for their willingness to take me to bars, giving me the opportunities to reflect on matters other than Neanderthal behaviour. Similar support was offered by Valentijn van den Brink whom I bored with musings about the state of Dutch archaeology in general and my thesis in particular for long hours.

My parents and brother are to be thanked for their patience and continued support.

Finally, Geeske thank you for dealing so patiently yet expertly with my continued laziness and indolence. As my final *stelling* says: Without a Graduate School this thesis would have been finished sooner. Without you, this thesis might not have been finished for years to come, or ever for that matter.

Curriculum vitae

Gerrit Leendert Dusseldorp werd op 5 augustus 1979 geboren te Eindhoven. Hij doorliep het atheneum aan het Lorentz Lyceum te Eindhoven en behaalde daar in 1997 zijn VWO diploma. In het najaar van 1997 begon hij met een propedeuse archeologie aan de Rijks Universiteit Leiden. Hij specialiseerde zich in de prehistorische archeologie van Noordwest Europa. In 2003 behaalde hij zijn doctoraaldiploma aan de Universiteit Leiden met een scriptie over grondstoftransport in het Oldowan in Afrika. Hierna was hij korte tijd werkzaam in de commerciële archeologie. Vanaf 2004 was hij werkzaam als promovendus aan de faculteit der Archeologie van de Universiteit Leiden teneinde het promotieonderzoek te doen waarvan deze dissertatie verslag doet.